CHICAGO
METROPOLIS OF THE MID-CONTINENT

THIRD EDITION

Irving Cutler

Chairman, Department of Geography
Chicago State University

published under the auspices
The Geographic Society of Chicago
and

KENDALL/HUNT PUBLISHING COMPANY
2460 Kerper Boulevard   P.O. Box 539   Dubuque, Iowa 52004-0539

Other books by Irving Cutler

The Chicago-Milwaukee Corridor
The Chicago Metropolitan Area: Selected Geographic Readings (editor)
Chicago: Transformations of an Urban System (coauthor)
Illinois: Land and Life in the Prairie State (contributor)
Urban Geography
Urban Communities (coauthor)
Ethnic Chicago (contributor)

Front Cover: Aerial view of the central area of Chicago looking northward from approximately Taylor Street (1000 S), 1980. The tallest buildings in the background from the river on the west to the lake on the east are Sears Tower (110 stories), First National Bank Building (60 stories), John Hancock Center (100 stories), Water Tower Place (74 stories), and Standard Oil Building (80 stories). The red high-rise is the 45-story CNA Plaza Building. (Photograph by Airpix)

Inside Front Cover: Aerial view of the central area of Chicago looking northwest, 1981. In the foreground is Grant Park and from left to right at the bottom is Soldier Field, Field Museum of Natural History, and Shedd Aquarium. Toward the center in the park fronting Michigan Avenue is the Art Institute. To the lower left, part of the land of the underutilized railroad facilities south of the Loop is now being redeveloped. On the right, north of the park, from Randolph Street to the Chicago River, are the new high-rise buildings of the Illinois Center development. The tallest buildings in the photo, from left to right, are Sears Tower (110 stories), First National Bank Building (60 stories), Standard Oil Building (80 stories), John Hancock Center (100 stories), and Water Tower Place (74 stories). (Photograph by Airpix)

Printed in the United States of America
10 9 8 7 6 5

Contents

Foreword

For the first edition of *Chicago: Metropolis of the Mid-Continent,* Herbert H. Gross, then president of the Geographic Society of Chicago, wrote the following Foreword:

> *Chicago: Metropolis of the Mid-Continent* is a dream of the Board of Directors of the Geographic Society of Chicago converted into reality by Irving Cutler, Professor of Geography, Chicago State University.
>
> Accelerating change demands that the story of a dynamic and influential city must be told and retold, each time with a modified or new perspective. Chicago is no longer the "hog butcher" of the world, but is truly the "Metropolis of the Mid-Continent." The diversity of its spatial relationships has regional, national, and international impacts and implications. Chicago interacts with a myriad of people and places. Its role in a world of increasingly dynamic cultures places on it the responsibility for dealing constructively with the complexities and challenges of change. How this is being accomplished provides the basic theme of this book.
>
> Throughout its history, the Geographic Society of Chicago has remained sensitive to the responsibility it must assume as a contributive agency. A primary concern has been the dissemination of the type of scholarly information about Chicago and its environs that is relevant to the needs of its members in particular and of society in general. Man's patterns of urban occupancy are growing increasingly complex; his understanding of these complexities is being made difficult by vocational specialization associated with a vibrant technology; the demands for responsive, intelligent citizenship are constantly expanding. These three related forces have pointed out the imperative need for improving the quality of citizenship in our city. May *Chicago: Metropolis of the Mid-Continent* enlarge and refine the perspective of those who commune with its contents.

That statement written in 1973 continued to be true for the second edition (1976), and now for this, the third edition. Three editions in less than ten years is indicative of the "accelerating changes" taking place in Metropolitan Chicago and the concern of the Geographic Society of Chicago that people be kept informed of these changes and their significance to the "Metropolis of the Mid-Continent, a dynamic and influential city." Our continuing appreciation goes to the author, Irving Cutler, for keeping us up-to-date.

Elizabeth Eiselen, President
The Geographic Society of Chicago

Preface

The first edition of this book was published in 1973 on the occasion of the seventy-fifth anniversary of the Geographic Society of Chicago. It was distributed primarily to the Society's thousands of members and to school libraries in the Chicago area. When it became evident that there also was a large demand for such a book from educational institutions and from the general public, the Society brought out a second edition, and now this up-dated and enlarged third edition. This broader treatment of the Chicago area should be of value to students and others, both within the city and its suburbs, who often know too little about the growth, characteristics, problems, and plans of their remarkable and changing Metropolis of the Mid-Continent.

In this third edition, the original single chapter on people and settlement patterns has been enlarged and divided into two chapters. These deal with the various ethnic and racial groups in Metropolitan Chicago in much greater detail than in earlier editions. All other chapters have been enlarged. There are new maps and photographs, as well as greatly increased supplementary material in the appendix. Population data from the 1980 U.S. census is used throughout the book, except where not yet available.

Numerous individuals and organizations facilitated the writing of this book, and their help is gratefully acknowledged. Edward B. Espenshade, Jr., as chairman of the Seventy-fifth Anniversary Publication Committee, skillfully organized and guided the original project. Herbert H. Gross of the Society supplied important material for the appendix. A very special acknowledgment must go to the representative of the Society for the project, Elizabeth Eiselen, for her wise counsel and perceptive editing of all three editions.

Many thanks are due Eugene Zucker for his critical reading of the manuscript and whose valuable advice was most helpful. Joseph Kubal rendered needed cartographic assistance by producing or modifying many of the maps. Sections of this latest edition on the various ethnic and racial groups were critically read by my colleagues Joseph Chada, John Hobgood, Walter Kelly, Albert Logan, Herbert Rau, Leonard Simutis, and Irwin Suloway, and also by Dominic Candeloro, Edwin Cudecki, Andrew Kopan, Carolyn Levy, Leonard Mishkin, and Henry Sokolow. I also express deepest appreciation to my wife, Marian, for her encouragement, discerning criticism, and untiring efforts in typing, retyping, and proofreading. My children, Dan and Susie, have also been helpful in numerous ways.

The photographs and maps in the book came from many sources, which are indicated in the captions. The largest number of illustrations are from the Chicago Historical Society.

Through the years I have had the opportunity to observe the city and its suburbs from diverse career vantage points, ranging from cab driver to employment in the area with the U.S. Army Corps of Engineers, the U.S. Department of Labor, and the Office of Economic Opportunity. I also learned about the metropolitan area from the excellent writings and teachings of many scholars, and particularly from my former professor, Harold M. Mayer.

Finally, I am most grateful to the Geographic Society of Chicago for affording me this opportunity to write on a subject that has interested and fascinated me all my life—Chicago.

Irving Cutler
January 1982

Figure 1.1. The Chicago Water Tower, one of the few structures to survive the disastrous Chicago fire of 1871. To the left, combining residential, retail, and office functions, is 100-story John Hancock Center, completed in 1970. To the right is 74-story Water Tower Place, opened in 1975, which contains an urban high-rise shopping center with many small shops and two major department stores, the 450-room Ritz-Carlton Hotel, and luxury condominiums. (Photograph by Mati Maldre, 1981.)

Chapter One

INTRODUCTION

Yesterday and Today

Stand on the busy Michigan Avenue Bridge over the Chicago River, in the locale where Chicago began, and look about you in any direction. At once you are aware of the vigorous growth and development of a great city.

From the north end of the bridge, where once the old Green Bay Road originated and the Du Sable cabin stood alone in a wilderness, now stretches the Magnificent Mile crowned by the John Hancock Center. This soaring skyscraper overshadows the Water Tower, the last landmark of the great fire that decimated the city more than a century ago.

To the south, where once Fort Dearborn stood and where the river arched southward sharply and the lake washed Michigan Avenue, now stand a park built on the debris of the Chicago Fire, railroad yards, and skyscrapers symbolic of Chicago's commerical growth.

Westward, along the Chicago River, where less than a century ago produce terminals, warehouses, and hundreds of ships and barges lined the channel, and where the tragic capsizing of the steamer *Eastland* occurred, there are now the Merchandise Mart, Marina Towers, and the Burnham Plan's double-deck Wacker Drive.

And to the east, on the former sites of grain elevators and the large McCormick Works, is a growing array of skyscrapers; farther on is the Outer Drive Bridge with its endless procession of vehicles; beyond is the lock which helps to reverse the flow of the river; and finally, Lake Michigan, Chicago's water gateway to the world.

Chicago's Geographic Attributes

Chicago's growth and change have been both swift and dramatic. It is the youngest of the world's largest cities, and, with a 1980 population of 3,005,072, it ranked second in the nation. The number of inhabitants in its burgeoning suburban area is now even greater than that of the city proper, resulting in a metropolitan area population of almost 8 million people—the tenth largest urban area in the world.

This remarkable population growth, greater than that attained by Paris in twenty centuries, was achieved in the last century and a half, although the area was first visited by Europeans three centuries ago. A bronze tablet on the Michigan Avenue Bridge commemorating the event bears this inscription:

> In honor of Louis Jolliet and Pere Jacques Marquette, the first white men to pass through the Chicago River, September, 1673.

The Canadian explorer and the French missionary were returning to Canada after exploring the Mississippi Valley for France. The Chicago region they passed through was essentially a flat, poorly drained wilderness blanketed with prairie grass, wild onion, clusters of trees, and foul-smelling marshes. Indians often would pass through in pursuit of game.

1

Figure 1.2. A major asset of Chicago is its excellent location. (Based on map from Chicago Association of Commerce and Industry.)

Despite the area's inauspicious setting, the essentials for its rapid growth were present when the first settlers arrived. These essentials included:

1. Location near the geographic center of the vast, flat, and fertile plains between the Appalachian Mountains to the east and the Rocky Mountains to the west. Chicago's situation enabled it to become the center of the most productive agricultural hinterland in the world. The flat terrain permitted easy access to this rich tributary empire by all modes of transportation. For Chicago, it offered no barriers for the laying out of streets in any direction and for the unimpeded expansion of urbanization.

2. Conveniently located and economically accessible important natural resources—the forests of the north, iron ore of Minnesota and Wisconsin, the coal of Illinois and nearby states, and an unlimited supply of fresh lake water.

3. Location at the southwestern tip of the world's greatest lake system. This made possible exceptionally low transportation costs and a great range of domestic and overseas connections. In addition, Chicago's location is at a natural point of convergence for land traffic between the east and northwest that had to find its way around the southern tip of Lake Michigan. Long before the coming of the white man, numerous Indian trails joined at Chicago.

4. The short natural waterways of Chicago eventually were modified and extended to provide the only all-water connecting link between the Great Lakes-St. Lawrence

Seaway and the rich Mississippi Valley. Louis Jolliet noted this important possibility when he portaged through the Chicago region in 1673. He wrote in his journal that "it would only be necessary to make a canal by cutting through but half a league of prairies to pass" from Lake Michigan to the Illinois River and on to the Mississippi River and the Gulf of Mexico.

Figure 2.1. The limestone bedrock underlying Chicago is revealed at the more-than-century-old Stearns Quarry at 28th and Halsted streets. Since 1971 the quarry has been used by the city as a dumping site for the residue of its incinerator operations. (Photograph courtesy Material Service Corporation, Chicago.)

Chapter Two

THE PHYSICAL SETTING

In the Beginning

The natural landscape of the Chicago region as viewed by Jolliet and Marquette, and by the Indians before them, was the result of millions of years of geologic action—for although the chronicle of man in Chicago is brief, the story of the land on which Metropolitan Chicago spreads began eons ago.

Many millions of years ago the first living creatures appeared in the ancient tropical sea that covered the mid-continent. Through the millennia of geologic eras the limy skeletons and the shells of countless sea creatures settled over the ocean bottom where, eventually, they formed the rock known as limestone. In time the ocean receded, but the limestone remained to form the bedrock upon which rest Chicago's skyscrapers.

The bedrock is visible in limestone quarries, some road cuts, and some waterway channels. The limestone from the numerous quarries in the area has provided a basic building material. In Chicago the limestone bedrock is visible at the more-than-century-old former Stearns quarry at 28th and Halsted (800 W) streets and also flanking the Kennedy Expressway around Addison Street (3600 N). Large limestone quarries were opened in Thornton, McCook, and other places throughout the area. Southwest of the city the bedrock is exposed along sizable segments of the Calumet Sag Channel and the Chicago Sanitary and Ship Canal.

In the mild and fertile swampy areas bordering the receding shallow inland seas, giant fern trees took hold, forming thick jungles of vegetation. As the plants and trees died, layer upon layer of dead vegetation, often buried by sediment, decomposed into peat. Millions of years later, the peat was compressed into the harder fuel, coal, which was eventually mined in the southwestern fringe of the Chicago region just beyond Joliet, at Coal City and Braidwood.

Effect of the Glaciers

Many thousands of years ago, changes in climate brought on the glacial period. At least four successive ice sheets crept down from Canada and covered much of the northern part of the United States, including most of Illinois. These glaciers, advancing and retreating, greatly altered the landscape.

The moving ice masses ground down elevations, polished rough surfaces, and gouged and deepened such areas as the basin of Lake Michigan. The glaciers left behind a covering of glacial drift—a jumble of clay, sand, gravel, and boulders over the limestone bedrock. In some places this drift reached a depth of more than 150 feet (45.7 m) with an average depth of between 50 and 60 feet (15.2-18.3 m). Later some of the drift was commercially quarried.

In the Chicago region, the last glacier receded about 13,500 years ago, having sculp-

Figure 2.2. Gravel pit along U.S. 45 in Lake County, Illinois, showing glacial till of the Valparaiso Moraine. (Photograph by Irving Cutler.)

tured the basic landscape surface. Chicago now occupies a lake plain which is hemmed in by a series of concentric ridges of glacial drift, called moraines, which are aligned generally parallel to the lake. The largest and most significant, especially in regard to the drainage pattern, is the outer crescent-shaped ridge around the southern end of Lake Michigan, stretching from southeastern Wisconsin into southwestern Michigan. Its surface exhibits substantial diversity. It is known as the Valparaiso Moraine (fig. 2.3) and borders the southern and western part of the Lake Plain. Its inner edge is followed approximately by the Tri-State Tollway. It averages about 15 miles (24.1 km) wide and in general stands 12 (19.3 km) or so miles from Lake Michigan. The elevation of the moraine ranges from less than 100 feet (30.5 m) to over 500 feet (152.4 m) above the level of Lake Michigan. The steep front of the moraine is used for the toboggan slide in the Palos Hills Forest Preserve.

The northern part of the Valparaiso Moraine is rugged and irregular, exhibiting a surface characterized by rounded hills and undrained depressions. In Lake County, Illinois, and crossing into Wisconsin many of these depressions are occupied by about one hundred small lakes and ponds. This inland lake region has become an important recreational and residential area with sizable settlements developing around some of the larger lakes, such as Fox Lake, Pistakee Lake, Round Lake, Long Lake, Grays Lake, and Lake Zurich.

On the lake side of the northern part of the Valparaiso Moraine is the much smaller Lake Border Upland, an elongated belt of nearly north-south ridges with a width of 5 to 15 miles (8.0-24.1 km). The main segment extends northward from about Des Plaines and Winnetka, with a narrow extension south into the Lake Plain as far as Oak Park. Some ridges rise to about 200 feet (61 m) above the lake level and are interspersed by gentle sags occupied by several small streams and an occasional marsh, such as the Skokie Lagoons. Lakeward of the Valparaiso Moraine and the Lake Border Upland—except between Winnetka and Waukegan where the bluffs rise abruptly from Lake Michigan—spreads the flat Lake Plain on which Chicago is situated.

The Lake Plain

As the last glacier retreated, water drainage to the north was blocked by the ice; consequently, the glacier meltwater filled the depression between the receding ice front and the Valparaiso Moraine. This created a lake, marginal to the ice, that at its highest elevation rose about 60 feet (18.3 m) above the present surface of Lake Michigan. This enlarged Lake Michigan, geologically known as Lake Chicago, covered all of the present city of Chicago as well as a portion beyond it. The boundary line of the lake reached from approximately what is now Winnetka through the present communities of Maywood, La Grange, and Homewood, crossing the state line at Dyer, and then continuing eastward beyond Chesterton, Indiana.

The accumulated water receded in stages, finding its way into the Illinois-Mississippi River drainage system by enlarging two outlets through the Valparaiso Moraine drainage divide. These outlets were later to become important transportation corridors. One of the outlets, which now holds the Calumet Sag Channel, was through the Sag Valley south and southwest of the city. The other outlet, to the southwest, sometimes known as the Chi-

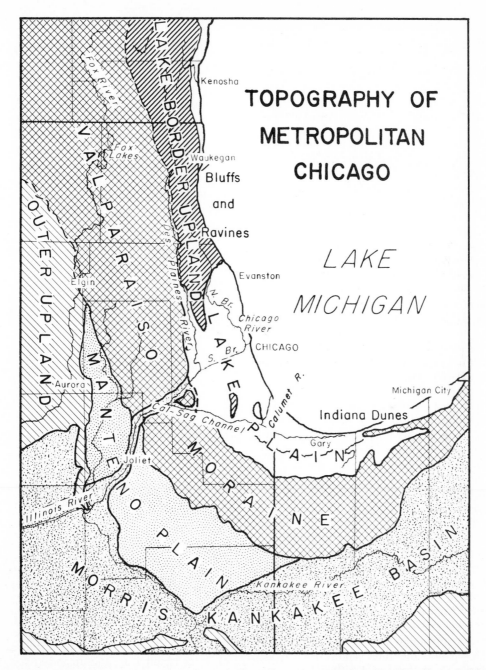

Figure 2.3. Topography of Metropolitan Chicago. (Reproduced by permission from *Open Land in Urban Illinois* by Rutherford H. Platt, Northern Illinois University Press, 1971. Based on F. M. Fryxell, *The Physiography of the Region of Chicago*.)

cago Portage, contained first the Illinois-Michigan Canal and later the Chicago Sanitary and Ship Canal, as well as other important transportation arteries, including railways and highways.

The lake bottom of Lake Chicago left the Chicago area remarkably flat—a lake plain—except for a few small islands that had existed in the lake, such as Mount Forest Island, Blue Island, and Stony Island, and some spits, sand bars, and crescent-shaped beach ridges that emerged as the water receded in three different stages (fig. 2.4). These ridges stand about 60 feet (18.3 m), 40 feet (12.2 m), and 20 feet (6.1 m) higher than the present approximately 580-foot (176.8 m) height above sea level of Lake Michigan. Driving away from the lake on an east-west street, such as Devon Avenue (6400 N) or 111th Street, will take one over each of the three beach ridges of Lake Chicago within a distance of 10 to 15 miles (16.1-24.1 km).

Because they were often the best-drained ground in an otherwise marshy area, some of the sandy spits, bars, and beach ridges of the area became Indian trails, and some are now parts of modern roads such as Green Bay Road, Gross Point Road, Ridge Avenue, North Clark Street, Vincennes Avenue, U.S. routes 6, 20, 30, and Interstate 94. The good drainage also made these areas attractive locations for cemeteries and golf courses. Both Graceland and Rosehill spits bear the names of large cemeteries on them.

Three small lakes near the Chicago-Hammond state-line boundary are isolated remnants of the glacial Lake Chicago. In recent decades these lakes have declined in size because of marginal filling and drainage alterations. Lake George, on the Indiana side, has virtually disappeared; Wolf Lake is a recreational area; and Lake Calumet has been developed as the major port of Chicago. Beach ridges separate the three lakes from Lake Michigan. A series of such ridges has hampered drainage in the Calumet district.

After the Glaciers

The basic topography of the Chicago area that developed through these ecological epochs resulted from the superimposition on the limestone bedrock of an uneven layer of glacial drift and, later, of the deposits of Lake Chicago. Since the Ice Age, a number of limited topographic changes have occurred. Through weathering, wind and water deposition, and vegetative growth, the present soils have been formed on the surface of the deposits of the glacial period. The soils are generally of good quality, very productive agriculturally except where there are major drainage problems or where extensive sand deposits have accumulated, such as along the shore at the head of Lake Michigan, especially in parts of northwestern Indiana. A magnificent concentration of dunes has developed there due to the continued action of the lake current and winds sweeping sand southward.

A dune is formed when sand from the beach is blown inland until it strikes an obstruction, such as a bush or tree, and piles up on the windward side. In time the sand dune becomes higher, often burying the obstruction. The wind may blow sand from the windward slope of the dune over to the leeward side, creating a "moving dune" which migrates slowly inland. Small dunes are found several miles inland from Lake Michigan; the large ones are found very close to the lake, where some approach a height of almost 200 feet (61 m).

Another noteworthy postglacial change has been the result of shoreline erosion which created very scenic bluffs with deep ravines along the lake between Winnetka and Waukegan. Some of the bluffs are almost 100 feet (30.5 m) high, and many of the more than twenty major, deep, V-shaped ravines extend a mile (1.6 km) or so inland. The ravines have been eroded by the downward-cutting action of water runoff from the upland area as the water seeks to reach the lake below.

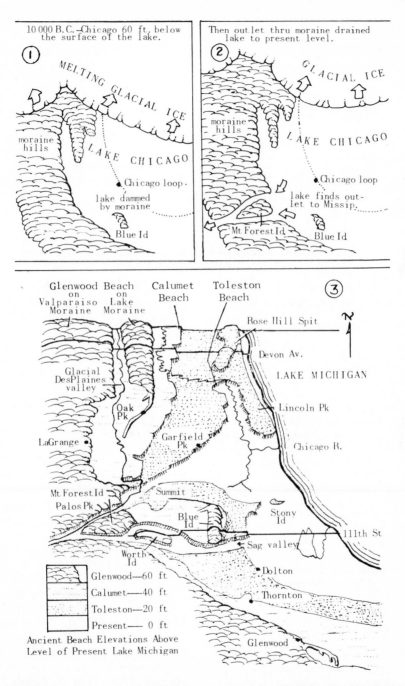

Figure 2.4. Stages and development in the Chicago area of the three ancient beach levels of Lake Chicago. (From "Lake Michigan's Ancient Beaches" by W. J. Beecher, Science Notes of the Chicago Academy of Science.)

Figure 2.5. Looking east along 115th Street where it drops down from the ancient beach ridge at the intersection of Michigan Avenue, 1895. (Photograph by Henry R. Koopman, courtesy Mrs. Walter Gindl.)

The effect of lakeshore erosion is dramatically illustrated by the following report:

> In 1845 and for about ten years following there was a village located in the southeast corner of what is now the Fort Sheridan grounds. This village was known as St. Johns. The chief industry was brick making, the yards employing as many as eighty men. . . . North of the clay pit remnants of a foundation and of an orchard are at the very margin of the lake cliff. Reports differ as to the amount of land that has been cut away at this point, but all agree that it was more than 100 feet. Some old settlers insist that 300 to 400 feet have been removed, and that the cliff and even overhanging are reported by some to have been in the yard to the west of the westernmost house in the village. If this is true, the entire site of the village of St Johns is east of the present shoreline.[1]

Today, even these meager traces of the village have vanished, prey to the attacking waves and currents.

The Chicago River

The Chicago River is the outstanding topographic feature of the rather featureless Lake Plain that contains the city of Chicago. Though short and sluggish (the important South Branch is only about 6 miles, or 9.7 km,

in length), the river has been a major factor in the establishment and growth of the city. It was the early connecting route between the East and the commercial wealth of the Middle Prairie. Early Chicago centered upon the river and consisted mainly of the rectangular peninsula about a mile square (2.6 sq km) which was enclosed on the north and west by the river and on the east by the lake. In the period of its greatest use, the river handled huge cargoes of grain, lumber, and manufactured goods.

The river's main channel with its two branches forms a Y, with the junction near the Merchandise Mart. This configuration has, by tradition, divided Chicago into three broad sections—the North, South, and West sides.

The North Branch of the Chicago River originates in Lake County, Illinois, as three small streams flowing southward in the sags of the moraines of the Lake Border Upland. The three streams—the Skokie River, the Middle Fork, and the West Fork—join in northern Cook County and flow southeast toward the junction with the main channel. The North Branch is joined just south of Foster Avenue (5200 N) by the North Shore Channel. This 8-mile (12.9 km) channel was completed in 1910 by the Metropolitan Sanitary

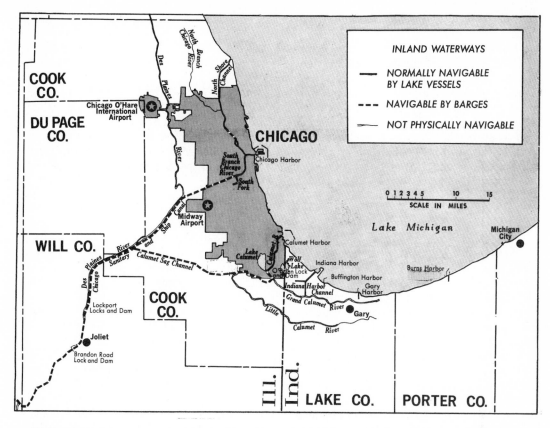

Figure 2.6. Harbors and waterways of the Chicago area. (Updated from *Mid-Chicago Economic Development Study*, Mayor's Committee for Economic and Cultural Development of Chicago, 1966.)

District of Greater Chicago to furnish an outlet for drainage and sewage for Wilmette, Evanston, and the adjacent area. Fresh water for the channel is drawn from Lake Michigan through the gates at Wilmette.

The South Branch was usually navigable only as far west as the present Leavitt Avenue (2200 W). Often, however, during spring high water it was possible to push canoes across the marshy divide all the way to the Des Plaines River (near 49th Street and Harlem Avenue, 7200 W), by using seasonal Mud Lake which bridged most of the 6-mile (9.7 km) portage between the two rivers.

The Chicago River has been greatly modified since it was navigated by the early explorers and was alive with fish, mink, muskrat,

turtles, and wading birds. It has been straightened and widened in parts. The sand bar which blocked the river's mouth and caused it to bend southward and flow into the lake opposite the foot of Madison Street has been removed. An artificial island, Goose Island, was created and a sharp bend by-passed by the construction of the mile-long (1.6 km) North Branch Canal. Most important, the portage was eliminated and the South Branch of the river was connected with the Illinois-Mississippi River waterway system, first by the Illinois and Michigan Canal in 1848, and later by the Chicago Sanitary and Ship Canal in 1900. And the flow of the Chicago River was reversed to flow into these connecting waterways instead of into Lake Michigan whose shoreline waters were being polluted by the unsanitary discharges of the river.

Unfortunately, during this period the river was largely walled off by industrial development and its aquatic life drastically curtailed. However, in recent years various environment-conscious groups have promoted limited improvements and have dedicated themselves to the rebirth of the river as a multipurpose, clean, pleasant, life-supportive waterway which could serve as a vibrant artery through the heart of the city as well as a controlled transportation and industrial corridor.

The Calumet River

At the southeastern end of the city is Chicago's other important river—the Calumet. It is formed by the confluence of the nearly parallel Grand Calumet and Little Calumet rivers. Joined to the Calumet River as a saclike attachment is Lake Calumet on Chicago's far South Side and the site of Chicago's major port. Unlike the Chicago River, the Calumet River played an insignificant role in Chicago's early history. Today, however, it is one of the most industrialized rivers in the world— "the Ruhr of America"—and carries considerable tonnage.

The early settlers found the Calumet to be a strange, erratic, meandering stream that had formed an elongated loop parallel to the lake. The river flowed westward from its source in Indiana and then looped back only 2 or 3 miles (3.2-4.8 km) to the north, flowing in the opposite direction to empty into Lake Michigan near Miller, Indiana. Frequently, the mouth of the river was nearly closed by sand drift.

Later, man altered the Calumet River also to suit his purposes. The mouth at Miller was blocked and a channel was dug from the river near Hegewisch to an outlet into Lake Michigan at about 90th Street in South Chicago. The river was again altered in 1922 when the 16 mile (26 km) Calumet Sag Channel was dug. The Calumet River was reversed to flow away from Lake Michigan into the

Chicago Sanitary and Ship Canal, and so eventually into the Illinois-Mississippi river system.

The Drainage Pattern

The reversal of the Chicago and Calumet rivers altered the unusual drainage pattern of the Chicago region. In creating moraines parallel to Lake Michigan, glacial action also created a divide parallel to the lake and relatively close to it. Water on one side of the divide flows into the Great Lakes-St. Lawrence River system; on the other side, into the Gulf of Mexico via the Illinois-Mississippi river system. The divide is less than 4 miles (6.4 km) from the lake in the Waukegan, Illinois, area, and at its farthest point, south of Hammond, Indiana, only about 20 miles (32 km) from the lake.

A few short rivers on the eastern side of the divide, such as the Chicago and the Calumet, broke through sand bars to reach Lake Michigan, but the major rivers, such as the Fox, Des Plaines, and Kankakee, never penetrated the moraines; instead, they flow into the Mississippi Basin. In places, the divide is less than 100 feet (30.5 m) above Lake Michigan. At its lowest point, the Chicago outlet at Summit, Illinois, the divide is a barely discernable 15 feet (4.6 m) above the lake.

The Kankakee, Fox, and Des Plaines rivers have the largest drainage basins in the area. The Kankakee drains the largest area—over 5,000 square miles (12,950 sq km), but only a small part, in Will County, is within the six-county metropolitan area. The river starts in Indiana, flows westward, and crosses the southwest corner of Will County, where it joins the Des Plaines River to form the Illinois River. In Indiana, the Kankakee is considered a drainage ditch, straightened and channelized to drain the old Grand Marsh, once one of the nation's most famous wildlife areas. The drainage project produced a million acres (405,000 ha) of rich Indiana farmland. In Illinois, the Kankakee is still a winding natural river, the home of a spectacular array of wildlife and where record-sized fish are caught. The river is an important source of drinking water, and recreation along the Illinois portion of the Kankakee adds an estimated $25 million annually to the economy of the area. The differences in use of the river in Indiana and Illinois have, on occasion, led to friction between the two states over the "waterway with a split personality."

The Fox River rises in Wisconsin and flows 70 miles (113 km) southward before entering the northwestern part of Lake County, Illinois. There it flows through the recreational Chain of Lakes, Fox Lake, and Pistakee Lake area. The Fox River then continues southward through McHenry and Kane counties before angling to the southwest and joining the Illinois River at Ottawa, Illinois. The drainage area of the Fox covers almost 2,000 square miles (5,180 sq km), about half in the Chicago Metropolitan Area. In Kane County the river is near the outward-pushing edge of the urban area, although some of the cities straddling the Fox River, such as Elgin and Aurora, are industrial cities almost as old as Chicago itself.

The Des Plaines River starts in the sloughs and marshes near the boundary between Kenosha and Racine counties in Wisconsin and flows south some 90 miles (145 km) through Illinois' Lake, Cook, DuPage, and Will counties before joining with the Kankakee River to form the Illinois River. The Des Plaines River drains about 1,000 square miles (2,590 sq km), mainly within the Chicago Metropolitan Area. It has two sizable tributaries, Salt Creek and Du Page River, both of which flow parallel to the Des Plaines River itself for many miles. At Summit the Des Plaines River turns to the southwest, descending toward Joliet. It is a small river in the relatively wide, deep, scenic valley formed by the mighty torrents that flowed through the Chicago outlet with the melting of the last glacier.

The 25 miles (40 km) of the Des Plaines River Valley between Summit and Joliet has been suggested as a most desirable site for a linear state or national park. Although dotted with scattered industry and settlements, the valley contains sizable natural areas and places of geologic and historic interest. These include virgin prairie and wetlands, dense forest growth, Indian archeological sites, interesting geologic formations, waters paddled by early explorers, rapids, river islands, abandoned spring-fed quarries replete with fish, historic trails, and towns, such as Lockport, rich in history and beauty.

Because the land of so much of the Chicago area is flat, the rivers tend to be sluggish and drainage of the land is poor, with some of the lowland river areas subject to occasional flooding. Furthermore, layers of impermeable clay left by the glaciers hampered the drainage of surface waters, created a high water table, and helped make early Chicago a virtual sea of mud for at least part of the year. To get adequate gradient for storm and sanitary sewers, the Metropolitan Sanitary District of Greater Chicago has had to provide more than a dozen pumping stations to enhance the flow to the extensive drainage canal system.

The Vegetation

The Chicago region is a transition zone between the vegetative patterns of the great eastern forests of North America and the prairies farther to the west. The transition zone once contained both forests and tall-grass prairies. An early settler, Gurdon S. Hubbard, wrote about the natural landscape with its grasslands and forests:

> The waving green, intermingling with a rich profusion of wildflowers, was the most beautiful sight I had ever gazed upon. In the distance the grove of Blue Island loomed up— beyond it the timber on the Des Plaines River.

The solid stands of forest diminished westward in Illinois largely because of declining rainfall. The zone's average annual rainfall of about 34 inches (86 cm) is substantially less than the 40 to 50 inches (102–127 cm) farther east that nurtured a beech-maple forest. However, there is enough rain to support drier oak-hickory stands and extensive tall-grass prairie. The percentage of forestland generally increased to the east and to the north and was prevalent and more varied in wet bottomlands, as along the rivers. Along the river floodplains are elms, hackberries, and basswoods.

The preferred choice of the earliest farmers in the area usually was well-drained prairie land that was partly forested. The forest supplied construction timber and fuel and was a protection against winds and floods, but it also presented problems of clearance. Later settlers had to choose mainly prairie land, but this generally was more productive than cleared forest land.

The natural vegetation of the Chicago area is indicative of its position as a meeting ground for plants of a number of regions. The plants fall chiefly into three categories: "hangovers" of species of the north that had persisted locally since the glacial era; returned plant migrants from the southeastern states that had been driven out during glacial times; and a few species that migrated from the semiarid Southwest.

Within a generation or two of the start of intensive settlement of the area, most of the forest and prairie grass had disappeared except in a few isolated patches and on the moraines and along the rivers where drainage was often poor. Many of the remaining wooded areas, especially along the rivers, later became part of the extensive 65,000 acre (26,325 ha) system of Cook County Forest Preserves.

The cosmopolitan character of the vegetation in the area was especially evident under the unusual and largely untouched conditions of the Indiana sand dune region. Professor H. C. Cowles, a pioneer plant ecologist, largely from his studies of these dunes, developed the concept of the dynamics of plant succession, especially the correlation between changes of vegetation as landforms are changed by the action of wind, wave, and the presence of vegetation. The following is his description early in this century of the vegetation of the Indiana dunes:

There are few places on our continent where so many species of plants are found in so small compass. This is in part because of the wide diversity of conditions prevailing there. Within a stone's throw of almost any spot one may find plants of the desert and plants of rich woodlands, plants of the pine woods, and plants of swamps, plants of oak woods and plants of prairies. Species of the most diverse natural regions are piled here together in such abundance as to make the region a natural botanical preserve, not only of the plants that are characteristic of northern Indiana, but also of the plants of remote outlying regions. Here one may find the prickly pear cactus of the southwestern desert hob-nobbing with the bearberry of the arctic and alpine regions. The commonest pine of the dunes, the jack pine, is far out of its main range, reaching here its farthest south. One is almost startled at the number of plants of the far north, many of which, like the jack pine, are not found to the southward of our dunes. Among such plants of the Canadian forest and tundra are the twin flower, the glandular willow, the poverty grass, and the northern rose. Northern plants are particularly characteristic of the dune swamps and embrace such interesting species as the larch, bunchberry, dwarf birch, sage willow, numerous orchids, cranberry, leather leaf, and many more. Many of these species are found nowhere for many miles outside of the dune region.[2]

The Climate

A major characteristic of the climate of Chicago is its variability from season to season, and even from day to day. The seasonal change in temperature is due to the northern latitude and the interior continental location. Seasonally the temperature ranges from an average daily reading of about 25°F (−3.9°C) in January to about 75°F (23.9°C) in July with a yearly mean of about 50°F (10.0°C). Individual daily extremes have officially been recorded ranging from $-27°F$ to $105°F$ ($-32.8°C$ to $40.6°C$).

The day-to-day changes are mainly the result of a procession of high and low pressure areas that move across Chicago at intervals of a few days and in a generally easterly direction. The succession of highs and lows gives to the weather its frequently changing aspects of warm and cold, rain and snow, cloudy and sunny.

The climate of the Chicago area is suitable for agriculture, and the region used to be very productive, especially in dairying and truck farming. Agriculture declined with the spread of urbanization, although it is still high in the surrounding rural areas.

The region averages 183 consecutive frost-free days a year. Summers are warm, but the lake, in addition to its welcome breezes, exerts a moderating influence to keep the city somewhat cooler than it is farther inland. The reverse occurs in the winter, with temperatures higher near the lake than to the west. Despite Chicago's "Windy City" reputation, the winds, predominantly from a westerly direction, are moderate in velocity, with an annual average of 10.4 miles (16.7 km) per hour. (Although some claim the "Windy City" nickname is even older and credit it to politicians, the title is often said to have been bestowed in 1893 by the editor of the *New York Sun,* Charles Dana, who was tired of hearing Chicagoans boast about the wonders of their World's Exposition.)

Precipitation is adequate, averaging 34.44 inches (87.5 cm) annually, with about one-third usually coming during May, June, and July. Droughts are rare, as are exceedingly prolonged rainy periods. Annual seasonal snowfall is 39.3 inches (99.8 cm), with extremes ranging from 9.8 inches (24.9 cm) in 1920–21 to 89.7 inches (227.8 cm) in the unusually severe winter of 1978–79. On the average, 10 inches (25.4 cm) of snow is considered the equivalent of 1 inch (2.54 cm) of rain.

There is some evidence that Chicago has slightly more rain than the nearby suburbs and rural areas. A recent study showed that the city produces atmospheric changes which increase local rainfall slightly. Two factors seem to account for this increased rainfall over the city. First, there is a greater prevalence of dust, water vapor, and tiny particles over the city. These provide nuclei for cloud condensation. Second, more heat rises from city surfaces, buildings, and automobiles and as this warm air rises, it is cooled and may form rain clouds over the city.

In summer, the Chicago area is subject to occasional severe thunderstorms with very strong winds. Once in a while a tornado will develop and touch down, usually in a suburban area. In 1967, for example, a tornado touched down in the southwest suburban area centered around Oak Lawn, killing 33, injuring 500, and causing $50 million damage. A dozen tornadoes have been recorded inside the Chicago city limits, but so far only the one in 1961 has resulted in serious damage. It moved across the South Side of the city from approximately 91st Street and Hoyne Avenue (2100 W) to 61st Street and the lake, killing one person and injuring 115.

Two possible explanations have been given for central Chicago's relative absence of tornadoes. One is the "heat island" theory which suggests that the rising warmer air from the city creates updrafts which cause tornadoes to skip over central Chicago. The more widely accepted theory is that tornadoes thrive on flat land and their force is dissipated somewhat by building obstructions. The built-up suburban sprawl seems to have created a relative "zone of safety" for the central part of Chicago.

Notes

1. Wallace W. Atwood and James Goldthwait, *Physical Geography of the Evanston-Waukegan Region.* Illinois State Geological Survey Bulletin no. 7 (Urbana, 1908), p. 4.
2. S. T. Mather, *Report on the Proposed Sand Dunes National Park, Indiana* (Washington, D.C.: Dept. of the Interior, National Park Service, 1917), p. 44.

Figure 3.1. Looking westward at the site of Chicago, 1779. North of the bend in the Chicago River is the cabin of Jean Baptiste Point du Sable, the first permanent settler (shown in insets). The sand bar at the river's mouth caused the river to bend southward and flow for almost a half mile along approximately what is now Michigan Avenue until entering the lake at about the present Madison Street. In the distant center are the forks of the river where the South Branch and North Branch of the Chicago River join to form the main channel. (Photograph courtesy Chicago Historical Society.)

Chapter Three

THE EVOLUTION
OF CHICAGO

Early Settlement

A century after Marquette and Jolliet had passed through the area in 1673, Chicago still did not have any permanent settlers. During the period of French rule, which lasted until the cession of the land to the British in 1763, there had been sporadic but limited activity in the area. Other explorers for France, notably Robert Cavelier, Sieur de La Salle, and his companion Henri de Tonti, had passed through the area around the 1680s. Later, because of its excellent geographic location and portage, a number of French voyageurs, trappers, and fur traders also traversed the area. Indians, mainly members of the Potawatomi, which was the most powerful tribe around the southern end of Lake Michigan, hunted, traded furs, and occasionally camped in the area they called "Checagou," evidently referring to the garlic, wild onion smell which permeated the air.

The territory was under British rule for twenty years, until the Treaty of Paris of 1783 ended the American Revolutionary War and made the area part of the new United States. The British, nonetheless, lingered on illegally until the Jay Treaty of 1794 pledged British evacuation.

Indian resentment at being driven from their lands continued to make permanent settlement of the area hazardous. A turning point for the Chicago area came with the defeat of the Indians at Fallen Timbers, Ohio, by the army of "Mad Anthony" Wayne. The ensuing Treaty of Greenville of 1795 forced the Indians to cede "one piece of land, six miles square at the mouth of the Chicago River." The treaty cleared the title to Chicago and opened to settlement a 36 square mile area (93.2 sq km) encompassed today by the lake, Cicero Avenue (4800 W), Fullerton Avenue (2400 N), and 31st Street. In 1803 the United States Army erected Fort Dearborn, at an elevated point in the bend near the mouth of the Chicago River, to secure the area and protect the important waterway linkage, which became even more important with the Louisiana Purchase the same year.

In the late 1770s, even before the building of the fort, Jean Baptiste Point du Sable had built a cabin on the north bank of the river in the vicinity of the present Tribune Tower. Du Sable's father is believed to have been French and his mother a Negro slave. Du Sable described himself as a "free Negro."[1] His home was probably Chicago's first permanent dwelling; from here, for about two decades, du Sable carried on trade with the Indians. Later, the house was occupied by another trader, John Kinzie, also a famous early settler of Chicago.

Despite the fort, settlement in this part of Illinois remained very sparse, whereas southern Illinois was rapidly being occupied by settlers. A major reason was the persistent

Figure 3.2. The original Fort Dearborn was erected in 1803 by Captain John Whistler and a company of United States soldiers. It was burned by the Indians in 1812. The site is now the intersection of Michigan Avenue and Wacker Drive. (Photograph courtesy Chicago Historical Society.)

hostility of the Indians who were angered by the continuing takeover of their lands. This was brutally manifested in the War of 1812 when a group of soldiers and settlers, who had been ordered to evacuate Fort Dearborn in order to contract the western military perimeter against the British, were ambushed by the Indians. This ambush took place along the shores of the lake at about what is now 18th Street and Calumet Avenue (344 E). Fifty-three men, women, and children were killed. The Indians burned Fort Dearborn to the ground and once more Chicago lapsed into a prairie wilderness.

In 1816 Fort Dearborn was reestablished following peace between Great Britain and the United States. News of the outpost's reestablishment attracted a few settlers, tradesmen, and agents to the vicinity of the fort. But large-scale settlement did not begin until the conclusion of the Black Hawk War in 1832. The treaty with the Indians provided for their relocation west of the Mississippi River in return for certain payments in cash and goods.

The Indians assembled in Chicago for their final payments in 1835. Gathering there also were a motley group of wayfarers—horse dealers and horse stealers, peddlers, grog sellers, and "rogues of every description, white, black, brown and red—half-breeds, quarter-breeds, and men of no breed at all." By ruse, whiskey, and thievery, they managed to separate the Indians from a good part of their money and goods. About 800 Indians joined in a last defiant dance of farewell before crossing the bridge over the South Branch of the Chicago River and heading westward until Chicago saw them no more.

Town and City

No longer impeded by fear of the Indians, the trickle of newcomers to the little military and trading outpost grew into a stream. The westward movement of people and trade was aided by the opening of the Erie Canal in 1825 and the subsequent establishment of regular, cheap, and convenient steamboat service from the east via the Great Lakes. Migration was also helped by improvements in land transportation to the Chicago area as competing Atlantic ports fostered the building of canals and roads westward to tap the growing midwestern hinterland.

The rapid push westward to this area was also due to a variety of difficulties experienced in other areas—especially in eastern United States and in western Europe. Men were drawn to Chicago by cheap land, jobs, and a speculative fervor stimulated by plans for a canal that would connect Lake Michigan with the Mississippi River.

Settlers came in increasing numbers, some to fan out into adjacent lands and some to remain in Chicago. In 1831 the first Methodist church in Chicago was establish, with a congregation of ten members. Services were held in a log cabin located on Wolf Point, at the fork of the Chicago River. In 1833, the first Baptist, Catholic, and Presbyterian churches were established. In 1833 also, Chicago, with a population of around 350, was incorporated as a town. The town was only ⅜ of a square mile (1 sq km) in size and was centered around the main channel of the Chicago River. Its boundaries were the present Kinzie Street (400 N) on the north, Madison Street (N and S baseline) on the south, State Street (E and W baseline) on the east, and Des Plaines Street (700 W) on the west. Also in the same year Congress appropriated $25,000 for major improvements of the harbor. In 1834, a channel was opened through the sand bar at the mouth of the river and, to protect the entrance to the harbor, 500 foot (152.4 m) piers were constructed on either side.

In the year of its incorporation Chicago was described by the Scottish traveler, Patrick Shirreff as follows:

> Chicago consists of about 150 wood houses, placed irregularly on both sides of the river, over which there is a bridge. This is already a place of considerable trade, supplying salt, tea, coffee, sugar, and clothing to a large tract of country to the north and west; and when connected with the navigable point of the river

> Illinois, by a canal or railway, cannot fail of rising to importance. Almost every person I met regarded Chicago as the germ of an immense city, and speculators have already bought up, at high prices, all the building-ground in the neighborhood.[2]

Chicago's rapid growth was reflected in a number of ways. In 1833 black bear were still being killed on the fringes of what is today's Loop. Only four lake steamers entered the harbor that year; by 1836 the number had increased to 450. A parcel of land at South Water (300 N) and Clark (100 W) streets costing $100 in 1832 was sold for $15,000 in 1835. And by 1837, when Chicago was incorporated as a city, the population exceeded 4,000 people.

The city, as incorporated in 1837, encompassed some 10 square miles (25.9 sq km). Its boundaries were North Avenue (1600 N) on the north, 22nd Street on the south, the lake on the east, and Wood Street (1800 W) on the west. Ten years later, as the population grew, the boundary was extended westward to Western Avenue (2400W).

The author John Lewis Peyton portrayed the burgeoning Chicago of 1848 as follows:

> . . . The city is situated on both sides of the Chicago river, a sluggish slimy stream, too lazy to clean itself, and on both sides of its north and south branches, upon a level piece of ground, half dry and half wet, resembling a salt marsh, and contained a population of 20,000. There was no pavement, no macadamized streets, no drainage, and the three thousand houses in which the people lived were almost entirely small timber buildings painted white, and this white much defaced by mud. . . .
> . . . Chicago was already becoming a place of considerable importance for manufacturers. Steam mills were busy in every part of the city preparing lumber for buildings which were contracted to be erected by the thousand the next season. Large establishments were engaged in manufacturing agricultural implements of every description for the farmers who flocked to the country every spring. A single establishment, that of McCormick employed several hundred hands, and during each season

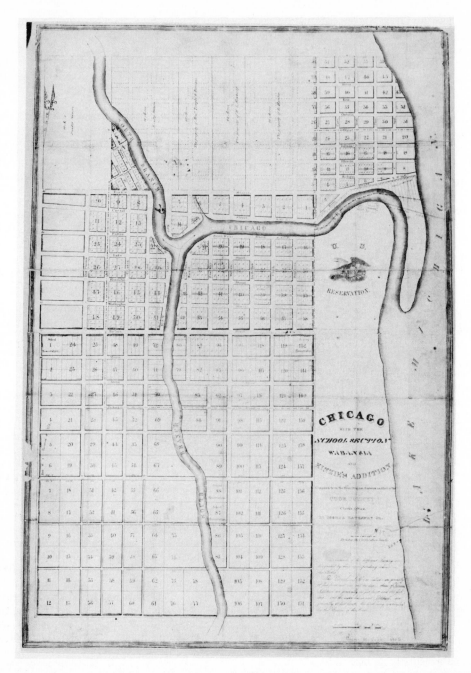

Figure 3.3. Map of Chicago streets and subdivisions, 1834. The United States Reservation included Fort Dearborn in the bend in the river. The same year an artificial canal was cut through the sand bar at the mouth of the river. (Photograph courtesy Chicago Historical Society.)

completed from fifteen hundred to two thousand grain-reapers and grass-mowers. Blacksmith, wagon and coachmaker's shops were busy preparing for a spring demand, which with all their energy, they could not supply. Brickmakers had discovered on the lake shore near the city and a short distance in the interior, excellent beds of clay, and were manufacturing, even at this time, millions of brick by a patent process, which the frost did not hinder, or delay. Hundreds of workmen were also engaged in quarrying stone and marble on the banks of the projected canal; and the Illinois Central Railway employed large bodies of men in driving piles and constructing a track and depot on the beach. Real estate agents were mapping out the surrounding territory for ten and fifteen miles in the interior, giving fancy names to the future avenues, streets, squares, and parks. A brisk traffic existed in the sale of corner lots, and men with nothing but their wits, had been known to succeed in a single season in making a fortune—sometimes, certainly, it was only on paper. . . .[3]

By 1850, Chicago's population had grown to about 30,000 and its future role as a great transportation and industrial center was already clearly evident. The Illinois and Michigan Canal opened in 1848 connecting the Great Lakes with the Mississippi Valley. It was 96 miles (154.5 km) long, from Chicago's southwest side near Ashland Avenue (1600 W) and the South Branch of the Chicago River, to the confluence with the Illinois River near La Salle, Illinois. Shortly thereafter, a period of vigorous railroad building brought railroad tracks to Chicago from almost every direction. By 1855, Chicago was already the focus of ten trunk lines. Ninety-six trains a day arrived or departed from the city, and on a single day the Michigan Central brought 2,000 immigrants into the city.

Chicago's location and its excellent transportation connections with the rich agricultural hinterland helped forge strong bonds of interdependence between the city and the farmers of the Midwest. The farmers funneled their produce to Chicago; the city provided stockyards, food processing, and grain elevators, as well as ships and trains to deliver the commodities eastward. And from Chicago the farmers were shipped clothing, processed food, household items, lumber, and farm equipment. Much of the farm equipment was manufactured by the McCormick Reaper factory which had been established in 1847 on the north bank of the river at the site of the former du Sable cabin. Cyrus McCormick from Virginia was among the first of a long line of commercial and industrial entrepreneurs who, together with their employees, were to help make Chicago "Hog Butcher for the World, Tool Maker, Stacker of Wheat, Player with Railroads and the Nation's Freight Handler."

On the whole, political and economic dominance was held initially by men from the eastern United States. With remarkable combinations of thrift, shrewdness, and drive, they acknowledged no barriers to successful expansion of a wide range of enterprises. Often with little regard for others in their climbing to the top, perhaps they did what had to be done to raise a city out of a swamp.

Among these early pioneer leaders was William B. Ogden of New York who was elected the city's first mayor in 1837. One of the earliest of many Chicagoans to promote the building of railroads, he later was the first president of the Union Pacific. Potter Palmer arrived in 1852. He made a fortune in dry goods and cotton speculation and added to his wealth by developing State Street. In 1867 Marshall Field, who came from Massachusetts, became a part-owner in the firm that was later to bear his name. Two farm youths from the East, Gustavus Swift and Philip D. Armour, helped make Chicago the meat packer of the nation. In 1892 the latter also founded the Armour Institute of Technology, now part of the Illinois Institute of Technology.

A new era in railroad travel began in 1864 when George Pullman invented the sleeping car. Later his shops for building passenger and freight cars spread over 3,500 acres (1,418 ha)

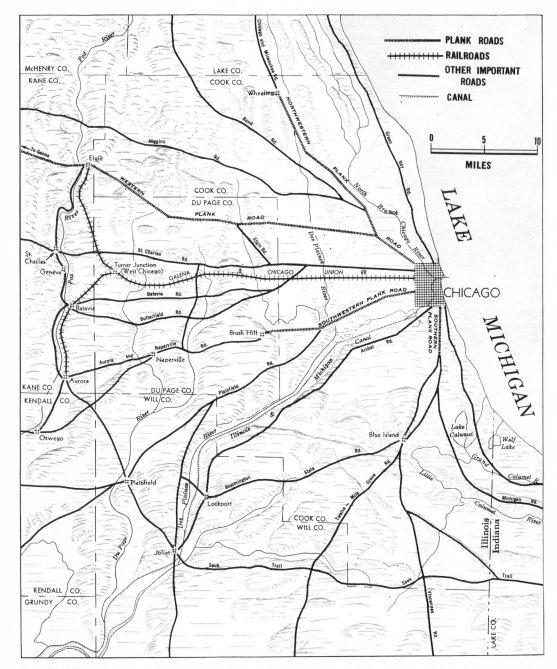

Figure 3.4. Transportation routes of the Chicago area, 1850. (From Harold M. Mayer and Richard C. Wade, *Chicago: Growth of a Metropolis*, 1969. Reproduced by permission of the University of Chicago Press.)

Figure 3.5. View west between Randolph and Washington streets from La Salle Street, 1858. This photograph was taken by Alexander Hesler, a pioneer Chicago photographer who took a series of panoramic views of Chicago. The clutter of retail establishments, livery stables, woodsheds, and cheap hotels is caught in this photograph. The four-story building on La Salle Street in the foreground housed an undertaker. Several ships are visible in the distance on the South Branch of the Chicago River. (Photograph, Alexander Hesler, courtesy Chicago Historical Society.)

Figure 3.6. The Chicago River as seen from State Street, looking eastward, 1868. In the background is the Rush Street Bridge. On the left is the grain elevator of the Galena and Union Railroad; in the lower right-hand corner is a canal boat being towed from the Illinois and Michigan Canal. (Photograph courtesy Chicago Historical Society.)

Figure 3.7. Lock of Illinois and Michigan Canal at Lockport. Photograph probably taken between 1900 and 1910 when canal traffic already had declined sharply. (Photograph courtesy Chicago Historical Society.)

Figure 3.8. View of Chicago in the 1860s. Prominent features of the city are the rectangular grid street pattern and the great activity on the lake and river. (Lithograph, Rufus Blanchard, Chicago. Photograph courtesy Chicago Historical Society.)

near Lake Calumet. Julius Rosenwald, a native of Springfield, Illinois, learned the clothing business, went to work for Sears, Roebuck and Company, and eventually became the president and board chairman as well as one of the nation's great philanthropists. Sears' major competitor was founded shortly after the Chicago Fire of 1871 by A. Montgomery Ward, who had lost everything in the conflagration but $65 and the clothes he wore. He later earned the nickname "watchdog of the lakefront" for his long but successful struggle to save the Grant Park area from being commercialized—thus upholding an 1836 legal provision which designated the area as "public ground, forever to remain vacant of building."

The Street Pattern

Fundamental to Chicago's internal development was its street pattern. The Federal Ordinance of 1785, with its land survey provisions, imparted to early Chicago a basic functional pattern of land subdivision and roads. Even today it is still a strong determinant in the pattern of streets, traffic flow, commercial development, and the arrangement of lots and parcels.

The survey divided the land into square-mile (2.59 sq km) sections using a rectangular grid system. The section lines were a mile (1.6 km) apart and ran either north-south or east-west. They became the city's main traffic thoroughfares and later the major routes of public transportation. The section-line streets also became endless ribbons of commercial development that ultimately became too extensive and inefficient. Major shopping areas often developed at the intersections of section lines, such as 63rd and Halsted (800 W), and Madison (N and S baseline) and Pulaski (4000 W).

In Chicago there are typically sixteen short blocks to the mile (1.6 km) in the east-west direction and eight long blocks in the north-south direction, although there are many variations from this pattern, especially in the older parts of the city. The street numbering system of Chicago was adopted in the early 1900s and, with a few exceptions, is based on a theoretical 800 numbers to the mile (1.6 km). Thus there are the section line streets of 31st, 39th, 47th, 55th, and so on, and in the other direction such streets as Halsted (800 W), Ashland (1600 W), Western (2400 W), and Kedzie (3200 W). Frequently, half-mile (0.8 km) streets, halfway between the section lines, became important thoroughfares and shopping streets, such as California Avenue (2800 W) and 51st Street.

In time, as a result of tradition, zoning laws, and actual development, this rigid rectangular grid system became virtually fixed as the basic pattern of Chicago. This had an advantage in that the right-angle pattern eliminated travel dangers associated with streets meeting at acute angles. Chicago's few diagonal streets were major exceptions. Many of these had begun as Indian trails which followed higher and drier land. The subdividing of lots and the assigning of street addresses were also simplified by this rectangular street pattern.

On the other hand, this street pattern led to a monotonous uniformity, made virtually all streets through streets, and fostered unneeded commercial ribbons. Furthermore, the grid system discouraged some pleasing patterns such as distance-saving diagonals, curvilinear streets, cul-de-sacs, streets following terrain, drainage, or scenic conditions, and planned housing and shopping developments—features that have been adopted in many of the newer suburbs of the metropolitan area.

Mudhole of the Prairies

Mud was the main problem of the streets of early Chicago. In 1848 Chicago

> could boast of no sewers nor were there any sidewalks except a few planks here and there, nor paved streets. The streets were merely graded to the middle, like country roads, and in bad weather, were impassable. A mud hole deeper than usual would be marked by signboards with the significant notice thereon, "No bottom here, the shortest road to China." . . . Wabash Avenue, between Adams and Jackson Streets, was regarded as out of town, where wolves were occasionally seen prowling about.[4]

The difficulty arose because Chicago was flat and low, being only about 2 feet (0.6 m) above the river level. Moreover, the sewage

Figure 3.9. A Chicago slough in the late 1880s. At the time of settlement Chicago contained numerous sloughs including a prominent one along South State Street. (Photograph courtesy Chicago Historical Society.)

Figure 3.10. View on Clark Street in 1857. In 1855 the city council had decided to raise the level of the streets and sidewalks to lift Chicago out of the mud. The raising proceeded unevenly for several years, with the result that there were often several levels in the sidewalk in a single block. (Photograph courtesy Chicago Historical Society.)

that did drain off into the Chicago River flowed into Lake Michigan, the city's source of drinking water. The resulting epidemics of cholera, typhoid, and other diseases were not finally curtailed until the flow of the Chicago River was reversed in 1900. Before that, Chicago tried to lift itself from the quagmire by actually raising the elevation of the city. After the death of 1,424 people in 1854 from cholera, the city council at the urging of community leaders including, particularly, a group of downtown businessmen and major industrialists, in a power pattern repeated many times since, decreed that the streets should be elevated. Street levels were raised by piling fill several feet deep; sometimes the fill was obtained from the dredgings of the waterways.

George M. Pullman in 1854 demonstrated successfully, with the help of 500 men and 2,500 jackscrews, how even one of the largest

of Chicago's buildings, the Tremont Hotel, could be lifted eight feet (2.4 m) "without disturbing a guest or cracking a cup." The idea caught on in this spirited community of ardent boosters and within two decades several thousand acres had been raised 3 to 5 feet (0.9 m-1.5 m) above its former level. For a time, however, Chicago exhibited a somewhat confusing pattern of disjointed sidewalks, some up and some down, depending on whether the owner had raised his property or not. And even today, especially in the inner city, one can find yards and homes below the raised street level, some with steps leading down to the first floor, and others with a small bridge-like platform or steps leading from the sidewalk to what was formerly the second floor but is now the main entrance. (See figure 4.22.) In some of the areas, the street was paved on top of solid fill, but the sidewalk was raised over hollow spaces

Figure 3.11. The Illinois Central Railroad in 1860. The railroad followed the lakeshore from the South Side to the Chicago River. Front row buildings in the background are on Michigan Avenue. (Photograph courtesy Chicago Historical Society.)

Figure 3.12. State Street in the late 1860s—looking south from Lake Street. (Photograph courtesy Chicago Historical Society.)

or "vaults" and was held in place by a retaining wall on each side. For a while the spaces under the sidewalks and bridge-like platforms were useful as places for outhouses or for the storage of coal; however, today some of the vaulted sidewalks are in need of costly repairs.

Despite such problems, Chicago continued to grow and prosper. It was buoyed by the opening of the Illinois and Michigan Canal, heavy lake traffic (13,730 ship arrivals in 1869), the coming of the railroads (13 by 1870), the development of substantial industry fueled somewhat by the Civil War, the further settling of its rich hinterland, and the accelerating influx of settlers. Chicago rapidly became the most important link between the industrial east and the rich agricultural land to the west. Between 1850 and 1870 the population increased tenfold, from 30,000 to about 300,000. The disastrous Chicago Fire of 1871, however, cast a temporary pall on the growth of Chicago.

Figure 3.13. The forks of the Chicago River looking north from Randolph Street before the Fire of 1871. The North Branch flows from the top left and the South Branch from the lower right to form the main stem of the river. Two of the major activities along the river are evident here: lumberyards and grain elevators. The open bridge on the right is at Lake Street: in the right background are Illinois and Michigan Canal barges tied up near Wolf Point on the north side of the main stem of the river. (Photograph courtesy Chicago Historical Society.)

The Fire

In the autumn of 1871, Chicago was a city of 334,000, partly a metropolis and partly a frontier town, six miles long and three miles wide. . . . It was known by various nicknames: Gem of the Prairie, Garden City, Queen City. And some considered it one of the wickedest cities in the land. No one thought to call it the Matchbox, with its thousands of wooden structures, wooden sidewalks and heavy streets paved with wooden blocks.

Chicago was divided into three divisions by its river, which was spanned by a dozen wooden bridges and which forked half a mile west of the lake, one branch running northwest and the other south. Nestling between the lake and the southern branch was the South Division, where the city's extremes of wealth and squalor were represented, the elegant houses along Michigan Avenue contrasting with the hovels of Conley's Patch and Healy Slough and Kilgubbin, the principal business establishments balanced by ramshackle barns and storage sheds. Between the north branch and the lake was the North Division, primarily an area of upper-middle-class and wealthy homes, although along the river stood grain elevators, the Chicago and Northwestern Railroad depot, the McCormick Reaper Works, the wholesale meat market and laborers' dwellings. To the west of the river's fork was the West Division, comprising industrial plants, hundreds of frame houses occupied by workers' families and a small, handsome residential area around Union Park.[5]

Figure 3.14. People crowding west across the Randolph Street bridge in an effort to flee the approaching flames of the Chicago Fire of 1871. The Lake Street bridge is on the left. An important means of escape from the downtown area, especially after the bridges over the river had been destroyed by the flames, were tunnels under the river. These had been built to handle the growing traffic and to circumvent the delays caused by the frequent opening of the bridges. The Washington Street Tunnel to the West Side had been opened in 1868, and the La Salle Street Tunnel to the North Side had been opened just three months before the fire started. (From an engraving in the October 28, 1871, issue of *Harper's Weekly.* Courtesy Chicago Historical Society.)

After an unusually long period of drought, the city became tinder dry. The stage was set for the fire that broke out on October 8 in Mrs. O'Leary's barn at 558 De Koven Street (1100 S at the site of the present Chicago Fire Academy). Fanned by a southwest wind, the fire spread rapidly. When it finally subsided two days later, it had thoroughly gutted about 4 square miles (10.4 sq km) of the city. The fire took more than 250 lives, destroyed some 17,000 buildings, and left almost 100,000 people, about a third of the population, homeless. Property loss reached nearly $200 million.

The fire virtually consumed the entire area from Taylor Street on the south to Fullerton Avenue (2400 N) on the north, and westward nearly to Halsted Street (800 W), including the entire downtown area. Only a handful of buildings were spared—including, ironically, the O'Leary house; of these the Chicago Avenue Water Tower is the only remaining landmark. Indeed the city's future appeared so bleak that a New Orleans newspaper wrote: "Chicago will never be like the Carthage of old. Its glory will be of the past, not of the present, while its hopes, once so bright and

Figure 3.15. Looking eastward along Randolph Street from Market Street (now Wacker Drive) after the Chicago Fire of 1871. Prominently visible are the gutted remains of the courthouse and the city hall on the site of the present City Hall-County Building. (Photograph courtesy Chicago Historical Society.)

cloudless will be to the end marred and blackened by the smoke of its fiery fate." Other editorialists reflecting on Chicago's notorious reputation for gambling, saloons, and brothels, especially in its Levee district just south of downtown, felt this was proper retribution: "Again the fire of heaven has fallen on Sodom and Gomorrah!"

The positive faith in Chicago, however, was underscored the day after the fire when Joseph Medill's *Chicago Tribune,* printing from an improvised plant in the unburned area, editorialized:

CHEER UP!
In the midst of a calamity without parallel in the world's history, looking upon the ashes of thirty years' accumulations, the people of this once beautiful city have resolved that CHICAGO SHALL RISE AGAIN!

And Deacon Bross, one of Chicago's greatest boosters and a former lieutenant governor declared:

I tell you, within five years Chicago's business houses will be rebuilt, and by the year 1900 the new Chicago will boast a population of a million souls. You ask me why? Because I know the Northwest and the vast resources of the broad acres. I know that the location of Chicago makes her the center of this wealthy region and the market for all its products.

What Chicago has been in the past, she must become in the future—and a hundredfold more! She has only to wait a few short years for the sure development of her manifest destiny!

Rebuilding and Further Expansion

Determined Chicagoans, who had already created a city on marshland, immediately

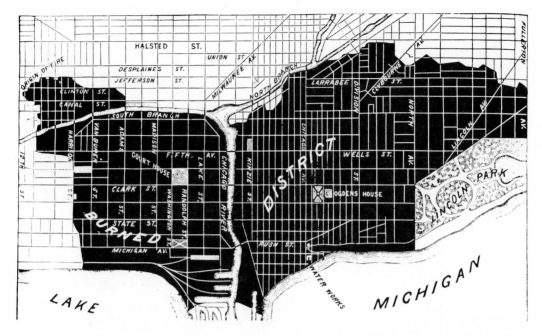

Figure 3.16. Map showing area destroyed by the Chicago Fire of 1871. (Courtesy Chicago Historical Society.)

turned to the task of rebuilding it. Five months after the fire, while some grain elevators and coal bins were still smoldering, Everett Chamberlain wrote in the *Lakeside Monthly* of April, 1872:

> . . . Chicago has, on this 9th day of March, 1872,—five months from the date of that conflagration,—near twenty miles frontage of solid stone and brick buildings in progress, while the number of less permanent structures, from one to three stories high, already built, is counted by tens of thousands. When we take into consideration the fact that those five months have been winter months of unusual severity, the temperature having been, on an average far below the freezing point, we have illustrated, in a single sentence, the extraordinary energy for which Chicago, as a type of the West, has become proverbial . . . . the joke which was in everybody's mouth just after the fire—the joke wherein a citizen of some far-off town was represented as rushing with mad haste to the railway station, and refusing to brook any delay, because, as he said, he

must reach Chicago on such a train, or they would have the whole town built up again before he could get a view of the ruins.

By 1875, little evidence of the catastrophe remained. The people's indomitable spirit and vitality, visions of a profitable future, and generous amounts of outside aid totaling over $5 million, including about $1 million from abroad, all contributed to building a new Chicago that was to emerge bigger and better than ever. Material contributions included 14,000 books donated by the British, with donors such as Queen Victoria, Carlyle, Ruskin, Tennyson, and others autographing their volumes.

The fire accelerated the movement of residential homes from the central business district. The new buildings in the downtown area were larger and higher, conforming to the new city ordinance outlawing wooden buildings in the downtown area. In other parts of the city thousands of homes were going up, many of brownstone and brick. The rebuilding activities attracted to Chicago thousands of laborers

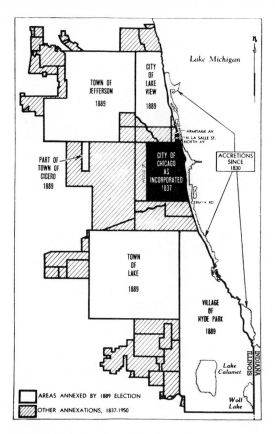

Despite the fire, depressions, and sporadic violent labor strife, such as the Haymarket Riot, Chicago continued to grow rapidly. Besides its commercial and transportation importance as a major handler of grain, cattle, and lumber, the city was becoming increasingly a major center of diversified manufacturing.

The annexation by Chicago in 1889 of four sizeable but relatively sparsely populated communities—the towns of Jefferson and Lake, the city of Lake View, and the village of Hyde Park—increased its size from 43 square miles to 168 square miles (111.4 to 435.1 sq km) and by 1890 the city had a population of 1,099,850. In the preceding decade the output of many of its major industries had more than doubled.

Protecting the People's Health

The rapidly increasing population and industrial growth created serious problems of waste disposal and protection of the city's water supply. Raw, untreated wastes from the Chicago area were being discharged into Lake Michigan through the Chicago River, thereby

Figure 3.17. Growth of Chicago, 1837–1950. In one year, 1889, Chicago increased its size about fourfold through a series of annexations. Since 1950 Chicago has annexed about 15 additional square miles (38.9 sq km), accounted for largely by the land of O'Hare International Airport plus a few small pieces of land on the northwestern and southwestern fringes of the city. (From *Chicago*, Chicago Board of Education, 1951.)

Figure 3.18. Pollution problems plague the wealthy as well as the poor. In recent years some of the North Shore suburbs have had to close their beaches periodically due to the discharge of pollutants into Lake Michigan by communities farther to the north. Steps are being taken to alleviate the problem. View is of the Lake Forest Beach, 1969. (Photograph by Irving Cutler.)

and numerous architects. In the 1880s many of them helped design and construct the world's first skyscrapers using the innovative steel skeleton, elevators, and somewhat later, the floating foundation. The "progenitor" of the true skyscraper was probably William Le Baron Jenney's Home Insurance Building, built in 1885 with an iron and steel framework. It was on the northeast corner of La Salle (150 W) and Adams (200 S) streets, where today the La Salle Bank Building stands.

Figure 3.19. The world's largest sewage treatment plant located at Stickney, Illinois on the western border of Chicago. It is one of the many facilities operated by the Metropolitan Sanitary District of Greater Chicago. The plant treats up to 2 billion gallons of sewage and produces at capacity 900 tons of sludge daily. Some of the sludge has been shipped by barge about 200 miles (322 km) southwest to Fulton County, Illinois, where it is being used to reclaim strip-mined land and to boost agricultural production. (Photograph courtesy Metropolitan Sanitary District of Greater Chicago.)

contaminating the city's own water supply. In the latter half of the nineteenth century, the Chicago area suffered extensively from waterborne diseases such as cholera, typhoid fever, and dysentery. In 1889, in the wake of one such epidemic, the Chicago Sanitary District was created; the name was later changed to the Metropolitan Sanitary District of Greater Chicago, as the district in time encompassed almost all of Cook County. It is an autonomous body, with elected officials and independent taxing authority.

The original purposes of the district were to protect the water supply and beaches of Lake Michigan from pollution, collect and dispose of all domestic and industrial wastes, provide a waterway which would carry runoff from storms, and develop navigation links to the inland waterway system. To prevent the discharge of waste materials into the lake, the flow of both the Chicago and Calumet rivers was reversed and an extensive 71-mile (114.2 km) drainage and flushing waterway system was developed, consisting of channels, rivers, and 52 miles (83.7 km) of constructed canals. These waterways include the Chicago Sanitary and Ship Canal, the North Shore Channel, and the Calumet Sag Channel. The building of the Chicago Sanitary and Ship Canal alone involved moving more earth than was dug in the construction of the Panama Canal.

The disposal of waste was based on the principle of dilution, using enough fresh water diverted from Lake Michigan and flowing through the waterways to the Illinois River to let natural purification processes do the work. A court decision in 1930 later reduced the amount of water diversion from Lake Michigan, forcing the district to use three major treatment plants to prepare the effluent to a level that could be safely handled by the decreased amount of water.

A bold new plan has been developed in recent years by the district to alleviate the flooding and resulting pollution that often occurs after very heavy rains. When the existing largely-combined sanitary and storm sewer system cannot handle all the storm runoff and sewage, the polluted excess flows untreated into basements and waterways, and sometimes backflows into Lake Michigan. Backflows occur when the gates of the North Shore Channel at Wilmette or those of the Chicago and Calumet rivers have to be opened to relieve the mounting water surplus. The plan envisions "bottling a rainstorm" by temporarily storing the contaminated storm water in a series of deep underground tunnels and chambers drilled in the solid rock at a depth of several hundred feet. After the storm the polluted water would be pumped to the surface where it would be treated before being discharged into the waterway.

This Tunnel and Reservoir Project (TARP), or "Deep Tunnel Project," is now well underway. If completed, it will be one of history's largest construction undertakings; however, the escalating cost of the total project, estimated in the billions of dollars, has helped make the project and its effectiveness

a controversial issue. Completion beyond the first phase, which alone includes 110 miles (177 km) of tunnels, drop shafts, connecting structures, pumping stations, and a new treatment plant, remains in doubt.

The Sanitary District has long lessened some of its disposal problems by using the treated waste to produce large quantities of fertilizer. A recent experiment of the district has been the recycling of solid sewage material into a treated sludge fertilizer that is shipped by barge to Fulton County in downstate Illinois. There it is spread on land that has been spoiled by strip mining operations, thus allowing the land to be put back into productive agriculture. The plan, however, has been opposed by some of Fulton County's residents.

The projects of the Sanitary District have eliminated the incidence of serious disease related to polluted drinking water. In addition, two city-owned modern water filtration plants located on the lakefront supply Chicago and many of its suburbs with wholesome low-cost water. The filtration plant adjacent to Navy Pier is the world's largest.

The filtration plants obtain their water from intake cribs that are located 2 to 3 miles (3.2–4.8 km) offshore in Lake Michigan. The cribs are connected with the filtration plants by large water-supply tunnels under the lake bed. After the water is filtered and purified at the two plants, it is pumped, with the aid of eleven strategically located pumping stations, through over 4,100 miles (6,597 km) of mains which supply water to about 40 percent of the people of Illinois.

While the problem of safe drinking water has been solved, the problem of garbage disposal is becoming more serious as an affluent and growing society produces more and more garbage. The average Chicagoan is responsible for about half a ton of garbage each year. Chicago, however, with three large incinerators, is in a more favorable position than the suburban areas which depend largely on sanitary landfills. The readily accessible landfills are rapidly becoming exhausted, resulting in the use of more distant and costly garbage hauling operations. There are some 30 sanitary landfill sites in the Chicago Metropolitan Area which accept municipal wastes, with the majority having as estimated site-life of fewer than five years. Recycling operations, including the use of garbage as a supplemental fuel to generate electricity, are still largely in the experimental high-cost stage. Unlike the operations of the Sanitary District, there is no area-wide garbage disposal agency, although a number of suburban communities have joint operations.

From Fair to Fair

In 1893, just twenty-two years after the fire had leveled the heart of the city, Chicago again attracted the attention of the world with its dazzling, classically-styled World's Columbian Exposition. The 684-acre (277 ha) fair, with its Greek-, Romanesque-, and Renaissance-style architecture, displayed the accomplishments of the nineteenth century and suggested what lay ahead in the twentieth century. Among the famous contributors to the fair were Daniel H. Burnham, chief of con-

Figure 3.20. World's Columbian Exposition, 1893. View is eastward from approximately 65th Street. The building to the left is the Manufactures and Liberal Arts Building and on the right is the Agricultural Building. In the six months the fair was open it attracted 27 million visitors—the equivalent of almost half of the total population of the United States at that time. (Photograph courtesy Chicago Historical Society.)

struction; Fredrick Law Olmstead, who designed the landscaping; Louis Sullivan and Dankmar Adler, who designed the Transportation Building; and Daniel Chester French, Augustus Saint-Gaudens, and Lorado Taft, who contributed statuary. In contrast to the imposing orderliness of the fair proper was the amusement section, located westward along the Midway. It featured exotic displays and entertainment from all over the world, and also contained a giant Ferris wheel which could carry more than 2,000 people at one time.

With its customary audacity, the city built the fair on an apparently impossible sandy site along the lakefront 8 miles (12.9 km) south of the river, and it drew over 21 million people. The fair sparked a feverish real estate boom on the South Side, especially in the Hyde Park-Woodlawn area around the Exposition grounds. As a legacy to the city, it left Jackson Park, the Midway, and the Museum of Science and Industry (the Fine Arts building of the fair).

The many contrasting facets of Chicago in the 1890s were depicted by George W. Steevens, an English journalist, who wrote this sprightly portrayal of the city in 1896:

> . . . Chicago! Chicago, queen and guttersnipe of cities, cynosure and cesspool of the world! Not if I had a hundred tongues, every one shouting a different language in a different key, could I do justice to her splendid chaos. The most beautiful and the most squalid, girdled with a twofold zone of parks and slums; where the keen air from lake and prairie is ever in the nostrils, and the stench of foul smoke is never out of the throat; the great port a thousand miles from the sea; the great mart which gathers up with one hand the corn and cattle of the West and deals out with the other the merchandise of the East; widely and generously planned with streets of twenty miles, where it is not safe to walk at night; where women ride straddlewise, and millionaires dine at midday on the Sabbath; the chosen seat of

public spirit and municipal boodle, of cutthroat commerce and munificent patronage of art; the most American of American cities, and yet the most mongrel; the second American city of the globe . . . the first and only veritable Babel of the age; all of which twenty-five years ago next Friday was a heap of smoking ashes. Where in all the world can words be found for this miracle of paradox and incongruity?[6]

The growth of Chicago continued unabated during the first three decades of this century despite periodic depressions, the turmoil of World War I, the curtailment of European immigration, and the gangster era of the Prohibition years, which created an image of lawlessness that the city's many accomplishments failed to overcome. The national and international notoriety of gangsters such as Al Capone was to reflect upon Chicago for several decades. Between 1900 and 1930 the population almost doubled, increasing from 1,698,575 in 1900 to 3,376,808 in 1930. By 1930 the entire city area, except for some small patches mainly on its fringes, had been occupied. In addition, especially since World War I, population was increasingly overflowing into the suburbs.

To celebrate a century of remarkable growth, Chicago staged the Century of Progress Exposition of 1933–1934. The very colorful and modernistic structures of the World's Fair were erected on artifically created land along the lakeshore from Roosevelt Road (1200 S) to 39th Street and covered 47.4 acres (19.2 ha). The fair emphasized science, technology, industry, and some innovative architecture. Its most popular entertainment attractions included the towering Skyride and Sally Rand's fan-dancing.

Although the fair was held in the depth of the Great Depression, it attracted over 39 million people and proved an unqualified financial success. More important, it showed the world how far the little muddy portagetown had come in one hundred years.

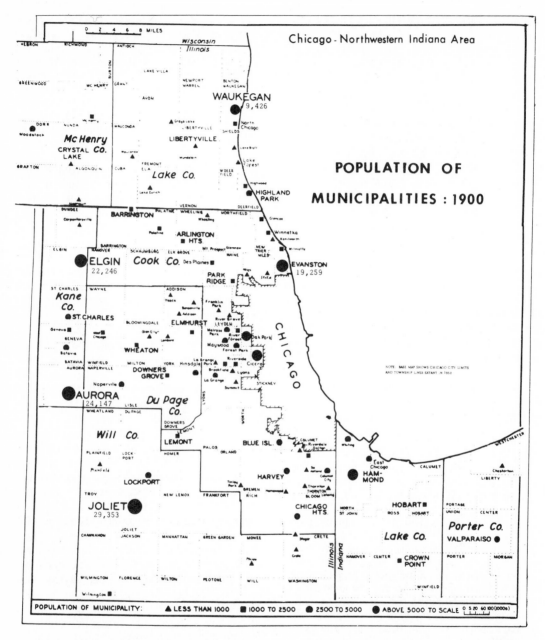

Figure 3.21. Population of municipalities in 1900. (Courtesy Northeastern Illinois Planning Commission.)

Figure 3.22. View of Century of Progress, 1933, looking northward. The fair was located on artificially created land along the lakeshore from Roosevelt Road to 39th Street. In the upper right are the two towers of the famous Skyride. (Photograph courtesy Chicago Historical Society.)

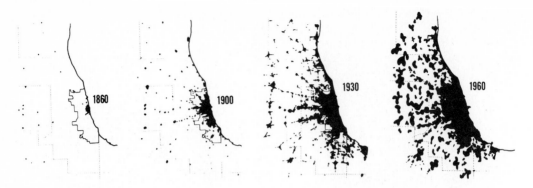

Figure 3.23. Metropolitan growth, 1860–1960. (From Pierre De Vise, *Chicago's People, Jobs, and Homes*, Vol. 1, Department of Geography, De Paul University, 1964.)

Notes

1. Milo M. Quaife, *Checagou: From Indian Wigwam to Modern City, 1673–1835* (Chicago: University of Chicago Press, 1933), p. 36.
2. Patrick Shirreff, *A Tour through North America; together with a Comprehensive View of Canada and the United States* (Edinburgh: Oliver and Boyd, 1835), p. 226.
3. John Lewis Peyton, *Over the Alleghenies and Across the Prairies. Personal Recollections of the Far West One and Twenty Years Ago* (1848) (London: Simpkin, Marshall & Co., 1869), pp. 325–29.
4. Joseph Kirkland and John Moses, *History of Chicago*, vol. 1 (Chicago: Munsell and Co., 1895), p. 119.
5. Herman Kogan and Robert Cromie, *The Great Fire: Chicago 1871* (New York: G. P. Putnam's Sons, 1971), p. 9.
6. George W. Steevens, *The Land of the Dollar* (New York: Dodd, Mead, and Company, 1897), p. 144.

Figure 3.24. Chicago has undergone many changes, including the straightening of the South Branch of the Chicago River, as seen looking northward from about 18th Street, 1929. The river's wide arc to the east from approximately Congress Street to 18th Street had resulted in tight reverse curves in the river, the blockage of through streets connecting the Loop, and awkward track layout for the railroad yards. Straightening the river, accomplished in 1928–30, alleviated some of these problems. Some of the adjacent land was underutilized, and the decline of railroad passenger and freight volume in the area has made much of the land available for redevelopment. (Photograph courtesy Chicago Historical Society.)

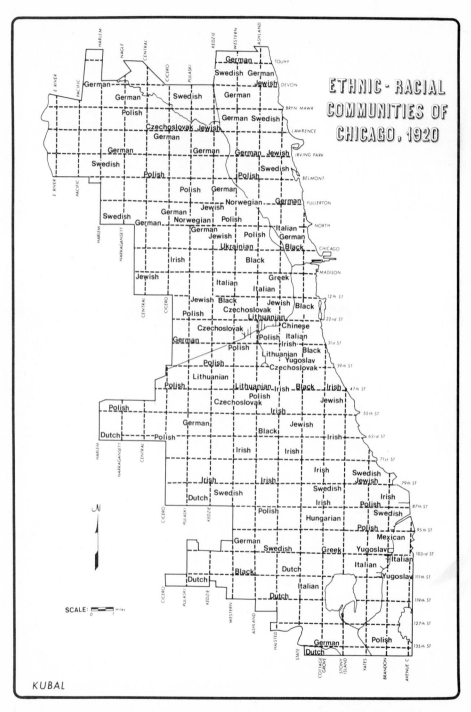

Figure 4.1. The approximate location of Chicago's ethnic and racial communities, 1920. None of the communities was totally homogeneous. Figure 5.1 shows the ethnic and racial communities of 1980. **(Map by Joseph Kubal is based largely on U.S. Census, church, and Chicago Department of Planning data.)**

Chapter Four

PEOPLE AND SETTLEMENT PATTERNS—THE EUROPEANS

Sources of Early Settlers

Chicago's unprecedented growth from a marshy wilderness to a city of well over 3 million people in less than a century and a half resulted largely from an almost constant flow of settlers into the area—settlers whose major points of origin, however, changed with the passing decades. At first settlers came mainly from eastern United States, then from northwestern Europe, later from eastern and southern Europe, and most recently from southern United States, the Caribbean areas, Mexico, and parts of Asia. In all, Chicago is an amalgam of about eighty identifiable ethnic and racial strains. Figure 4.1 shows the approximate location of the major ethnic and racial communities in 1920; figure 5.1 shows the major ethnic and racial communities in 1980.

They came because opportunities in Chicago were much brighter than in their home areas where they had often encountered economic, political, and religious difficulties. They came because Chicago's network of waterways, roads, and rails made it highly accessible. And they contributed with brawn and brains to the development of the great Mid-Continent Metropolis.

The first permanent settlers in the city and surrounding farmland came mainly from New England, the Middle Atlantic States, and nearby Ohio and Indiana. Many were sons and daughters of pioneers emulating their parents. Unlike southern Illinois, very few of Chicago's early settlers came from the South.

In the early decades of Chicago's growth, some of the settlers from the East became the city's political and economic leaders. Many lived in the fashionable areas along Michigan and Wabash avenues in what is now the downtown area. Although their role in the development of Chicago was very important, it was probably never as great as that of the "native elite" in such cities as New York, Philadelphia, or Boston whose roots in their cities sometimes went back two centuries or more. Chicago, especially in its early history, was largely a city of immigrants who came directly from overseas and who became a major force in creating the city.

European Immigration

European immigration into Chicago started on a large scale in the 1840s. The first large group was the Irish fleeing from potato crop failures and from the burden of absentee landlords. The Irish were followed by large numbers of Germans, especially after the

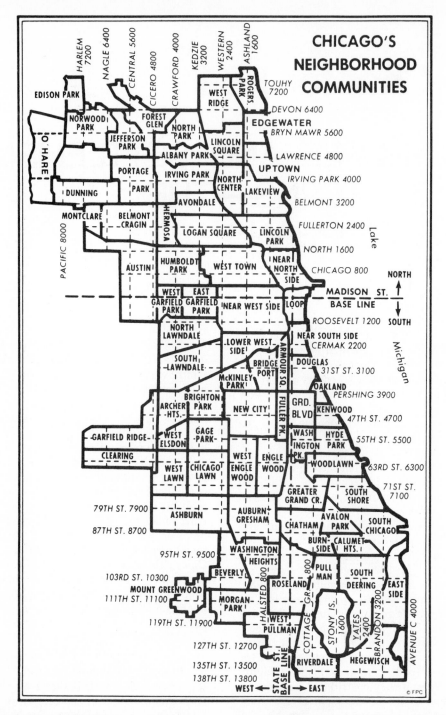

Figure 4.2. The boundaries of Chicago's neighborhood communities were first delineated over 50 years ago through the work of the Social Science Research Committee of the University of Chicago. Since then only minimum boundary refinements have been made, although an additional community, O'Hare, was created largely out of land annexed in the 1950s for the airport, and recently the community of Edgewater was separated out of the northern part of Uptown, making a total of 77 communities. Over the years most of these neighborhood communities have been changing ethnic/racial communities. (Adapted from M. S. Ratz and C. H. Wilson, *Exploring Chicago,* Follett Publishing Co., 1958.)

Figure 4.3. Chicago Avenue, with its street car tracks, brick paving, and wooden sidewalks, looking westward near Franklin Street, 1900. (Photograph courtesy Chicago Historical Society.)

suppression of the democratic revolutions of the 1840s. Scandinavians also began to come in large numbers, together with smaller numbers of English, Welsh, and Scots. By 1860, over half of Chicago's population of 112,172 was foreign-born.

The movement of immigrants to Chicago had been spurred by the opening of the first rail connection between New York and Chicago in 1853, as well as by organized solicitation of settlers and by the glowing reports of Chicago's opportunities that the city's foreign settlers sent to their homelands. By 1890, about 79 percent of Chicago's 1 million people were either immigrants or the children of immigrants. The Germans, Scandinavians, and

Irish, in that order, were the three largest foreign-born groups in 1890. In 1900 Chicago had more Poles, Swedes, Czechs, Dutch, Danes, Norwegians, Croatians, Slovaks, Lithuanians, and Greeks than any other American city.

The flow of Europeans to Chicago continued unabated until the outbreak of World War I in 1914, but the geographic sources of immigration began to shift markedly about 1880. For about the next half century, until national immigration quotas went into effect in 1927, the majority of the immigrants came from eastern and southern Europe. Poles, Italians, eastern European Jews, Czechs, Slovaks, Lithuanians, Ukrainians, Greeks, Croatians, Ser-

TABLE 4.1
European-born in Chicago

Country	1920	1980
Poland	137,611	43,338
Italy	59,215	18,593
USSR	102,095	17,497
Germany	112,288	16,075
Ireland	56,786	8,372
United Kingdom	37,932	5,589
Austria	30,491	4,370
Czechoslovakia	50,392	3,443
Sweden	58,568	2,155

Source: U.S. Bureau of the Census.

bians, and Hungarians were among the largest groups, although there were newcomers from almost every area in Europe. At the peak of immigration, Chicago was the largest Lithuanian city in the world, the second-largest Czech city, and the third-largest Irish, Swedish, Polish, and Jewish city. The concentrations of Irish along with large groups from eastern and southern Europe helped to make Chicago the largest Roman Catholic archdiocese in the United States.

When immigration was sharply curtailed in 1927, European-born whites comprised about 27 percent of Chicago's total population. This figure fell to 20 percent in 1940, 15 percent in 1950, and was 5 percent in 1980. The contrast between the number of European-born in Chicago in 1920 and in 1980 by major country of origin is shown in table 4.1. The table shows that the number of European-born is now comparatively small and that the proportion from northwestern Europe has declined markedly.

In 1970 the median age of European-born was 62 years, thus foreshadowing a further decline of the group which at one time had constituted a majority of the people of Chicago. Their decrease also marked the decline of one of Chicago's most colorful eras—a period when much of Chicago was a microcosm of Europe and when Chicago was probably the most ethnically-rich city in the country. The city had been enriched by many cultures and filled with the sounds of dozens of languages, exotic dress, and a myriad of ethnic shops, schools, churches, synagogues, theaters, cafes, coffeehouses, and newspapers. The immigrants cherished the security of their own institutions in their own neighborhoods.

Who are the Chicagoans? . . . they come from almost every race and people. . . . Germans form solid districts all over, but chiefly in the north and northwest, like the working-class quarters of Hamburg. Poles with their pseudo-baroque Catholic churches with green cupolas make whole areas look like Cracow or Lodz. Czechs and Slovaks keep their homes and little gardens more neatly and reproduce Brunn or Pilsen. . . . Lithuanians, Latvians, and Estonians have their homes out in the southwest, looking severe and North European in winter. There are Scandinavians of all kinds; Italians of all kinds, too, who keep their feast-days and market days as if in the old country and live in solid blocks of the city; Greeks, Yugoslavs, and Syrians mainly on the west side; Mexicans, Chinese, and Japanese, in their characteristic quarters; Hungarians down in the south and also on the north side, mixed in with the Czechs and Germans and Yugoslavs, whom in Europe they dislike; British, Dutch, Belgians, Spaniards, Portuguese, Russians, Ukrainians, and Armenians; and of course the Negroes. . . . Here is a potent source of variety and difference as well as vigor and restlessness.[1]

Figure 4.4. Although their number and circulation have declined steadily through the years, Chicago still had about two dozen foreign language newspapers in 1975. Changes in ethnic numbers have had their effect. Sixty years ago there were four German language newspapers and no Spanish. Today there are one German and five Spanish language newspapers. Most of the newspapers are tabloids put out by tiny two and three member staffs and sold at newsstands in neighborhoods where there are heavy ethnic concentrations. Two of the Spanish newspapers have the largest circulation, around 40,000 each. (Collage by John Downs and Jack Bruza. Courtesy *Chicago Daily News*.)

As the immigrants endeavored to work their way upward economically and socially, they occasionally encountered hostility from those who considered themselves "native Americans," many of whom were themselves the children or the grandchildren of European immigrants.

An Ethnic Checkerboard

The newcomers generally worked at unskilled and menial jobs with minimal remuneration. They usually found housing in congested, low-rent areas around the Loop, areas abandoned by earlier immigrant groups

Figure 4.5. Hull House on South Halsted Street, 1910. It was founded by Jane Addams in 1889. Only a small remnant of the complex was preserved when the campus of the University of Illinois at Chicago Circle occupied the site. (Photograph courtesy Chicago Historical Society.)

who had moved upward economically and outward geographically. The Near West Side community area has been home for a succession of groups—Irish, Germans, Czechs, Jews, and now blacks and Hispanics.

The desire of the immigrants to be close to their countrymen and to establish in their new land the institutions that they had cherished in their homelands led to the formation of numerous ethnic neighborhoods. Some were even formed on the basis of subgroups, such as Venetian, Neapolitan, and Sicilian neighborhoods. A traverse in the vicinity of Halsted Street (800 W) around the turn of the century from the North Side going south would have taken one successively through Swedish, German, Polish, Greek, Italian, Jewish, Czech,

Lithuanian, and Irish neighborhoods. Centrally located on Halsted Street was Jane Addam's Hull House, which catered to immigrants who were often needy, poorly educated, and bewildered by the unfamiliar setting.

Jane Addams described the conditions of the immigrant groups as follows:

Between Halsted Street and the river live about ten thousand Italians. To the south on Twelfth Street are many Germans, and side streets are given over almost entirely to Polish and Russian Jews. Still farther south, these Jewish colonies merge into a huge Bohemian colony. To the northwest are many Canadian-French and to the north are Irish and first-generation Americans. The streets are inex-

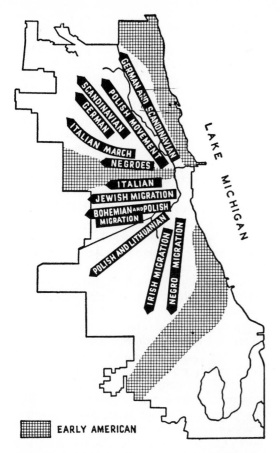

Figure 4.6. Outward expansion of race and nationality groups in Chicago. (Reprinted from Samuel C. Kincheloe, *The American City and Its Churches*, Friendship Press, New York, 1938.)

pressibly dirty, the number of schools inadequate, sanitary legislation unenforced, the street lighting bad, the paving miserable and altogether lacking in alleys and smaller streets, and the stables foul beyond description. The older and richer inhabitants seem anxious to move away as rapidly as they can afford it. They make room for newly arrived immigrants who are densely ignorant of civic duties. Meanwhile, the wretched conditions persist until at least two generations of children have been born and reared in them.[2]

The immigrants helped each other find jobs and spouses and to adapt to the new way of life. In time, with some acculturation and economic success, the immigrant groups and especially their offspring moved outward from their crowded islands near the downtown area. These groups often migrated in an axial pattern with many eventually settling in the suburbs. On weekends some would return to the old neighborhood to visit their parents, attend church, and shop at a delicatessen or bakery. However, each migration outward was usually accompanied by a further loosening of Old World ties as each new generation became more assimilated, more geographically dispersed, and more active in its community's civic and economic affairs.

The Irish

The Irish were the earliest European immigrants to come to Chicago in large numbers. In 1803 the builder and commander of Fort Dearborn was Irish-born Captain John Whistler. (He was also to become the grandfather of the famous painter, James McNeill Whistler.) There was a small group of Irish pioneers in Chicago in 1833 when Chicago was first incorporated. That same year they helped found Chicago's first Catholic church, St. Mary's, on the southwest corner of State and Lake streets. The cost of the little frame building was $400. The first of the annual St. Patrick's Day parades was held ten years later when Chicago had 773 residents of Irish birth. The marchers paraded from the "Saloon Building" on Lake and Clark streets to the new site of St. Mary's on Madison Street near Wabash Avenue.

The disastrous potato famines in Ireland during the 1845 to 1860 period and the perennial problems of overpopulation, political dissatisfaction, and an oppressive land system helped to greatly increase Irish migration to the United States. Many were unskilled or semiskilled, unlike the earlier Irish immigrants who were often craftsmen. In 1850 the Irish-born population in Chicago constituted 6,093 of Chicago's total population of 29,963, or about 20 percent, and they were the largest foreign-born group in Chicago. Although the

Germans surpassed the Irish in numbers in the 1860s and succeeding census years, the Irish-born population continued to grow rapidly, reaching a peak of 73,913 in 1900.

Numerous organizations were formed to aid the immigrants. They ranged in scope from nationalist groups to fraternal, cultural, and athletic organizations. Among the groups represented in the United Irish Societies were the Hibernian Benevolent Society, St. Patrick's Society, Irish American Club, and the Ancient Order of Hibernians. A secret nationalist group, Clan-na-Gael, was dedicated to the absolute independence of Ireland.

The earliest Irish communities were largely along the Chicago River. The start of construction of the Illinois and Michigan Canal in 1836 resulted in a settlement along the South Fork of the South Branch of the Chicago River ("Bubbly Creek") in the "Hardscrabble" area. Somewhat later came settlement in the nearby "Canaryville" section of Canalport (later known as Bridgeport), close to the canal route and employment. In 1847, while working on the canal, the Irish staged the first labor strike in the Chicago region. They were unsuccessful in their demands for $1.25 a day wages and a more agreeable foreman. The early Irish settlers grew cabbages for their dinner tables in the square block area at 30th and Halsted which is now part of McGuane Park. Until St. Bridget's Church was organized in 1850 to serve the needs of this growing Irish community around Archer Avenue, many of the Irish would row down the Chicago River on Sunday to attend mass at St. Patrick's Church, which was originally located at Randolph Street (150 N) and Desplaines Avenue (700 W).

St. Patrick's Church served the largest Irish community in the city. This settlement was located in the present downtown area mainly along the east bank of the South Branch of the Chicago River. In 1856, a new building for the church was completed at Desplaines and Adams (200 S). The building survived the Chicago Fire and today is the oldest church building in the city. It has been designated a Chicago landmark. In the vicinity of the church, around Adams and Franklin (300 W), was "Conley's Patch", the birthplace of two colorful, but corrupt politicians, Michael "Hinky Dink" Kenna and John "Bathhouse" Coughlin, who ruled the downtown First Ward for many years.

Toward the end of the 1850s, about a mile to the southwest of St. Patrick's at 12th Street near Morgan (1000 W), another church was built that was to become a bastion of Irish culture. Holy Family rose out of the West Side prairie to a height of 246 feet, making it the fourth largest church in North America at the time. A few years later, St. Ignatius College Preparatory school was established next to the church. Most Catholic parishes set up their own parochial schools to teach their religious views and because they were apprehensive about the public schools of early Chicago, which they felt were under Protestant domination.

Another area of early Irish settlement was to the east of the North Branch of the Chicago River in a shantytown section known as "Kilgubbin." It lay between Chicago Avenue (800 N) and Division Street (1200 N). This was an impoverished settlement of ramshackle houses, the premises of which often contained pigs, cows, chickens, and geese. Far to the south in South Chicago, amidst the growing industrial area, a small Irish settlement started around midcentury.

The early Irish in Chicago, largely a rural people with limited education transplanted into an urban setting, worked mainly in unskilled occupations—canal diggers, teamsters, railroad builders, factory and stockyard workers, domestic servants, and washerwomen. In the dominantly Anglo-Saxon Protestant business environment of Chicago they sometimes encountered "No Irish Need Apply" signs. But unlike most of the other immigrants, they knew the English language, understood the Anglo-Saxon political system, and showed a flare for public service. They overcame the initial discrimination and improved their lot. In time many Irish became policemen, firemen, streetcar employees, teachers, priests, labor leaders, and politicians, and some advanced

Figure 4.7. St. Patrick's, Chicago's oldest church building, at 718 West Adams Street on the western fringe of the downtown area, was built in 1856 and survived the Chicago Fire. The church and its school once served the sizable Irish community of the area. Today the landmark church attracts downtown workers and visitors and is the traditional starting point of the St. Patrick's Day Parade. In 1953 some of its properties were razed for the Kennedy Expressway. (Photograph by Irving Cutler.)

rapidly in these fields. In 1900 an estimated 40 percent of the policemen and firemen were Irish and many held high positions. Some Irish became doctors, lawyers, professors, writers, and architects. In the latter profession, Louis Sullivan is regarded as one of the fathers of modern American architecture and is particularly associated with the aesthetics of the skyscraper. Among his more famous Chicago buildings are the Auditorium (designed with Dankmar Adler), 1889, and the Carson Pirie Scott store, 1899.

Among the successful Chicago businessmen of Irish descent were Cyrus H. Mc-Cormick (farm machinery), John M. Smyth (furniture), Edward Hines (lumber), and Edward A. Cudahy (meatpacking). Charles A. Comiskey was president of the Chicago White Sox from its founding until his death in 1931.

The Irish of Chicago were depicted in the writings of Finley Peter Dunne and James T. Farrell. Born of Irish-immigrant parents, Dunne (1867–1936) wrote a satirical Chicago newspaper column in which he commented on the affairs of the day with humor and insight through his legendary character, Mr. Dooley, a saloon keeper on "Archey Road" (Archer Avenue). "Dooley poked fun at Irish vices such as clannishness, volubility, flamboyant American and ethnic patriotisms, the ability to condone political corruption, and their excessive thirst for beer and whiskey. But he also praised virtues like courage, generosity, sentimentality, a sense of humor, family solidarity, and hard work."[3] James T. Farrell (1904–1979) is most famous for his *Studs Lonigan* trilogy (1932–1935) which fictionally depicted the life of the lower middle-class Irish Catholics in a neighborhood on the South Side where Farrell grew up in the vicinity of St. Anselm's Church (Michigan Avenue and 61st Street). The Irish often retained their identity through the parish structure rather than through the formation of strong ethnic communities.

As the Irish increased in numbers and moved upward financially more rapidly than most European groups, they also began to disperse outward geographically. Many eventually settled in largely middle-class and upper-middle-class suburbs, where much of their Irish identity has disappeared. From the Near North Side community they moved into the Lincoln Park, Lake View, and Uptown areas. Some moved to the Northwest Side where a small number still live. But the greatest movement was to the south and west (fig. 4.1). From the Lower West Side and Bridgeport communities they moved southwest into McKinley Park, Brighton Park, and Chicago Lawn. Others moved south into New City, Kenwood, Hyde Park, Woodlawn, South Shore, West Englewood, Grand Crossing, Avalon Park, Chatham, and Auburn Gresham. The wealthiest lived even farther south in Beverly. Similarly, to the west, more affluence was evident as parish addresses advanced westward toward Austin and Oak Park—St. Malachy (2200 W), Our Lady of Sorrows (3100 W), Presentation (3900 W), St. Mel (4300 W), St. Thomas Aquinas (5100 W), and St. Catherine of Siena on Austin Boulevard (6000 W) in Oak Park, where the "lace curtain Irish" lived. Unlike many of the other ethnic groups, however, the Irish usually were a minority in the neighborhoods in which they lived.

Dispersal to the suburbs increased rapidly after World War II. Many Irish areas on the South Side and in Austin experienced a rapid racial change. A 1975 survey showed that 110,000 Chicago residents considered themselves of Irish extraction, but there were almost twice as many (210,000) in the suburbs. Two suburbs in particular, Oak Park and Oak Lawn, had relatively high concentrations of Irish residents. Hardly any Irish neighborhoods are left in the metropolitan area. The Irish were the first European group to come to Chicago in large numbers, and having no language problem, they were one of the first immigrant groups to melt into the established society. But some Irish social, fraternal, and benevolent aid organizations and clubs are still

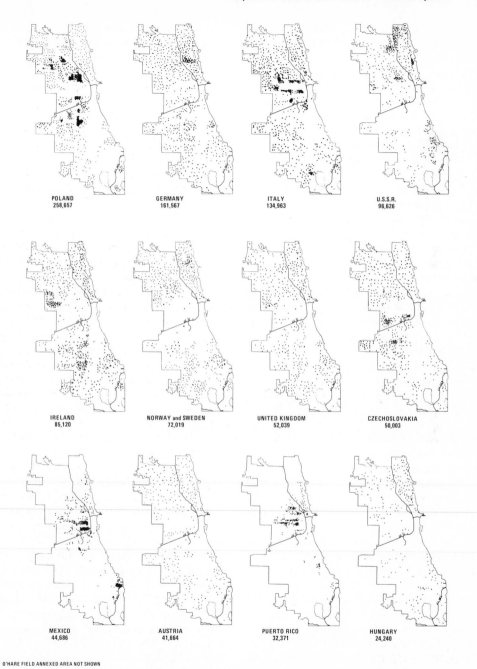

Figure 4.8. Locational pattern of major ethnic groups, 1960. (From Harold M. Mayer and Richard C. Wade, *Chicago: Growth of a Metropolis,* 1969. Reproduced by permission of the University of Chicago Press.)

active, and there has been a recent revival in such cultural activities as the Irish theater and Irish dancing.

The influence and leadership of the Irish are great, especially in the Catholic Church, politics, and education. Among the Chicago Irish, 65 percent of the high school and 81 percent of the elementary school students attended parochial or private schools compared with 27 percent and 24 percent respectively for the total student population. The Irish have been very active in building Loyola and De Paul universities.

All of the bishops of the Catholic church from 1855 to 1915, with one exception, were of Irish descent. This led to some resentment on the part of other Catholic groups which was somewhat alleviated by the establishment of national parishes for non-English speaking immigrants, in addition to the territorial parishes. After about 1900 the high percentage of Irish Catholics in the church declined with the arrival of more and more immigrants from eastern and southern Europe.

Many of the noted members of the Catholic church hierarchy have Irish lineage including Samuel Cardinal Stritch and Bishop Bernard J. Sheil, the latter being born in Chicago. In 1970 16 percent of Irish workers in Chicago held government jobs compared with 6 percent for the remainder of the population. All of Chicago's mayors from 1933 to 1976— Kelly, Kennelly, and Daley—were of Irish descent, and all were born in the community of Bridgeport. Daley served for a record 21 of these years (1955–1976). Bridgeport is believed to have produced more priests and politicians than any other neighborhood in Chicago. In 1969, 11 of the top 16 government offices in Chicago and Cook County were held by men of Irish descent. These were the positions of mayor, city collector, president of the Cook County Board, county clerk, sheriff, assessor, state's attorney, and the heads of the Chicago police, fire, school, and park systems. The descendants of the laborers of early Chicago who lived in Kilgubbin, Conley's Patch, Canaryville, and Hardscrabble now occupy

positions of power and prominence, and every St. Patrick's Day, when all of Chicago is said to be Irish, they are given their due recognition.

The Germans

In the latter half of the nineteenth century and the first decade of the twentieth century, the Germans were the largest foreign-born group in Chicago. During this period the percentage of foreign-born who were German was as high as 38.9 percent in 1860 and in 1890 was still 35.7 percent. In this century the percentage has steadily declined due to decreasing German immigration and to increased immigration from eastern and southern Europe. Today Germans comprise only about 6 percent of the total foreign-born population. Over the years, however, far more Germans have come to Chicago than any other European group. In 1975 a survey showed that the number of people of German extraction totals about 150,000 in the city and an additional 430,000 in the suburbs. The combined population total was larger than that of any other European ethnic group in the metropolitan area except for the Poles.

Table 4.2 based on U.S. Census data shows the percentage of total foreign-born of major foreign-born groups in Chicago by 30 year intervals during the peak period of immigration. Table 4.3 shows the percentage of the total population of Chicago of the major foreign groups during the same years.

Germans first settled in Chicago in the 1830s, but it was not until 1848, when the revolts in Germany failed, that they started to come in larger numbers. In 1845 there were only about 1,000 Germans in Chicago; by 1850 the number had increased to 5,073; and by 1860 the number was 22,230, or almost 20 percent of the entire population. The number of foreign-born Germans in Chicago reached a peak of 191,168 in 1914.

In general, those who came in 1848 or soon thereafter—the "Forty-Eighters"—were articulate, well educated, reform minded, with

TABLE 4.2
Major Foreign-born Groups As Percentage of Total Foreign-born in Chicago

	Germans	Irish	Scandinavians	East Europeans	South Europeans
1860	38.9	36.3	4.0	0.25	0.2
1890	35.7	15.5	16.0	12.5	1.8
1920	13.9	6.0	11.1	35.8	11.9

TABLE 4.3
Major Foreign-born Groups As Percentage of Total Population in Chicago

	Germans	Irish	Scandinavians	East Europeans	South Europeans
1860	19.4	18.2	2.0	0.13	0.1
1890	14.7	6.3	6.5	5.3	0.62
1920	4.1	2.1	3.2	10.6	3.4

a small, vocal minority friendly to the socialist philosophy. Although their immediate reason for leaving Germany was political, the main underlying motive, like that of later German immigrants, was largely economic. As a whole, however, they arrived much less destitute than did the Irish. The religious motive was unimportant.

Many Germans became active in antislavery movements, in founding radical political groups, and in organizing labor unions that were based partly on their experience with the guild system in Europe. Antiforeign feeling (fanned by the Know-Nothing movement) and cultural misunderstandings about such activities as keeping theaters and saloons open on Sunday brought the Germans into conflict with the city establishment on a number of occasions, including the "German Beer Riots" of 1855. In that year Mayor Levi Boone ordered that all saloons and beer gardens be closed on Sundays. German workers, who had traditionally relaxed on Sunday with a stein of beer and the camaraderie of their countrymen, considered this an affront to their freedom. Two hundred German saloon keepers were arrested when they refused to obey the edict. Large numbers of Germans, some armed, marched to the courthouse downtown to protest. In a confrontation with the police, one German was killed, several were hurt, and many were arrested before peace and Sunday beer sales were restored.

A much graver event which attracted international attention was the Haymarket Riot of 1886. The preceding years had witnessed labor turbulence and a number of strikes aimed mainly at bringing about an eight-hour day and other improvements in poor working conditions and low wages. Some of the labor leaders were German socialists and anarchists. A number of the strikes were marked by violence, including one at the McCormick factory, where a clash involving strikers and police on May 3, 1886, resulted in two fatalities and a number of serious injuries. The following evening a bomb was thrown into a group of policemen who had come to disperse a labor protest meeting being held in Haymarket Square (Randolph Street and Desplaines Avenue). Many died, including seven policemen. The bomb thrower was never positively identified, but ten men characterized mainly as anarchist leaders were indicted. Eight of them were Germans.

Eight of the defendants in the Haymarket Riot were eventually convicted, more on the basis of their inflammatory rhetoric inciting to murder than on any proven direct connection with the bomb throwing. Four of the convicted were hung, including Albert Spies, the fiery editor of an anarchist German language newspaper, the *Arbeiter Zeitung;* one committed suicide; and in 1893 John Altgeld pardoned the remaining three, stating that the defendants had not received a fair trial and had not been guilty of the crime as charged. This act of the very able, liberal, and first foreign-born (German) governor of Illinois ruined his very promising political career.

Another result of the Haymarket Riot was the establishment in 1887 of Fort Sheridan on some 600 acres (243 ha) of land along the shore of Lake Michigan 28 miles (45 km) north of downtown Chicago. The land was donated to the federal government by the Commercial Club of Chicago, whose members evidently felt that the presence of federal troops nearby would help to protect their interests against further threat of violence.

By 1890 the number of German-born living in Chicago had reached 161,039 and comprised about 15 percent of the city's total population. At first there had been numerous small German settlements, such as those just north and west of the Chicago River and those south along both sides of the South Branch of the river between 12th and 22nd streets and into the Bridgeport area. The greatest concentration by 1890, however, was on the North Side from Clark Street westward to the North Branch of the Chicago River, and from about Division Street northward, eventually extending into Lake View, Uptown, and Rogers Park. The area was filled with frugal Germans who owned their own homes and who made first North Avenue (1600 N) and then Lincoln Avenue the center of their activities.

For a number of decades the most commonly heard language on North Avenue was German, and for a while "Keep Off the Grass" signs in Lincoln Park were printed in both English and German. On Clark Street near North Avenue was the famous Red Star Inn and the still functioning Germania Club, built in 1888 (on the fringe of today's Carl Sandburg Village complex). Farther south on Clark Street was the old Turner Hall, the home of several German and Swiss Turnverein (physical fitness societies). Streets in the area bore such names as Goethe, Schiller, Lessing, Wieland, Germania, Siebens, and Beethoven.

North Avenue in the 1920s was largely a north European—mainly German—thoroughfare, though many of the wealthier Germans had moved farther north.

> Its many German cafes—Wein Stube (with a bunch of huge gilded grapes over the door), Pilsner, Wurzń Sepp Family Resort, Komiker Sepp—give it a distinctive color. . . . The windows of the many delicatessen shops plainly proclaim Swiss, German, or Hungarian; and they have little tables about which men eat lunches of rye bread, sauerkraut, and pickles, perhaps with alpenkrauter, and talk in German. . . . At the corner of Larrabee and North Avenue is the Immigrant State Bank (with name in German, Hungarian, and Italian, as well as in English). . . . To the east are building and loan associations and several steamship agencies. On Halsted, near North Avenue, are two German labor newspapers, and St. Michael's Bavarian Church. North Avenue has a few chain grocery stores, but most of its groceries are neighborhood stores. . . . The names along the street are nearly all northern European: Carl Bocker, Cigars and Tobacco; Stroup & Happel, Architects; A. Schlesinger, Schiffskarten.[4]

Many of Chicago's approximately thirty breweries were found in this area, most of them German owned. (Chicago's first brewery had been established by Germans in a tenement building at what is now Michigan and Chicago avenues). Some of the breweries even produced beer surreptitiously during the Prohibition era. In recent years they have closed down, partly because of a declining German population but mainly because of competition from large national brands. One of the last, the Sieben Brewery at 1470 North Larrabee Street (600 W), with its extremely popular "Sieben Bierstube", closed in 1967.

Although the largest German concentration was on the North Side, by 1920 Germans were scattered throughout most of the Northwest Side, with centers in such communities as Humboldt Park, Logan Square, Irving

Figure 4.9. Yondorf Block Building at the northeast corner of North Avenue and Halsted Street, 1963. Built in 1887, the building once housed numerous German organizations and included a theater and dance hall. (Photograph, Tom H. Long. Courtesy Chicago Historical Society.)

Park, Avondale, and Albany Park (fig. 4.1). There were also settlements west and southwest of the stockyards in Gage Park and surrounding areas. And there were small communities to the southeast in Avalon Park and South Chicago.

A measure of the dispersion of the German population is revealed by the location of German churches. Curiously, the German churches were even more dispersed than the German population. Almost half of the ethnic churches erected in Chicago in the latter half

of the nineteenth century were German. The peak building of German churches took place between about 1880 and 1900. After that, German church building, especially Catholic churches, slowed somewhat, as German immigration had started to taper off and German Catholics increasingly attended non-German Catholic churches. In 1900 there were 122 German churches of a variety of denominations within the city. Seventy-four of the churches could be classified as Lutheran or Evangelical, 24 were Catholic, 13 Methodist,

Figure 4.10. Beer tanks for sale mark the end of Chicago's last brewery, the Peter Hand Brewing Company at 1000 West North Avenue, 1979. (Photograph by Irving Cutler.)

4 Baptist, 3 Congregational, 2 Reformed, and 2 Adventist.[5] At that time there were 15 German churches in the suburbs, mainly Catholic.

Virtually all of the German churches had parochial schools with instruction given in German. World War I, with its anti-German sentiment, brought about a decline in the number of German parochial schools and the elimination of the German language from the public grade school curriculum. In 1920 a survey revealed that the churches were split about evenly between the North and Northwest sides and the South and Southwest sides, although the bulk of the German population lived to the north. Today there are about forty predominantly German churches in the metropolitan area, most of which have some services in German. One of Chicago's most prominent religious leaders of German descent was George Cardinal Mundelein, the first Cardinal of the Archdiocese of Chicago, who served in the area from 1915 until his death in 1939.

Figure 4.11. St. Paul's Catholic Church was founded in 1876 by Germans. The present church at 2127 West 22nd Place was started in 1897 and completed a few years later with the help of parishioners who were masons. Today about 70 percent of the church membership is Mexican, the remainder being largely Polish, Lithuanian, Slovenian, and Italian. (Photograph by Irving Cutler.)

Germans were employed in virtually every type of occupation, but basically they were skilled craftsmen, mechanics, technicians, and small shop owners. For example, in 1900 the Germans

> formed over one-half of the bakers and butchers. More than one-third of the boot and shoemakers and repairers were German; also the masons. They made up about one-third of the iron and steel workers and the machinists and nearly one-third of the blacksmiths, painters, glaziers, varnishers, printers, lithographers, pressmen, and of the manufacturers and officials.[6]

Among the larger present-day concerns that were founded by Germans are the Wieboldt stores and Oscar Mayer & Company, the meat packer. Among the Germans in the field of planning and architecture were Charles H. Wacker and Ludwig Mies van der Rohe. Wacker, a second-generation German-American, was chairman for 17 years of the Chicago Plan Commission and the most vigorous proponent of the Burnham Plan of 1909. Mies van der Rohe was an internationally known architect who left Germany in 1937 and became head of the School of Architecture at the Illinois Institute of Technology. His work and that of his many students have helped alter the skyline of Chicago.

The Germans were always somewhat group conscious and this led to the early establishment of German churches, theaters, restaurants, unions, and stores handling German goods. Their varied activities are perhaps best exemplified by their many clubs and organizations. In 1935, well past the peak of major German immigration, a German newspaper listed 452 active German clubs in the Chicago area. These included lodges and fraternal organizations, mutual and immigrant aid societies, soccer clubs, "turner" or gymnastic groups, professional and labor organizations, compatriot clubs and Old World city clubs, ladies clubs, literary societies, drama groups, veterans' organizations, and choral groups. They reflected such differing German

backgrounds as Bavarian, Saxon, Rhenish, and Prussian. Germans were especially active in music, and the founding of the Chicago Symphony Orchestra in 1891 was due largely to their enterprise. Initially the ninety-member orchestra was predominantly German and was led by the famed German-born conductor Theodore Thomas. The orchestra performed in the Auditorium until it moved into its new home, Orchestra Hall, in 1904. Thomas's assistant director, Frederick Stock, also German-born, became the conductor in 1905 and directed the distinguished orchestra for the next 37 years.

Membership in many of the German organizations was adversely affected by the Americanization of younger German generations and by the unpopularity of some of these organizations during the two World War periods. The organizations were also hurt somewhat by the dispersal of the German population into the suburbs, where almost three-quarters of the people of German extraction lived in the 1970s. Today there are only about a hundred German organizations in the Chicago area. There is only one German-language newspaper remaining in the city, the *Abendpost,* founded in 1889. It is the only paper of its kind left in the United States.

The German population in the area surrounding Chicago has been significant for more than a century, although the big increase has taken place in the last few decades with the general movement of population to the suburbs. At one time there were many German farmers on land around Chicago who produced for the city's people and carried on a sizable trade in the city's markets. Some of the areas that now bear names of German origin include Schiller Park, Hanover Park, Bensenville, New Trier Township, Schaumburg, Hoffman Estates, Bremen Township, Bloom Township, and Frankfort. There were also early German settlements in such places as Addison, Arlington Heights, Blue Island, Chicago Heights, Crete, Country Club Hills, Des Plaines, Elmhurst, Flossmoor, Franklin Park, Hillside, Homewood, Itasca, Lincolnwood, Markham, Matteson, Morton Grove, Mount Prospect, Niles, Northbrook, Palos Heights, River Grove, Riverwoods, Sauk Village, Skokie, Thornton, Villa Park, Westmont, Wheeling, and Winnetka.

Today the German population in the metropolitan area is more evenly spread out than that of other ethnic groups and there are no great concentrations of German stock in any of the larger suburbs. According to the 1970 census several communities in the metropolitan area had between 2,000 and 3,000 residents of German descent. These were Arlington Heights, Aurora, Des Plaines, Elgin, Elmhurst, Evanston, Homewood, Joliet, Oak Park, and Skokie.

In Chicago in the 1970s, the approximately 150,000 people of German extraction lived scattered mainly on the North and Northwest sides of the city, with smaller numbers on the Southwest side. The main commercial concentration is along Lincoln Avenue—the diagonal street along which German farmers once hauled their produce from their northwest-area farms to Chicago markets. Although the highly concentrated German neighborhoods broke up about half a century ago, an influx of many post-World War II immigrants has helped to maintain some German commercial strips, especially along two stretches of Lincoln Avenue. One of these is from Lincoln and Southport (1400 W) northwest for a few blocks; the other is along Lincoln from approximately Montrose (4400 N) to Lawrence (4800 N) avenues. In these areas are German delicatessens, bakeries, restaurants, music stores, meat markets, sport shops (featuring soccer equipment), import and gift stores, bars, meeting houses, travel bureaus, and the Davis Theater where German language movies are still shown.

The Chicago communities with the greatest population of Germans as shown by the 1970 census were all on the North and Northwest sides—Lake View, Uptown, Lincoln Square, North Center, Irving Park, Logan Square, and Portage Park. Chicago's German population was much older than the general Chicago population. The median age of 59.8 years for the German population contrasted with the 29.6 years median age for the general population, the latter reflecting a relatively large number of young blacks and Hispanics. Politically, the present German population has changed drastically from a century ago when many were socialists or anarchists. Surveys show that a large majority of the people of German descent now vote Republican.

The Scandinavians

Another sizable group of northern Europeans to settle relatively early in Chicago were the Scandinavians. By 1870 they comprised 9.5 percent of the city's large foreign-born population, and by 1890, 15.9 percent, surpassing the Irish in number. From 1850 to 1870 the largest group of Scandinavians came from Norway, but thereafter the Norwegians were outnumbered by those from Sweden. Danes constituted a small fraction of the Scandinavian immigrants. In 1890 there were 43,032 Swedes, 21,385 Norwegians, and 7,087 Danes in Chicago who were foreign-born.

Many more thousands of Scandinavians fanned out from Chicago to settle in Illinois, Wisconsin, Minnesota, Iowa, and the Dakotas; some had first worked in Chicago temporarily to accumulate capital for the purchase of farmland. In Illinois Norwegians settled in the lower Fox River valley in Kendall and La Salle counties, as well as adjacent areas. Farther west in Illinois a Swedish religious community was established at Bishop Hill near Kewanee. A sizable number of Danes settled north of Chicago in Racine, Wisconsin.

The earliest Scandinavians to settle in Chicago were two Norwegians who arrived in 1836. Even before this, however, many of the Norwegian sailors on the Great Lakes had been familiar with Chicago. By 1860 there were 1,313 Norwegians in Chicago, and their numbers started to increase rapidly. In 1862, after a 71-day trip, the schooner *Sleipner* arrived in Chicago with 107 passengers and 350 tons of cargo direct from Bergen, Norway, via the St. Lawrence River and the Great Lakes— the first such vessel to arrive direct from the mainland of Europe. (The trailblazing voyage of the *Sleipner* is now commemorated by a bronze plaque at the State Street Bridge, the site of the ship's first arrival.) The trip was repeated in each of the next three years.

The first Norwegian settlement was south of Chicago Avenue (800 N) between Orleans (340 W) and the lake.[7] In 1847, when their numbers were still small, the Norwegians joined with the Swedes in establishing the first Scandinavian Lutheran Church located at Superior (732 N) and La Salle streets (150 W). In 1849 the Norwegian community was especially hard hit by a cholera epidemic. It was later discovered that all of the victims had used water from the same well into which the drainings of an outhouse had flowed.

As the Norwegians increased in number they moved west of the river into an area bounded approximately by Milwaukee, Grand (530 N), Halsted (800 W), and Racine (1200 W). A number of Norwegian churches were built in the area. Two Norwegian churches, one Lutheran and the other Methodist, were founded in 1870 in the Grand and Sangamon (932 W) area. The first Norwegian newspaper, *Skandinaven,* started in 1866 and survived until 1935. At its peak it had a circulation greater than that of any newspaper in Norway.

Like their fellow Scandinavians, the Norwegians were a frugal, hard working, very law-abiding people with a relatively high literacy rate. Many were skilled tradesmen. Many found employment in the mills, railyards, and factories along the North Branch of the Chicago River. Some of the young girls worked as domestics in the homes of prosperous Chicagoans. In time, many Norwegians set up their own shops, small manufacturing plants, and professional offices. Chicago companies founded by men of Norwegian heritage include the Olson Rug Company, the Nester Johnson Skate Company, and the Gulbransen Company which manufactures pianos. Many

Norwegians also served aboard lakeships, some as captains. The Norwegians' continuing interest in sailors was evidenced by their sponsorship of seamen's missions, including one in the Lake Calumet area.

Before the turn of the century many Norwegians moved northwest into the newer, less crowded, attractive areas of Humboldt Park and Logan Square. The wealthier Norwegians, including doctors, lawyers, and businessmen, settled into beautiful homes in the Wicker Park area around Damen Avenue (2000 W) to the south of North Avenue. North Avenue, westward from Wicker Park to Humboldt Park and on to Pulaski Road (4000 W), became the main Norwegian business street. (Figure 4.1.) There the chief languages spoken were Norwegian and Danish. Humboldt Park was an important center for gatherings, and in 1893 a statue of Leif Eriksson, the Norse discoverer, was erected there. Half a century ago most of the 26 Norwegian churches in Chicago were located in and around the Humboldt Park-Logan Square areas.

Later many Norwegians moved farther northwest, especially into Irving Park, Portage Park, and Jefferson Park, with many in recent decades moving into the suburbs. At present there are about 10,000 foreign-born Norwegians and their children in Chicago, down from over 52,108 in 1930. However, despite this outward migration and despite the rapid influx of Puerto Ricans, the Humboldt Park area and especially the Logan Square area is still the home of many Norwegian institutions and societies. These include the Norwegian-American Hospital; the last Norwegian language newspaper, *Vinland;* many churches of Norwegian origin; and the Norway Center at Kedzie near Fullerton (2400 N), a meeting place for athletic, social, singing, folk dancing, and literary Norwegian organizations. An illustrious resident of the Logan Square area was Knute Rockne, the famous Notre Dame football coach. Other famous Chicagoans of Norwegian descent include Victor F. Lawson, for many years publisher of the *Chicago Daily*

News; Arthur E. Anderson, founder of the nationally known accounting firm that bears his name; and Ludwig Hektoen, the famous pathologist who is noted for his cancer research.

The smaller Danish population's first Chicago settlement was north of the Chicago River around La Salle (150 W) and Kinzie (400 N). Later, like the Norwegians, the Danes moved into the Northwest Side communities of Wicker Park, Humboldt Park around the Trinity Danish Lutheran Church at Cortez (1032 N) and Francisco (2900 W) avenues, and adjacent Logan Square. The Dania Society of Chicago, founded just north of downtown in 1862 as the city's first Scandinavian club and the oldest Danish society anywhere outside Denmark, was located from 1912 until recent years in the area on Kedzie Avenue north of North Avenue. The Humboldt Park-Logan Square Danish area started changing after World War II and now virtually no Danes live there. The three Danish Lutheran churches of the area have closed. A small pocket of Danes also existed on the far South Side, around 85th and Maryland (832 E), where in 1875 Danish Lutherans opened St. Stephan's Lutheran Church.

Many of the Danes were artisans and journeymen who found employment in the building trades. A large Chicago contractor is the S. Nielsen Co. Some Danes opened little shops. A company that became nationally known is the market research firm of A.C. Nielsen. Chicagoans of Danish stock reached a peak of 28,695 in 1930 and then declined to 5,887 in 1970. Few new Danish immigrants come to Chicago, and, like other ethnic groups, many Danes have moved to the suburbs. Because of their small numbers and dispersal, no strictly Danish churches are left in the Chicago area. Economic advancement and Americanization have virtually eliminated the vestiges of Danish culture that the immigrants brought to America.

By far the greatest number of Scandinavians arriving in Chicago came from Sweden, and Chicago soon had the largest number of Swedes of any city in America. However, as Table 4.4 shows, the Swedes initially lagged behind the Norwegians in numbers.

The first "Swede Town" in Chicago was from just north of the river to about Erie Street (658 N) and from Wells Street (200 W) west to the North Branch of the Chicago River. Danish and especially Norwegian settlers were also in this area. It was an area that had been inhabited mainly by the Irish, and it was already assuming the characteristics of a slum. In this area the building of St. Ansgarius Swedish Episcopal Congregation in 1850 on the corner of Franklin (300 N) and Grand (520 N) gave the Swedes their first center. The world renowned singer, Jenny Lind, "the Swedish Nightingale", assisted in the building of the church by giving a donation of $1500. This first Swedish church was followed in a few years and in the same general locale by a Lutheran and a Methodist church. The miserable shacks which housed the early Swedish immigrants in the area were gradually replaced by little wooden houses.

As immigration increased, Swede Town pushed northward to Division Street causing the earlier German inhabitants of the area to

TABLE 4.4
Foreign-born Scandinavians in Chicago

	Swedes	Norwegians	Danes
1860	816	1,313	150
1870	6,154	6,374	1,243
1900	48,836	22,011	10,166
1930	65,735	21,740	12,502
1970	7,005	3,094	1,708

move on to the North Avenue area. By 1870, the Swedish Club at 1258 N. La Salle (still in existence) and the Immanuel Lutheran Congregation at Sedgwick near Division had become important centers of Swedish community life. Chicago Avenue, the main Swedish business street, was known as "Swedish Clodhoppers Lane."

Some of the Swedes of the area worked as maids, cooks, or gardeners for the rich to the east. Many of the men worked in construction as laborers and carpenters, and eventually as engineers, architects, electricians, and contractors. The Gust K. Newberg Construction Company has become one of the largest in the Chicago area. It is estimated that Swedes may have been involved in the building of as many as half of the buildings in Chicago.

The Chicago Fire of 1871 destroyed much of the Swedish community, including four Swedish churches and as many Swedish newspapers.[8] With hard work, their great experience in construction, and outside financial aid, including some from Sweden, the Swedes quickly rebuilt their area.

Many Swedes soon began to move farther north, especially into Lake View which, by the turn of the century, became the major Swedish community with close to 20,000 Swedes. The Lake View community centered around the intersection of Belmont (3200 N) and Clark. Swedish businesses dominated the commercial stretch along Clark Street, and the area contained Swedish churches, meeting halls, cafes, singing clubs, the Swedish Engineers' Society of Chicago, and other facilities and organizations.

By the early 1900s the once sizable Swede Town around Chicago and Division streets had given way to an influx of other immigrant groups, especially Sicilians. The Swedes kept moving farther north and northwest beyond Lake View, where the Swedish population had declined to 14,000 by 1930. A very large Swedish community, Andersonville, had developed by 1900 in Uptown, around Clark and Foster (5200 N). They also moved farther west into West Ridge, Lincoln Square, Albany Park, and North Park. In North Park, Swedish Covenant Hospital and Covenant Home, at California (2800 W) and Foster, began its operations in 1886 as a combination hospital, old people's home, and orphanage. In 1894 North Park College and Theological Seminary was built at Kedzie (3200 W) and Foster by the Evangelical Covenant Church. Today the college is an important Swedish-American cultural and religious center. Between 1900 and 1920, encouraged by Swedish builders and by the opening of the Irving Park streetcar line, Swedes also moved into the communities of Irving Park, Portage Park, and Norwood Park.

Although the bulk of the Swedish population lived on the North and Northwest sides, there were also Swedish communities on the West and South sides of the city. These were areas of wooden houses that had been untouched by the Chicago Fire. By 1880 some 2,500 Swedes lived in an enclave between Kinzie (400 N)-Milwaukee-Division-Ashland, a neighborhood where many Norwegians had already settled.[9] Some Swedes later settled farther west in Austin.

The initial Swedish community on the South Side was in an area predominantly populated by Germans and Irish, and the Swedes remained a minority in the area. In 1880 they were concentrated especially between Clark (100 W) and Stewart (400 W) and 21st and 27th streets. To serve the Swedes in this area, four denominations—Lutheran, Baptist, Methodist, and Evangelical Covenant, which had also been established among the North Side Swedes—started churches there. Physically the area was similar to Swede Town, with generally ramshackle, wooden buildings.

As industry and the expanding black ghetto encroached upon the area, some Swedes moved farther south into the Armour Square area to the east of Bridgeport and some moved into the "Stockholm" area near the McCormick reaper factories which were located around Western (2400 W) and Blue Island. Others settled near the industrial areas of South Chicago and Pullman. Swedes who had

Figure 4.12. Andersonville, Clark Street just north of Foster Avenue, is the only important Swedish community left in Chicago. In addition to numerous Swedish stores, a Swedish museum and Chicago's last Swedish newspaper are also located on Clark Street. (Photograph by Irving Cutler.)

worked their way up economically also began to settle in other communities to the south, especially in Englewood, Greater Grand Crossing, South Shore, Chatham, Beverly, and Roseland.

As the Swedes dispersed to the North, South, and West sides until there were about two dozen identifiable enclaves, so, too, did their numerous social, humanitarian, labor, and religious organizations. Early in the history of the Chicago Scandinavian community there had been a joining together of Swedes, Danes, and Norwegians in various social causes and common organizations, including some of the early churches. However, as the size of each Scandinavian group increased, there was a trend toward each nationality developing its own facilities and organizations. The various Scandinavian nationalities were especially productive in the erection of hospitals and old people's homes to take care of their own.

The Swedes were also active in building churches throughout their communities. By 1905 the Chicago area contained 41 Swedish Lutheran congregations, 18 Swedish Methodist, 11 Swedish Baptist, and 12 Evangelical Covenant churches. Their combined membership was almost 25,000. Before World War I most of these churches held their services in Swedish, but thereafter services were increasingly held in English until the Swedish language was almost completely replaced. Today what were Swedish Lutheran and other Swedish Protestant churches are more and more becoming community churches serving a variety of ethnic groups. Like the other Scandinavians, the Swedes had confidence in American secular education, but unlike other immigrant groups, they generally did not push the teaching of their native language in the schools.[10]

There are now an estimated 300,000 people of Swedish descent in the Chicago area. Immigration from prosperous Sweden is small. Many Swedes live in such suburbs as Evanston, Skokie, Morton Grove, Park Ridge, Des Plaines, Wheaton, Glen Ellyn, Oak Lawn,

Homewood, and Lansing. In Chicago the Swedes were easily assimilated and became scattered, so that today the only important Swedish community left in the city is Andersonville, around Clark and Foster. Even there the Swedish population is now small, mainly elderly, and intermixed with other groups, including a recent influx of Asians. Nevertheless, a few blocks on Clark Street north of Foster Avenue have been revitalized as a special Swedish commercial street. Bedecked with banners in the Swedish national colors of blue and yellow, the shops attract many who come to savor the smorgasbord of Nordic offerings. A bell is rung every morning to remind shopkeepers to clean their sidewalks. The merchants foster an annual October parade.

Arrayed along the street are numerous Swedish gift shops, restaurants, bakeries, delicatessens, fish stores, and grocery stores with Scandinavian delicacies. Also there is the office of Chicago's last Swedish newspaper and the only all-Swedish-language one in the United States, the 104-year-old *Swedish American Tribune*. (There were once seven Swedish newspapers in Chicago.) Interspersed among the stores is a new Swedish museum with a simulated log cabin exterior. Here one can learn about Polycarpus von Schneidau, the Swedish immigrant engineer who supervised construction of Chicago's first railroad—the Chicago and Galena; Charles R. Walgreen, who built the largest retail drug chain in the United States; Gloria Swanson, the movie star, who was born in the Swedish community around Ashland Avenue; and, of course, Carl Sandburg, the Pulitzer Prize winning historian, newspaperman, and poet who in a famous poem vividly portrayed Chicago as the "City of the Big Shoulders."

The Jews

Jews came to Chicago from almost every country in Europe. In Chicago they formed a type of melting pot within the larger immigrant melting pot. Because of harsh discriminatory treatment in many European countries, sometimes culminating in out-right massacres, the Jewish immigrants, despite some sentimental attachment to the old country, were less interested in returning to their homelands than were the members of any other immigrant group. Whereas the most affluent and educated members of other immigrant groups usually remained in their native land where they occupied secure and respected positions, in most central and eastern European countries the Jews of all economic and educational levels welcomed the opportunity to settle in American communities. Although limited somewhat by occasional open anti-Semitism and by more frequent covert discrimination, especially in the earlier periods of their settlement in Chicago, the Jews were able to flourish when given the opportunity in a free land.

Jews who came to Chicago could be divided into two relatively distinct groups. The first group to come were German-speaking Jews from central Europe—from Bavaria, Prussia, Austria, Bohemia, and the German-occupied part of Poland. In general, these Jews were more secular, urbane, and affluent than the second group—the eastern European Jews who came in much larger numbers somewhat later. The latter spoke Yiddish and were mainly from Russia, Poland, Romania, and Lithuania in which persecution was often especially severe and where there was little in the way of political or economic emancipation. They were a poor, deeply religious people, mostly from small towns and villages (shtetls) where they had frequently been confined to government-imposed ghettos. Despite their varied backgrounds and homelands, which resulted in occasional internal discord, the two groups in time achieved a degree of unity.

Among the earliest settlers in Chicago were small numbers of German Jews, mainly from Bavaria, who started trickling into the area in the late 1830s and early 1840s. In 1841 one of the settlers was Henry Horner, who became an organizer of the Chicago Board of Trade and helped found a major wholesale grocery company. His grandson of the same name was to serve as governor of Illinois from 1933 to 1940. By 1845 there were enough Jews

to hold the first High Holy Day services and to purchase an acre of land for use as a Jewish cemetery in what is now Lincoln Park. In 1847, upstairs of a dry goods store owned by Rosenfeld and Rosenberg on the southwest corner of Lake (200 N), and Wells (200 W), a small group of about 15 Jews agreed to form the first congregation, which they called Kehilath Anshe Mayriv (K.A.M., Congregation of the Men of the West). In 1851 the congregation erected a small frame synagogue on Clark Street, just south of Adams Street (200 S).

The *Daily Democrat* of June 14, 1851, reported the dedication of the synagogue as follows:

> The ceremonies at the dedication of the first Jewish synagogue in Illinois, yesterday, were very interesting indeed. An immense number had to go away, from inability to gain admittance. There were persons of all denominations present. We noticed several clergymen of different religious denominations.
>
> No person that has made up his mind to be prejudiced against the Jews ought to hear such a sermon preached. It was very captivating and contained as much real religion as any sermon we ever heard preached. We never could have believed that one of those old Jews we heard denounced so much could have taught so much liberality towards other denominations and earnestly recommended a thorough study of the Old Testament (each one for himself) and entire freedom of opinion and discussion.

The revolutionary movements that swept central Europe in 1848 increased Jewish immigration to the United States and by 1860 there were about 1,500 Jews in Chicago. Most lived around Lake and Wells streets where a few owned clothing and dry goods stores. Some of these store owners had started out as almost penniless backpacking peddlers. Later, large scale retailers such as Mandel Brothers, Goldblatt Brothers, Maurice L. Rothchild, Maurice B. Sachs, Polk Brothers, Aldens, and Spiegel were to grow from similar modest beginnings, as were such manufacturers as Hart Schaffner & Marx, Kuppenheimer, and Florsheim.

By 1870 the Jewish community had diffused somewhat, with largest concentration between Van Buren (400 S) and Polk (800 S) streets and between the river on the west and the lake on the east. There were enough Jews in the city to support seven synagogues scattered throughout what is today the central business district. One congregation was as far north as Superior Street (732 N); today it is Temple Sholom on North Lake Shore Drive. Another one was as far west as Desplaines Street (700 W); it is today's Oak Park Temple on Harlem Avenue (7200 W).

The Fire of 1871 and another on the Near South Side in 1874 destroyed most of the Jewish community, including more than half of the synagogues.[11] The German Jews, increasing rapidly due to the continual influx of immigrants, moved out of the rapidly spreading downtown business area. They settled mainly one or more miles south of downtown along such streets as Michigan, Wabash, and Indiana; later in the Grand Boulevard, Washington Park, Kenwood, and Hyde Park communities; and eventually in South Shore. Large orphanages and homes for the aged were built, and in 1880 Michael Reese Hospital was founded at 29th Street and Ellis Avenue (1000 E). After World War I Jews of eastern European descent also moved into these areas.

At their peak in the years after World War II, the communities of Hyde Park and South Shore each contained about a dozen synagogues; a few were Orthodox, but most were either Conservative or Reform. The Orthodox congregations adhered strictly to the traditional, fundamentalist Judaism; the newer Conservative and Reform movements conceived Judaism as more of a developmental religion that needed to adjust to contemporary conditions. The Conservative movement retained more of the traditional practices than did the Reform movement. Today only Hyde Park-Kenwood with three synagogues still has an active Jewish community on the South Side of Chicago.

The movement of the German Jews southward can be traced by the movement of the K.A.M. Congregation. From the downtown area it moved to 26th and Indiana (200 E) in 1875. In 1891 it occupied the beautiful temple at 33rd and Indiana built by renowned architect Dankmar Adler (whose father was rabbi of K.A.M.). In 1920 the congregation moved to 50th and Drexel. Today it is part of K.A.M./Isaiah Israel located at 1100 Hyde Park Boulevard (5100 S). The large Sinai Congregation followed a similar path from downtown to Hyde Park. The congregation was headed from 1880 to 1923 by the very prominent Rabbi Emil Hirsch, whose grandson, Edward Levi, became president of the University of Chicago and a member of President Ford's cabinet.

In 1880 eastern European Jews comprised only a small fraction of Chicago's 10,000 Jews. But when Russia's especially brutal pogroms of 1881 were followed in 1882 by the very repressive so-called "May Laws", which expelled Jews from their homes and towns, a wave of Jewish emigration from eastern Europe was set off which lasted for almost half a century. In 1900 Chicago's Jewish population reached about 80,000, of whom an estimated 52,000 were from eastern Europe, 20,000 were German Jews, and the remaining 8,000 were largely from northwestern Europe and the Middle East. By 1930 the Jewish population of the Chicago area was estimated at about 275,000, of whom over 80 percent were of eastern European descent.

The Russian-Polish Jews crowded into the area southwest of downtown, a district formerly occupied by German, Bohemian, and Irish gentile communities. The Jews moved south along Canal (500 W) and Jefferson (600 W) streets and westward to Halsted, and then still farther west as new immigrants increased the congestion. By 1910 Jews were found in a ghetto that stretched approximately from Canal Street west to almost Damen Avenue (2000 W) and from Polk Street (800 S) south to about 15th Street. Of the estimated 50,000

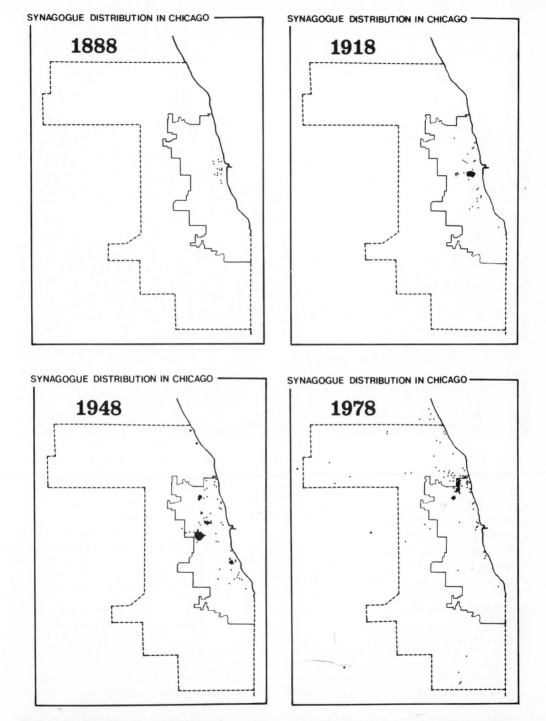

Figure 4.13. The changing distribution patterns of Chicago-area synagogues, by 30-year periods, reflects the changing residential locations of Jews in the area. Today it is estimated that slightly more than half of the Jews live in the suburbs. (Map by Joseph Kubal.)

Figure 4.14. An Eastern European Jewish immigrant settlement around Twelfth and Jefferson streets, 1906. (Photograph courtesy Chicago Historical Society.)

immigrant Jews who arrived in Chicago during the last two decades of the nineteenth century, most settled in this area.

Like other immigrant groups, the eastern European Jews initially found living in a big city quite difficult. In 1907 an article in the *Jewish Daily Courier* discussed the feelings of these Jewish immigrants:

The "hurry up" spirit of the city overwhelmed him at first. The strangeness of the city left him lonely; and the longing to return "home" increased. "What kind of memories could the immigrant fleeing from a land of persecution have?" asked a *Courier* writer. Why was it that something reminding the immigrant of

the old home, like a pouch of tobacco, tea, or a European utensil brought forth a sigh and a tear? How could one compare the little village with the straw-bedecked houses and its crooked streets of dirt with the great American cities where noise, turmoil, hustle and bustle reigned, he quoted older immigrants querying the "greenhorn".

Furthermore how could one help but scoff at the longing of the immigrant for his old home when here in a city like Chicago he found himself in the center of a civilization that was prepared to offer him everything with a broad hand? The writer answered these questions in a typical Jewish manner. When one digs a little deeper, he said with a Talmudical flourish of his hand, he will see that there were certain

Figure 4.15. Vendors in the Maxwell Street area about 1906—a type of old world retailing transplanted to America. The market still exists, but on a much smaller scale, the victim of redevelopment, expressway construction, a changing neighborhood, and changing shopping patterns. (Photograph courtesy Chicago Historical Society.)

values in the little town that are still lacking in the big city. In a small town everybody was friendly and knew everybody else. In the big city the houses are "cold" inside, no matter how much better built, and how superior in other ways they may be to the little cottages. Moreover, the social recognition given to men of learning and of honorable ancestry was lacking in the city.[12]

The main commercial arteries of the ghetto were north-south Halsted and Jefferson streets and east-west 12th and Maxwell (1330 S) streets. Maxwell Street, especially, was well-known for its crowded, bustling, Old-World-style, open-market bazaar. The focal point of the community was around Halsted and Maxwell. In the blocks around this intersection the population was about 90 percent Jewish. In many ways the community resembled a teeming eastern European ghetto. It contained kosher meat markets and chicken stores, matzo bakeries and ones with bread and bagels, Yiddish newspaper offices, bookstores, cafes with intellectuals discoursing,

Yiddish theaters, Hebrew schools, literary organizations, tailor and seamstress shops, bathhouses, and peddlers' stables. Conspicuously missing were the large number of saloons that could be found in other ethnic communities.

There were more than 40 Orthodox synagogues (for the Orthodox the synagogue had to be within walking distance of the home). These synagogues were usually small, only a few having over a hundred members, and were made up largely of immigrants who came from the same community in Europe.[13] Religiously, the eastern European Jews tried to cling to the old, whereas the German Jews espoused the new.

Even the dress was largely that of eastern European ghettos. One could speak Yiddish, wear a beard, a long black coat, and a Russian cap and boots without being ridiculed. But those who ventured into other neighborhoods often encountered scorn and even physical harassment.[14]

Ghetto life was hard and living conditions deplorable. The crowded wooden shanties and brick tenements of the area usually had insufficient light and few baths, and were surrounded by areas of poor drainage and piles of garbage. Despite the slum conditions, crime was almost nonexistent and the death and disease rate was one of the lowest of the various immigrant groups.

To support themselves the eastern European Jewish immigrants worked in the sweatshops of the clothing industry and in cigarmaking factories. Many became peddlers, tailors, butchers, bakers, barbers, small merchants, and artisans. As they became more Americanized they organized to fight for better working conditions. They comprised about 80 percent of the 45,000 workers involved in the prolonged and successful garment strike of 1910, which resulted in the organization of the Amalgamated Clothing Workers of America under the leadership of Sidney Hillman.

The more affluent and established German Jews of the South Side "Golden Ghetto" were embarrassed by some of the Old World ways and beliefs of their eastern European Jewish brethren. They tried to aid in their Americanization by founding the Jewish Manual Training School, a settlement house, a dispensary, and other community facilities. Julius Rosenwald, who was of German Jewish descent, and the president of Sears, Roebuck and Company, contributed sizable sums for these institutions as well as for other worthy causes, including black housing and institutions, the University of Chicago, and the Museum of Science and Industry. The proud Russian-Polish immigrants sometimes resented the paternalistic attitude of their more "aristocratic" German brethren, but nevertheless, accepted their help.

Jews of the Maxwell Street area exhibited a physical and mental vitality that was sustained by a long tradition of hard work and learning. They strove for success, if not for themselves, then for their children. A surprising number of people with roots in this ghetto area became well known:

> Joseph Goldberg was one of these immigrants. He came to America from Russia and eventually landed on Maxwell Street. He bought a blind horse, the only horse he could afford. He became a fruit-and-vegetable peddler; his son, Arthur, would serve in President Kennedy's cabinet and became a Supreme Court Justice of the United States.

> Samuel Paley became a cigar maker in America, as did Max Guzik. Samuel's son William, born in the back room of the modest family cigar store near Maxwell Street, is founder, president and chairman of the board of the Columbia Broadcasting System. Mr. Guzik's son, Jake, known as "Greasy Thumb," became the brains behind the Capone gang. . . .

> Eastern European immigrants David Goodman and Abraham Rickover took jobs in Chicago as tailors. Their sons are Benny Goodman and Admiral Hyman G. Rickover.

> Paul Muni's father owned a Yiddish theater near Maxwell Street. Jack Ruby's father was a carpenter there.

> John Keeshin, once the greatest trucking magnate in America, is the son of a man who owned a chicken store on Maxwell Street, as did the father of Jackie Fields, former welterweight champion of the world. The father of Federal Court Judge Abraham Lincoln Ma-

rovitz owned a candy store near Maxwell Street.

Colonel Jacob Arvey, once a nationally prominent political power broker, is the son of a Maxwell Street area peddler.[15]

By 1910, improvements in their economic status, the encroachment of industry and railroads, and an influx of blacks, caused the Jews to start moving out of the Maxwell Street area. By the 1930s only a small remnant of older Jews and businessmen remained. Today the population of the area is almost wholly black and the bazaar-like Maxwell Street commercial strip has been reduced to a couple of short blocks. Vacant lots and abandoned buildings dominate the area. But on Sunday throngs of curiosity seekers and shoppers still crowd the area looking for bargains and odd merchandise that can range from rusty nails and used toothbrushes to antiques.

The Jews of the Maxwell Street area dispersed in a number of directions. A few joined the German Jews on the South Side. A small number moved into the lakefront communities of Lake View, Uptown, and Rogers Park, joining Jews who had been moving northward from their small settlements on the Near North Side. A large number moved to the Northwest Side where the nucleus of a Jewish community had been established in the late 1800s in the West Town area. There many lived near their retail stores on Milwaukee Avenue and on Division Street (1200 N). The first synagogues in the area were built in the 1890s and eventually about twenty served a Jewish community which in time spread to the western side of Humboldt Park. Many of the Jews of this area were more inclined to emphasize Yiddish culture and somewhat radical philosophies, rather than the religious orthodoxy of the Near West Side. Ideologically the area was split among adherents of socialism, secularism, Zionism, and orthodoxy. These differences declined markedly among their more Americanized children.

The main commercial street was Division Street with its numerous Jewish stores and the Deborah Boys Club. Although the Jews were a minority of the population, which included large numbers of Poles, Scandinavians, Ukrainians, and Russians, this area was the home of such well known Jews as comedian Jackie Leonard (Fats Levitsky), movie impressario Michael Todd, columnist Sidney J. Harris, and Nobel prize winning novelist Saul Bellow. Harris and Bellow were among a distinguished group of Chicago writers of Jewish descent which also included Edna Ferber, Ben Hecht, Meyer Levin, Leo Rosten, Studs Terkel, and Louis Zara.

Some Jews moved farther northwest into Logan Square and Albany Park, but the vast majority of the Jews leaving the Near West Side leapfrogged over the railroad and industrial area and settled some three miles to the west in the Lawndale-Douglas Park-Garfield Park area. This became the largest and most developed Jewish community that Chicago ever had. At its peak in 1930 this Greater Lawndale area contained an estimated 110,000 Jews out of the city's Jewish population of about 275,000. Other areas with significant Jewish population in 1930 included the Lake View-Uptown-Rogers Park area, 27,000; West Town-Humboldt Park-Logan Square, 35,000; Albany Park-North Park, 27,000; and on the South Side the Kenwood-Hyde Park-Woodlawn-South Shore area, 28,000. The South Side area had the highest economic status followed by the North Side and Northwest Side communities. Smaller Jewish communities were found in Austin, 7,000; Englewood-Greater Grand Crossing, 4,000; and Chatham-Avalon Park-South Chicago, 3,000. The Jewish population was served by 105 synagogues of which 84 were Orthodox, 8 Conservative, and 13 Reform.

About 1910 the Jews started moving out of the crowded Near West Side ghetto into the Greater Lawndale area, a quieter residential area with comparatively spacious streets, yards, and parks. The German and Irish residents initially refused to rent to them. Jews then bought many of the one- and two-story

Figure 4.16. Numerous Jewish institutions lined Douglas Boulevard. The Jewish People's Institute (left), on Douglas Boulevard and St. Louis Avenue, was a major cultural, social, and recreational center of Chicago Jewry from 1926 to 1955. It is now listed in the National Register of Historic Places. The Hebrew Theological College (right) was located on Douglas Boulevard from 1922 to 1956. It now is in Skokie. The two buildings are presently the Julius Hess Elementary School. (Photograph by Irving Cutler.)

homes in the area and also built numerous three-story apartment buildings. By 1920 Greater Lawndale had become largely Jewish. The area stretched approximately from California Avenue (2800 W) west to Tripp Street (4232 W) and from Washington Street (100 N) south to 18th Street, although the greatest Jewish concentration was south of Roosevelt Road (12th Street).[16] The Greater Lawndale area more than doubled in population between 1910 and 1930 to become one of the most densely populated communities in the city and the one with the greatest proportion of foreign-born—mainly Jews from Russia and Poland. By 1933, in the central core of the area, Herzl, Penn, Howland, Bryant, and Lawson public

schools each averaged around 2,000 Jewish students, probably more than 90 percent of each school's enrollment.

The L-shaped parkway formed by Douglas Boulevard (1400 S) and Independence Boulevard (3800 W) was the heart of the area. Each boulevard extended for about a mile with Douglas Park at the east end of Douglas Boulevard and Garfield Park at the north end of Independence Boulevard. Many of the major Jewish institutions of the community were along these boulevards, including some dozen synagogues, most of imposing classical architecture and all but one Orthodox. Located there also were a huge community center—the Jewish People's Institute; the Hebrew The-

Figure 4.17. Banquet at Orthodox Jewish Home for the Aged, Albany Avenue near 18th Street, about 1925. Most of the larger immigrant groups built facilities to care for their old, sick, and needy. (Photograph courtesy Chicago Historical Society.)

ological College; a home for the Jewish blind; and a number of other religious, cultural, and Zionist organizations.

On the side streets were about four dozen more synagogues, all Orthodox, with many bearing the name of some community in Russia, Poland, Lithuania, or Romania from which the founders had come. In 1944 about half of the city's synagogues were located in this area. On Kedzie Avenue (3200 W) were a Yiddish theater, the offices of the Workmen's Circle, and the building of a Jewish Daily newspaper. On the east and west sides of Douglas Park—on California and Albany (3100 W) avenues—was an imposing array of social service institutions supported by the Jewish community. They included Mt. Sinai Hospital, a rehabilitation hospital, a convalescent home, a day and night nursery, a large

orphanage, and a home for elderly Orthodox Jews.

The Greater Lawndale area was bisected by Roosevelt Road (1200 S), the main commercial street. Jews came from all over the city to shop there. In the mile from approximately Kedzie Avenue to Crawford (Pulaski) Avenue (4000 W) were half-a-dozen movie houses, Jewish bookstores and food stores, meeting halls, restaurants, and political organizations. The 24th Ward was the top Democratic stronghold in the city. In the 1936 presidential election the ward gave Roosevelt 29,000 votes to Landon's 700, leading President Roosevelt to call it "the number one ward in the entire Democratic Party."

About as rapidly as the area had changed from gentile to Jewish earlier in the century, a rapid, peaceful, and complete change from

Jewish to black occurred from about 1946 to 1954. The Jews did not leave this area of second settlement because it had deteriorated. They left because they had attained relatively high incomes and desired to raise their growing young families in homes of their own in areas with more amenities and higher status. The move was helped by improved mobility provided by the automobile. The younger Americanized Jews, especially, were not interested in clinging to the magnificent institutional structures that their parents and grandparents had built. They moved to the better and more prestigious areas of the North Side—some to Albany Park and Rogers Park, but more to West Rogers Park (West Ridge)—and to parts of the northern suburbs. A much smaller number went to the western suburbs.

Jews started moving into Albany Park a few years after the completion of the Ravenswood elevated line in 1907, with its terminal at Lawrence (4800 N) and Kimball (3400 W) avenues. By 1930 Albany Park contained about 23,000 Jews, or almost half the population of the community. Many came from the older and less affluent Jewish areas of the West and Northwest aides. They viewed Albany Park as a more Americanized community. In religious matters it was a transitional community between the Orthodoxy of the West Side and the Reform Judaism of the South Side. Orthodox, Conservative, and Reform synagogues and other Jewish institutional facilities dotted the area, with a strong concentration around Kimball Avenue. The main business street, Lawrence Avenue, was somewhat similar in character to Lawndale's Roosevelt Road.

During the post-World War II exodus from Lawndale, many Jewish families, including some of the most Orthodox groups, still settled in Albany Park, while some of the more affluent earlier Jewish settlers of Albany Park moved farther north. The Jewish movement out of Albany Park accelerated during the 1960s, and by 1975 only an estimated 5,000 Jews remained, most of them elderly and of limited means.

Until the northward extension of an elevated line to Howard Street (7600 N) in 1909, Chicago's most northeasterly community, Rogers Park, had been largely an area of single-family frame houses. The community started to grow rapidly with the improvement of transportation, and numerous large apartment buildings and apartment hotels were built, especially in the eastern portion adjacent to Sheridan Road and the lake. Jews began to move into the area after 1910, and by 1930 about 10,000 lived there. After World War II the area contained about 20,000 Jews who constituted about one-third of the community's population. Thereafter, the Jewish population in the area gradually declined to an estimated 13,000 in 1979. Most of the remaining Jews are elderly and there are very few Jewish children. The average age of the Jewish population in Rogers Park is about 60.

Since World War II the big intracity movement of the Jews who have left their former communities on the South, West, and Northwest sides has been into West Ridge. This area, popularly referred to as West Rogers Park, lies between Rogers Park and the Albany Park-North Park area.

There were fewer than 2,000 Jews in West Rogers Park in 1930; by 1950 there were about 11,000. Then in the 1950s the Jewish population quadrupled, and in 1960 it reached an estimated 48,000, or about three-fourths of the community's total population. Most were Jews of Russian-Polish descent. They had come from Lawndale and Albany Park and had purchased new single-family homes in the northern part of the community. Today West Rogers Park is the largest Jewish community in Chicago. There are about ten synagogues, many of which were founded almost a century ago in the Maxwell Street area and reached West Rogers Park via the Lawndale area. Most of the synagogues are Orthodox. Many are aligned along California Avenue, between Peterson (6000 N) and Touhy (7200 N) avenues, in a manner slightly reminiscent of Douglas Boulevard in the Lawndale area. Devon Avenue (6400 N), the main business street, houses many merchants who were once located on Roosevelt Road or on Lawrence Avenue.

Compared to the rest of the city's population, the Jewish population of West Rogers Park is older and has a higher median income and educational level. But like the population of the city as a whole, it has been declining in numbers. At present there are about 35,000 Jewish residents. Young Orthodox Jewish families continue to maintain their strength and institutions in the community. But increasingly, Greeks, East Asians, Slavs, and others have been moving into the community. Devon Avenue is becoming a street of many nations.

The major movement of Jews in recent years has been out of Chicago into the north and northwest suburbs. Small numbers of Jews, mainly descendants of the early German immigrants, moved into such North Shore suburbs as Glencoe and Highland Park shortly after World War I. But by 1950 only about 5 percent of Chicago area Jews were living in the suburbs. By the early 1960s, however, some 40 percent of the Jewish people were living in the suburbs; today the proportion exceeds 50 percent. It is estimated that more than 80 percent of the Jews in the entire metropolitan area now live north of Lawrence Avenue. (See fig. 4.12.) The bulk of the remainder reside in the high-rise complexes along Chicago's lakeshore south to the Near North Side. Some Jews also live in Hyde Park; a few are scattered in other Chicago communities. And there are small numbers of Jews in most western and southern suburbs, with some concentration to the west in Oak Park, River Forest, and Westchester and to the south in Glenwood, Homewood, Flossmoor, Olympia Fields, and Park Forest.

The first major suburban move was into Skokie and adjacent Lincolnwood. These communities were near the Jewish concentrations in Rogers Park, West Ridge, Albany Park, and North Park. By the 1960s Skokie and Lincolnwood were estimated to be about half

Jewish. In 1980 these two suburbs contained about a dozen synagogues, mainly Orthodox or Conservative, in contrast to the greater concentration of Orthodox synagogues in West Rogers Park and the prepreponderance of Reform temples in the more distant suburbs. Skokie also has two rabbinical colleges.

In place of the previous divisions of the city into North, South, and West side Jewish communities, today's Chicago-area Jewish community is being concentrated increasingly in the northern suburbs and is moving outward over a wide geographic area. Based on survey data compiled in the mid 1970s by the Jewish Federation of Metropolitan Chicago, the northern suburbs of Niles, Evanston, Wilmette, Winnetka, Morton Grove, Northfield, and Deerfield are estimated to be from 10 to over 20 percent Jewish. Glencoe and Highland Park are about 50 percent Jewish. Some of the Jews moving into these suburbs continue to come from Chicago; some however, come from other suburbs, especially from Skokie, whose Jewish population has declined some 15 percent in the last dozen years.

The latest settlement pattern has been for young Jewish families to move to outlying suburbs to the northwest, where there is still vacant land and more reasonably priced housing. Serving these newer Jewish communities are synagogues in Hanover Park, Schaumburg, Hoffman Estates, Des Plaines, Buffalo Grove, and Vernon Hills. The Buffalo Grove area, some 30 miles northwest of the Loop, with some 4,000 Jews, now has three synagogues, one for each major branch of Judaism.

The Jewish population of Metropolitan Chicago has declined in recent years to an estimated 253,000 in 1975, or about 4 percent of the total population. The decline has been due mainly to a low birth rate, movement to the Sunbelt states, intermarriage, lack of Jewish identity, and an alienation from Judaism among some of the youth. There has also been the elimination of most immigration, although some European Holocaust survivors came to the area after World War II, and several thousand Russian-Jewish immigrants have arrived in more recent years.

With some exceptions, the Jewish community today is relatively prosperous, comprising many successful professional and business people. The abandoned Jewish institutions in the city have been replaced by new ones scattered mainly in the northern fringes of the city and in the suburban areas where Jews live. Active Jewish Community Centers serve the people in about a dozen places. They are under the sponsorship of the Jewish Federation of Metropolitan Chicago, an umbrella-type community organization. From the contributions of many thousands to the Jewish United Fund, the Jewish Federation supports dozens of community, social welfare, cultural, religious, and educational services and organizations.

With the passing from the scene of the original immigrants, there has been a sharp decline in the hundreds of *landsmanshaften* fraternal organizations and synagogues that banded together Jews from the same towns in Europe. They have been replaced by numerous local, regional, and even national institutions and organizations. There now is a greater diversity in religious beliefs, though religious convictions are no longer always the motivation for joining a particular congregation. In 1981 there were approximately 125 synagogues in the metropolitan area—about 50 were Orthodox or Traditional, 35 Conservative, 30 Reform, and the remainder essentially independent. The Conservative and Reform congregations usually have larger memberships than the Orthodox congregations; consequently it is estimated that of the religiously affiliated Jews, 30 percent are Orthodox, 35 percent are Reform, and 35 percent are Conservative.

The once sharp division between the German and eastern European Jews has largely disappeared. The transition from European *shtetls* to Chicago suburbs took less than a century.

The Czechs and Slovaks

The first group of Czech immigrants, from Bohemia and Moravia, started filtering into Chicago in 1851 and 1852, shortly after the suppression by the Austrians of the 1848 Czech revolution. Their kinsmen to their east, the Slovaks, started coming to Chicago several decades later, in about 1890.

The earliest Czechs were squatters on what is now the southern part of Lincoln Park in an area called "The Sands." After being evicted in 1855, they moved temporarily into the area around Van Buren (400 S) and Clark (100 W) streets. By 1860 they had moved into an area bounded approximately by Canal (500 W), Halsted (800 W), Harrison (600 S), and 12th Street. By 1870 this community known as Praha (Prague) contained some 10,000 Czechs and a number of Czech institutions. The first Czech Catholic church in Chicago, St. Wenceslaus, was founded in 1863 at De Koven (1100 S) and Desplaines (700 W) streets. The first Czech daily newspaper in America, *Svornost,* began publication in 1875 on Canal Street. The first Bohemian Sokol (Falcon) in Chicago was established in 1868 at Canal and Taylor (1100 S) streets. Its major purpose was to develop physical fitness through gymnastics, and its organization was paramilitary, but it also fostered cultural development and served as a social and national unifying force.

After the Chicago Fire, which started in Praha about a block from St. Wenceslaus Church, the Czechs started to move southwest. Meanwhile newer immigrant groups, such as eastern European Jews and later Italians and Greeks, moved into Praha. The area into which the Czechs moved became known as Pilsen, named after the local "Pilsen" tavern, which, in turn, had been named after Bohemia's second largest city. By 1895 the Pilsen area, bounded approximately by 16th, 22nd, Halsted, and Western, contained about 60,000 Czechs and was the center of their culture.

A focal point of the Pilsen community was the vicinity of 18th and Allport (1234 W). On

Figure 4.18. Thalia Hall on the southeast corner of 18th Street and Allport Avenue, 1963. The building had been a major institutional center for the Czech Pilsen community. It housed a Czech theater, meeting rooms, and the offices of numerous Czech organizations. (Photograph, Sigmund J. Osty. Courtesy Chicago Historical Society.)

one corner was the stately St. Procopius Church with its green copper tower. The church was organized in 1876 and soon became a great religious, educational, and cultural complex, even including a Benedictine abbey. In the 1880s Sunday church attendance averaged about 6,000 people. The first Bohemian Catholic Literary Society of Chicago was organized there. Its boys' high school was the forerunner of Illinois Benedictine College, now located in Lisle, Illinois. Associated with the church were vocational and commercial classes and a Catholic Bohemian press, one of whose purposes was to counteract the large number of Bohemians who were antireligious free-thinkers or secularists—people who had often resented the Catholic church's close ties with the politically oppressive Austrian regime in their homeland.

Across the street from St. Procopius Church was Thalia Hall which housed a theater, meeting rooms, and offices for Czech organizations, many of which were destined to play an important role in exerting pressure for the creation of an independent Czechoslovakia after World War I. Further west at 18th Place and Paulina (1700 W) was St. Vitus Church, founded in 1888 by the Bohemian Benedictine Fathers. Near the church was the Leader Store, a famous ethnic-type department store where thousands of immigrants had their "perinys" (Czech feather comforters) made annually. Nearby on Blue Island Avenue was Pilsen Auditorium, and on Ashland Avenue was the Pilsen Sokol Hall.

By 1900, about 75,000 first- or second-generation Czechs lived in Chicago. There were then six Czech Catholic parishes and one

Slovak Catholic parish in the city. By 1910 there were about 110,000 Czechs in Chicago. Chicago was sometimes referred to as "Czechago" because it contained more Czechs than any other city in the United States. It soon would be the second largest Czech city in the world after Prague. The Czech immigrants were not as poor as many of the other immigrant groups. Their illiteracy rate was very low, only about 2 percent compared with an illiteracy rate of 24 percent for all immigrants. By the 1920s, at the height of Czech culture in the city, Chicago had four Czech daily newspapers representing the divergent views of Catholics, freethinkers, Socialists, and the unaffiliated and business community. In addition, there were a number of Czech periodicals. One common denominator of the press was its fight for the liberation and preservation of the original homeland, Bohemia and Moravia. In an effort to preserve their heritage, classes were held throughout the community on Saturdays for thousands of children to teach them the Czech language, culture, and history.

Many of the Czechs were skilled workers, such as carpenters, tailors, butchers, musicians, weavers, and smiths. Some worked in lumber and grain facilities along the Chicago River and in furniture factories, breweries, and garment shops. Others worked at the huge McCormick Works or the Western Electric plant to the west, the latter being the largest employer of Czech workers. Some worked in offices or owned stores, shops, or saloons. In 1900, 1,521 such facilities were Czech owned.[17]

The Czechs were noted for their reliability, hard work, and thrift, and thus were readily hired as workers. They usually took advantage of overtime, and their job stability built seniority. Many became foremen in factories. Even at the prevailing low wages, many Czechs were able to prosper as shown by the following account written in 1895:

> Often good artisans were compelled to work for low wages, even $1.25 a day; still, out of this meager remuneration they managed to lay

a little aside for that longed-for possession,— a house and lot that they could call their own. When that was paid for, then the house received an additional story, and that was rented so that it began earning money. When more was saved, the house was pushed in the rear, the garden sacrificed, and in its place an imposing brick or stone building was erected, containing frequently a store, or more rooms for tenants. The landlord, who had till then lived in some unpleasant rear rooms, moved into the best part of the house; the bare but well-scrubbed floors were covered with Brussels carpets, the wooden chairs replaced by upholstered ones, and the best room received the added luxury of a piano or violin.

> In those early days rent was high and flour ten dollars a barrel, but they bought cheap meat at four cents a pound, coffee at twelve cents; and thus by dint of great economy many were able to lay aside money each year, and some of those early settlers now own property ranging in value from fifty thousand to two hundred thousand dollars.[18]

The Czechs were especially prominent in building and loan associations. In 1910, 94 of 197 such associations in Chicago were Czech owned. Zeal for saving enabled Czechs to become homeowners and to move westward into some of the city's better residential areas and eventually into the western suburbs.

Sickness and death benefits were provided by many of the 500 Czech lodges and clubs that existed in the 1920s in Chicago. These organizations were usually formed by people from the same Czech village or town. In the 1920s there were also some 20 Czech soccer clubs in the city.

As early as 1880 they began moving into what was to become the largest Czech community in Chicago. Known as "Czech California," it derived its name from California Avenue (2800 W). The settlement encompassed mainly the community of South Lawndale, and was bounded approximately by Rockwell (2600 W) to the east, the city's boundary with the community of Cicero to the west, 14th Street to the north and 33rd Street to the south. By 1910 Czechs owned about 80 percent of the dwellings in Czech California.

The major artery of this community was 26th Street, which was lined with Czech facilities, especially between Rockwell and Pulaski. At Lawndale Avenue (3700 W) was the three-story Sokol Havlíček-Tyrš which contained a large hall that doubled as a gymnasium. At Albany Avenue (3100 W), adjoining the Pilsen Brewery, was Pilsen Park where for more than half a century many Czechoslovakian organizations held picnics, dances, festivals, and political rallies—especially rallies for the independence of Czechoslovakia. A number of Czech churches were established in the area, including Catholic St. Ludmila at 24th Street and Albany Avenue and Blessed Agnes at 26th Street and Central Park (3600 W), and Protestant John Hus Church at 24th Street and Sawyer Avenue (3232 W).

Partly due to differing views on religion among the Czechs, somewhat competing and duplicating facilities were often erected. In 1916 the Bohemian Freethinkers of Chicago completed the John Hus Memorial Hall on 22nd Street near Keeler Avenue (4200 W). The Bohemian Freethinkers also helped organize the Bohemian National Cemetery at Foster Avenue and Pulaski Road. In 1893 they helped found the nearby Bohemian Old People's Home and Orphanage. Today it is the Bohemian Home for the Aged and is run by a consortium of Czech organizations.

Czech influence permeated Czech California. The Czech language was taught at Farragut and Harrison high schools, and streets in the area, such as Kostner, Karlov, and Komensky, were named for prominent Czechs. Twenty-second Street was changed to Cermak Road to honor Chicago's first foreign-born mayor, Anton J. Cermak, who was killed in 1933 during the attempted assassination of President-elect Franklin D. Roosevelt. The Douglas Park elevated line which traversed both Pilsen and Czech California was dubbed the "Bohemian Zephyr."

On the periphery of the community, located in 1912 at 3659 Douglas Boulevard (1400 S) was the prestigious Bohemian Club ("Ceska Beseda") whose members were the leaders of the arts, professions, and commerce in Chicago's Czech community. The club's programs included concerts, plays, lectures, dances, and social receptions. The club hosted Thomas G. Masaryk, the first president of Czechoslovakia, and his son, Jan Masaryk, who later became the Czech foreign minister. Mayor Cermak, Judge Otto Kerner and his son Otto, who served as governor of Illinois, were members of the club. The composer Rudolph H. Friml, who lived in Chicago for several years, also visited the club. Other well-known Chicago-area Czechs include George Halas, founder and owner of the Chicago Bears football team, and the American astronaut, Eugene Cernan, who landed on the moon in 1972.

The Czechs were very active politically. Between 1890 and 1920, for example, they elected some 80 public officials ranging from city aldermen to state legislators to United States congressmen.

In addition to the three major Czech settlements of Chicago—Praha, Pilsen, and Czech California, there were smaller settlements in other parts of the city. One such settlement was south of the stockyards around Saints Cyril and Methodius Church which was established in 1891 at 50th Street and Hermitage Avenue (1732 W). Some Czechs lived in the Bridgeport area, some near the steel mills in South Chicago, some in the "Merigold" area around Our Lady of Lourdes Church at 15th Street and Keeler Avenue, and a small settlement was established on the northwest side around Milwaukee and Foster avenues, not too far from the Bohemian National Cemetery. By 1940 there were about a dozen Czech parishes in Chicago, all with parochial schools. There were also about two dozen Free Thought schools which met in the afternoon or on the weekends to teach Czech children the language, literature, and history of Czechoslovakia. After World War I, there were also several Czech Protestant churches and missions, and some of the Czech freethinkers joined them.

After World War II the Czechs began to move into the western suburbs. First they moved into Cicero and Berwyn, and then, generally following Cermak Road, Ogden Avenue, and the Burlington Railroad, they moved into Riverside, North Riverside, Westchester, Lyons, Brookfield, La Grange, La Grange Park, Hinsdale, Downers Grove, Naperville, and even out to Aurora. Generally the more affluent lived farther out.

By 1930 over one third of the combined population of Cicero and Berwyn, 113,629, was of Czechoslovak descent, and today they contain the greatest concentration of Czechs in the metropolitan area. Many of the Czech organizational facilities are concentrated there. These include the Czechoslovak National Council of America in Cicero, which attempts to keep Czech traditions and language alive and strives for a truly independent Czechoslavakia, and the Czechoslovak Society of America in Berwyn, with its fraternal insurance and benefit program for lodges across the country, a monthly "Journal", and a small museum.

The main commercial street of Cicero and Berwyn is Cermak Road. At the Chicago boundary with Cicero, where the black residential population ends abruptly, stands the huge Hawthorne Works complex of the Western Electric Company, Cicero's largest employer. Large numbers of Czechs and Slovaks are employed there. Nearby, on Cermak Road just west of Cicero Avenue (4800 W), stands the hotel where the gangster Al Capone had his headquarters in the 1920s. Capone terrorized Cicero and controlled its gambling, bootlegging, and even some of its elections and public officials.

Farther west on Cermak Road today is "downtown Bohemia," with numerous store signs bearing Czech names, babushka-wearing women, bakeries displaying Bohemian pastries, and restaurants such as Old Prague with its multi-colored Old World exterior. Because of its numerous savings and loan associations, often spaced only a block or two apart and

Figure 4.19. Cermak Road in Cicero, "downtown Bohemia," with its Bohemian restaurants, bakeries, and food shops, and numerous savings and loan associations. (Photograph by Irving Cutler.)

sometimes even on adjoining corners, Cermak Road has been referred to as the "Bohemian Wall Street." Next to almost every savings and loan association is a real estate office with pictures of modest bungalows and two-flats in the window. The penchant for thrift is reflected in a *Cicero Life* newspaper survey in the 1960s which showed that "18 out of every 19 Bohemians in the two communities paid cash for their cars—either 100 percent down immediately or within 90 days of purchase." Off the main street are rows of similar two-story red or brown brick houses, modest but neat and well-kept, on 25- or 30-foot lots, and usually debt free.

Today the majority of people of Czech descent in the Chicago area live in the suburbs. Unlike the suburban population of many other groups, the Czech suburban population is not dispersed, being largely concentrated in a few western suburbs. The rapid and continuing movement to the suburbs, however, has largely depleted the old Czech neighborhoods of the city. Praha, on the southwestern fringe of the Loop, has long been an industrial area. Pilsen is now almost wholly Mexican, though a very few, largely elderly Czechs still live there. St. Procopius is the only church that conducts the Sunday mass in the Czech language. A Czech daily newspaper is still located on 18th Street, but the six remaining Sokol groups are all in the suburbs. The Czech movement out of Czech California has been more recent and is still continuing. Here, too, Mexicans now occupy most of the area. Some Czech institutions are still functioning there, but others have passed from the scene. Pilsen Park, the great Czech gathering place, has been replaced by a steel-and-glass shopping center with a large parking lot.

While Praha, Pilsen, and Czech California have become legends to many of the descendants of the people who came from Bohemia and Moravia, there are other communities in Chicago which still have Czechs. These are mainly communities on the Southwest Side such as New City (the Back-of-the-Yards area), Gage Park, Garfield Ridge, and Ashburn.

Some of the Czechs in these communities, and also in the suburbs, are refugees and political exiles who came as a result of the Nazi or communist takeover of their country. But despite this more recent infusion, the tempo of Czech ethnic life in the Chicago area has slowed considerably as the processes of Americanization, ethnic intermarriage, and assimilation continue unabated.

It is estimated that there are fewer than one-third as many Slovaks as Czechs in the Chicago area. The Slovaks started arriving in Chicago after 1890. Because the Slovaks and Czechs had some language, cultural, and historical differences, the Slovaks generally formed their own separate organizations in the United States. Coming from a more rugged, rural, and isolated part of Europe, most Slovaks lacked the educational opportunities of the Czechs.

Many Slovak immigrants settled and worked in the coal mining and steel mill areas of Pennsylvania and Ohio. Of those who settled in Chicago, many also worked in the steel mills. Some settled in the heavily industrialized part of northwestern Indiana—in Hammond, Whiting, East Chicago, and Gary. Some worked in the Chicago stockyards; others worked as carpenters, masons, and cabinet makers; and some found jobs in a field in which they excelled—that of wireworkers who either mended pots and pans or produced new wire products.

Unlike most of the Czechs, the Slovak men frequently came to America alone. They came with the idea of making some money which they would take back home or use to bring their families to the United States. Most of them remained, however, built churches, and soon owned their own homes with the aid of their savings and loan associations. Each of their communities and parishes soon had fraternal, charitable, social, dramatic, and athletic clubs. Being predominantly Catholic, there were fewer divisions among the Slovaks than among the Czechs who had sizable freethinker and secular groups.

Many Slovaks settled in or near the Czech communities, but they were generally more

Figure 4.20. Steel workers' homes in South Chicago in the early 1900s. (Photograph, R. R. Earle. Courtesy Chicago Historical Society.)

widely dispersed in smaller communities. In the early days, Slovaks from the same section of Slovakia often settled close to one another.

The first Slovak church, St. Michael Archangel, was organized in 1898, and a church building was erected near the stockyards at 48th and Winchester (1932 W). It contained a large parochial school, and until St. Simons was built in 1926 at 52nd and California, St. Michael Archangel was the largest Slovak Catholic parish in America. St. Joseph was built in Pilsen near the Czech St. Procopius Church. Slovak churches were also established in Bridgeport, South Chicago, Roseland, South Lawndale, and on the Northwest Side in the West Town and Humboldt Park communities. In time, as the Slovaks moved upward economically, they moved into the same western suburbs as the Czechs, especially into Cicero and Berwyn.

The Poles

Although the Poles were the last of the major European immigrant groups to arrive in Chicago in large numbers, they now constitute the largest European ethnic group in the Chicago area. With an estimated 700,000 people of Polish descent currently in the area, Chicago has become the fourth largest Polish city in the world.

Until the end of World War I, Poland had been partitioned among Germany, Austria, and Russia; consequently, precise figures of Polish immigration are somewhat difficult to obtain inasmuch as immigrants were listed in some censuses by country of origin. Supplementary data, however, indicate that there were relatively few Poles in Chicago before the late 1860s and only about 2,000 in 1870, or less than 1 percent of the city population. Thereafter, until 1930, more Poles arrived in

Figure 4.21. St. Stanislaus Kostka, the first Polish Roman Catholic parish in Chicago, was organized in 1867 and the church at Noble and Bradley (now Potomac) streets was started in 1877. In the 1890s it was one of the largest Polish parishes in the world. Today the membership is a mixture is Hispanics, Poles, and some blacks; separate masses are celebrated in Spanish, Polish, and English. One of the twin green cupolas was damaged by lightning and never replaced. (Photograph by Irving Cutler.)

Chicago than any other ethnic group. Most of them were landless, poorly educated, rural people fleeing poverty, military conscription, and foreign domination.

The first major Polish community in Chicago started to develop in the 1860s around Division (1200 N) and Noble (1400 W) streets, about two miles northwest of the city's business center and just west of the North Branch of the Chicago River. Here in 1867 St. Stanislaus Kostka, the first Polish Roman Catholic parish in Chicago was organized, and in 1877 its massive, baroque-style, cathedral-like church with twin green cupolas was started at Noble and Bradley (now Potomac, 1300 N). The St. Stanislaus district, or "Stanislawowo" (sometimes called the "Polish Downtown"), expanded rapidly, with some of the precincts around the church being over 90 percent Polish. This highly congested area consisted mainly of streets lined with two-story wood or wood-brick bungalows and tall, narrow three-story brick tenements, usually built on 25-foot lots, and often containing shoddy wooden shacks on the rear of the lot. Usually at the corner, but often also in the middle of the block, were small stores on the ground level of residential buildings. These might house a "ma and pa" grocery, a bakery, a butcher shop, or the local tavern.

The "Main Street" of the community was Noble Street, lined with small shops and stores of all kinds, and with religious and other institutional facilities. The business hub became the nearby triangle bounded by Milwaukee, Ashland, and Division streets. It was in this area that many of the growing number of Polish fraternal, religious, financial, and commercial organizations opened their offices, among them an increasing number of Polish newspapers and some of the largest Polish national organizations.

In the 1890s, the parish of St. Stanislaus Kostka had about 40,000 parishioners, making it one of the largest Roman Catholic parishes in the world. In 1893 over 2,000 baptisms, almost 400 weddings, and about 1,000 funerals were held in the church. The church complex eventually contained a rec-

tory, convent, parish school which enrolled some 4,000 students at its peak, huge auditorium, and parish hall which accommodated various activities, ranging from Polish singers to political meetings. The parish also had its own savings and loan association. Much of the growth of the church took place under the direction of a vigorous immigrant pastor, Father Vincent Barzynski. He also played a role in organizing some 25 other parishes in Chicago.[19]

Although St. Stanislaus Kostka remained the parent church of the Polish Roman Catholic churches in Chicago, other churches were soon built nearby to handle the burgeoning Polish population. Holy Trinity, organized in 1873 as a mission of overcrowded St. Stanislaus Kostka, was just two blocks to the south. Within a mile (1.6 km) of St. Stanislaus Kostka were St. John Cantius (1893), St. Mary of the Angels (1899), and Holy Innocents (1905). The architecture of these churches was also essentially baroque-style, with large green domes dominating the landscape.

The Poles were more church oriented than most of the other immigrant groups, and nearly all of them were Roman Catholic. The fusion of religion with culture was part of their way of life. The churches were landmarks that reflected the Old World and were built as if the people were going to remain in the neighborhood forever. Polish parishes channeled more of their revenue into church buildings than did almost any other group.

By 1910 this Polish community had expanded to include the area bounded approximately by the river on the east, California Avenue (2800 W) on the west, Fullerton Avenue (2400 N) on the north, and Chicago Avenue (800 N) on the south. Many worked in the factories in the river area, including the many tanneries. Of the 200,000 people then in the area, about half were Polish. These 100,000 Poles represented 40 percent of the quarter million Poles in the city in 1910.

The Poles kept moving northwest on both sides of Milwaukee Avenue, the Polish commercial corridor. Early in this century, aided

Figure 4.22. A cottage in the 1880s in an immigrant area on the Near North Side. Adjustment had to be made to the home because of the raising of the grade of the street and sidewalk. (Photograph courtesy Chicago Historical Society.)

by improving public transportation along Milwaukee Avenue, some Polish families leaped over German and Scandinavian settlements in the Logan Square area to settle farther out in such areas as Avondale, Irving Park, and Portage Park.

Most of the other Poles in Chicago lived in a few other sizable Polish communities on the West or South sides. A large church was the focal point of each community. Each community was near numerous factories. Lack of industrial experience (80 percent of the Polish immigrants had been farmers or farm laborers), as well as the language barrier, forced them to take unskilled, low-paying jobs that were usually strenuous and often dangerous. A survey in 1911 found that a foreign-born Pole earned about one-third less than a foreign-born German.

One such community developed around St. Adalbert's Church at 17th and Paulina (1700 W), organized in 1874. Jobs were available in nearby quarries and breweries and in the many factories along the Burlington Railroad and the ship canal. By 1910 there were about 15,000 Poles in the area. On the other side of the waterway around the bad-smelling stockyards, were the Bridgeport and Back-of-the-Yards areas with a 1910 Polish population of almost 30,000. They contained five Polish-language Catholic churches, the oldest being St. Mary of Perpetual Help (1883) in Bridgeport and St. Joseph (1887) in the Back-of-the-Yards area. Five Holy Martyrs Church, organized in 1908 and located at 43rd and Richmond (2932 W), was visited by Pope John Paul II during his visit to Chicago in 1979.

A dozen or more miles south of the Loop, the area stretching from South Chicago to Hegewisch contained some 18,000 Poles in 1910. There, church steeples and factory smokestacks dominated the skyline. Although remote and isolated from the main Polish communities, this heavily-industrialized, smoke-filled steel area offered many employment opportunities. Immaculate Conception Parish was organized there in 1882 and a church was built at 88th Street and Commercial Avenue (3000 E), a few blocks from the steel mills.[20]

In none of these communities was there quite as high a population density or as high a proportion of Poles as there was in the Stanislawowo area. Instead of tenements, most of the people lived in frame cottages which often housed two or more immigrant families plus boarders. In none of the areas other than Stanislawowo did the Poles comprise much more than a quarter of the population. Their neighbors usually included Germans, Czechs, and Lithuanians, and frequently also Irish and Italians. From 1910 to 1930, however, while the Stanislawowo area's Polish population remained relatively static, the Polish populations in the St. Adalbert, Bridgeport-Back-of-the-Yards, and South Chicago-Hegewisch areas were each increasing about 50 percent, and in the newer Brighton Park-McKinley Park area on the Southwest Side it rose sharply to some 25,000 Poles. The Polish community on the far Northwest Side grew even more rapidly until in 1930 it contained some 90,000 Poles.

As the Polish population grew, so too did the number of their organizations, which at their peak probably numbered over 4,000. These included religious, educational, immigrant aid, cultural, fraternal, financial, veteran, social, and athletic organizations. Today the two largest organizations, both with national headquarters in Chicago, are the Polish Roman Catholic Union, founded in 1873, and the larger Polish National Alliance, founded in 1880. The Polish Museum of America at 984 North Milwaukee Avenue is maintained by the former organization. Although the aim of both organizations was to promote the welfare of Polish Americans through insurance and social and cultural programs, the approach of the rival organizations differed. The Polish Roman Catholic Union, a Catholic fraternal order, was organized along parish lines and was dominated by the clergy. The Polish National Alliance, more of a nationalistic fraternal order, implemented its programs through local secular institutions and laymen. Other major national organizations headquartered in Chicago include the Polish Women's Alliance, the Polish Alma Mater (youth work), and the Polish American Congress. The latter is a nationwide "umbrella" of Polish organizations.

With its large Polish immigrant population, Chicago supported a flourishing Polish-language press. In 1920 there were five Polish daily newspapers, but with the subsequent decline in immigration, the press gradually dwindled until today only one Polish daily remains, *Dziennik Zwiazkowy (Polish Daily Zgoda)*.

The larger social welfare agencies operated by the Polish community include St. Mary of Nazareth Hospital, Guardian Angel Day Care Center, St. Joseph Home for the Aged, St. Vincent's and St. Hedwig's orphanages, and the Polish Welfare Association. Over 100 building and loan associations were Polish owned, and in time about two-thirds of the Polish families owned their own homes, about double the city average. Poles found it difficult to achieve land-ownership in the old country; here hard work and thriftiness could achieve the security, status, and neighborhood stability that came with home ownership.

Behind many of these Polish organizations stood the Polish-language Roman Catholic churches of which there were eventually 43 in the city. The church, however, was not without its dissenters. Around the turn of the century a splinter group broke from the Roman Catholic Church and formed the Polish National Church, which today has some 10,000 to 15,000 members and nine congregations in the city. Conflict within the church frequently centered on the efforts of Poles to establish more Polish parishes and separate Polish dioceses, to maintain the use of the Polish language and religious traditions, to obtain financial control of church property, to achieve national autonomy within the American Roman Catholic Church, and to end the underrepresentation of the Poles in the Roman Catholic hierarchy. The Roman Catholic church hierarchy in Chicago was dominated largely by two earlier immigrant groups, the Irish and the Germans, although in time the

Poles comprised between one-third and one-half of the Catholic parish membership and about one-sixth of the parishes. Today Alfred L. Abramowicz, of Polish descent, is an Auxiliary Bishop of the Roman Catholic Archdiocese in Chicago.

The Poles have felt that they have been underrepresented also in political office, considering that people of Polish descent have made up 12 to 18 percent of the city's population in recent decades. Poles have never held some of the highest offices, including that of mayor. Among the more prominent Polish officeholders have been Judges La Buy and Jarecki, State's Attorney Adamowski, and Congressmen Kluczynski, Derwinski, Pucinski, and Rostenkowski.

In proportion to their numbers Poles have also lagged in commerce and industry. But in the last few decades they have fared somewhat better in the business, professional, and educational worlds, though they are still more likely to be employed as laborers, operatives, and craftsmen than is the general population. Poles are proud that their unemployment rate has been consistently below the city average, their median income has been about 20 percent above the city average, and the number of Poles on welfare has been far below the city average. They have been far more likely to attend private and parochial elementary schools than the city average (52 percent versus 24 percent in 1970), but they have had somewhat less total schooling than that of the general city population. In 1970, only 30 percent of all Polish adults in Chicago had completed high school, compared to 44 percent for all Chicagoans. However, this disparity was due in part to the lesser educational attainments by the older generation of Poles.[21]

The World War II period brought a temporary renewal of Polish immigration to the Chicago area, mainly of refugees. Most were younger, better educated, more articulate, and more aggressive than the rural Polish immigrants who came earlier in the century. Many were professionals, and their attitude toward the established institutions and organizations often conflicted with that of older Polish generations.

A bigger change in the Polish community had started even before World War II. This was the tendency of Poles of the second and third generation to move out of the once stable Polish communities into much more mixed areas, although the Poles generally remained in their old neighborhoods longer than most ethnic groups. Higher income, changed lifestyles, the desire for better surroundings, improved transportation, and pressure from expanding minority groups all helped to accelerate the geographic dispersion of the Poles, especially after World War II. In the desire to become more Americanized, the younger generations of Poles lost some of their tenuous attachment to the established Polish communities and institutions. Through the years, as with other ethnic groups, there has been a declining interest among Poles in their language, newspapers, and radio programs. There has also been a tendency of some to "Americanize" their names. The 1970s, however, witnessed a renewed interest on the part of the young of various ethnic groups to learn more about their heritage. A few Chicago public high schools offer Polish language classes. The Poles, in particular, were interested in upgrading their image and combating the disparaging effects of the Polish jokes.

The movement and scattering of the Poles outward has been mainly to the southwest and northwest and into the suburbs. Archer Avenue leading to the southwest and especially Milwaukee Avenue to the northwest have been the main commercial corridors of this movement. The 1970 census revealed that in addition to the old Polish concentrations in the Chicago communities of West Town, Logan Square, and Humboldt Park, Poles reside in large numbers in communities to the northwest, such as Belmont Cragin, Dunning, Avondale, Irving Park, Portage Park, Jefferson Park, and Norwood Park. To the south

from the Bridgeport, New City, and Lower West Side communities, Poles have moved into such Southwest Side communities as South Lawndale, Brighton Park, Gage Park, Archer Heights, and Garfield Ridge.

Sizable numbers of Poles live in such communities as Cicero, Berwyn, Elmwood Park, Norridge, Harwood Heights, Park Ridge, Niles, Posen, and Oak Lawn. They are also in the industrial suburbs of the Calumet steel area of northwestern Indiana. The suburban area now contains an estimated 40 percent of the people of Polish descent of Metropolitan Chicago. The suburbanites are far less likely to be officially affiliated with the ethnic-oriented churches, although some retain a sentimental or "weekend" attachment to certain parishes.

The old Stanislawowo district is undergoing rapid change, due especially to an influx of blacks and Puerto Ricans. On both Milwaukee Avenue and Division Street signs in Polish and newer signs in Spanish are seen side by side. One drugstore carries a sign that reads "Mowimy po Polsku. Se hablo Espanol. We also speak English." Noble Street, where it still exists, is no longer a Polish "Main Street."

The parent church, St. Stanislaus Kostka, still stands across Pulaski Park as the landmark of the original Polish settlement in Chicago. It successfully withstood an effort to demolish it to make way for the Kennedy Expressway—a project which helped in the disruption of the old community, as did Noble Square, a major urban renewal project. The once large membership of the church is now down and is divided among Hispanics, blacks, and Poles, the latter mainly older people. Nearby the Polish Museum of America still remains, as do the headquarters of a number of Polish institutions, including the Polish Roman Catholic Union. However, the recent move of the Polish National Alliance headquarters and the *Polish Daily Zgoda* from the Division-Milwaukee-Ashland triangle to 6100

Figure 4.23. The intersection of Division, Milwaukee, and Ashland, once the crossroads of the Polish community, 1980. The changing neighborhood is reflected by the Hispanic food store and the former home of the *Polish Daily Zgoda.* The newspaper and the nearby Polish National Alliance headquarters have moved in recent years to 6100 North Cicero Avenue on the northwest fringe of Chicago. (Photograph by Irving Cutler.)

North Cicero Avenue, on the northwest fringe of the city, symbolizes the outward migration of the Polish population. The numerous prominent Polish churches which can be seen on a drive northwestward along the Kennedy Expressway are striking evidence of a century of outward Polish migration from the original cradle on Noble Street near Division Street.

The Lithuanians

Chicago's Lithuanian community is the largest outside of the Soviet Union. And probably due to the occupation of their homeland by the Soviet Union and the resultant restrictions, the Lithuanians of the Chicago area are one of the most determined of the ethnic groups to retain their identity, culture, and customs. Chicago has become a focal point of Lithuanian culture, where the language is being preserved and where there is a strong nationalistic spirit.

An estimated 100,000 people of Lithuanian descent live in Chicago today, a small number in comparison to such groups as the Poles, Italians, and Germans, but a large number for a people whose homeland contains only about 3 million people. Proportionately the emigration from Lithuania was larger than that from most European countries, exceeded perhaps only by the emigration from Ireland. During the last decades of the nineteenth century and the beginning of the present century, some 20 percent of the Lithuanian population migrated from their homeland, the greatest number coming to America. Czarist oppression of Lithuania, the inability of urban industry to absorb Lithuania's landless peasants, and periods of famine spurred the migration to America.

Figure 4.24. Lithuanian Polish Butcher at 3355 West 38th Street, 1913. Tall man is Stanley Balzekas whose son, Stanley Balzekas, Jr., founded the Balzekas Museum of Lithuanian Culture in 1966 in Brighton Park. (Photograph courtesy Chicago Historical Society.)

The first Lithuanians to appear in Chicago were a group of 18 men who came to help lay railroad tracks. Finding no Lithuanians with whom to live, many of them boarded with Polish families in the growing Polish community around Division and Noble streets. Although historically there had been some conflict in Europe between Poles and Lithuanians, in Chicago the Polish culture was the closest to that of the Lithuanians, and some Lithuanians understood the Polish language from their contacts with Poles in the Old World. As a result, the Lithuanians initially used some of the facilities of the Polish churches and organizations, although there was occasional friction between the groups. Many Lithuanians attended services at St. Stanislaus Kostka, the first of the Polish churches in the city. The only Lithuanian Catholic church on the North Side, St. Michael, was established in 1904 at 1644 West Wabansia (1700 N). Although a small Lithuanian community existed in this area for many years, by far the largest Lithuanian communities developed and continue to exist on the South and Southwest sides.

The largest early Lithuanian communities were in the vicinity of the stockyards—in Bridgeport to the northeast of the stockyards and in the Back-of-the-Yards area to the west. Since most of the early immigrants were peasants with no particular skills for working in the big city, they found jobs mainly as common laborers in freight yards, breweries, brickyards, factories, foundries, and especially in the stockyards. It is estimated that during the little over a century of the stockyards' existence, approximately 100,000 Lithuanians worked there. Before World War I they were second only to the Poles in numbers of workers employed there.[22] Thus it was not accidental that the main character of Upton Sinclair's novel *The Jungle* (1906), depicting the inhuman conditions in the stockyards, was a Lithuanian.

Since very few Lithuanian immigrants had any experience in business, by 1910 only a very small percentage of the Lithuanians were self-employed. However, as their communities developed, Lithuanians began to own groceries, saloons, barbershops, restaurants, and even savings and loan associations and banks. Ultimately, they became numerous in many of the professions, and among the various ethnic groups, Lithuanians came to have one of the higher proportions of people with graduate school training.

The first Lithuanians moved into the Bridgeport area in the 1880s. In 1892 they established St. George's Catholic Church on the corner of 33rd Street and Auburn Avenue (now Lituanica Ave., 900 W). In 1896 this small wooden church was replaced by a tall-spired, beautiful church which was then probably the largest Lithuanian church in America. Affiliated with the church was a parochial school where courses in the Lithuanian language were taught along with the major part of the public school curriculum. Lithuanian-owned stores and facilities of various types soon stretched along Halsted Street near the church, especially between 31st and 35th streets. Antanas Olšauskas, who came to America in 1889, opened Chicago's first Lithuanian bank in 1896 in Bridgeport. He also founded a Lithuanian newspaper and and published about 130 Lithuanian books. In addition, he bought and built numerous buildings in Bridgeport.

To the west of the stockyards, Lithuanians settled in the communities of New City and Brighton Park in what had been the Town of Lake. Holy Cross Parish was organized in 1904 at 46th and Wood (1800 W) and a new church was consecrated there in 1915. In 1914, about a mile to the west at 44th and Fairfield (2732 W), Immaculate Conception Parish was organized and a church soon completed. Its membership later reached about 1,000.

A small Lithuanian community existed around the Providence of God Church, built in 1915 at 18th and Union (700 W). The church is now used by the surrounding Mexican community and was visited by Pope John Paul II in 1979. The area still contains the office of *Naujienos* (News), founded in 1914 as a socialist newspaper. It is one of Chicago's two remaining Lithuanian daily newspapers. Almost two miles to the west another small Lithuanian community existed around Our Lady of Vilna Church, 2323 West 23rd Place, which was organized in 1904, and around the Lithuanian Zion Evangelical Lutheran Parish, organized in 1903. The latter had a church at Bell Avenue (2232 W) and Cermak Road (2200 S). Some of the members of the congregations worked at the nearby International Harvester and Crane plants.

Other Lithuanian communities developed around the South Chicago steel mills. In some iron and steel plants the workers spoke only Polish or Lithuanian. In 1900 St. Joseph Church was established in this area at 8801 South Saginaw Avenue (2638 E). In the Roseland-Pullman area, All Saints Church was founded in 1906. Like those of the Polish communities, the Lithuanian churches were mainly Roman Catholic. From the end of the nineteenth century until the late 1920s, the peak period of their church building, the Lithuanians established eleven Roman Catholic parishes and one Lutheran parish. Later two more Protestant churches were built. Many of their churches were large with unique steeples decorated with the ancient Lithuanian sun cross.

The churches offered numerous services to their members, including the establishing in 1903 by nine Lithuanian churches of St. Casimir Lithuanian Cemetery. It is located on 111th Street between Pulaski Road and Cicero Avenue in extreme southwestern Chicago. In 1912 the denominational Lutheran National Cemetery was located in Justice, Illinois.

In time there was some conflict between the Lithuanians and the Catholic church hierarchy concerning use of the Lithuanian language in the liturgy. As among the Poles, there was also some conflict between the ardent nationalists and the religionists, although Lithuanians have been almost unanimous in their strong desire for an independent Lithuania.

Living standards were low in the various early Lithuanian communities. Homes were often simple wooden structures, and few Lithuanians owned their own homes. In time, however, aided by their savings and loan associations, home ownership became extremely high and the houses were improved and well kept. Lithuanian neighborhoods had increasing numbers of Lithuanian-owned stores. On some streets, such as on Ashland Avenue near the stockyards, taverns were so numerous that according to the Lithuanian newspaper *Draugas,* they were literally "cropping up like mushrooms after the rain."

The Lithuanian population in Chicago increased rapidly after the turn of the century. In 1900 there were an estimated 14,000 people of Lithuanian descent in Chicago; by 1910 there were some 50,000; and in 1924 about 80,000. During World War I, Lithuanian immigration largely ceased. Then after Lithuania achieved independence in 1918, in a burst of patriotism for their newly independent homeland, there was actually a very short period when Lithuanians left the United States and returned home.

In 1940, however, Lithuania was forced to become part of the Soviet Union. This action resulted in many thousands of Lithuanian refugees coming to Chicago after World War II. Many settled in the Marquette Park area of the community of Chicago Lawn. They helped to enhance the Lithuanian cultural life in Chicago and to perpetuate the intense nationalistic spirit. Many were white collar workers and professionals; some had been among Lithuania's foremost intellectuals. The Marquette Park area contained a larger per-

Figure 4.25. Interior of an immigrant's residence, probably a Lithuanian bachelor, about 1920. (Photograph courtesy Balzekas Museum of Lithuanian Culture and Chicago Historical Society.)

centage of such people and also of skilled workers and mechanics than did the older Lithuanian neighborhoods.

Today the largest concentration of Lithuanians in Chicago, and perhaps in the United States, is in the Marquette Park area. Here more than 30,000 people of Lithuanian descent (out of a total community population of about 45,000) live and maintain major Lithuanian institutions. This area is bounded approximately by California Avenue (2800 W) and Marquette Park on the west, Western Avenue (2400 W) on the east, 63rd Street on

the North, and 71st Street on the south. The heart of the area—between Marquette Road (6700 S), 69th Street, Rockwell Avenue (2600 W), and California Avenue—has been given the honorary designation of "Lithuanian Plaza" by the city of Chicago.

In 1911 the Sisters of St. Casimir, a Lithuanian Catholic order, led by Mother Marija, built a convent, part of which was used as a girls' academy. It was built on land between 67th and 68th streets and between Washtenaw (2700 W) and Talman (2623 W) avenues. Although the site was then somewhat marshy and largely unsettled, it was close to the many Lithuanian parishes on the South Side. The convent became the nucleus for a number of major Lithuanian institutions located in a couple of square blocks in the heart of the Marquette Park area and for a neighborhood of numerous brick homes, mainly one-story, which were built by the Lithuanians after World War I. The institutions built by the Lithuanians included Holy Cross Hospital, Nativity BVM Church, and Maria High School. The latter, a girls' preparatory school for the Lithuanians, was also attended by Poles and members of other eastern European groups. Nativity BVM Church has the distinction of being the largest and wealthiest Lithuanian church in Chicago today. A new building was erected in 1957 to handle the increased membership. The parish also has a parochial school.

Three-hundred-acre (122 ha) Marquette Park on the western edge of the community is the site of numerous Lithuanian meetings, outings, and soccer games. At the northeast corner of the park is a monument to Darius and Girenas, two Lithuanian-American flyers who in 1933 attempted to fly non-stop from the United States to Kaunas, Lithuania, in a plane named Lituanica. They died when their plane crashed in Germany just short of their goal.

Lithuanian-owned facilities in the Marquette Park area include a Lithuanian bookstore, real estate offices, overseas parcel-shipping services, savings and loan associations, flower and plant stores, grocery stores, restaurants, bakeries, delicatessens, and taverns. Also located there is the Lithuanian consulate. The main commercial street is 69th Street, and, to a lesser extent, 71st Street. Along 69th Street from Western to Washtenaw are about a dozen taverns, many catering to different Lithuanian clientele such as soccer players, artists, intellectuals, young people, and older people.

Surrounding areas also contain Lithuanian facilities. At 4545 West 63rd Street is the modern plant of *Draugas,* founded in 1916, a daily Lithuanian newspaper which serves not only the Chicago Lithuanian community but also national, Canadian, and Latin American Lithuanian communities. As the elderly immigrants have passed from the scene, the circulation of the paper has dropped to about 16,000 from more than double that number in the 1960s. Leonard Simutis (1892–1975), a leading Lithuanian spokesman in the United States, was the editor of *Draugas* from 1927 until his retirement in 1967.

About a mile to the northeast of the Marquette Park area is the Lithuanian Jesuit Youth Center, built in 1957–1958 at 56th Street and Claremont Avenue (2333 W). Although geographically in Gage Park, culturally it is part of Marquette Park, for it is a major focal point of Lithuanian culture. Plays, vocal and instrumental recitals, and art exhibits are held in its auditorium. The center has a Saturday high school, an Institute of Lithuanistics, and it hosts numerous secular and religious clubs and societies. It is part of a vigorous effort, together with family upbringing, to keep ethnic vitality alive among young Lithuanian-Americans by teaching them the language, history, literature, and folkways of their parents and grandparents. Generally the effort has been successful, as Lithuanians still usually marry Lithuanians, and even if they move to the suburbs, they still bring their children to the city every Saturday for Lithuanian cultural instruction. To the northwest at 4012 South Archer Avenue in Brighton Park is the Balzekas Museum of Lithuanian Culture, the only such museum in North America.

The Lithuanian community of the Chicago area is very active with more than 300 cultural, fraternal, and political organizations, most of which are in the Marquette Park area. There are numerous Lithuanian choral, dance, art, and literary groups. There are radio and TV programs. There is even a Lithuanian Opera Company which annually performs an opera in Lithuanian, some of the operas being original. In 1940 a Lithuanian newspaper discerningly discussed the importance of transmitting the Lithuanian cultural heritage to the second generation of immigrants to America:

> When many people speak of new immigrant groups, they refer not only to the foreign born, but to their children. There is probably no group in our population that is making a more distinguished contribution to American life than the sons and daughters of immigrant parents.
>
> There is no group, also, which is so much a "lost generation" as many of these native-born Americans. They are without roots, many of them, either in the new world or the old.
>
> They may learn in our schools about the Pilgrim Fathers and the farmers who stood at Lexington, but whose historic events and traditions find no echo in their personal or home life.
>
> Their vital American background is Ellis Island, the immigrant steerage, city slums, the mine and sweatshop.
>
> On the other hand, their parents, too often, have not the background or education to give them a sense of the cultural heritage they have brought from the old country—a heritage, which, if they were able to share it, would help to give these young people a new dignity and self-reliance and to make them more effective Americans.[23]

The Lithuanian population has declined in most of the older neighborhoods. Hispanics have moved into the Lower West Side and some of the Back-of-the-Yards area. Blacks have moved into the Roseland area on the far South Side. Sizable, but generally declining numbers, still live in the Chicago communities of Bridgeport, New City, Gage Park, and especially Brighton Park. Some live in the peripheral Southwest Side communities of Ashburn and Garfield Ridge. Some live in such western and southwestern suburbs as Burbank, Evergreen Park, Oak Lawn, Orland Park, Palos Heights, and Palos Hills. Farther out, Lemont has become the newest hub of Lithuanians in suburbia. Cicero contains an old established community of Lithuanians, many of whom work at Western Electric. St.

Anthony's Church, which has a large Lithuanian parochical school, was established in Cicero in 1911.

By far the largest concentration of Lithuanians in the Chicago region continues to be found in the Marquette Park area. But even there change has been taking place, especially on the eastern periphery of the area. Not too long ago Lithuanians were as far east as Damen Avenue (2000 W), but now blacks occupy homes a half mile to the west. Thus the Lithuanian Marquette Park area, reluctant to change, is in the direct path of the westward movement of the blacks, and the Lithuanian area's stability has been challenged. Racial tension and violence have punctuated a number of summers for almost a decade.

Although no mass exodus from the Marquette Park area has yet occurred, some of the younger Lithuanian-Americans, whose ethnic ties may not be very strong, have joined the trek to the suburbs. But the bulk of the Lithuanians seem determined for the present to stay where they, their parents, or grandparents settled and built at great cost many of the city's major Lithuanian institutions, creating a little Lithuania. Many see the Marquette Park area as the last major truly Lithuanian community in the city. With an eye to the effects of Russian domination over their homeland, they have become more determined than ever to preserve a viable Lithuanian culture in the area and to keep the spark burning for the eventual freedom of Lithuania.

The Italians

In the 1680s the Italian Henri de Tonti, the lieutenant of La Salle, the explorer, became one of the first white men to pass through the Chicago area. Two centuries later in 1880, when Chicago's population was already over half a million, there were only 1,357 foreign-born Italians in the city. This was up from 4 in 1850. In contrast, the German-born population in 1880 numbered 75,205 and the Irish-born 44,411. Thereafter,

Italian immigration increased very rapidly as part of the last great wave of European immigration, which came largely from eastern and southern Europe. The peak period of Italian immigration was from 1899 to 1924. Chicago's Italian population increased almost tenfold from 13,000 in 1890 to 124,000 in 1920. Today the Chicago area numbers about half a million people of Italian descent, a number exceeded among the European groups only by the Polish and German communities.

Until the 1880s the bulk of Italian immigrants came from relatively prosperous northern Italy—from the regions of Tuscany, Genoa, Lombardy, Piedmont, and Venetia. They generally came as family units. Some of the men worked at skilled or semiskilled jobs, some in the service and trade fields, and some became street vendors and small retailers.[24]

The first Italian settlements were in the heart of what is now the downtown area, along the south bank of the Chicago River and around Clark (100 W), Plymouth Court (31 W), Harrison (600 S), and Polk (800 S). Another settlement, predominantly Genoese, was just north of the river around Wells (200 W) and Illinois (500 N) in the angle formed by the river and its North Branch. Here in 1880 construction started on the Assumption of the Blessed Virgin Mary Church. It was completed in 1886. Resembling an Italian village church in design, the building still stands at 313 West Illinois Street, amid multistory commercial and factory buildings and in the shadow of the Merchandise Mart.

The great influx of Italian immigrants started in the 1880s. More than 75 percent of these immigrants came from the poor rural districts and small towns of Southern Italy— the Mezzogiorno. This area lying south of Rome included the provinces of Lucania, Apulia, Campania, Abruzzi, Calabria, and Sicily. About a quarter of the immigrants came from Sicily. Between 1899 and 1910, one-fifth of all the immigrants to the United States were southern Italians. Most of them were struggling financially, in debt, and heavily taxed and had little or no education. They

were extremely village and family oriented, with strong and expressive feelings and pride. Sometimes almost an entire village came to the United States, occasionally bringing the village priest with them. A majority of these Italians settled along the eastern seaboard, but many came to Chicago. In Chicago they usually moved into neighborhoods where friends and relatives from their town or province already lived. These were neighborhoods which had previously been lived in and then abandoned by German, Irish, and Swedish immigrants. Many of the southern Italians were single males who moved in with their friends and relatives as roomers.

To obtain employment, the southern Italians frequently turned to the padrone, a labor agent or boss. The padrone, often an earlier arrival from the same home province, spoke some English and understood Old World traditions as well as the business operations of the New World. He had established contacts with American businessmen who needed unskilled laborers, so he was usually able to provide the newly arrived immigrants with jobs, especially in construction or with the railroads. Chicago became a major padrone operations center partly because of its geographic location and because it was the country's greatest railroad center. The city served as a clearinghouse for seasonal railroad and construction jobs throughout the Midwest and much of the rest of the United States. The workers would return to Chicago during the winter season, often as boarders.

Although many of the eastern and southern European immigrants had some type of labor boss system, the influence of the padrone on workers from southern Italy was especially strong. Around the turn of the century many of these immigrant workers were not only beholden to the padrone for their jobs, but in some cases even for their passage tickets from Italy, although the total probably never approached half of the work force.[25] The padrone system became notorious because of the abuses of some unscrupulous padrones. They took exorbitant commissions, overcharged for inferior food and lodging at railroad and construction camps, secretly pocketed some of the money provided by employers for the workers, and exploited the workers in numerous other ways. The system started to decline rapidly starting about 1900, after revelations of fraud by a number of social agencies and governmental investigative commissions resulted in new labor legislation. Pressure applied to the railroads and construction officials caused them to change their labor practices. In addition, as the immigrants became familiar with the English language and with American labor practices, as the Italian community became better established, and as more and more immigrants had relatives who could help them find jobs, there was less need for an intermediary to obtain employment. The immigrants no longer were easy prey for the padrone.

In time the Italian-Americans branched out into a wide range of economic activities. In 1916 almost 50 percent were still common laborers; in 1931, 30 percent; in 1950, only 11 percent.[26] The railroads decreased in importance as a source of employment. Italians became stonecutters, masons, hod carriers, and the like. Many obtained jobs in public service, becoming garbage collectors, streetsweepers, streetcar employees, policemen, and so on. Increasing numbers worked in factories—about a third of the garment workers in Chicago were Italian, usually women, some of whom worked at home. Although as new immigrants the Italians had sometimes been used as strikebreakers, they later became very active in a number of unions, including the garment workers' union.

Many Italians opened small businesses of their own. They were grocers, fruit merchants, bakers, barbers, painters, carpenters, tailors, musicians, candy store owners, street vendors, restaurant owners, saloon keepers, and small factory owners. John F. Cuneo, whose grandparents came from Genoa in 1847, built one of the nation's largest printing concerns— Cuneo Press. Anthony J. Paterno rose from owner of a small grocery store, in the vicinity of Grand and Western avenues, to become one of the largest wine distributors in the country and also a prominent civic leader in the Italian community. A number became wealthy in the real estate business. During the prohibition era a few became financially successful by organizing gangs to control the distribution of illegal beverages to a thirsty public. The highly publicized operations of these gangs reflected unfavorably on the image of an immigrant group whose crime rate was not significantly different from the national average.[27]

Two Italian immigrants to Chicago became world renowned. Enrico Fermi (1901–1954), a distinguished Nobel Prize winning physicist, came to Chicago in the 1930s as a refugee from Mussolini's Italy. He led the team of eminent scientists at the University of Chicago who achieved the first man-controlled nuclear reaction. Mother Frances Cabrini (1850–1917) founded the Missionary Sisters of the Sacred Heart and did social work among the poor Italian immigrants in Chicago. Her order established hospitals, orphanages, and schools for the immigrants. In 1946 she was canonized by the Roman Catholic Church, the only American citizen to have been raised to sainthood.

In recent years, based on the 1970 United States Census figures, "Italians in Chicago were more likely to be employed as operatives and laborers (31%) and as craftsmen (17%) than the general employed population (26% and 13% respectively); less likely to be professionals and managers (12% vs. 18%), or sales and clerical workers (27% vs. 30%), and just as likely to be service workers (13%)."[28] Forty percent of employed Italians worked in manufacturing compared to 32 percent for the general employed population. Because they arrived late, the number of Italians who have held church or political office is relatively small compared to the size of the Italian population. However, in recent years a number of well known Italians have served in legislative bodies, including Alderman Vito Marzullo, State Representatives Victor Arrigo and Anthony Scariano, and Congressmen Frank Annunzio and Martin Russo. Especially prominent in the academic world is John Rettaliata who served for many years as president of the Illinois Institute of Technology.

As the Italian population increased from less than 1 percent of the foreign-born in Chicago in 1870 to over 8 percent in 1970 and as many worked their way upward financially, they began to move outward from the downtown area. Sometimes they were pushed outward by expanding industry. The Italian enclave in the area around Plymouth Court and Polk Street near the Dearborn Street railroad station (where some of the immigrants disembarked from the trains that brought them from the East) gradually began to expand westward between Harrison and 12th streets—first to the South Branch of the Chicago River, then to Canal Street (500 W), later to Halsted (800 W), and in 1905 into the area between Morgan (1000 W) and Racine (1200 W). To the north was a Greek community and to the south was the eastern European Jewish community. After 1910 the Italians began to move westward from Racine to Western Avenue (2400 N), then to Cicero Avenue (4800 W), and beyond into the Austin area in the 1920s.

"Little Italy" on the Near West Side was the largest Italian concentration in Chicago. The percentage of Italians in the total population was especially high in the vicinity of Halsted and Taylor (1000 S), but it decreased as one went farther west. Unlike many other Chicago Italian communities, this one was a melting pot of all the regional subcultures of Italy—combining Venetians, Neapolitans, Sicilians, Tuscans, and so on. Some of the regional groups clustered on certain blocks within the community. In the early 1920s the West Side area, encompassed by the Chicago River west to Paulina Street and from Van Buren Street south to 12th Street, contained perhaps half of Chicago's Italian population and included two large Italian parishes.[29]

The first Italian church in the area was Guardian Angel, founded in 1899 at 717 West Arthington (900 S), just east of Halsted. It had been preceded by the Guardian Angel

School, which was just a block west of Hull House. As the Italian population west of Halsted Street grew, the Guardian Angel parish was divided and Our Lady of Pompeii Church, staffed by the Scalabrini Fathers, was erected in 1910 at Lexington (732 S) and Racine. Feast days and festivals were important and colorful religious events among the Italians of the area.

After reaching a peak in the 1920s, the population of the Near West Side Italian community gradually declined. In the 1960s the community's existence was threatened by the intrusion of the campus of the University of Illinois at Chicago Circle, which was built despite the vehement protests of the community. But unlike the former Greek community to the north, a small Italian community has survived in the area between Circle Campus to the east and the giant medical complex to the west. The institutional influence has greatly increased land value in the area and has brought about much redevelopment and new construction. Nevertheless, glimpses of Little Italy are still visible, for example along stretches of Taylor Street and around Arrigo Park (formerly Vernon Park), with its Italian churches, Mother Cabrini Hospital, and its recently installed statue of Columbus. This statue originally had been exhibited at the Italian Pavilion during the 1893 World Columbian Exposition.

What was probably the second largest Italian area extended westward from the river along Grand Avenue (520 N) and adjacent streets. It was in the vicinity of the Chicago Commons Settlement House which was at Grand Avenue and Morgan Street. This had been an Irish and then a Swedish area. In the 1890s sizable numbers of northern Italians moved into the area, followed by others from southern Italy and Sicily. In 1899 the Swedish Lutheran Church at Grand Avenue and Peoria Street (900 W) was purchased and converted into an Italian Catholic church, Santa Maria Addolorata. In 1904, almost two miles to the west, Holy Rosary Church was established at 612 North Western Avenue. The community later moved farther west, paralleling Grand and Chicago avenues to Kedzie Avenue, and then out toward Cicero. Some Italian-Americans still live in this Northwest Side area.

The Near North Side had an area of chiefly Sicilian settlement to the east of the North Branch of the Chicago River and less than a mile west of the lakefront Gold Coast apartments. It was in the vicinity of Division (1200 N), Oak (1000 N), Cambridge (528 W), and diagonal Clybourne. This "Little Sicily" had previously been known as "Little Hell" because of its blight and the lawlessness of its previous residents, a pattern of behavior that did not readily change with the coming of the newer residents. In 1910 more than 8,000 Italians (almost all from Sicily) lived in Little Sicily. In 1929 the area was described as follows:

> . . . Little Hell, or Little Sicily, is a world to itself. Dirty and narrow streets, alleys piled with refuse and alive with dogs and rats, goats hitched to carts, bleak tenements, the smoke of industry hanging in a haze, the market along the curb, foreign names on shops and foreign faces on the streets, the dissonant cry of the huckster and peddler, the clanging and rattling of railroads and the elevated, the pealing of the bells of the great Catholic churches, the music of marching bands and the crackling of fireworks on feast days, the occasional dull boom of a bomb or the bark of a revolver, the shouts of children at play in the street, a strange staccato speech . . . on every hand one is met by sights and sounds and smells that are peculiar to this area, that are "foreign" and of the slum.
>
> Two generations ago this district was an Irish shanty town called Kilgubbin. A generation ago it was almost equally Irish and Swedish. Then the "dark people" began to come. At first they came slowly, meeting no little resistance. . . .
>
> But the Sicilians pushed slowly into the district. Industry was demanding cheap labor. Sicilians came in great numbers, especially in 1903–4, the tremendous Italian immigration

year. In this river district of the Near North Side they found cheap living quarters. It was the old story of a competition of standards of living, colored somewhat by national antagonisms. The Irish and Swedish, more prosperous, moved out of the district and northward. And by 1910 Kilgubbin and Swede Town had become Little Sicily. . . .

> The colony centers about the church of St. Philip Benizi. . . . West Division Street, the colony's principal street, is lined with Italian businesses and shops; numerous grocery stores and markets, florist shops, the Sicilian pharmacy, undertaking establishments, cobbler's shops, macaroni factories, cheap restaurants, pool rooms and soft drink parlors which are the lounging places of the second generation, and the barber shops which have replaced the saloon as the center of gossip for the older people. On the corner of Elm and Larrabee is a curb market. Along Oak Street are numerous stalls where fruit, vegetables, coal and wood, and oysters on the half-shell are sold. The shingles of the doctor and the midwife are frequently seen. The vicinity of Oak and Townsend is the center of the colony's population. Many of the influential Sicilians live along Sedgwick however, the colony's eastern boundary and more prosperous and fashionable street.
>
> Because of its isolated situation, due to poor transportation and the barrier of river and industry, Little Hell remained until the war relatively untouched by American custom, a transplantation of Sicilian village life in the heart of a hurrying American city. . . .
>
> During the last four years there has been a great change; the colony is slowly disintegrating; old customs are giving way. Contacts with the outside world, through work and school, have given boys and girls a vision of freedom and new opportunity. They are going to night school and making their friends outside the old circle. They are out of patience with the petty interests and quarrels of the older group, and refuse to have their lives ordered by their parents, whom they know to be ignorant and inexperienced. Families are not being broken up; the deep affections still persist; and though the old folks have misgivings,

Figure 4.26. Italian religious festival at Cambridge Avenue and Oak Street in front of St. Philip Benizi Church, 1947. The area now contains the Cabrini-Green Homes, low-income high-rise public housing. (Photograph, James D. McMahon. Courtesy Chicago Historical Society.)

in their indulgent way they are letting the new generation take the lead and are proud of their progressive sons and daughters. Young married couples are making their homes north of the old district, within easy reach of their parents, but away from the old associations. Evidences of refinement are seen in their homes and in their manner, and their children are dressed and fed according to most modern standards.[30]

In recent decades the Italians in the community have been replaced by blacks, many of whom live in the large Cabrini-Green public housing complex, a name that still partially reflects the former Italian character of the area.

In addition to the three large Italian communities, there were perhaps another twenty smaller Italian communities scattered throughout the city. These included a group mainly from Tuscany around 25th Street and Oakley Avenue near the large International Harvester plant. In this community St. Michaels Church was established in 1903 at 24th Place and Western Avenue. Another community was in the Roseland, Pullman, and Kensington areas on the far South Side where the Italian residents were largely from Venetia and Lombardy, and where the church of St. Anthony of Padua was established in 1904 at 216 Kensington Street (11552 S). Italians also settled south along Clark and Wentworth (200 W) into Armour Square and part of the Bridgeport area. Santa Maria Incoronata Church was founded in 1899 at Clark and 18th Streets. In 1914 the church was moved to Wentworth and Alexander streets (2246 South). This community had many Neapolitans as well as some northern Italians.

Some of these Italian communities declined significantly in numbers as blacks or Hispanics moved into the areas. One vibrant community that still continues is the Italian enclave around 25th Street and Oakley Avenue which is noted citywide for its numerous Italian restaurants. With the change in population the Italian membership in the local churches also declined. In addition, many more mobile and affluent second and third generation Italians turned away from Italian-dominated churches in favor of Americanized churches. With the decline of the Italian-born population and with the development of government social welfare programs, most of the hundreds of Italian mutual-aid societies, often started by immigrants from the same home region, ceased to exist.

In 1970 the largest concentrations of Italian-Americans in Chicago were on the West and Northwest sides in such communities as Portage Park, Dunning, Belmont Cragin, Humboldt Park, Austin, and West Town. But an estimated 55 percent of the Italian-Americans, mainly second and third generation, now live in the suburbs. With the exception of Chicago Heights to the south and Highwood to the north, the suburbs with a significant percentage of people of Italian American descent are to the west and the northwest. These suburbs include Melrose Park, Elmwood Park, Franklin Park, Cicero, Berwyn, Oak Park, River Forest, Stone Park, and Northlake.

Today important Italian-sponsored organizations and activities are still found in Chicago, but many are now in the suburbs. Among the latter is the Scalabrini Fathers

senior citizens' home in Northlake. Villa Scalabrini was the dream of Father Armando Pierini. Stone Park has an Italian cultural center. Elmwood Park has the Italian American Sports Hall of Fame and the Italo-American Soccer Club. There are also a number of Italian civic organizations, with the Joint Civic Committee of Italian-Americans having an office in the Loop.

The Greeks

Greek immigration to Chicago started slowly and relatively late. Small numbers of Greeks began coming during the 1880s and 1890s; the number increased rapidly during the first few decades of the twentieth century, reaching a peak from 1900 to 1920. In 1890 there were only 245 people of Greek birth in Chicago; in 1900 there were 1,493; by 1920 the number had risen to 11,546. Since World War II, due partly to internal strife in Greece, Greeks have been among the most numerous of the European groups arriving in the city. They have probably been the largest group of European immigrants in the past few years. By the late 1970s the metropolitan area contained an estimated 125,000 people of Greek ancestry, giving the Chicago area the largest urban Greek population in the world outside of Greece.

The Greeks came from a small scenic country with a glorious history and proud traditions, but it was largely a nation of peasants, poverty, and frequent wars. The first immigrants came mainly from southern Greece—Peloponnesus, first from around Sparta in the province of Laconia and then from the province of Arcadia. Later they started coming from almost all parts of Greece.

About 95 percent of the early immigrants were males, mainly young peasants, often very poor and with a minimum of education. In some cases whole villages were virtually emptied of men. The Greek immigrants came to Chicago primarily for economic betterment, often with the idea of making money and then returning home. An estimated 40 percent of the earlier immigrants did return home, but many remained and, like other immigrant groups, used their savings to help support relatives in Greece or to help finance their passage to America.[31] Others returned to Greece to marry and then came back to Chicago with their wives.

Although most of the early Greek immigrants had been peasants in their home country, in America they preferred to settle in big cities like Chicago. There, employment was readily available, wages were paid weekly, and they could share the companionship of their fellow countrymen. Later, the better educated Greeks, including merchants and those trained in the professions, joined the movement to Chicago.

Around the turn of the century there were small Greek concentrations in three areas—on the Near North Side around Clark and Kinzie, on the Far South Side in Pullman, and on the Near West Side in what was known as the "Delta," the triangle formed by Harrison,

Halsted, and Blue Island. There the first permanent Greek Orthodox church, Holy Trinity, was established in 1897.[32] For more than half a century the Delta area was the site of the main Greek community in Chicago, attaining at its height a Greek population of about 30,000.

The Delta was essentially a self-contained Greek community. The main streets of this "Greek Town" were Blue Island and Halsted. For several blocks these streets were lined with groceries, newspaper offices, barbershops, bookstores, labor agencies, travel agencies, and coffeehouses whose windows contained signs with Greek characters. The community had its church and school and numerous fraternal organizations. A large office building on the corner of Blue Island and Harrison housed the offices of Greek doctors, dentists, lawyers, and businessmen.[33]

The Delta's numerous coffeehouses, a familiar institution in Greece, filled a gap in the lives of the many lonely immigrant men. There

Figure 4.27. The old Greek Town on South Halsted Street between Jackson Boulevard and Van Buren Street, 1976. The commercial strip contains a number of Greek restaurants, bakeries, groceries, and import stores, but the once sizable Greek residential community was displaced by the construction of the Eisenhower Expressway and the campus of the University of Illinois at Chicago Circle. (Photograph by Irving Cutler.)

for the price of a cup of thick black Turkish coffee, men—and men only—could sit at a table, smoke, read Greek newspapers, play cards, gamble, reminisce about Greece, and discuss politics with great animation while sitting beneath the framed picture of the Parthenon on the Athenian Acropolis. The coffeehouse also often served as an informal post office as Ernest Poole noted in *Everybody's Magazine,* October 1910:

> Here many come to seek news from home. On the wall at one spot were pinned some score of letters, the addresses in strange Greek scrawl. When the postman came in with the evening mail, a half dozen rose and crowded around him, but came back disgusted; except for one chubby-faced man who took a blue letter—also chubby—back to his corner table, and sat complacently smiling down, lighting a fresh cigarette before beginning to read. Stories cluster thick round this rough, simple post office, but of these you can get only hints. There was a boy of eighteen who walked in every night for over six months, never asking for letters, but simply glancing up at the place on the wall—for the missive which never came. On the wall are some envelopes dingy with months of waiting for readers, the stories still hidden inside. And here one night an anxious group of big workmen sat breathing hard over a letter to be sent to a mother in Greece, to say that her son had lost his leg, in a tunnel explosion, that by passing the hat in the cafe for the past five evenings they had collected enough for his passage, and that he would soon start for home.

Greek Town lay in the very shadow of Jane Addams' social settlement complex at 800 South Halsted Street. Jane Addams had started her pioneering social reform movement there in 1889, and through the years she had fought to improve the condition of the succession of peoples in the area and had helped to educate and Americanize them. As she had to other groups, Jane Addams opened Hull House to the Greeks, befriended them, and tried to help them solve their adjustment problems. Hull House became a second home to thousands of young Greek immigrants, and

many of their numerous organizations met there. When Jane Addams died in 1935, Greek businesses closed for her funeral. A major event for the Greeks of the area occurred in 1910 at Hull House when President Theodore Roosevelt addressed the Greek community urging them to perpetuate their "incomparable Greek heritage" while becoming Americans.[34]

The Greek Town of the Delta area was displaced in the early 1960s by the erection of the campus of the University of Illinois at Chicago Circle, though its decline had started some years before. Still remaining is a thriving Greek commercial strip of a few blocks, mainly along Halsted Street between Adams (200 S) and Van Buren (400 S) streets. This strip contains a concentration of Greek restaurants, some featuring entertainment, and a number of Greek groceries, bakeries, and import and other stores. Greeks from throughout the metropolitan area come to shop and dine in the area in which many had their roots. However, many of the diners are non-Greeks, such as Loop workers who lunch at the many fine Greek restaurants located so near the Loop. Or they are people who want an evening of Zorban enjoyment.

Although today Greek-Americans are found in every profession and all types of businesses, they are best known for their great success in the restaurant business and other related food enterprises. As far back as 1919 the Greeks were believed to own one of every three restaurants in Chicago, including a large number in the Loop.[35] At one time John Raklios owned or operated 32 restaurants in the Chicago area. Today Greeks run some of the area's most famous restaurants. Successful Greek-owned restaurants, including many that do not specialize in Greek cuisine, are found throughout the metropolitan area.

A possible explanation for the heavy Greek concentration in the restaurant business is that the early Greek immigrants, almost all male, arrived alone and poor. They arranged to live in groups, cooking for themselves in community kitchens. In this way some of them became expert cooks and when they found they could make money selling meals to the public, they eventually opened their own restaurants. Moreover, it required little financial investment.

In numerous cases newly arrived Greek immigrants were hired on arrival to work in the Greek-owned restaurants. In time, through frugality and hard work, they too became restaurant owners. A number owned chains of restaurants. Immigrants and their descendants from one village in Greece, Nestani, now own or control almost a hundred restaurants in the Chicago area.

Many Greeks started out as street peddlers selling candy, flowers, fruit, and sandwiches from pushcarts and lunch wagons. Some worked as busboys, dishwashers, cooks, and countermen. A large percentage were self-employed; a very small percentage worked in factories. Few Greek women entered the labor market. When they had saved enough money, the immigrants often went into the retail business by opening a candy store, ice cream parlor, floral shop, restaurant, grocery, or fruit and vegetable store. From grocery and fruit and vegetable retailing, many eventually moved into the wholesale produce business, with Greeks now comprising about one-third of the merchants in the South Water and Randolph Street produce market districts. Greeks were also active in the entertainment field. They owned theaters, night clubs, and ballrooms—including the famed Aragon and Trianon ballrooms. Their dominance, however, continued greatest in the restaurant business.

The economic success of the Greeks was due to a large extent to their willingness to work very hard for many hours a day. Success in turn allowed them to help the second generation to rise into the professions and also to extend a helping hand to their relatives in Greece. Second-generation Greek Americans ranked very high in educational achievement.

With the continuing influx of immigrants, the Greeks grew in number and prospered. Many joined Greek national organizations such as the American Hellenic Educational and Progressive Association (AHEPA) which focused on Americanization and adaptation. Others joined the rival Greek American Progressive Association (GAPA) which emphasized the preservation of the Greek language, church, and traditions.

New Greek communities were established and the population began to disperse. On the South Side, Saints Constantine and Helen Church was established in 1909 at 61st Street and Michigan Avenue, and became one of the largest Greek Orthodox parishes. In 1946 it moved to 7351 South Stony Island. As the neighborhood changed, the building was sold in 1972 and the church moved to suburban Palos Hills.

A Near North Side Greek settlement established Annunciation Church in 1910 at 1017 North La Salle Street. It became the Cathedral for the diocese. After 1920, as other Greek settlements developed, many Greek Orthodox parishes were established throughout the city and the suburbs. In Chicago small Greek communities developed around Clark and Diversey (2800 N), Harrison and Central (5600 W), and in the Diversey and Austin (6000 W) neighborhood. As some of the Greek population dispersed, churches were built in a number of suburbs, including Des Plaines, Elmhurst, Glenview, Oak Lawn, Olympia Fields, Summit, and Westchester. The Greek community also established a number of elementary day and afternoon schools whose chief objectives included the transmission of the Greek language and cultural heritage. The schools bore such revered names as Socrates, Plato, Solon, Aristotle, Pythagorus, and Archimedes.

At present the largest concentration of Greeks is in the Lincoln Square community, fanning out from the Lincoln-Western-Lawrence avenues area into adjacent communities. Today an estimated 40,000 Greek-Americans live in this new Greek Town. Like the former Delta area, the main streets are lined with Greek establishments, including numerous restaurants, some of which offer entertainment.

Figure 4.28. The new Greek Town in the community of Lincoln Square. Looking eastward on Lawrence Avenue near Washtenaw Avenue. (Photograph by Irving Cutler.)

Although there have been Greeks in the area since the 1920s, the surge of Greeks into what was once a predominantly German community, took place mainly after World War II. Greeks were attracted both by the community's residential possibilities and by the presence of the imposing St. Demetrios Church at 2727 West Winona Avenue (5132 N). The church has been in the area for about half a century, and its membership of about 1,500 families makes it the largest of its kind in the nation.

Like other ethnic groups in the area, the Greek community has experienced conflicts regarding the language and ritual used in the church; conflicts between recent immigrants and second and third generation Greek-Americans; and conflicts over assimilation. But perhaps more than many ethnic groups, the Greeks have made a determined effort to maintain some of their native culture, and they continue to have a deep interest in their Greek homeland. There is a steady infusion of Greek culture from the homeland, with people traveling back and forth. Although one of the smaller ethnic groups and a relative latecomer to Chicago, the Greek-American community today is very active, highly organized, generally prosperous, and very well educated. Its history in Chicago has been beautifully depicted in the novels and short stories of one of its sons, the renowned writer Harry Mark Petrakis.

Other European Groups

There were numerous other European groups who came to Chicago in smaller numbers. French and French Canadians were among the earliest explorers and settlers of the

Chicago area. Their numbers were never very large, although there were a few small French settlements. One was in the Halsted-Congress (500 S) area around Notre Dame Church, established in 1864, and another in Brighton Park in the parish of St. Joseph and St. Anne Church, founded in 1889. The National Shrine of St. Anne, located in the church at 38th Place and California Avenue (2800 W), is an important center for French religious life in the United States.

English and Scots were important in the early settlement of Chicago. Through the 1890 census they both ranked among the ten largest foreign-born groups in Chicago. Unencumbered by language barriers, neither the English nor the Scots developed the type of ethnic neighborhoods characteristic of most of the other European groups, though there was a Scottish concentration near the Presbyterian McCormick Theological Seminary which until recently was in the Lincoln Park area.

Dutch settlers started coming to Chicago in the 1840s, and the peak number of Dutch foreign-born in Chicago was reached in 1900 when there were almost 20,000 of them. Many of the Dutch in the Chicago area were truck farmers to the south and southwest of the city, especially in the South Holland-Lansing-East Chicago Heights area and to a lesser extent in Riverdale, Alsip, Evergreen Park, Oak Lawn, and Summit. In areas that were to become part of Chicago, the Dutch were concentrated especially in Roseland and in the adjacent West Pullman community, and to a lesser extent in Mount Greenwood and Englewood. Many were truck farmers until the last decades of the nineteenth century when the gradual disappearance of the Dutch farming communities began. Small numbers worked for the railroad and in the great industrial plants around Roseland, such as International Harvester, Sherwin-Williams, Pullman, and in the Illinois Central yards—facilities whose establishment helped change the character of the area. Some worked in the building trades, and many others went into private businesses of various kinds.

A Dutch community, which at one time numbered almost 2,000 people, was located on the Near West Side around 14th Street and Ashland Avenue; it lasted well into the twentieth century. Many of the Dutch in this community had teams of horses and drifted into garbage collecting for the Loop area and other parts of the city.[36] Waste Management, Incorporated, the largest waste service company in the United States, with both national and international operations, evolved from a small family operation that began in this community. The Reformed church was well established in this and other major Dutch communities. The largest of the Dutch communities, in Roseland, continued to exist until recent decades when the community started to become predominantly black.

The Belgians and Luxembourgers in Chicago were never as numerous as their European neighbors, the Dutch. At their peak in 1930, there were over 4,000 Belgians and almost 2,000 Luxembourgers of foreign birth in Chicago. The Luxembourgers had arrived early in Chicago. Many became truck farmers in the vicinity of the first St. Henry's Church which they built in 1851 at Devon and Ridge avenues. Luxembourgers were also truck farmers and among the earliest settlers in what was later to become the suburbs of Lincolnwood and Skokie. The Belgians were somewhat more scattered than the Luxembourgers, but there was a small colony around St. John Berchmans Church at 2517 West Logan Boulevard (2600 N), which was organized in 1903 as a national parish for Belgian Catholics. In 1916 the church was opened to all nationalities.

Austrians and Hungarians started coming to Chicago in large numbers in the 1880s. They reached their greatest population in Chicago in 1920 with 30,000 foreign-born Austrians and 26,000 foreign-born Hungarians. They were located in scattered parts of the city, with the Austrians often in close proximity to or intermingled with the German population. Some Hungarians also settled around the older German community on the North

Side; they organized St. Stephen King of Hungary Church at 2015 West Augusta (1000 N). A major Hungarian colony developed in the Burnside area around 95th Street and Cottage Grove Avenue, with many of the immigrants working in the nearby railroad yards and steel mills. Our Lady of Hungary Church was established in the area in 1904, and the Hungarian Center was built in 1927. They also spread into the nearby communities of South Chicago, West Pullman, and Roseland. As these communities started changing racially, most of the Hungarians moved out. Some relocated in Hegewisch, Chicago's most southeasterly community, and others moved into such south suburbs as Lansing, Calumet City, and Burnham.

Croatians, Serbians, and Slovenes started coming to Chicago around the turn of the century. After World War I their homeland became Yugoslavia, but their old nationalistic feelings generally continued to survive. By 1930 there were about 20,000 Croatian, Serbian, and Slovene immigrants in Chicago, the largest number being Croatian. Most settled on the South Side where they worked in the stockyards and the steel mills. In the steel mills they generally replaced the original workmen from northwestern Europe—the British, Irish, Germans, and Scandinavians. Many initially lived as lodgers and were delayed in bringing over their families from Europe by the Balkan Wars of 1912 and 1913 and World War I.

There were a number of sizable South Side Croatian settlements, each served by a Croatian-founded Roman Catholic church. The largest church, St. Jerome's in the Bridgeport area, was founded in 1912 at 28th and Princeton Avenue (300 W). Former Mayor Michael A. Bilandic, of Croatian descent, is a member of this church. In 1914 two other churches were founded by the Croatians. One was Holy Trinity in the Pilsen area on Throop Street (1300 W) near 18th Street; the other, Sacred Heart, was in the South Deering steel

mill area at 96th Street near Exchange Avenue. Croatians also live in the adjacent communities of Hegewisch and East Side. Many Croatians now live north in Rogers Park and West Ridge, and some farher north in Skokie, Morton Grove, and Northbrook. In recent years the large Croation Cultural Center of Chicago was established at 2845 West Devon Avenue. Also serving to perpetuate Croatian customs and culture are some 20 Chicago lodges of the National Croatian Fraternal Union and a dozen more of the Croatian Catholic Union. Today Chicago is the fourth-largest Croatian city in the world.

The Serbians also established a church in the steel mill area at 9805 South Commercial Avenue. This was the Serbian Eastern Orthodox Church of St. Michael the Archangel. The Serbians also had small settlements on the Northwest Side, including one on Clybourne Avenue near Fullerton Avenue and another in the Wicker Park area in the vicinity of Damen and Evergreen (1332 N) streets. A new Serbian Orthodox Cathedral, Holy Resurrection, was built in 1973 near O'Hare Field. A prolonged and bitter conflict in the Serbian Community between the Belgrade wing of the Serbian Orthodox Church and the anti-communist Free Serbian Orthodox Diocese involves the ownership of the beautiful $2 million Serbian monastery near Libertyville, Illinois.

The Slovenes, the smallest of the Yugoslav groups in Chicago, also had one of their most important settlements in the steel mill district. Between 2,000 and 4,000 Slovenes lived around St. George's Slovenian Church on Ewing Avenue near 96th Street.

The Bulgarians were another small Balkan ethnic group. Like the Serbians, Croatians, and Slovenes, the Bulgarians lived near the steel mills of the South Chicago area. They also had a small colony around Halsted and Adams streets (200 S) with Bulgarian coffeehouses, food stores, and lodging houses for the numerous non-family men. Employment

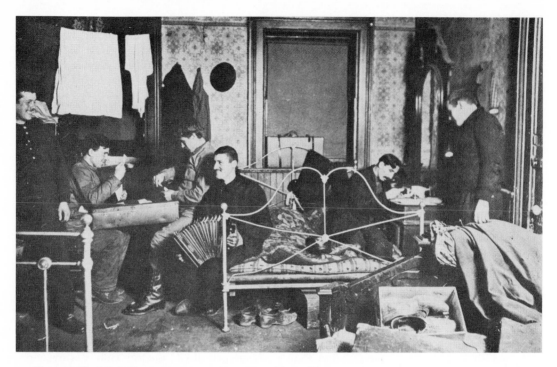

Figure 4.29. A Bulgarian lodging group on the West Side of Chicago in the early 1900s. Nine men occupied two rooms. (Photograph, R. R. Earle. Courtesy Chicago Historical Society.)

agencies in the area often shipped these Bulgarians out to work on the railroads, to lay pipes, or to pave roads. Many of the Bulgarians in this colony returned to their homelands to fight in the Balkan Wars.

Although the number of Russians coming to Chicago through the years is given as relatively high, many of the immigrants actually have not been Russians, but such national groups as Ukrainians, Poles, Lithuanians, and Belorussians who were under Russian rule. Many of the immigrants from Russia were Jews. The "true" Russians were found in small numbers in a few parts of the city. These included the Calumet steel area on the Southeast side, as well as the Northwest Side, where there are two Russian Orthodox churches. These are St. George's on Wood Street (1800 W), south of Augusta Boulevard (1000 N),

and Louis Sullivan's landmark Holy Trinity Orthodox Cathedral, at 1121 North Leavitt (2200 W).

The Ukrainians were an immigrant group who started coming in the late 1800s from Russia, and to a lesser extent from the Austro-Hungarian Empire. The first Ukrainian community was established west of the Loop and then gradually moved northwestward into West Town, which still contains the city's largest Ukrainian community. Other Ukrainian communities developed near areas of employment in the Back-of-the-Yards district near the stockyards, in West Pullman, and in Burnside near the steel mills. In these communites the Ukrainians established churches of various denominations (Orthodox, Catholic of Eastern Rite, and Protestant), as well as schools, organizations, and other institutions.

Figure 4.30. Holy Trinity Orthodox Cathedral 1121 North Leavitt Street was built in 1903 by the Russian community in the area. It received some financial aid from the Czar of Russia. The architect was Louis Sullivan and the stuccoed church is now an official Chicago landmark. In the tradition of the homeland, the church contains no pews and the congregants remain standing during the services. The Slavic services are now sparsely attended, but the English services are crowded and attract people from a wide area, as well as the revitalized Wicker Park area. (Photograph by Irving Cutler.)

Figure 4.31. The gold-domed Sts. Volodymyr and Olha Ukrainan Catholic Church, 739 North Oakley Boulevard, was dedicated in 1973. The building is the shape of a Byzantine cross. It was organized by a splinter group from nearby St. Nicholas Ukrainan Cathedral (left background), located at 2238 West Rice Street, who became upset when the traditional calendar and ritual were changed. St. Nicholas, with its 13 green domes, was completed in 1915. (Photograph by Irving Cutler.)

The South Side Ukrainian communities have declined in size in recent years, while the Ukrainian population has increased on the northwestern fringes of the city and in the suburbs. There are now Ukrainian parishes in Palatine, Niles, Roselle, Palos Park, and Joliet, plus five parishes in adjacent heavily industrialized Lake County, Indiana. The largest Ukrainian settlement in Chicago continues to be in the West Town community, with the core area centered around Chicago Avenue and Oakley Boulevard (2300 W), a neighborhood which received a large influx of Ukrainian displaced persons after World War

II. Occupying about a square mile area, there continues to be a stable, well-kept, and viable Ukrainian community, despite the fact that much of it borders on deteriorated and often arson-afflicted areas occupied by poor minority groups. The main commercial axis is Chicago Avenue near Oakley, with its Ukrainian publishing companies, import shops, savings and loan associations, food stores, art museum, and national museum.

On Oakley Boulevard, in a stretch of less than half a mile, are three of the community's six Ukranian churches. St. Vladimir's Ukranian Orthodox Church has been at the corner of Cortez (1032 N) and Oakley since 1945. The largest is the thirteen dome St. Nicholas Ukrainian Catholic Cathedral, at the corner of Rice Street (832 N), completed in 1915 and ordained a cathedral in 1960. Presently it serves 1,600 families and has a parochial school of 500. Two blocks to the south at the corner of Superior Street (732 N) is the new, gold-domed Sts. Volodymyr and Olha Ukrainian Catholic Church which was dedicated in 1973. It was organized by a splinter group of St. Nicholas parishioners who became upset when the traditional calendar and ritual were altered. Built at a cost of over $2 million, the members of the new church also showed dedication and confidence in their ethnic community—qualities that have often been lacking recently in Chicago's other European ethnic communities, many of which have all but disappeared. Like the Lithuanians, the Ukrainians seem determined to keep their culture and religion alive in their Chicago enclave despite Soviet suppression in their homeland.

Chicago's European Neighborhoods

The European ethnic neighborhoods of Chicago, though distinct culturally from one another in many ways, have exhibited certain common characteristics and problems. Each newly arrived ethnic group usually met hostility in varying amounts from the established groups before it learned the manners and style of a new society and finally gained tolerance and acceptance. The various ethnic groups generally developed a similar mix of religious, cultural, and social service institutions. These were usually based on Old World patterns, of which the religious institutions were the most influential. Bickering and fractionalization occurred within almost all the ethnic groups, often over religious differences, including the secular versus the nonsecular, but also sometimes over economic or political issues. In addition, different immigrant groups often did not relate well to each other.

Virtually all of the groups were originally situated in the central part of the city where they developed major ethnic neighborhoods and smaller, scattered ethnic clusters. In time these areas were taken over by newer, poorer immigrant groups as the earlier arrivals prospered and dispersed outward geographically. The earliest ethnic groups have also generally moved the farthest outward. Many of the later arriving ethnic groups reached suburbia only in recent decades. Forty suburbs now have a higher percentage of first- and second-generation ethnics than does Chicago. Meanwhile the percentage of such European ethnic families still living in Chicago declined from 30 percent in 1960 to 19 percent in 1970. But as the European roots of the younger generations of Chicago's ethnic groups became more distant and obscure, ties with the old country and Old World ways became of less consequence. In every group it is the older generation that is most concerned about marriage outside the ethnic group and about the too rapid assimilation of their young.

Some people did approve of the weakening of Old World cultures which they felt often fostered clannishness, occasionally fanned nationalistic prides and prejudices, and sometimes made Americans suspicious of one another. Others, however, have felt that one of America's greatest strengths has been the diversity of backgrounds and cultures of its various peoples, each of which contributed in its own way to the remarkable vitality and success of the nation.

Mike Royko, in his book on the late Mayor Richard J. Daley, with humor and insight depicted the characteristics and significance of Chicago's ethnic neighborhoods and the feelings of their people:

> . . . Chicago, until as late as the 1950s, was a place where people stayed put for a while, creating tightly knit neighborhoods, as small-townish as any village in the wheat fields.
> The neighborhood-towns were part of large ethnic states. To the north of the Loop was Germany. To the northwest was Poland. To the west were Italy and Israel. To the southwest were Bohemia and Lithuania. And to the south was Ireland.

It wasn't perfectly defined because the borders shifted as newcomers moved in on the older settlers, sending them fleeing in terror and disgust. Here and there were outlying colonies, with Poles also on the South Side, and Irish up north.

But you could always tell, even with your eyes closed, which state you were in by the odors of the food stores and the open kitchen windows, the sound of the foreign or familiar language, and by whether a stranger hit you in the head with a rock.

In every neighborhood could be found all the ingredients of the small town: the local tavern, the funeral parlor, the bakery, the vegetable store, the butcher shop, the drugstore, the neighborhood drunk, the neighborhood trollop, the neighborhood idiot, the neighborhood war hero, the neighborhood police station, the neighborhood team, the neighborhood sports star, the ball field, the barber shop, the pool hall, the clubs, and the main street.

With everything right there, why go anywhere else? If you went somewhere else, you couldn't get credit, you'd have to waste a nickel on the streetcar, and when you finally got there, they might not speak the language.

Some people had to leave the neighborhood to work, but many didn't, because the houses were interlaced with industry.

On Sunday, people might ride a streetcar to visit a relative, but they usually remained within the ethnic state, unless there had been an unfortunate marriage in the family.

The borders of neighborhoods were the main streets, railroad tracks, branches of the Chicago River, branches of the branches, strips of industry, parks, and anything else that could be glared across.

The ethnic states got along just about as pleasantly as did the nations of Europe. With their tote bags, the immigrants brought along all their old prejudices, and immediately picked up some new ones. An Irishman who came here hating only the Englishmen and Irish Protestants soon hated Poles, Italians, and blacks. A Pole who was free arrived hating only Jews and Russians, but soon learned to hate the Irish, the Italians and the blacks.[37]

According to Royko another good reason for staying close to your home and in your own ethnic neighborhood was that you could never tell what would happen to you if you entered the territory of another ethnic group. But in your own neighborhood

. . . you were safe. At least if you did not cross beyond, say, to the other side of the school. While it might be part of your ethnic state, it was still the edge of another neighborhood, and their gang was just as mean as your gang.

So, for a variety of reasons, ranging from convenience to fear to economics, people stayed in their own neighborhood, loving it, enjoying the closeness, the friendliness, the familiarity, and trying to save enough money to move out.[38]

Notes

1. Graham Hutton, *Midwest at Noon* (Chicago: University of Chicago Press, 1946), pp. 143–44.
2. Jane Addams, *Twenty Years at Hull House* (New York: Macmillan Co., 1910), pp. 81–82.
3. Lawrence J. McCaffrey, *The Irish Diaspora in America* (Bloomington: Indiana University Press, 1976), p. 84.
4. Harvey Warren Zorbaugh, *The Gold Coast and the Slums* (Chicago: University of Chicago Press, 1929), pp. 149–50.
5. Rudolph A. Hofmeister, *The Germans of Chicago* (Champaign, Ill.: Stipes Publishing Co., 1976), p. 202.
6. Andrew Jacke Townsend, "The Germans of Chicago," *Deutsch-Amerikanische Geschichtsblätter,* 32 (1932), p. 141. Reprinted from Ph.D. dissertation, University of Chicago, 1927.
7. A. E. Strand, *A History of the Norwegians of Illinois* (Chicago: John Anderson Publishing Co., 1905), p. 180.
8. Ernst W. Olson, ed., *History of the Swedes of Illinois, I* (Chicago: Engberg-Holmberg Publishing Co., 1908), p. 311.
9. Ulf Beijbom, *Swedes in Chicago: A Demographic and Social Study of the 1846–1880 Immigration* (Sweden: The Historiska Institutionen at the University of Uppsala/Chicago Historical Society, 1971), p. 95.
10. Bessie Louise Pierce, *A History of Chicago,* vol. 3 (Chicago: University of Chicago Press, 1957), p. 28.
11. Morris A. Gutstein, *A Priceless Heritage* (New York: Bloch Publishing Co., 1953), pp. 38–39.

12. Seymour Jacob Pomrenze, "Aspects of Chicago Russian-Jewish Life, 1893–1915," *The Chicago Pinkus,* ed. Simon Rawidowicz (Chicago: College of Jewish Studies, 1952), pp. 130–31.

13. Louis Wirth, *The Ghetto* (Chicago: University of Chicago Press, 1928), pp. 205–6.

14. Hyman L. Meites, ed., *History of the Jews of Chicago* (Chicago: Jewish Historical Society of Illinois, 1924), pp. 150–51.

15. Ira Berkow, *Maxwell Street* (Garden City: Doubleday & Co., 1977), pp. 10–11.

16. Sentinel Publishing Co., *The Sentinel's History of Chicago Jewry, 1911–1961* (Chicago, 1961), p. 127.

17. Czechoslovak National Council of America, *Panorama: A Historical Review of Czechs and Slovaks in the United States of America* (Cicero, Ill., 1970), p. 33.

18. Residents of Hull-House, *Hull-House Maps and Papers* (New York: Thomas Y. Crowell & Co., 1895), p. 117.

19. Edward R. Kantowicz, *Polish-American Politics in Chicago, 1888–1940* (Chicago: University of Chicago Press, 1975), pp. 31–32.

20. Kantowicz, *Polish-American Politics in Chicago, 1888–1940,* p. 22.

21. City of Chicago, Department of Development and Planning, *Chicago's Polish Population: Selected Statistics* (Chicago, 1976), pp. 1–2.

22. David Fainhauz, *Lithuanians in Multi-Ethnic Chicago until World War II* (Chicago: Lithuanian Library Press and Loyola University Press, 1977), p. 99.

23. "The Second Generation," *Jaunimas* (Chicago), December 1–15, 1940.

24. Rudolph Vecoli, "Chicago's Italians Prior to World War I: A Study of Their Social and Economic Adjustment," Ph.D. dissertation, University of Wisconsin, 1962), pp. 16–17.

25. Humbert S. Nelli, *Italians in Chicago, 1880–1930* (New York: Oxford University Press, 1970), p. 66.

26. Ronald P. Grossman, *The Italians in America* (Minneapolis: Lerner Publications Co., 1966), p. 28.

27. Grossman, *The Italians in America,* p. 25.

28. City of Chicago, Department of Development and Planning, *Chicago's Italian Population: Selected Statistics* (Chicago, 1976), p. 2.

29. Edith Abbott, *The Tenements of Chicago, 1908–1935* (Chicago: University of Chicago Press, 1936), pp. 95–96.

30. Zorbaugh, *The Gold Coast and the Slums,* pp. 159–61, 164–65, 166, 170.

31. Jayne Clark Jones, *The Greeks in America* (Minneapolis: Lerner Publications Co., 1969), p. 55.

32. George A. Kourvetaris, *First and Second Generation Greeks in Chicago* (Athens, Greece: National Centre of Social Research, 1971), p. 49.

33. Abbott, *The Tenements of Chicago, 1908–1935,* p. 97.

34. Andrew T. Kopan, "Education and Greek Immigrants in Chicago, 1892–1973: A Study in Ethnic Survival" (Ph.D. dissertation, University of Chicago, 1974), p. 152.

35. Theodore Saloutos, *The Greeks in the United States* (Cambridge: Harvard University Press, 1964), p. 267.

36. Amry Vandenbosch, *The Dutch Communities of Chicago* (Chicago: Knickerbocker Society of Chicago, 1927), pp. 75–76.

37. Mike Royko, *Boss: Richard J. Daley of Chicago* (New York: E. P. Dutton & Co., 1971), pp. 24–25.

38. Royko, *Boss: Richard J. Daley of Chicago,* p. 26.

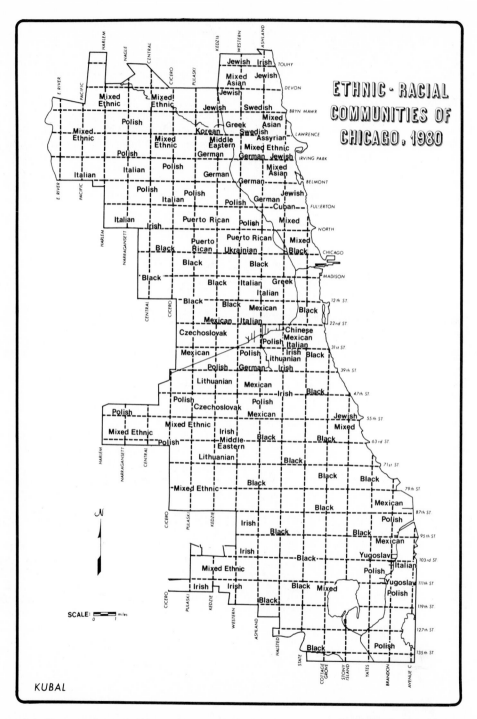

Figure 5.1. The approximate location of Chicago's larger ethnic and racial communities, 1980. Almost none of the communities was completely homogeneous. Figure 4.1 shows the ethnic and racial communities in 1920. (Map by Joseph Kubal is based largely on U.S. Census, church, and Chicago Department of Planning data.)

Chapter Five

PEOPLE AND SETTLEMENT PATTERNS—RECENT MIGRATION AND TRENDS

Population Changes

The 1980 census figures for the city of Chicago indicated a population of 3,005,072, down substantially from the 1950 peak of 3,620,962. The 1980 census also showed that substantial changes had taken place in the racial composition of Chicago. The changes resulted from two factors. One was the sizable exodus of white families to the suburbs. The other was the substantial increase in the population of the non-white groups. However, the total increase of non-whites did not equal the total loss of whites. In addition, the city has lost some population due to clearance and redevelopment. Chicago's population density declined from a peak of 17,011 per square mile (6,568 per sq km) in 1950 to 13,173 per square mile (5,086 per sq km) in 1980.

In 1980 Chicago had 1,490,217 whites (49.6 percent of the total population), down 716,783 from 1970. The blacks numbered about 1,197,000 (39.8 percent of the population), an increase of 95,000 during the decade. Hispanics, many of whom also classified themselves as either black or white, numbered 422,061, or 14 percent of the city's population, up substantially from the 1970 census count

of 247,343 Hispanics. In the 1970s increasing numbers of immigrants came from Asian countries, such as Korea, India, Pakistan, Philippines, Thailand, South Vietnam, Cambodia, Laos, and also from Middle Eastern countries. As a result the Asian population increased to over 100,000, or about 3 percent of the total population. In 1980 there were about 6,000 American Indians in Chicago, or 0.2 percent of the city's inhabitants.

The changing composition of Chicago's population results from the fact that the most recent wave of migration to the city has largely been from the South, mainly blacks but also some whites, especially from Appalachia, and Hispanics from Mexico, Puerto Rico, and to a lesser extent Cuba. The Asians are much fewer in number but growing rapidly. The more recent migrants have come to a much more structured city than did those who came a century ago when it seemed that almost everyone was a recent European immigrant.

Recent migration to Chicago by these groups was spurred by the continuing demand for labor, especially during World War II and the boom years that followed. As the 1980s started, the ethnic checkerboard, which had

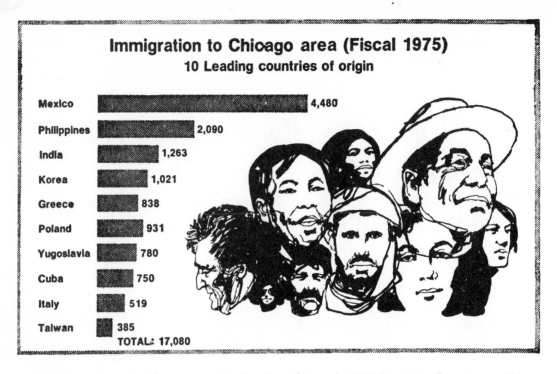

Immigration to Chicago area (Fiscal 1975)
10 Leading countries of origin

Mexico	4,480
Philippines	2,090
India	1,263
Korea	1,021
Greece	838
Poland	931
Yugoslavia	780
Cuba	750
Italy	519
Taiwan	385

TOTAL: 17,080

Figure 5.2. Of the ten leading countries in immigration to Chicago in 1975, six were non-European countries, including the four countries that sent the most immigrants. For most of the earlier history of Chicago, the leading sources of immigrants to Chicago had consistently been European countries. (Courtesy *Chicago Daily News.*)

characterized Chicago for about a century, had largely given way to a tripartite division of the city into black, white, and Hispanic.

The Blacks

Blacks have lived in Chicago since its earliest days. Jean Baptiste Point du Sable built his cabin in the late 1770s near the mouth of the Chicago River and was spoken of by the Potawatomi Indians as "the Negro who was the first settler of Chicago."

After Chicago was incorporated as a city in 1837, its black population increased slowly but steadily. Some blacks came via the Underground Railroad for fugitive slaves, which had a number of stops in the Chicago area, including one at what is now 9955 South Beverly Avenue in Chicago and another at the Old Grau Mill in what is now Oak Brook.

Chicago was labeled by the editor of the *Cairo (Ill.) Weekly Times* as "a sinkhole of abolition."

Just prior to the Civil War, the 1860 census listed 955 blacks, or slightly less than 1 percent of the city's total population of 112,172. A half century later, in 1910, the census listed 44,130 blacks, but this still constituted only 2 percent of the city's rapidly growing population, which had passed 2 million persons as a result of the very rapid influx of various European groups.

The first significant black settlement developed generally along the South Branch of the Chicago River during the 1840s and was composed of both free blacks and fugitive slaves. To serve the community a number of small black churches, mainly Baptist and Methodist, were established. They also often served as stations on the Underground Rail-

Figure 5.3. Quinn Chapel of the African Methodist Episcopal Church, 1980. It was officially organized in 1847 in the downtown area as Chicago's first black church. Quinn Chapel has occupied its present site at 2401 South Wabash Avenue since 1891 and is a city landmark. Those who have spoken from its pulpit include the educator Booker T. Washington, poet Paul Lawrence Dunbar, Dr. Martin Luther King, Jr., William McKinley, and Theodore Roosevelt. (Photograph by Irving Cutler.)

road. The first black church, Quinn Chapel, was officially organized in 1847 in the downtown area, with about 50 members. Since 1891, Quinn Chapel of the African Methodist Episcopal Church has been located at 2401 South Wabash Avenue. One of the church's most illustrious leaders was Archibold J. Carey, who became its pastor in 1898. He gained renown as an accomplished speaker and as a powerful black political figure. His well-known son, Archibold J. Carey, Jr., also served as pastor of this church as well as serving as a city alderman and county judge.

A few years after the founding of Quinn Chapel, Olivet Baptist Church, and Bethel African Methodist Episcopal Church were established. By 1910 there were almost two dozen black churches in Chicago. At least initially most of the black Baptist churches were offshoots of Olivet, the city's oldest and largest black Baptist church, while the African Methodist Episcopal churches were generally founded by dissident parishioners from Quinn Chapel and Bethel Church.[1]

During the latter half of the nineteenth century, Chicago's black population was small and attracted little significant attention. Although there was some prejudice and discrimination, many of the city's whites openly fought and disobeyed the federal Fugitive Slave Acts and Illinois' oppressive Black Code laws. With the ending of the Civil War, the Black Code laws were repealed, thus officially, although not always in reality, banning school segregation and discrimination in public accommodations, and giving blacks such civil rights as the right to vote, to serve on juries, and to testify against whites. But even with these legal rights, as well as the advantage of native birth, a common language, and religious beliefs generally similar to those of the native whites, the blacks still occupied a social and economic position inferior to the European immigrants who were streaming into Chicago. Although blacks were only 1.3 percent of Chicago's population in 1890, they comprised 37.7 percent of the city's male servants and 43.3 percent of the female servants.

Very instrumental in repealing the Illinois Black Code laws was one of Chicago's first civil rights leaders and the early leader of Chicago's blacks, John Jones (1816–1879). Of mixed free black and white parentage, Jones came to Chicago from North Carolina in 1845 and opened a downtown tailoring shop which soon became very successful. His home became a frequent meeting place for such fellow abolitionists as John Brown, Fredrick Douglass, and Wendell Phillips. His pamphlet *The Black Laws of Illinois and a Few Reasons Why They Should Be Repealed,* published in 1864, helped influence the vote of the state legislature. In 1871, with white support, he was elected to the Cook County Board of Commissioners, the first black to hold public office in the county.

Another prominent black civil rights activist was Ida B. Wells (1869–1931). Born in Mississippi, she became a crusading journalist and lecturer who tried to arouse public opinion against the horror of lynching. She first came to Chicago in 1893 and soon married Ferdinand L. Barnett, a journalist, who in 1878 founded the *Conservator,* the first black newspaper in Chicago. She helped start many black organizations, became the first black woman adult probation officer in Chicago, and was the first black woman admitted to the bar in Illinois. She wrote for the *Conservator* and for the *Chicago Defender,* which had been founded by Robert S. Abbott (1870–1940) in 1905 and was to become one of the largest and most successful of black newspapers. In 1940 a South Side public housing project built by the Works Progress Administration (WPA), in the vicinity of the present Martin Luther King Drive (400 E) and Pershing Road (3900 S), was named for Ida B. Wells.

As Chicago grew and the number of its blacks remained relatively small, much of the black population of the late 1800s lived in scattered small groups, interspersed with the white population, mainly on the Near South Side. They often lived in poor areas on the fringes of wealthy white residential districts, where many blacks worked as domestics. One

TABLE 5.1
Black Population of Chicago, 1840–1980

Year	Total Population	Black Population	Percent Black
1840	4,470	53	1.2%
1850	29,963	323	1.1
1860	112,172	955	0.9
1870	298,977	3,691	1.2
1880	503,185	6,480	1.3
1890	1,099,850	14,271	1.3
1900	1,698,575	30,150	1.8
1910	2,185,283	44,103	2.0
1920	2,701,705	109,458	4.1
1930	3,376,438	233,903	6.9
1940	3,396,808	277,731	8.2
1950	3,620,962	492,265	13.6
1960	3,550,404	812,637	22.9
1970	3,369,359	1,102,620	32.7
1980	3,005,072	1,197,000	39.8

such small isolated enclave existed farther south on Lake Park Avenue near 55th Street in Hyde Park until the early 1900s, when it dwindled due partly to pressure from some elements of the surrounding white community.

As the black population started increasing rapidly after the turn of the century, as is shown in table 5.1, the blacks became concentrated and segregated in older neighborhoods of the inner city that had been abandoned by earlier immigrant groups. Some of the European immigrant colonies tended to break up with the passage of time, but the black areas became increasingly crowded because the blacks had nowhere to move. Especially congested was a strip three miles (4.8 km) long and barely one-fourth mile (0.4 km) wide, from south of downtown to 39th Street and bounded by the Rock Island Railroad on the west and the South Side Elevated on the east.

The black population in the city increased 148 percent in the World War I decade (1910–1920), when many blacks started coming from the South, especially after 1915. They were lured by the jobs that became available in Chicago as immigration from Europe was virtually cut off by the war. The blacks also fled the South at this time because their traditional poverty was being intensified by low cotton prices, the damage to cotton plants by the boll weevil, a series of disastrous floods, and racial discrimination. Southern blacks were urged to go north not only by some northern industrialists, but by black newspapers, especially the *Chicago Defender*.

Thousands of blacks sometimes arrived during a single week, usually at the 12th Street Illinois Central Station or in later years at the 63rd and Stony Island Avenue (1600 E) bus station. They came mainly from such southern states as Mississippi, Louisiana, Georgia, Alabama, and Arkansas. Previously the largest numbers of blacks had come from such upper southern states as Kentucky, Tennessee, and Missouri. In 1915 the Chicago Urban League was established specifically to help resettle the migrants. It collaborated with the National Association for the Advancement of Colored People whose first Chicago chapter was organized in 1911. The NAACP was devoted primarily to legal and legislative action dealing with equal rights and integration, while the Chicago Urban League concerned itself more with housing and employment.

With the huge increase in Chicago's black population during the World War I period, the relatively benign equilibrium that had existed between the blacks and whites began to change drastically. Blacks, who had previously been employed chiefly as workers in hotels and restaurants, as domestics in private homes, as janitors in big buildings, and as porters on trains, now began to compete with white immigrant workers for factory jobs. In 1910 more than 51 percent of the male black labor force was employed in domestic or personal service jobs; by 1920 this figure had dropped to 28 percent. Barred from membership in most unions, the blacks had been used as scabs in a number of strikes, including those of the meat packers and teamsters. This created further ill will between blacks and whites, although the blacks usually were fired after the strike.

Competition for housing, which was in short supply during the war period, caused the most tension between the races. Bombings and other forms of violence occurred as the rapidly increasing black population attempted to move beyond the confines of the crowded black ghetto. On a scorching Sunday in July 1919 a stone-throwing melee between blacks and whites broke out on the beach at 29th Street near the unofficial line of racial segregation. This resulted in the drowning of a 17-year-old black youth, which in turn touched off Chicago's most violent race riot. It lasted six days before order was restored by the state militia. The toll was 23 blacks and 15 whites dead and 537 injured.

The race riot dealt a severe blow to whatever hope remained for a more integrated city. It did, however, for the first time focus serious attention on the blacks and their problems, especially in regard to housing. Until then the black community usually had been neglected by social reformers.

The increased racial tension also brought to light the resentment of some Old Settler blacks against the more recent, less educated black migrants from the rural south. The Old Settler blacks looked back wistfully and perhaps somewhat unrealistically to the days before the great migration from the South.

The southern migrants reacted enthusiastically to the economic opportunities and the freer atmosphere of the North. But the Old Settlers were far from enthusiastic over the migrants, despite the fact that many of them were eventually to profit by the organization of the expanding Negro market and the black electorate. The Riot, to them, marked a turning point in the history of Chicago. Even today, as they reconstruct the past, they look back on an era before that shattering event when all Negroes who wanted to work had jobs, when a premium was placed on refinement and gentility, and when there was no prejudice to mar the relations between Negroes and whites. As they see it, the newcomers disturbed the balance of relationships within the Negro community and with the white community. From their point of view, the migrants were people who knew nothing of the city's traditions, were unaware of the role which Negroes had played in the political and economic life of Chicago, and did not appreciate the "sacrifices of the pioneers."[2]

Some black leaders felt, however, that it was the self-help, "accommodationist" attitude of some of the Old Settlers rather than that of the militant protest of the newcomers which brought about the segregation of the blacks into the black ghetto.

The great migration from the South during the World War I period also greatly affected the religious tenor of the black community in whose life religion played an extremely important role. It was observed that the blacks had more churches in relation to their population than did any other ethnic community.

Before the war, the large middle-class Baptist and Methodist churches had dominated Negro religious life in Chicago. Although they had not completely discarded the emotionalism of traditional Negro religion, these churches had moved toward a more decorous order of worship and a program of broad social concern. The migration, however, brought into the city thousands of Negroes accustomed to the informal, demonstrative, preacher-oriented churches of the rural South. Alienated by the formality of the middle-class churches, many of the newcomers organized small congregations that met in stores and houses and that maintained the old-time shouting religion. Often affiliated with the more exotic fringe sects, Holiness or Spiritualist, these storefront churches became a permanent force in the Chicago Negro community and secured a powerful hold on thousands of working-class Negroes.[3]

As the tensions of the Race Riot period began gradually to subside, a new and increased wave of more than 120,000 blacks came to Chicago from the southern states during the 1920s. Among these migrants were some of the best educated and most skilled blacks of the South. The decade was a relatively prosperous one.

The five years from 1924 to 1929 were no doubt the most prosperous ones the Negro community in Chicago had ever experienced. A professional and business class arose upon the broad base of over seventy-five thousand colored wage-earners and was able for a brief period to enjoy the fruits of its training and investment. Throughout the Twenties, additional migrants from the rural South swelled the size of the Black Belt market. The Fat Years were at hand.

The Negroes spread along the once fashionable South Parkway and Michigan Boulevard, closing up the pocket which existed in 1920, taking over the stonefront houses and the apartments, buying the large church edifices and opening smaller churches in houses and stores, establishing businesses, and building a political machine as they went. By 1925 the Black Belt business center had shifted two miles southward, and those who could afford to do so were trying to move from the slums into more stable residential areas. The masses flowed along persistently as the Black Belt lengthened.[4]

However, the 1920s were characterized not only by such signs of progress, but also by restrictions on the activities of Chicago's blacks.

There were stores and restaurants that didn't like to serve Negroes. To walk into certain downtown hotspots was unthinkable. To run for any state office higher than Senator from the Black Belt just wasn't done. To hope for a managerial or highly skilled job in industry was ridiculous. To buy or rent a house out of the Black Belt precipitated a storm. But after all, Chicago was in America, not in France or Brazil. It was certainly different from slavery sixty years ago, or from the South today. Negroes liked Midwest Metropolis.

There were evidences on every hand that "the Race was progressing." Here were colored policemen, firemen, aldermen, and precinct captains, state representatives, doctors, lawyers, and teachers. Colored children were attending the public schools and the city's junior colleges. There were fine churches in the Negro areas, and beautiful boulevards. It seemed reasonable to assume that this development would continue with more and more Negroes getting ahead and becoming educated. There were prophets of doom in the Twenties, but a general air of optimism pervaded the Black Belt, as it did the whole city.[5]

By 1930 the blacks lived in seven densely populated concentrations. Six of these were small enclaves, and the seventh was larger than the other six combined. Some of these areas had been occupied by blacks for decades and none of them was even close to the far North Side. Of the small enclaves, the one farthest north was around Division Street (1200 N) and Larrabee Avenue (600 W), in what had been a Sicilian area until after World War I. A survey in the 1930s revealed that about 90 percent of the blacks in this area had been born in rural parts of the South. One settlement straddled Lake Street (200 N) from about Ashland Avenue (1600 W) to west of Western Avenue (2400 W). This was an older black community which had started in the 1880s. Another was south of Roosevelt Road in the Maxwell Street area, which had previously been occupied by eastern European Jews. There was a small community in Englewood around 61st Street between Racine (1200 W) and Loomis (1400 W) avenues. Blacks had lived in Englewood since 1870, when the area was a railroad center. Farther south there was a small settlement in Lillydale around 95th and State streets and also one in Morgan Park within an area bounded approx-

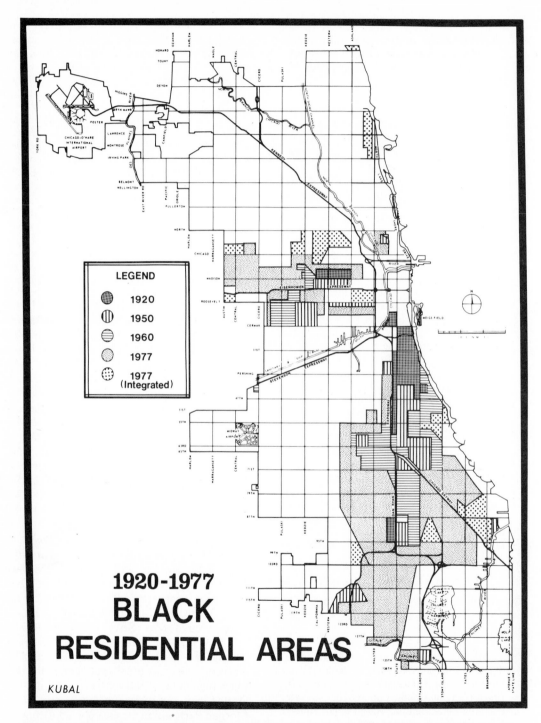

Figure 5.4. The expansion through more than half a century of the virtually all-black residential areas in Chicago. The expansion pattern in the city was largely southward and westward from the inner city until the city boundaries were reached. The movement outward was especially rapid after 1950. (Map by Joseph Kubal based largely on research by the Chicago Urban League.)

imately by 107th and 119th streets and by Halsted Street and Ashland Avenue. Many of these small areas were bounded by transportation corridors, in particular by railroads.

The major Black Belt was a narrow strip of land that started south of downtown, wedged between railroad yards, factories, the ethnic communities west of Wentworth Avenue, and the fashionable homes east of Wabash Avenue. By 1900 this Black Belt stretched south to 39th Street; by 1930 it had reached approximately 63rd Street. It had also expanded eastward to Cottage Grove Avenue, except for the area immediately south of Washington Park to 63rd Street. The first black settlement in the area usually was on side streets; later it was to include the better homes along the boulevards. Increasing immigration from the South, coupled with only limited opportunity for expansion, kept increasing the population density.

Over 80 percent of Chicago's blacks lived in the major Black Belt. Unlike the various European ethnic groups, even the blacks of wealth and education usually found it impossible to move out of this Black Belt into higher status areas. Higher rents, restrictive real estate practices, threats, and even violence were used to keep blacks out of parts of such adjacent communities as Hyde Park and Woodlawn. A total of 58 racially motivated bombings occurred between 1917 and 1921. The result was an economic stratification within the Black Belt. As was generally the case with white settlement patterns, the quality of neighborhoods and homes, educational level, and job status within the Black Belt tended to improve as one proceeded outward from downtown. Differences in economic and social status within all the black areas were often reflected in such factors as the quality and types of stores, the number of storefront churches, and the frequency of gambling establishments.

The 1920s also focused attention on the strides some of the blacks were making in business, the professions, and politics. Efforts were made by black groups to encourage blacks to patronize black-owned businesses. There were two black banks, seven black insurance companies, as well as numerous small black-owned businesses. These included groceries, beauty parlors, barber shops, restaurants, taverns, wood and coal dealerships, and funeral establishments. From small beginnings, some large black-owned Chicago firms arose and became prominent, among them John H. Johnson's Johnson Publishing (*Ebony, Ebony Junior, Black Star,* and *Jet*); George Johnson's Johnson Products Company, a cosmetics firm; and J. H. Parker's Parker House Sausage Company. Jesse Binga, an ex-Pullman porter, opened a bank and owned valuable South Side real estate. Anthony Overton, an ex-slave, owned a chain of businesses that included a bank, newspaper, insurance firm, and manufacturing plant. Renowned entertainment places developed on the South Side, such as Club De Lisa, the Regal Theater, and the Savoy Ballroom—they attracted some of the best black talent in the country.

Among prominent black professionals was Dr. Daniel Hale Williams (1858–1931) who helped found Provident Hospital on the South Side in 1891, a facility that gave young blacks a place to train as nurses and doctors. Dr. Williams in 1893 was the first physician to close a heart wound successfully. Percy Julian (1899–1975), a distinguished research chemist with more than fifty patents to his credit, founded the firm of Julian Laboratories. Despite his accomplishments, Dr. Julian was initially harassed when, in 1951, he purchased a home in the Chicago suburb of Oak Park. Theodore Lawless (1893–1971) was a nationally-known dermatologist who attracted patients from throughout the Chicago area, regardless of race. A South Side housing development is named after him.

Some blacks became wealthy operating in "protected businesses," notably in the numbers or policy racket that usually operated under the benevolent patronage of the city hall machine. In politics, Oscar De Priest (1871–1951), a prominent black Republican political figure and real estate dealer, was elected in 1915 as Chicago's first black alderman. In 1928 he became the first black to be elected to the U.S. House of Representatives from a northern state. He represented his South Side district until 1935. Thereafter, the number of blacks holding public office increased steadily, although not in proportion to their members. Until the 1930s and Franklin D. Roosevelt's New Deal, the blacks traditionally voted Republican, identifying themselves with the party of Abraham Lincoln.

Black politics generally was similar to the prevalent ethnic political context of Chicago. There were rewards for party loyalty, although usually not proportionate to those received by other groups. Some black political figures had strong commitments to black civil liberties and their social and economic advancement.

The depression years of the 1930s hit the black community of Chicago especially hard. Blacks, who often were the last to be hired by white-owned companies, were the first fired. And black businesses had few reserves to rely upon. Angered by their rising unemployment, blacks boycotted and picketed those white-owned stores in black neighborhoods that hired few or no black workers. And they vigorously protested the eviction of blacks from their homes and apartments. The same policy of eviction was also applied against thousands of Chicago's poor white families who also could not meet their rent or mortgage payments during the depression.

Despite the dire economic conditions that prevailed in the city during the 1930s, more than 43,000 blacks from the South migrated to Chicago during that decade. Even with its problems, Chicago looked better to them than the South, where the blacks suffered from the collapse of cotton tenancy and also from the discriminatory distribution of relief and emergency employment. In Chicago, however, as the policies of the New Deal began to take effect, relief and work in the form of such federally funded programs as the WPA began to alleviate the economic situation of the blacks somewhat. And toward the end of the 1930s

and into the 1940s the war-stimulated economy greatly improved the employment opportunities of the blacks.

Between 1940 and 1970, a period of general economic prosperity in the city, the black population in Chicago almost quadrupled, increasing from 277,731 to 1,102,620. Similarly the percentage of blacks in the population increased from 8.2 percent in 1940 to 32.7 percent in 1970. At the start of the 1980s, the percentage of blacks was about 40 percent, and Chicago had become the second-largest black city in the nation, exceeded only by New York. Black Chicagoans had a higher birth rate and, on the average, were much younger than non-blacks. The median age for blacks in 1970 was 22.4 and for non-blacks was 34.1.

The large black migration to Chicago during and after World War II taxed the inferior recreational facilities and the overcrowded schools of the black areas and built up a strong demand for housing. The artificial ghetto boundaries, such as Cottage Grove, Stony Island, and Ashland avenues, began to give way. Today the main segment of the black residential area has reached south to the city limits. The other major segment reached the western city limits as the black population moved into North Lawndale, East and West Garfield Park, and finally Austin. (See figure 5.4.)

The expansion of the black areas has almost always been on a block-by-block basis outward from the edges of the established ghetto. That expansion has often been into adjacent ethnic communities which resisted the arrival of the blacks, with resultant friction and even occasional violence. But once a number of black families had established themselves, the whites moved out. Their departure was often hastened by unscrupulous panic-peddling real estate dealers who bought houses from the whites at extremely low prices and then sold the houses to incoming blacks at a much higher price.

Along with the growth of the black population and the expansion of the black residential areas came an increasing number of public housing projects. By 1979 the Chicago

Figure 5.5. 3543-45 South Ellis Avenue, 1954. Recent redevelopment in the area has resulted in a variety of greatly improved, new housing. On the site of these houses is the Lake Grove Village housing development. (Photograph, Mildred Mead. Courtesy Chicago Historical Society.)

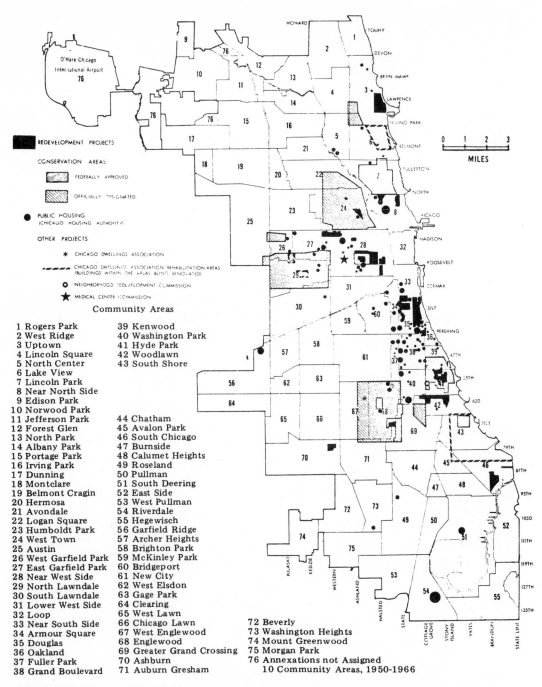

Community Areas

1 Rogers Park	39 Kenwood
2 West Ridge	40 Washington Park
3 Uptown	41 Hyde Park
4 Lincoln Square	42 Woodlawn
5 North Center	43 South Shore
6 Lake View	
7 Lincoln Park	
8 Near North Side	
9 Edison Park	
10 Norwood Park	
11 Jefferson Park	44 Chatham
12 Forest Glen	45 Avalon Park
13 North Park	46 South Chicago
14 Albany Park	47 Burnside
15 Portage Park	48 Calumet Heights
16 Irving Park	49 Roseland
17 Dunning	50 Pullman
18 Montclare	51 South Deering
19 Belmont Cragin	52 East Side
20 Hermosa	53 West Pullman
21 Avondale	54 Riverdale
22 Logan Square	55 Hegewisch
23 Humboldt Park	56 Garfield Ridge
24 West Town	57 Archer Heights
25 Austin	58 Brighton Park
26 West Garfield Park	59 McKinley Park
27 East Garfield Park	60 Bridgeport
28 Near West Side	61 New City
29 North Lawndale	62 West Elsdon
30 South Lawndale	63 Gage Park
31 Lower West Side	64 Clearing
32 Loop	65 West Lawn
33 Near South Side	66 Chicago Lawn
34 Armour Square	67 West Englewood
35 Douglas	68 Englewood
36 Oakland	69 Greater Grand Crossing
37 Fuller Park	70 Ashburn
38 Grand Boulevard	71 Auburn Gresham

72 Beverly
73 Washington Heights
74 Mount Greenwood
75 Morgan Park
76 Annexations not Assigned
   10 Community Areas, 1950-1966

Figure 5.6. Chicago urban renewal and related activities, 1967. Most of the public housing projects are in black areas. (From Harold M. Mayer and Richard C. Wade, *Chicago: Growth of a Metropolis*, 1969. Reproduced by permission of the University of Chicago Press.)

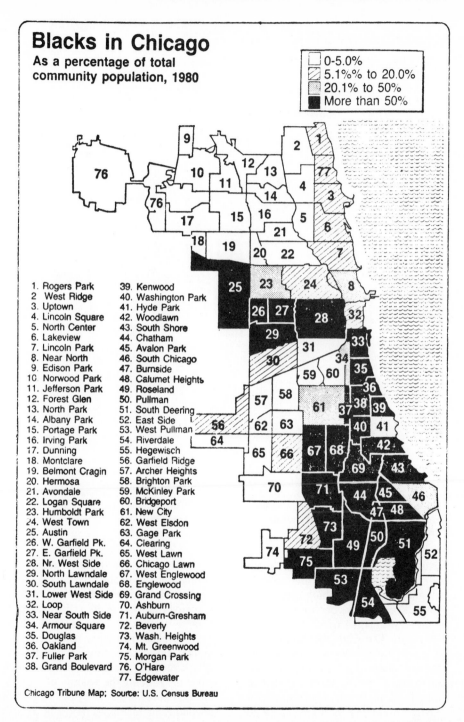

Blacks in Chicago

As a percentage of total
community population, 1980

- ☐ 0-5.0%
- ▨ 5.1%% to 20.0%
- ▨ 20.1% to 50%
- ■ More than 50%

1. Rogers Park
2. West Ridge
3. Uptown
4. Lincoln Square
5. North Center
6. Lakeview
7. Lincoln Park
8. Near North
9. Edison Park
10. Norwood Park
11. Jefferson Park
12. Forest Glen
13. North Park
14. Albany Park
15. Portage Park
16. Irving Park
17. Dunning
18. Montclare
19. Belmont Cragin
20. Hermosa
21. Avondale
22. Logan Square
23. Humboldt Park
24. West Town
25. Austin
26. W. Garfield Pk.
27. E. Garfield Pk.
28. Nr. West Side
29. North Lawndale
30. South Lawndale
31. Lower West Side
32. Loop
33. Near South Side
34. Armour Square
35. Douglas
36. Oakland
37. Fuller Park
38. Grand Boulevard

39. Kenwood
40. Washington Park
41. Hyde Park
42. Woodlawn
43. South Shore
44. Chatham
45. Avalon Park
46. South Chicago
47. Burnside
48. Calumet Heights
49. Roseland
50. Pullman
51. South Deering
52. East Side
53. West Pullman
54. Riverdale
55. Hegewisch
56. Garfield Ridge
57. Archer Heights
58. Brighton Park
59. McKinley Park
60. Bridgeport
61. New City
62. West Elsdon
63. Gage Park
64. Clearing
65. West Lawn
66. Chicago Lawn
67. West Englewood
68. Englewood
69. Grand Crossing
70. Ashburn
71. Auburn-Gresham
72. Beverly
73. Wash. Heights
74. Mt. Greenwood
75. Morgan Park
76. O'Hare
77. Edgewater

Chicago Tribune Map; Source: U.S. Census Bureau

Figure 5.7. Black population in Chicago communities, based on 1980 U.S. Census data. (Copyright, 1981, *Chicago Tribune*. Used with permission.)

Figure 5.8. The Cabrini-Green Homes on the Near North Side of Chicago, 1959. This is one of a number of such high-rise housing projects for low-income families operated by the Chicago Housing Authority. Such developments have generally tended to be isolated, segregated, crowded, noisy, unsafe, and with only limited facilities for the large number of children who live in them. This complex now contains 23 high-rise buildings and 55 rowhouses on 70 acres (28 ha) and houses almost 14,000 people. (Photograph, Betty Hulett. Courtesy Chicago Historical Society.)

Housing Authority had constructed about 45,000 low-rent public housing units, mainly in the black ghetto areas, in which more than 135,000 people lived. Blacks occupied 84 percent of the units; whites, 14 percent; and Hispanics, 2 percent. The high-rise complexes, especially, tended to be isolated, segregated, unsafe, crowded, noisy, and with unsuitable and limited facilities for the large number of children who lived in them. The complexes had the basic ingredients in many cases to become instant ghettos.

Efforts to build new, usually low-rise, public housing in the city outside of the ghettos have been blocked by legal and political maneuvering that often reflect racial feelings. Sizable but diminishing parts of Chicago still have no black residents, and the city remains highly segregated. Ironically, well-intentioned urban renewal programs have often had the effect of reducing the amount of low-cost housing available for blacks by pushing up the rents beyond their means to pay. Blacks still spend a much higher percentage of their income on housing than do whites, even though much of the city's substandard housing is in black neighborhoods. The City of Chicago Housing Assistance Plan of 1979 estimated that 281,300—24.9 percent—of the city's 1,128,000 dwelling units were substandard. Census data for 1980 revealed that in the decade of the 1970s, the black areas of the West and South sides lost almost 10 percent of their housing stock. North Lawndale on the West Side and Englewood on the South Side each lost over one-third of their population during the decade.

The 1960s was a turbulent decade that witnessed many civil rights demonstrations advocating open housing, greater employment opportunities for blacks, and the elimination of school segregation. Many of the demonstrations were led by Dr. Martin Luther King, Jr. His assassination in Memphis in the summer of 1968 brought on two days of rioting, arson, and looting in Chicago's depressed West Side ghetto. The intervention of the National Guard and federal troops was required to restore order. Whole blocks of businesses and housing along some streets—especially Roosevelt Road and Madison Street—were burned out. Many still have not been fully restored. Fires and abandoned buildings are a continuing problem in many parts of the West Side.

Mayer and Wade in 1969 summarized living conditions for the blacks as follows:

> Staggering congestion resulted. Blocks virtually burst at the seams; the deterioration of already substandard buildings accelerated. In its train came the long list of social ills that afflict blighted areas—poor health, inferior education, unskilled jobs or none at all, fragile family life, delinquency, and much more. The old became discouraged; the young despaired; hopelessness pervaded the ghetto. Finding a footing in the city had never been easy for any group; discrimination based on color added another high hurdle; for some it made advancement impossible.

Despite all the obstacles, increasing numbers of Negroes contrived to hold family and careers together, and began the long trek out of the worst areas. By 1968 over a third of Chicago's nonwhite population was listed by the social statisticians as "middle class." This achievement often involved dependence on more than one breadwinner in the family, but it made possible a more satisfying, hopeful life. Some moved into good neighborhoods recently abandoned by the whites at the edge of the ghettoes. Other successful Negroes found housing on a nondiscriminatory basis in Lake Meadows, Prairie Shores, Sandburg Village, or Hyde Park-Kenwood.

Yet the numbers who escaped the ghetto were still small. The Negro's confinement continued, increasing the bitterness of those who were successful and sought a housing market free of discrimination, and reenforcing the despair of those who seemed hopelessly caught in the teeming tenements of the south and west sides. A few Negro families moved into white suburbs without incident; others clustered in the isolated ghettoes within other suburban communities. Fair housing ordinances in the city and in a number of the smaller surrounding communities indicated a growing official determination to end this demeaning practice. But sporadic outbreaks of violence on the west side and civil rights marches into outlying neighborhoods in 1966 and large scale rioting in 1968 were grim reminders of the distance Chicago had still to travel before it became an open metropolis.[6]

Partly because of the civil rights movement, more and better opportunities have been made available for Chicago blacks in housing, employment, education, and politics. Because of increasing economic opportunities, there has been a marked increase in black home ownership and movement into good neighborhoods that were previously segregated. However, the movement of inner city blacks into the outer ethnic ring sometimes still causes racial friction. In 1946 blacks owned only about 5 percent of the dwellings they occupied; by 1960 the figure had reached 15 percent;

and in the mid-1970s black home ownership was estimated to be about 25 percent, compared, however, with about 40 percent for the non-black population.

The rapid expansion of black areas in the post-World War II years brought about the merging into the large Black Belt of former isolated black enclaves, such as those in Englewood, Lillydale, and Morgan Park. Attractive new black communities were established in such areas as in Avalon Park, Chatham, Calumet Heights, Auburn Gresham, Washington Heights, Roseland, and South Shore. Most of the blacks still live in highly segregated communities. The exceptions to segregation are Hyde Park (where the University of Chicago is located); some poorer areas around the Loop; and the north lakefront communities of Lincoln Park, Lake View, Uptown, Edgewater, and Rogers Park, where there has been an increasing, but scattered, black population.

At the time of the 1980 U.S. Census, 31 of the city's 77 community areas had no blacks, while 17 community areas were more than 95 percent black. The patterns of segregation, however, seem to be less rigid than in the past. Some blacks now live in most parts of the city, the major exceptions being much of the Northwest and Southwest sides. The recent movement of small but increasing numbers of blacks into the North Side lakefront communities has been without any noticeable incidents. Also some residential intergroup mixing seems to have occurred in recent years in communities with a sizable Spanish-speaking population such as Uptown, West Town, Humboldt Park, and South Chicago. In some cases whites have been moving into certain well-located black neighborhoods, particularly around the downtown area, raising the fear among some blacks that the low and moderate-income black residents of these areas will be displaced.

In the 1970s further expansion of black residential areas on the South Side continued in Roseland, West Pullman, South Deering, West Englewood, Auburn Gresham, South Chicago, Burnside, Calumet Heights, and into Chicago Lawn in the Marquette area. The West Side black area expanded westward in Humboldt Park and central Austin to the city limits.

In recent years, blacks have been facing increasing job competition, especially from the growing number of Hispanics in the area. In addition, the movement of manufacturing jobs out of Chicago into the suburbs has especially hurt the large numbers of unskilled or semi-skilled city blacks who had been dependent on these factory jobs. For example, in 1970, 53 percent of Chicago's blacks were in blue collar occupations, compared with 34 percent of the non-blacks. Reaching suburban jobs from the city's black areas is often difficult and costly. Moving into the suburbs so as to be near the jobs is often financially infeasible for blacks compared with whites, for the median income of the black family in Chicago is only about 70 percent of the median income of non-black families. Moreover, some tacit forms of housing discrimination are still practiced in some suburban areas.

Although most of the suburbs have enacted open housing laws and the number of blacks in the suburbs keeps increasing, the percentage of the total metropolitan area black population living in the suburbs has increased only moderately. Only about 11 percent of the blacks of the metropolitan area now live in the suburbs. These blacks represent about 6 percent of the total suburban population. Some of the suburbs still house no blacks at all, and a few have merely token integration. Fairly sizable black populations in predominantly white suburbs are found in some communities, including Evanston, Zion, Summit, Broadview, Oak Park, Bellwood, Matteson, Country Club Hills, Calumet Park, Hazel Crest, Justice, Glenwood, Park Forest, and Park Forest South. Blacks now comprise a majority of the population of Maywood, Markham, Harvey, and Dixmoor. However, two-thirds of the suburban blacks still live in older industrial satellites such as Gary, East Chicago, Chicago Heights, Waukegan, North

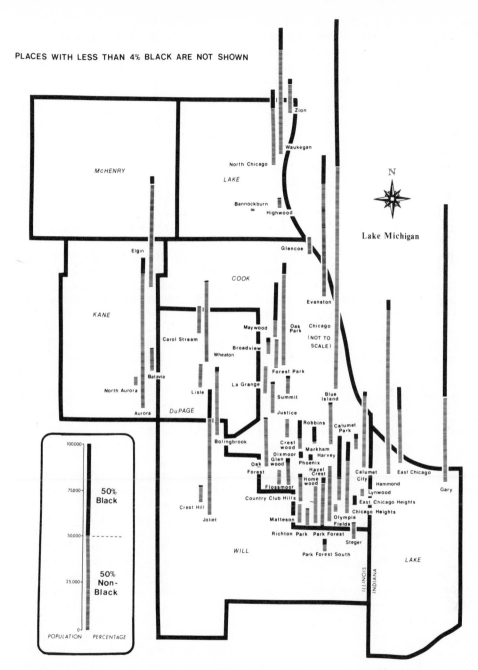

PLACES WITH LESS THAN 4% BLACK ARE NOT SHOWN

PERCENT OF BLACK POPULATION BY MUNICIPALITY
1980

Figure 5.9. Black population in the Chicago area, based on 1980 U.S. Census data. (Map by Joseph Kubal.)

Chicago, Aurora, Elgin, and Joliet or in such black-ghetto suburbs as Robbins, Phoenix, and East Chicago Heights. Most of the largely all-white suburbs have steadfastly resisted the construction of any public housing, at least partially because of the fear that it would attract low income black residents.

In the 1970s a declining birthrate, dwindling migration from the South, and some reverse migration to the South, coupled with continuing expansion of blacks into former white neighborhoods, took some pressure off some of the crowded black ghettos. In recent years the expansion of black residential areas within Chicago has been much more rapid than the growth of the black population. Though much still needs to be accomplished, in recent decades the blacks of the Chicago area, as a whole, have achieved significant gains in housing, employment, education, and political power. But while the expanding black middle class has made substantial progress, there still remains a sizable number of blacks who live in poverty and despair.

The Spanish-Speaking Peoples

Chicago's Spanish-speaking people more than doubled in number during the 1960s, and almost doubled again during the 1970s, reaching 422,061 in 1980, or 14 percent of Chicago's population. These figures generally do not include illegal aliens, mostly Mexicans, who may number as many as several hundred thousand according to U.S. Immigration and Naturalization Service data. The Spanish-speaking community is now the second-largest minority group after the blacks, and in recent years it has been by far the most rapidly growing segment of Chicago's population. Chicago now ranks third nationally in the number of its Spanish-speaking residents, behind New York and Los Angeles.

Chicago is the only major city in the United States that has a sizable representation of each of the nation's three major Spanish-speaking groups (Hispanics)—Mexicans, Puerto Ricans, and Cubans. It has the largest Mexican population in the United States except for Los Angeles and the largest Puerto Rican population in the country outside of New York. In addition, smaller numbers of immigrants from more than a dozen other Latin American countries, many of whom are well-educated professionals, have settled in various parts of Chicago. In 1980 it was estimated that of the Hispanics in the city, 60 percent were Mexican, 27 percent Puerto Rican, and 3 percent Cuban, with the remainder coming from the other Latin American countries.

Although they have come from different geographic backgrounds, there are certain characteristics that are common to the various Hispanic groups in addition to their common language. They are relatively recent arrivals in Chicago, but like their European predecessors, they came mainly for the economic opportunities and to a lesser extent because of political and social oppression. Because of the lack of sufficient education and urban job skills, and because of some cultural and racial discrimination, most find themselves competing for the poorer-paying and often menial jobs of the unskilled laborer. Many are unemployed. They live in the decaying older areas that have been abandoned by previous immigrant groups.

Many Hispanics lack an adequate knowledge of the English language; indeed, Spanish is the second language of the city, with public telephone, transit, and emergency directions written in the two languages. The lack of adequate knowledge of the English language hinders the Hispanics both economically and politically. They are also handicapped by their relative newness to Chicago; the frequent lack of cooperation among the various Hispanic groups; and the fact that many, especially the Mexicans, cannot vote because they are not citizens. These handicaps plus skillful gerrymandering by the entrenched political machine have prevented Hispanics from having more than one of their own as an alderman in

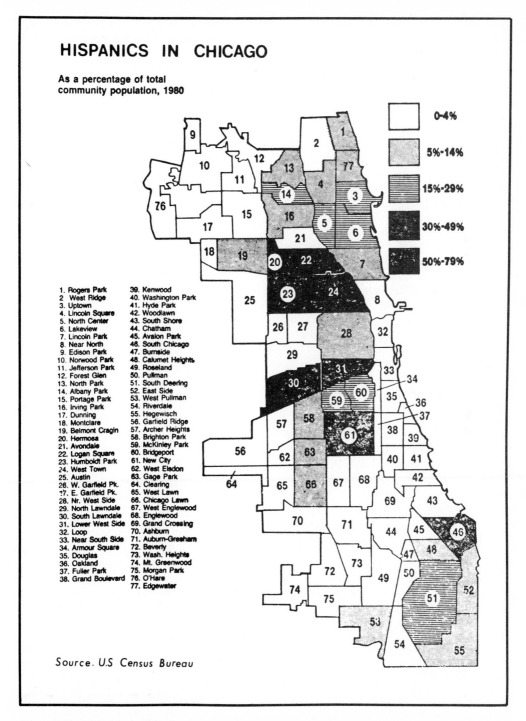

HISPANICS IN CHICAGO

As a percentage of total community population, 1980

Legend:
- 0-4%
- 5%-14%
- 15%-29%
- 30%-49%
- 50%-79%

1. Rogers Park
2. West Ridge
3. Uptown
4. Lincoln Square
5. North Center
6. Lakeview
7. Lincoln Park
8. Near North
9. Edison Park
10. Norwood Park
11. Jefferson Park
12. Forest Glen
13. North Park
14. Albany Park
15. Portage Park
16. Irving Park
17. Dunning
18. Montclare
19. Belmont Cragin
20. Hermosa
21. Avondale
22. Logan Square
23. Humboldt Park
24. West Town
25. Austin
26. W. Garfield Pk.
27. E. Garfield Pk.
28. Nr. West Side
29. North Lawndale
30. South Lawndale
31. Lower West Side
32. Loop
33. Near South Side
34. Armour Square
35. Douglas
36. Oakland
37. Fuller Park
38. Grand Boulevard
39. Kenwood
40. Washington Park
41. Hyde Park
42. Woodlawn
43. South Shore
44. Chatham
45. Avalon Park
46. South Chicago
47. Burnside
48. Calumet Heights
49. Roseland
50. Pullman
51. South Deering
52. East Side
53. West Pullman
54. Riverdale
55. Hegewisch
56. Garfield Ridge
57. Archer Heights
58. Brighton Park
59. McKinley Park
60. Bridgeport
61. New City
62. West Elsdon
63. Gage Park
64. Clearing
65. West Lawn
66. Chicago Lawn
67. West Englewood
68. Englewood
69. Grand Crossing
70. Ashburn
71. Auburn-Gresham
72. Beverly
73. Wash. Heights
74. Mt. Greenwood
75. Morgan Park
76. O'Hare
77. Edgewater

Source. U.S Census Bureau

Figure 5.10. Hispanics in Chicago as a percentage of total community population, 1980. (Copyright by *Chicago Sun-Times*, 1981. Chart by Laslo Vespremi. Reprinted with permission.)

the 50-member city council. They still have no state representative, no state senator, and no Democratic ward committeeman—a key position that controls patronage—despite large contiguous sections of the city being occupied by Hispanics.

While having much in common, each of the major Hispanic groups has its own history of development and settlement in the city. Each group generally lives in its separate and distinct community.

Mexicans were the earliest Hispanic migrants to Chicago and still comprise the largest segment of the Spanish-speaking community. The 1970 Census recorded 82,057 Mexicans, an increase of 84 percent from the preceding decade. In the 1970s the Mexicans more than doubled in number.

Mexicans began to arrive in Chicago after the start of the Mexican Revolution in 1910. Many came from rural areas. The migration accelerated greatly during the World War I period when there was a great demand for labor, especially in the steel mills, but also by the railroads and in the stockyards. Migration accelerated again during World War II and the ensuing years of industrial prosperity.

In many ways the Mexicans who settled in Chicago followed the same patterns and encountered the same problems as other immigrant groups. The Reverend Patrick J. McPolin traced the history of Mexican immigrants in a speech delivered in 1975 entitled "Mexicans in Chicago":

> . . . the slow trickle of Mexican laborers crossing the border in 1911 rapidly enlarged to the proportions, first of a river, then a flood. Letters began to make their way back into the homes of those families whose relatives or friends had gone to the United States, and they told of a land of peace and plenty, where men in those times were paid $3.00 to $6.00 a day in wages. Often the marvelous character of the story grew as it was repeated and people came in ever-increasing numbers. First the single men, followed by those family men who could arrange to leave their families behind until growing wealth would justify bringing them

into a new home in Chicago. Lastly came the family groups who moved North as units. This immigrant flood began in 1922 and continued through the twenties. . . . all moving here for one basic reason—in search of a life better both economically and socially than the one they had known. In brief, the roads they traveled were these:

> 1. As workers in maintenance gangs of railroads, where they transferred from point to point until they reached a railroad workers' camp in the outlying section of Chicago.
> 2. Employment agents of the steel mills hired them and brought them here.
> 3. They themselves came directly to Chicago to find work on the representations of friends who were already working here.
> 4. And at the close of the various harvest seasons in Michigan and Minnesota they came to Chicago rather than return south.

> In the beginning there were difficulties—many difficulties. The Chicagoans in the twenties and thirties, in general, made little effort to integrate the Mexicans into their society. We find the Mexicans live in the shabbiest quarters in the city, not from choice but from economic necessity. And thus, it was mostly and only in the manufacturing and commercial quarters that the Mexicans found welcome.

> Once started within a given neighborhood, the colony grew by ties of race, and the bewildered newcomer naturally seeks out a place to live among his own. He finds within the colony a strong spirit of group cohesion and an element of group consciousness exercising a governing control over the entire colony through the force of public opinion . . . also in the field of industry, the Mexican soon found that he was welcome only as an unskilled laborer at jobs which were the dirtiest and most uncomfortable.

> The first areas they came into were the railroad neighborhoods of Clyde—Cicero and around the McCormick and Crane Works. There were also hundreds who lived in boxcars in the shadow of what is now the Merchandise Mart. They moved from these temporary quarters to areas like Lake Street, Polk Street, and finally Roosevelt Road. This latter group was the beginning of the largest Mexican colony— the west side colony. In addition to this area,

the Mexicans moved into the South Chicago steel mill area, and into the stockyards district. . . .

Along came World War II. It was a great leveler. . . . The first generation of Mexicans began to move away from the barrio into neighborhoods where previously Mexicans were unwelcome. Even the traditional Mexican neighborhoods changed—and we find the shift from 12th Street to 18th Street . . . and now to the Lawndale area.

In 1910 the U.S. Census listed only 102 foreign-born Mexicans in Chicago; by 1920 the number had increased to 1,224; and by 1930 it had swelled to 14,733, but they still were only about 0.4 percent of the city's population. During these prosperous decades Mexicans were hired because they were hard working, reliable laborers who accepted lower wages than did the incoming European immigrants. As their numbers increased, they clustered in colonies near their work. Because many Mexicans hoped to return eventually to their homeland, they initially adhered strongly to their own traditions instead of integrating into American cultural patterns.

The oldest Mexican settlement was in South Chicago, where in 1925 a Catholic chapel was constructed which later became Our Lady of Guadalupe at 3100 East 91st Street. Most of the Mexicans in this settlement lived near the U.S. Steel plant in the Mill Gate and Bush areas or around the Wisconsin Steel plant at 106th Street and Torrance Avenue (2634 E). Their main shopping area was and continues to be around 92nd Street and Commercial Avenue (3000 E). At present, mostly second- and third-generation Mexicans live in this area, as do increasing numbers of blacks and some Puerto Ricans. In 1980 Mexicans comprised 39 percent of the population of South Chicago, and they are also increasing in adjacent South Deering where they now are about 25 percent of the population.

Some Mexicans have been living in the ethnically diverse Back-of-the-Yards area of the New City community since they started working in the stockyards during the World War I period. A larger Mexican community, but one that has all but disappeared, was in the very poor Hull House-Halsted Street area near the railway yards. The Mexicans in this area numbered 7,000 to 8,000 and were aligned sporadically along Halsted Street from Harrison Street (600 S) to 15th Street. The area contained a number of Mexican churches, the most important being St. Francis of Assisi at 813 West Roosevelt Road. This community diminished in numbers during the depression years of the 1930s when many Mexicans returned home. It then grew somewhat during World War II when employment was high. At that time some 15,000 Mexican contract laborers were brought in temporarily under international treaty and there was also an influx of Mexican-Americans from Texas. Subsequently, the neighborhood was largely demolished with the construction in the 1960s of the campus of the University of Illinois at Chicago Circle.

In recent decades a major Mexican settlement developed in the Pilsen area and then spread farther west to the La Villa Chiquita (Little Village) area. Both of these areas had been predominantly Czech and Polish until after World War II when Mexicans from the Halsted-Hull House area began moving in, along with large numbers of new arrivals from Mexico, many coming illegally. The large influx of immigrants created a need for larger Mexican communities and slowed the dreams of assimilation of earlier Mexican-Americans. Today the illegal status of many of the newcomers also means that they are willing to work at jobs that other groups have refused and for very low wages. These wages, however, are still much higher than they could earn in Mexico. They often work as dishwashers, bus boys, bellhops, janitors, and as non-union factory workers.

Pilsen has been transformed into a vibrant Mexican community. Signs and banners in Spanish are everywhere, as are colorful patriotic, religious, and political wall murals. Mexico's Independence Day is marked by pa-

Figure 5.11. Blue Island Avenue near 18th Street looking southwest, 1975. The street is one of the main business thoroughfares of the growing Mexican community in the Pilsen area of Chicago. The population of the community formerly consisted mainly of people of Czech and Polish descent. (Photograph by Irving Cutler.)

rades and bands. Barber shops have become barberias, groceries are supermercados, and hot dog stands are now taco stands. Churches founded by the Czechs, such as St. Procopius at 18th and Allport (1234 W) and St. Vitus at 18th Place and Paulina (1700 W), are now used chiefly by the Mexicans. The main business streets of the Pilsen community are 18th Street from Halsted to Western, Blue Island from 18th Street to Cermak Road, and Ashland from 16th Street to Cermak Road. At the intersection of Blue Island, Cermak, and Ashland, the first public school constructed in the area in this century—Benito Juarez High School—was recently opened. Pilsen contains some of the oldest housing in the city, but architecturally it has some of the most interesting and varied buildings. Much of the housing in the area is rental.

In the 1950s the Mexicans started to overflow to the west, mainly into South Lawndale. They replaced the Czechs who were moving into the western suburbs. The Mexicans who moved into this area, La Villa Chiquita, were generally wealthier than their Pilsen counterparts. Many were second- or third-generation Mexican-Americans; many owned their own homes and shops. If Pilsen is like a poor, crowded Mexican barrio, La Villa Chiquita is like a Mexican "suburb." About 4 square miles (10.4 sq km) in size, its main shopping streets are Cermak Road from about Western Avenue to Kedzie Avenue, and 26th Street from about Kedzie to the city limits at Cicero Avenue (4800 W). Although many Czechs and other Slavs, mainly elderly, still live in the area, an increasing majority of the people of South Lawndale are now of Mexican descent.

There has also been some recent Mexican movement to the south of Pilsen and South Lawndale. For example, the 1980 census data revealed that the late Mayor Richard J. Daley's Bridgeport community contained 21 percent Hispanics, mainly Mexicans. Similarly, there are sizable and growing numbers of Mexicans in McKinley Park—16 percent; and New City—39 percent.

Puerto Ricans are the second-largest Hispanic group in Chicago. They numbered 78,963 in 1970, an increase of 144 percent over the 1960 figure. It is estimated that Chicago's Puerto Rican population may have nearly doubled during the 1970s decade.

The Puerto Ricans are relative newcomers to Chicago even though they have been citizens of the United States for many decades. The Census Bureau first enumerated Chicago's Puerto Ricans as a separate classification in 1960. They entered the Chicago area mainly after World War II, some via New York City whose job market became saturated in the 1960s. Also, after 1960, low-cost direct air service was established between Chicago and San Juan. As American citizens, Puerto Ricans can move freely between the United States mainland and their sunny, but relatively poor and crowded island. Many move back and forth between Chicago and Puerto Rico, shifting between two cultures and never establishing deep roots in Chicago. Their movement frequently depends on the respective economic conditions of the two areas. Some of the movement, however, is due to homesickness, and a small amount is seasonal, with some Puerto Ricans returning home during the middle latitude winter.

During some years migration of Puerto Ricans out of Chicago has been greater than migration into Chicago. Many Puerto Ricans have returned to their island because of unemployment in Chicago or the low pay for unskilled jobs. Others have left because of difficulties with language, overcrowded housing, and a desire to remove their youth from areas with gang, drug, and crime problems. At present the Puerto Ricans have the lowest average income and the least amount of schooling of any minority group in Chicago. Many work in restaurants, hotels, and hospitals; some work in factories and steel mills.

Despite improving economic conditions in Puerto Rico, many still find conditions in Chicago more favorable. Their continuing migration to Chicago together with their large families account for the large increase of

Puerto Ricans in Chicago. They, like most Hispanics, have strong family ties.

Some of the earlier Puerto Rican settlers lived in scattered areas, including the South Side communities of Woodlawn and South Chicago. Some lived near already established Mexican communities, and initially still others lived near black communities. The Puerto Ricans had a stronger racial association with the blacks than did the Mexicans. Unlike the blacks, however, there were comparatively very few Hispanics in public housing.[7]

The vast majority of the Puerto Ricans, however, soon concentrated on the North and Northwest sides, miles north of the major Mexican communities. Today the major Puerto Rican community extends westward from Lincoln Park and Lake View, especially, into West Town, Logan Square, and Humboldt Park, and is continuing to expand northward into Hermosa, Avondale, and Albany Park. Puerto Ricans now comprise a majority of the population in West Town and Logan Square. Division Street (1200 N) is the main

Figure 5.12. Division Street near Damen Avenue looking eastward, 1975. The street is one of the main business thoroughfares of the growing Puerto Rican community on the Northwest Side of Chicago. In the background is the San Juan Theater which features Spanish language films. The population of the community formerly was predominately of Polish descent. (Photograph by Irving Cutler.)

business street. On Division at Western is the new Roberto Clemente High School. Unfortunately, one of the major problems of the area has been the large number of fires, many of suspicious origin, that have destroyed many hundreds of homes.

A number of churches dot the Puerto Rican community, but their influence is not as great as in the Mexican community. Puerto Ricans have very few of their own clergy. The Puerto Ricans have no elected major political representatives. Ideological differences and a certain degree of disunity among the various Hispanic groups have hampered their political efforts, although they are generally united in their efforts to secure more jobs, better housing, and some bilingual education. Poverty, overcrowding, and a lack of political power have probably been among the underlying causes of a number of Northwest Side riots that have resulted in confrontations between the police and some Puerto Ricans, mainly youths.

The Cuban community of Chicago, which began in the early 1960s with refugees from Castro's Cuban Revolution, is the smallest of the city's Hispanic groups, numbering 14,117 persons in 1970. Its growth in the 1970s was relatively slow, but in 1980 there was again an influx of refugees from Cuba.

The Cubans live mainly in five North Side communities—Uptown, Logan Square, Lake View, Lincoln Square, and Rogers Park. Because of their smaller numbers, Chicago has no large Cuban settlements comparable to those of the Mexicans or Puerto Ricans. Most live interspersed in communities of reasonable quality that have considerable ethnic and racial mixture. Compared to the other Hispanic groups in Chicago, the Cubans have tended to be older and better educated, and to possess greater employment skills. The early arrivals, in particular, included physicians, lawyers, and other professionals. Consequently, Cuban income has been the highest of the Hispanic groups, and the percentage of Cubans on welfare has been much lower than that of Puerto

Ricans, Mexicans, or blacks. Unlike the Mexicans and Puerto Ricans, the ties of the Cubans with their homeland were largely severed and there has been virtually no back-and-forth movement.

In 1970 the median income for all Spanish-speaking families in the Chicago area was slightly higher than that of black families but only about three-fourths that of white families. Spanish-speaking adults in Chicago average 8.7 years of schooling as opposed to 11.3 years for non-Spanish-speaking adults.

Although Hispanics and blacks have many problems in common, occasionally there have been differences or even some friction between the two groups. The differences have often resulted from competition between the two largest minorities in the city for jobs, housing, government aid programs, and political power.

At first slowly, but of late more rapidly, Hispanics have been moving into suburbs where there are now almost 150,000 of them. At least 1 percent of the population is Hispanic in 211 of the city's 256 suburbs; in contrast, only 81 of the suburbs are at least 1 percent black. Some of the Hispanic professionals live in the more affluent suburbs, but most of the suburban Hispanics live in industrial areas such as Gary, Chicago Heights, Blue Island, Joliet, Aurora, Melrose Park, Elgin, Waukegan, and Cicero. In these communities they comprise between 7 and 18 percent of the population. In the steel mill community of East Chicago, Indiana, Hispanics constitute 42 percent of the population. Finding adequate but reasonably priced housing in the suburbs, as well as suitable transportation, are problems for many of the poorer Hispanics.

Not all of the suburban Hispanics moved to the suburbs via Chicago. Mexican-Americans, in particular, mainly from Texas, began coming to some urban-rural fringe areas decades ago as migrant workers employed on farms and nurseries or by the railroads. Some eventually settled in the suburbs where they now work, especially in factories and in landscaping.

The Asians

In the late 1960s and through the 1970s there was a large influx of people from East and South Asia and from the Middle East—Filipinos, Chinese, Koreans, Indonesians, Indians, Pakistani, Thai, Vietnamese, Cambodians, Iranians, and Arabs. Their coming had been especially spurred by the turmoil in Southeast Asia and by the reduction of immigration restrictions. By 1980, combining the various U.S. Census classifications for that area, there were probably over 100,000 people of Asian descent in the Chicago area. Their growing number of small shops, restaurants, and religious and cultural facilities have added significantly to the cosmopolitan atmosphere of Chicago.

Many of the Asian immigrants were initially handicapped in their adjustment to life in Chicago by language and cultural differences, climatic factors, and by some still lingering employment and housing discrimination. However, with characteristic hard work and self-reliance, and because many of them were professionals, business people, or skilled craftsmen, most were able to overcome the obstacles they initially encountered.

The largest concentration of Asians in Chicago is on the North Side where they live under varying circumstances. Most of Chicago's estimated 4,500 refugees from the recent fighting in Indochina live in the poorer sections of Lake View, Uptown, and Rogers Park where the rent is cheaper. Most are Vietnamese with small numbers being from Cambodia and Laos.

There were a few hundred Japanese living in Chicago prior to World War II, mainly in the Hyde Park-Kenwood area. Many were students at the University of Chicago. After the war their numbers increased as West Coast Japanese released from internment camps found haven in Chicago, although some later returned to the West Coast. A small Japanese community, "Little Tokyo," developed around Clark and Division streets until it fell victim to urban renewal that included the large Sandburg Village development. The magnificent Midwest Buddhist Temple is located just to the north at 435 West Menomonee (1800 N). About 60 percent of the Japanese of the Chicago area work in white-collar occupations.

The Japanese community in the city today is largely scattered in North Side lakefront communities, especially in the vicinity of Clark Street in Lake View and Uptown. In recent years there has been little immigration from Japan, and the Japanese population has not increased significantly from 1970 when the census showed over 10,000 people of Japanese descent living in the city and another few thousand, especially the younger generation, living in suburbs such as Evanston, Skokie, and Des Plaines. Additionally, several thousand Japanese, representing Japanese business concerns, are usually residing temporarily in Chicago.

People from Thailand first started trickling into Chicago in the early 1950s and were largely college students. In the last 15 years the Thai population has increased until today an estimated 10,000 live scattered across the North and Northwest sides and in the suburbs. Over half of those employed work in the health field, many as doctors and nurses. Medical personnel found it easy to obtain visas during the period when there was a shortage of health professionals in the United States. The Thai have established the Thai Buddhist Temple at 1000 North Hoyne (2100 W) to serve as a religious and cultural center and also as a service center for the immigrants adjusting to the new land. They also help support about a dozen Thai groceries and almost that number of Thai restaurants, many located on Lincoln Avenue or Clark Street. Because of the difficulty of adapting to an American diet, some produce is flown in regularly from Bangkok.

Filipinos first came to Chicago in the 1920s when their homeland was still an American possession and immigration was unhampered. But William Howard Taft's "little brown brothers" found discrimination in employment and were confined largely to subordinate positions in the post office, or to menial

Figure 5.13. Japanese children attending Saturday morning classes at Loyola University where they learn about their culture, 1977. (Photograph by Irving Cutler.)

work for Pullman or in hotels and restaurants. By 1930 there were about 2,000 Filipinos in the city, and they formed a small colony on the near South Side. The Filipino population remained small until the immigration laws were liberalized in 1965. The ensuing wave of immigration increased their estimated numbers by the late 1970s to over 30,000. The Filipinos had an advantage over other Asians in that they had been introduced to American culture, government, and language during the more than four decades of United States rule of their homeland.

The Filipinos who have arrived in recent years have generally been well educated, with many professionals among them, including, like the Thai, many in the medical field. Most live on the North (especially in Uptown and Edgewater) and Northwest sides, often near the hospitals where they work or near the CTA elevated lines. They are relatively well off

economically, and like most of the other Asian people, they keep a low profile. Because the Filipinos usually take care of their own, they have very few public welfare cases. They also have few delinquency problems and the crime rate is exceptionally low. The Filipino-American Council umbrella organization at 1332 West Irving Park Road (4000 N) counts some 34 member organizations representing different homeland provincial groups and various cultural and professional groups. The facility is also used by other Asian groups of the area.

The Korean population in Chicago has grown from a few dozen families in the late 1950s to an estimated 35,000 persons in the late 1970s, making it now the largest Asian ethnic group in the city. Like the recent Thai and Filipino immigrants, the Koreans are well educated, with many holding college degrees. Their number also includes many doctors and nurses. Many of the Koreans settled in Lake

Figure 5.14. The changing ownership, from Jewish to Korean, of an institutional facility in the 4900 block of North Kimball Avenue, 1979, reflects the recent population shift in the Albany Park community. (Photograph by Irving Cutler.)

View and Uptown, and Korean commercial establishments were opened along Clark Street. In recent years, as they have become established economically, the Koreans have moved outward geographically, some into the suburbs, but their greatest concentration is now found in the former largely Jewish community of Albany Park. The mile stretch of Lawrence Avenue between Kedzie Avenue (3200 W) and Pulaski Road (4000 W) now has numerous Korean-owned commercial establishments. There are now more than 30 Korean restaurants in the city. And several dozen Korean churches are scattered in the various neighborhoods where Koreans live. Most of the churches are of the Christian faith, partly reflecting the intensive work of American missionaries in Korea.

Among the smaller Asian groups in Chicago, but also growing in number, are immigrants from India, Pakistan, and Indonesia. Small numbers of Assyrians, Armenians, Iranians, Syrians, and others from the Middle East have been living in the Chicago area for many decades. In recent years increasing numbers of Jordanian and Palestinian Arabs have been settling in Chicago. Most of the immigrants from South Asia and the Middle East have scattered on the city's North and Northwest sides, with a small number in the suburbs. A small Arab community also exists on the Southwest Side, especially around 63rd Street and Western Avenue.

The city's oldest, most distinct, and most concentrated Asian community is the compact Chinese neighborhood about two miles (3.2

Figure 5.15. A Korean commercial strip in the 3300 block of West Lawrence Avenue, 1980. There are many such stores on Lawrence Avenue between Kedzie Avenue and Pulaski Road. (Photograph by Irving Cutler.)

km) south of the Loop—Chinatown. Today's Chinatown was preceded by Chicago's first Chinese community which was started in the late 1880s in downtown Chicago along Clark Street south of Van Buren Street. Most of the early Chinese were men who had come via San Francisco and had worked on railroads. In Chicago many initially could find work only in restaurants or as laundrymen. In 1912, because the community was being compressed by the expanding downtown business district, Chinese businessmen bought property and established a new Chinatown around Cermak Road (2200 S) and Wentworth Avenue (200 W). About a third of Chicago's approximately 15,000 Chinese now live in this enclave where

more than two dozen restaurants, three noodle factories, numerous small shops, and many institutional facilities cater to the local people and to thousands of tourists who can purchase anything from herbal medicine to jade. Many buildings have pagoda-style architecture with Mandarin red and green trimmings. Street signs are printed in both English and Chinese—indicative of the two worlds that meet there. In 1975 an ornamental tile gate spanning Wentworth Avenue was erected by the community.

There has been some limited recent expansion of this Chinatown despite the area's tight encirclement by major transportation arteries. New housing, including a nine-story

Figure 5.16. Looking north in Chinatown on Wentworth Avenue, near Cermak Road, 1952. Original area of Chinese settlement was in the downtown area on South Clark Street. (Photograph, J. Sherwin Murphy. Courtesy Chicago Historical Society.)

senior citizen home, has recently been completed. In recent years, however, with increased immigration, especially from Hong Kong and Taiwan, an effort has been made to develop a Chinatown North along Argyle Street (5000 N) in Uptown to relieve some of the pressure on the South Side Chinatown. The latter area has also been affected commercially by the change and decline of the city's population and by the opening of hundreds of Chinese restaurants and takeout shops throughout the city and suburbs. However, additional improvements are being planned for the South Side's Chinese business area.

About 6,000 Native Americans also live in Chicago. They come from over 40 Indian tribes representing diverse cultures and geographical areas. They are especially concentrated in the Uptown area. Many have found it initially difficult to adjust from their tribal, rural life to the complicated life of the big city. They often have more problems than those who have come from foreign lands.

Socioeconomic Patterns

The Chicago Metropolitan Area consists of several hundred communities, of which 77 are recognized neighborhood community areas in Chicago, and the remainder are suburban municipalities (fig. 4.2). These communities have a great range of socioeconomic conditions. This range is indicative of the diverse racial, ethnic, and educational backgrounds of their inhabitants and of the wide variation in the opportunities available to them. Median annual family income in the Chicago Metropolitan Area in 1970 ranged from about $5,000 in some inner-city communities to more than $40,000 in several affluent suburbs. In general, the lowest income levels are found in the overcrowded inner-city black areas on the South and West sides. (See table 5.2 and figure 5.17.) Chicago's average family income is highest near the lake and also increases to the north, northwest, and southwest. It is also high in the later-settled peripheral communities in the city, such as Beverly and Forest Glen. However, average family income reaches its peak in the suburbs (fig. 5.18).

There is marked variation in the economic status of the communities of Chicago; similarly, there is great variation among the suburbs. Of the twenty-five wealthiest suburbs, fifteen are to the north, six are to the west, and four are to the south. The North Shore suburbs have such natural amenities as Lake Michigan and an interesting topography, as well as good commuter transportation to the Loop and extensive areas that are free of polluting industries. The poorest suburbs are virtually all to the south of the city, with the largely black suburbs of Robbins, East Chicago Heights, and Phoenix having some of the lowest incomes.

Many of the economic elite of early Chicago once lived on the Near West Side along fashionable Washington (100 N), Ashland (1600 W), and Jackson (300 S) boulevards, and on some of the adjacent streets, including the Union Park area. In the 1880s Potter Palmer led the way northward along the "Gold Coast" of the lakeshore (just as in the 1860s his actions had established State Street as the retail heart of the city). This high-income axial development eventually reached the North Shore suburbs, including Kenilworth, which in 1976 was the Chicago suburb with the highest median family income. Table 5.2 shows that in 1970 the eastern part of Chicago's Near North Side had top socioeconomic ranking in the city. An almost solid array of very expensive high-rise apartments and condominiums, overlooking Lake Michigan, line most of North Lake Shore Drive. In 1960 the western part of the Near North Side had been near the bottom in socioeconomic ranking, but by 1970, with some redevelopment, it had moved up substantially.

To the south by the 1880s high grade housing had spread from its location on Wabash (45 E) and Michigan (100 E) avenues, within the confines of today's downtown, southward along Indiana (200 E), Prairie (300 E), and Calumet (344 E) avenues to about 26th Street. On Prairie Avenue near 18th Street, the location of the 1812 Fort Dearborn Massacre, there stood in the 1880s the mansions of some of the social and economic leaders of Chicago—Pullman, Armour, Glessner, Kimball, and Field—an area recently restored as an historic landmark. In time, with the spread of industry and immigrant groups toward the area, and the growing "Levee" vice area to the west, some of the economic elite moved farther south along Grand Boulevard, now Dr. Martin Luther King, Jr. Drive (400 E), and Drexel Boulevard (900 E) into Kenwood and Hyde Park. Later they moved into South Shore, Beverly, and by-passing the older Calumet industrial satellites, into Homewood, Flossmoor, and Olympia Fields. A trend was developing for many of the higher income and better educated people—those who would ordinarily form a solid tax and

TABLE 5.2

Socioeconomic Status Ranking of Chicago Communities

No.	Community Name	Rank 1960	1970
1A	Rogers Park A	11	18
1B	Rogers Park B	20	23
2	West Ridge	8	11
3A	Uptown A	7	12
3B	Uptown B	39	44
4	Lincoln Square	23	25
5	North Center	53	60
6A	Lake View A	5	5
6B	Lake View B	57	53
7A	Lincoln Park A	18	3
7B	Lincoln Park B	58	39
8A	Near North Side A	1	1
8B	Near North Side B	73	41
9	Edison Park	9	16
10	Norwood Park	14	17
11	Jefferson Park	29	27
12	Forest Glen	4	7
13	North Park	13	10
14	Albany Park	43	48
15	Portage Park	33	32
16	Irving Park	35	34
17	Dunning	32	29
18	Montclare	40	26
19	Belmont Cragin	42	50
20	Hermosa	47	56
21	Avondale	52	59
22	Logan Square	62	64
23	Humboldt Park	61	67
24	West Town	74	77
25	Austin	27	46
26	West Garfield Park	70	78
27	East Garfield Park	78	81
28	Near West Side	68	74
29	North Lawndale	80	76
30	South Lawndale	67	68
31	Lower West Side	77	79
32	Loop	21	4
33	Near South Side	84	72
34	Armour Square	79	73
35A	Douglas A	10	9
35B	Douglas B	72	66
36	Oakland	83	83

No.	Community Name	Rank 1960	1970
37	Fuller Park	82	82
38	Grand Boulevard	81	84
39A	Kenwood A	22	2
39B	Kenwood B	54	58
40	Washington Park	76	80
41A	Hyde Park A	3	8
41B	Hyde Park B	25	24
42	Woodlawn	59	71
43A	South Shore A	6	20
43B	South Shore B	38	49
44	Chatham	28	33
45	Avalon Park	12	19
46	South Chicago	55	54
47	Burnside	66	65
48	Calumet Heights	19	13
49	Roseland	31	31
50	Pullman	51	43
51	South Deering	36	38
52	East Side	48	51
53	West Pullman	45	42
54	Riverdale	64	75
55	Hegewisch	56	52
56	Garfield Ridge	41	35
57	Archer Heights	49	47
58	Brighton Park	63	62
59	McKinley Park	65	57
60	Bridgeport	75	63
61	New City	69	69
62	West Elsdon	37	36
63	Gage Park	44	45
64	Clearing	46	37
65	West Lawn	34	28
66	Chicago Lawn	30	30
67	West Englewood	60	61
68	Englewood	71	70
69	Greater Grand Crossing	50	55
70	Ashburn	16	14
71	Auburn Gresham	26	40
72	Beverly	2	6
73	Washington Heights	15	22
74	Mount Greenwood	24	21
75	Morgan Park	17	15

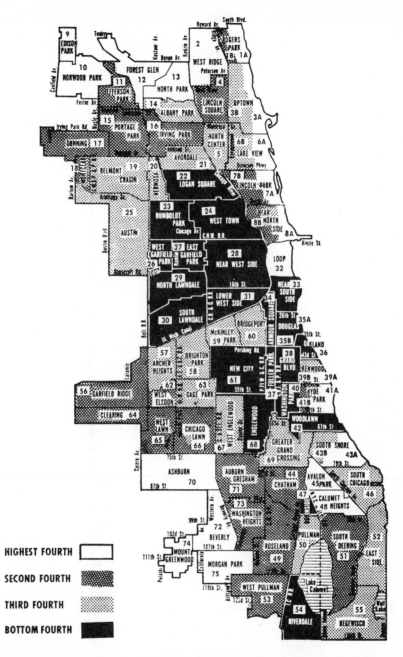

HIGHEST FOURTH

SECOND FOURTH

THIRD FOURTH

BOTTOM FOURTH

Figure 5.17. Socioeconomic or status ranking of Chicago communities based on income, education, and occupation data of the 1970 census. Some of Chicago's traditional communites along the lakeshore have been divided into "A" (eastern section) and "B" (western section) based on differing characteristics in each area, bringing the total communities studied to 84. (Data compiled by Pierre De Vise, director of the Chicago Regional Hospital Study; map reprinted, courtesy of *Chicago Daily News.*)

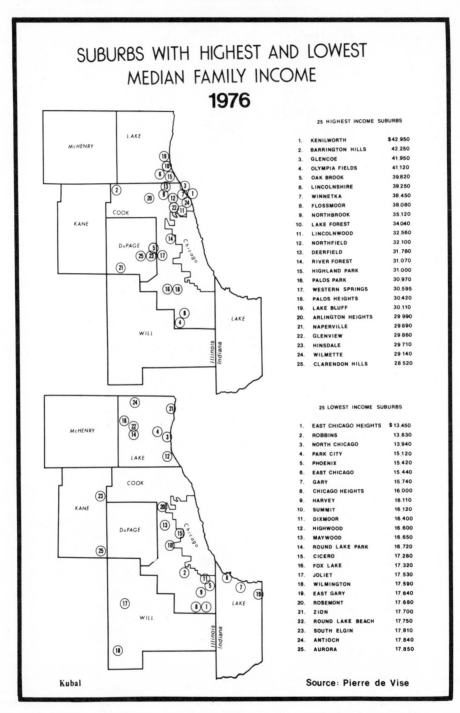

Figure 5.18. Suburbs with highest and lowest median family income, 1976. (Source of data: Pierre De Vise. Map by Joseph Kubal.)

Figure 5.19. Brownstones along North Dearborn Parkway on the Near North Side in a high-income area near Lincoln Park. Many of the interiors retain memories of bygone Victorian elegance although high-rise condominiums are encroaching on the area. (Photograph courtesy Chicago Convention and Tourism Bureau.)

Figure 5.20. 700 North Green Street, 1949. Before the development of zoning laws, homes and industry crowded together. (Photograph, Mildred Mead. Courtesy Chicago Historical Society.)

Figure 5.21. Michigan Avenue north from Eighth Street about 1911. The 22-story Blackstone Hotel had just been completed in 1909. The site of the homes was later to be occupied by one of the world's largest hotels, the Stevens (Conrad Hilton). (Photograph courtesy Chicago Historical Society.)

leadership base for the city—to move to the suburbs.

In time some of the older, high-income parts of the city deteriorated into the city's worst slums as the rich left and their mansions were subdivided to accommodate the poorer migrants. However, in the post-World War II period, some of these areas experienced massive urban renewal and redevelopment, reemerging as highly desirable residential locations, such as Lake Meadows, Prairie Shores, and South Commons south of downtown, and the Carl Sandburg Village area to the north. The massive redevelopment south of the Loop resulted from the coordinated efforts of various governmental bodies, civic groups, financial agencies, and local institutions, such as Michael Reese and Mercy hospitals and the Illinois Institute of Technology. In the Hyde Park-Kenwood area, the University of Chicago helped promote a redevelopment and conservation program that

Figure 5.22. Fashionable South Side residential areas, 1892. Bottom view is looking **eastward** on 26th Street from Wabash Avenue. Top view is looking **northward** on Prairie Avenue from Cermak Road. This section of Prairie Avenue, in particular, contained the mansions of Chicago's social and economic leaders including Marshall Field, George Pullman, Philip Armour, William Kimball, John Glessner, and others. After the turn of the century the encroachment of industry and of immigrant groups, a vice area to the west, and improved transportation to other areas caused an exodus of the wealthy from the area. In time most of the stately homes were replaced by industry. The city has restored part of Prairie Avenue as an historic landmark. (Photograph courtesy Chicago Historical Society.)

transformed the area. Important urban renewal programs have also been taking place in the Near West Side and Near North Side communities, and elsewhere.

Urban redevelopment, generally radiating outward from the downtown area, has been upgrading the older inner-city areas with more expensive high-rise housing. At the same time, however, the poor who had lived in these areas before redevelopment, were pushed out. Once again the poor crowded into what were once stable neighborhoods, creating new slums.

Theoretical Internal Arrangement of Chicago

More than half a century ago, Professor Ernest Burgess of the highly respected Chicago school of urban sociology, proposed his

Figure 5.23. View eastward from the Ogden Avenue viaduct north of Division Street, 1954, showing part of the near North Side area that Harvey Zorbaugh discussed in 1929 in his book entitled *The Gold Coast and the Slums.* The Gold Coast consists of the luxury high-rise apartment buildings along the lakefront, visible in the background. (Photograph, Lillian Ettinger. Courtesy Chicago Historical Society.)

Figure 5.24. Aerial view of Lake Meadows apartment community looking northwest from 35th Street with the Illinois Central Railroad tracks at the lower right. The integrated community was developed under the urban renewal program by the New York Life Insurance Company on what had been one of the worst slum areas of the city. The development contains a shopping center, elementary school, public park, community center, and an office building. The high-rise apartment complex in the right background is the adjoining Prairie Shores apartment development, also integrated. More than a century ago much of this land was owned by Senator Stephen A. Douglas who lies buried in the small park just west of the tracks with a tall pillar topped by his statue capping his tomb. (Photograph courtesy Department of Urban Renewal, City of Chicago.)

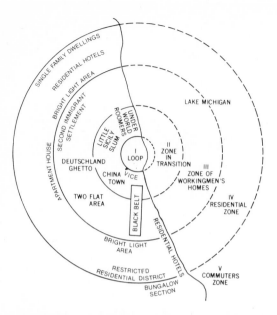

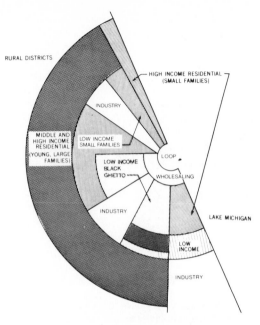

Figure 5.25. The Burgess concentric zone theory of the internal arrangement of cities as applied to the Chicago of the 1920s. This theoretical model suggests that a city expands radially from its center to form a series of five concentric zones each having certain distinguishing characteristics. The Chicago model is semicircular because of the presence of Lake Michigan. (From Park, Burgess, and McKenzie, editors, *The City*, 1925. Reproduced by permission of the University of Chicago Press.)

Figure 5.26. Generalized social and land use areas of Chicago, 1960, showing some evidence of the internal arrangement theories. (Adapted from Philip Rees, "The Factorial Ecology of Metropolitan Chicago, 1960," M. A. Thesis, Department of Geography, University of Chicago, 1968.)

concentric zone theory of the internal arrangement of cities. This theoretical model of urban structure, based largely on his studies of Chicago, postulated that the modern city consists of a pattern of five concentric zones or circles, with each zone having certain distinguishing characteristics. Figure 5.25 shows the model as applied to the Chicago of the early 1920s, semicircular because of the presence of Lake Michigan.

Zone I, the center and the original core of the city, is the downtown area or the Loop. This core is surrounded by Zone II, an area in transition, which contains principally wholesale and light manufacturing activities interspersed with areas of cheap hotels, rooming houses, and some tenements. This zone has

deteriorating and neglected facilities that are often held for speculative purposes on the assumption that the downtown area will expand outward, making the land more valuable. Next come a series of residential zones whose economic status improves as one moves away from the older inner core of the city to the newer commuters' or suburban zones. Planned social change and the dispersal of various groups and facilities have affected the pattern postulated by this theory, but in general the idealized pattern, as applied to Chicago, can still be detected.

Other theoretical models have also been advanced to help explain the internal arrangement of cities. One such model, the sector theory of internal growth, assumes that a city develops largely in a series of sectors or wedges radiating out of the downtown area and that each sector is dominated by a certain type of land use. Figure 5.26 shows a combination of the concentric circle and the sector theories. In Chicago such sectors are evident in the expensive apartments lining the lakeshore from the Loop north, in the industrial wedges along many of the rivers and railroads, and in the black ghettos radiating south and west of the Loop.

Chicago's internal arrangement also reflects the multiple nuclei theory which postulates that a city is made up of a number of cells or nuclei having basically similar functions. For example, there is a cell that contains the University of Chicago complex. There are numerous types of residential cells of varying economic, ethnic, and racial composition. And there are entertainment district cells, a steel area cell, an airport complex, and so on. The formation of cells is based on the tendency of like activities and people to cluster together. This is sometimes in response to zoning laws or because certain groups and activities profit by being near each other.

Chicago reflects, in many ways, characteristics of all three of these theories. Whatever the theory used to describe and explain the internal arrangement of Chicago's settlement and people patterns, the city's patterns are the result of a century and a half of immigration, internal growth and development, and continuous change.

Notes

1. Allan H. Spear, *Black Chicago: The Making of a Negro Ghetto, 1890–1920* (Chicago: University of Chicago Press, 1967), p. 91.
2. St. Clair Drake and Horace R. Cayton, *Black Metropolis,* vol. 1 (New York: Harcourt, Brace & World, 1945), p. 73.
3. Spear, *Black Chicago: The Making of a Negro Ghetto, 1890–1920,* pp. 174–75.
4. Drake and Cayton, *Black Metropolis,* vol. 1, pp. 78–79.
5. Drake and Cayton, *Black Metropolis,* vol. 1, p. 80.
6. Harold M. Mayer and Richard C. Wade, *Chicago: Growth of a Metropolis* (Chicago: University of Chicago Press, 1969), pp. 406–10.
7. Gerald William Ropka, "The Evolving Residential Pattern of the Mexican, Puerto Rican and Cuban Population in the City of Chicago" (Ph.D. dissertation, Michigan State University, 1973), p. 132.

Figure 6.1. McCormick Reaper Works plant, 1906, on the West Side along the South Branch of the Chicago River. The huge plant, as part of International Harvester, continued in operation for about another half century after this photograph was taken. (Photograph courtesy Chicago Historical Society.)

Chapter Six

THE ECONOMY OF CHICAGO

Early Industry

On one of the great buildings at the World's Columbian Exposition of 1893 in Chicago was inscribed the statement by Lord Bacon that three things make an area "great and prosperous: a fertile soil, busy workshops, and easy transportation for men and goods from place to place." Chicago fits this description.

A century and a half ago Chicago was a small trading and military post. Buoyed by its excellent geographic location in a growing area, it soon evolved into a bustling lake and river port, then into a canal terminal and railroad center, and into a major commercial and distribution center. The city's industries developed more slowly at first but generally paralleled its commercial development, and Chicago grew from a small manufacturing city a century ago to the nation's second-largest industrial center. Today, it is the nation's leading producer of a variety of items ranging from snuff to steel. Moreover, Chicago's location is such that within a 500-mile (804.5 km) radius of the Loop are found about 33 percent of the nation's wholesale and retail trade, 40 percent of its manufacturing, and 30 percent of its population.

The earliest industries of Chicago—milling, meat packing, tanning, and woodworking—were closely related to the products of the surrounding fields and forests. Other industries arose in response to the need of the area's growing population for printed matter, household utensils, clothing, wagons, boat supplies, building materials, and quarry products.

Chicago early developed a lucrative symbiotic relationship with its rich hinterland. It received, processed, and distributed the products of the farms; it also produced and sent back to the farms clothing, furniture, and agricultural machinery and implements.

One of Chicago's earliest major industries was the farm machinery company (the forerunner of International Harvester) established by Cyrus McCormick in 1847 on the north bank of the Chicago River on the present site of the Equitable Building. After the Chicago Fire of 1871, an enlarged McCormick Works was built on the West Side near Blue Island and Western (2400 W) avenues where it flourished for almost a century. It closed in 1961, having been supplanted by International Harvester plants in the suburbs, in other parts of the country, and indeed throughout the world.

Business directories show that in Chicago in 1856 the largest group of related firms, some 86, were in food processing, meat packing, and industries using animal by-products such as leather. The printing industry ranked second, with 65 firms; next, with more than

50 firms each, came the textile-garment-millinery industry and the building trades industry. The latter included brickyards, planing mills, lumberyards, and door and sash factories.

Certain industrial location patterns were already apparent. The area north of the river contained the fewest factories. Those that were there included the McCormick Reaper and Mower Works and a number of breweries which clustered in this area because of its large German population. The present downtown area, south and east of the river, contained the printing industry and numerous handicraft industries, such as dressmaking, shoemaking, tailoring, and cigar manufacturing. West of the river, on the Near West Side, were numerous metal-using and metal-manufacturing firms.

Many of the early industries congregated along transportation routes—first along the waterways, later along the railroads. Lumber, grain, and tannery facilities were concentrated along the Chicago River. More than 500 acres (202.5 ha) of land between Halsted Street and Western Avenue along the South Branch of the Chicago River became the largest lumber distribution center in the world. The lumberyards, stocked from Wisconsin, Michigan, and Canadian forests, supplied the booming home building and furniture industries of the city and the needs of the prairie farmers. Today a residual maze of tracks and lumber slips still occupy the area—but there are few lumberyards and Chicago's importance as a furniture mart has declined.

In 1867 manufacturing in the Chicago area was described as follows:

> At first Chicago began to make on a small scale the rough and heavy implements of husbandry. That great factory, for example, which now produces an excellent farm wagon every seven minutes of every working day, was founded twenty-three years ago by its proprietor investing all his capital in the slow construction of one wagon. At the present time, almost every article of much bulk used upon railroads, in farming, in warming houses, in

building houses, or in cooking, is made in Chicago. Three thousand persons are now employed there in manufacturing coarse boots and shoes. The prairie world is mowed and reaped by machines made in Chicago, whose people are feeling their way, too, into making woolen and cotton goods. Four or five miles out on the prairie, where until last May the ground had never been broken since the creation, there now stands the village of Austin, which consists of three large factory buildings, forty or fifty nice cottages for workmen and two thousand young trees. This is the seat of the Chicago Clock Factory. . . . A few miles farther back on the prairies, at Elgin, there is the establishment of the National Watch Company, which expects soon to produce fifty watches a day. . . . They are beginning to make pianos at Chicago, besides selling a hundred a week of those made in the East; and the great music house of Root and Cady are now engraving and printing all the music they publish. Melodeons are made in Chicago on a great scale.[1]

The Union Stock Yards

Probably the most famous of Chicago's older industries were the stockyards. Originally there were a number of small stockyards scattered throughout the city. Growing up with these stockyards were small handicraft shops, dependent on by-products from meat packing, which produced shoes, gloves, saddles, soap, candles, and glue. Some of the tanneries that grew in conjunction with nearby meat packing still exist on the North Branch of the Chicago River around Goose Island.

By the 1860s the scattered stockyards were too small and inefficient to handle the increasing numbers of animals shipped to Chicago with its growing market and unexcelled means of distribution. Furthermore, as the city grew, the stockyards became an undesirable source of odor and sanitation problems within the city proper.

The scattered stockyards were consolidated in 1865 when a consortium of nine railroads joined with packing interests to establish the Union Stock Yards. At the time the huge yards were located outside the Chicago city

Figure 6.2. The Union Stock Yards, about 1905, looking west on Exchange Avenue, with sheep being driven to the slaughter pens. After more than a century of operation the yards closed in 1971. (Photograph courtesy Chicago Historical Society.)

limits, south of 39th Street and west of Halsted Street. They eventually occupied about a square mile (2.59 sq km) of land, with numerous related companies developing on the periphery.

Almost from the start, the stockyards were the largest and busiest in the world, and Chicago became the meat capital of the world. A peak was reached in the years soon after World War I, when the yards employed over 30,000 people and received nearly 19 million head of livestock annually.

The Union Stock Yards in itself was almost a city, with its own newspaper, bank, "Board of Trade," electric plant, water wells, post office, inn, office building, fire department, amphitheater, and canal. But mainly the yards consisted of thousands of pens in the eastern part and the big packing plants in the western Packingtown section—Armour, Swift, Wilson, Cudahy, and Libby, McNeil & Libby. The yards were interlaced by dozens of miles of railroad tracks with trains delivering the animals, miles of overhead ramps for the circulation of the animals within the yards, and a branch of the city's elevated line to transport the workers.

The stockyards, in one way, were a model of efficiency, for it was claimed that only the squeal of the hog was wasted. As "Mr. Dooley," the famed fictional character created by Chicago's Finley Peter Dunne, put it:

A cow goes lowin' softly into Armour's an' comes out gelatin, fertylizer, celooloid, joolry, sofy cushions, hair restorer, washin' sody,

Figure 6.3. The smoking Union Stock Yards' meat packing plants, about 1912, looking eastward across a cabbage patch near Ashland Avenue. Upton Sinclair had exposed conditions in the stockyards in his book *The Jungle,* published in 1906. (Photograph courtesy Chicago Historical Society.)

soap, lithrachoor an' bed springs so quick that while aft she's still cow, for'ard she may be anything fr'm buttons to pannyma hats.

The Union Stock Yards for years was the city's greatest employer. Hundreds of thousands of European immigrants and later blacks from the South found employment there. A number of future mayors worked there also. But the stockyards also at one time contained horrifying unsanitary working conditions, which were exposed by Upton Sinclair in *The Jungle,* and they were surrounded by shoddy, often stench-filled neighborhoods such as the old Back-of-the-Yards area.

The stockyards declined rapidly after World War II. By then the yards were in the geographic center of Chicago, with its congestion and high taxes. There were labor problems, and a trend toward the decentralization of the packing industry was discernible. Furthermore, the yards' facilities had become obsolete since they had been designed to be served by railroads and most animals were now being shipped by truck. In 1971, after 106 years of service, the Union Stock Yards closed, although a few small meat product plants still exist on the periphery of the former stockyards. In recent years the city and industrial developers have greatly improved the street network on the land previously occupied by the yards. Today the land is occupied by numerous new, one-story, small plants with a great variety of activities, but virtually none of them is related to meat packing.

Pullman

Until the 1860s Chicago industry produced mainly for the local market and the market of the surrounding farm area. The requirements of the Civil War, however, helped to propel Chicago into the larger national market. After the Civil War, the city's industrial expansion continued uabated through an era of great technological advances and industrial consolidation. Manufacturing rapidly surpassed commerce in importance in the city's economy and became the dominant source of employment.

A variety of new industries developed in Chicago, one of the most important being the manufacture of railway equipment. Chicago provided many attractions for this industry; it was already the railroad center of the nation, and it offered, as well, a growing steel industry and a central location.

Foremost among the numerous railroad equipment manufacturers was the company founded by George Pullman, the inventor of the sleeping car. Its operations were unique, not only in size, but in being centered in a privately constructed "total community" erected in the early 1880s on the west shore of Lake Calumet, a dozen miles (19.3 km) south of downtown Chicago. The bold and original new model town, designed by the architect Solan S. Beman, occupied over 3,500 acres (1,417.5 ha) of once swampy land and housed the factories of the Pullman Palace Car Company as well as its workers. Pullman was a company town, but it was one of the first to be totally planned—and exceptionally well planned for its time, gaining for the community an international reputation.

Using some of the mass production techniques that had made his railroad car company the prosperous giant of the field, Pullman erected 1,400 residential units and all of the facilities of a self-contained community—a shopping center, church, theater, library, firehouse, school, hotel, and bank. The houses, all of brick and with indoor plumbing, were of three categories for the various levels of em-

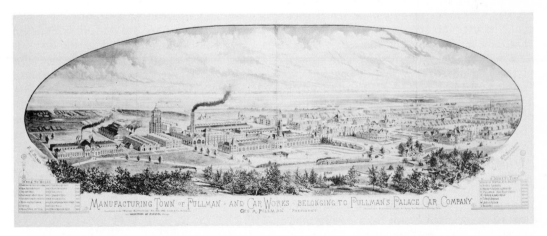

Figure 6.4. Pullman, in the 1880s, looking eastward. In the distance is Lake Calumet. Some of the prominent landmarks, such as the water tower (left), the small lake (center), and the Arcade (right), are no longer in existence and the Illinois Central tracks have been raised. But many other prominent features, such as the clock tower (center) and the Florence Hotel and Greenstone Church (both right of center), are still in existence. (Illustration courtesy Chicago Historical Society.)

ployees: fine single-family homes for the executives, and row houses and block houses (tenements) for the bulk of the workers. In 1884 some 8,000 people resided in the community, which was largely concentrated in the area now bounded by 103rd and 115th streets and by Lake Calumet and Cottage Grove Avenue.

The factories were separated from the residences, and the community was beautifully landscaped with gardens, parks, and even a small artificial lake. Many of these features were forerunners of modern suburban developments. Pragmatism was the principle of the planning. Bricks for the Pullman community were baked from clay dredged from the bottom of adjacent Lake Calumet. Steam from the plants heated some of the homes. And the sewage from the community was converted into fertilizer and then pumped to a company farm just south of Pullman. This 175-acre (70.9 ha) farm provided vegetables for the town market.

George Pullman designed his community to be clean, decent, beautiful, and modestly priced, but at the same time to be profitable in all aspects. He tried to increase sobriety and godliness in his workers by banning all taverns (except for one in the Florence Hotel that could be used by the executives). He purchased the surrounding land and kept it vacant as a buffer against the encroachment of any of the vices of society. Such a community, Pullman believed, would attract the finest craftsmen of Europe. He believed also that its advantages and surroundings would make "better workmen by removing from them the feeling of discontent and desire for change which so generally characterizes the American workman, thus protecting the employer from the loss of time and money consequent upon intemperance, labor strikes, and dissatisfaction which generally result from poverty and uncongenial home surroundings."

Pullman's paternalism, however, made some workers resentful. One worker said: "We were born in a Pullman house, fed from a Pullman shop, taught in a Pullman school, catechized in the Pullman church, and when we die we shall be buried in the Pullman cemetery and go to a Pullman hell!" When the depression of 1893 brought the curtailment of railway car orders, Pullman severely cut the pay of his workers but did not lower their rent or food prices. The following year the bitterness of the workers culminated in a prolonged and violent strike that also curtailed railroad operations. The strike ended only after President Cleveland sent in federal troops to move the mail.

The town was never the same after the strike. Annexation by the city of Chicago a few years earlier had already started a change in the private character of the town. Then an Illinois Supreme Court order of 1898 forced Pullman to sell the town because it was "opposed to good public policy and incompatible with the theories and spirit of our constitution." Most of the homes were sold to the Pullman workers.

Today, the basic pattern and the homes of this century-old, sturdily-built community remain largely intact, although time has wrought its changes. The population has dropped to about half of what it was at its peak; the operations of the Pullman Company have long been drastically curtailed and many of its facilities are utilized by other companies; a few new structures are evident, but some of the famous landmarks, such as the lake, the water tower, and the Arcade are gone. However, over 90 percent of the residences are still there, as is the Greenstone Church, the Florence Hotel, and the administrative clock tower. And they should continue to be there for a long time as Pullman has been declared a National Historic Landmark. There are also very active civic and historic organizations working hard at preserving and restoring the community.

Present Industry

In this century the Chicago area's industrial growth has been so rapid that it now ranks second among United States metropolitan areas in the number of manufacturing employees. In 1980 the area had about 3.5

TABLE 6.1
Manufacturing Employment and Sales in Metropolitan Chicago

Manufacturing Industry	Employment			Gross Manufacturers' Sales (millions of dollars)		
	1979	1974	% Change	1979	1974	% Increase
Primary Metals	128,000	142,000	− 9.9%	$16,328	$ 9,656	69.1%
Electrical Machinery	126,000	147,000	−14.3	9,463	6,157	53.7
Non-electrical Machinery	123,000	125,000	− 1.6	8,645	5,981	44.5
Fabricated Metals	113,000	114,000	− 0.8	8,272	6,752	22.5
Printing and Publishing	83,000	89,000	− 6.7	5,264	3,989	32.0
Food and Kindred Products	74,000	80,000	− 7.5	10,249	7,964	28.7
Chemical and Allied Products	55,000	53,000	+ 3.8	6,817	4,748	43.6
Transportation Equipment	37,000	33,000	+12.1	4,190	2,176	92.6
Instruments and Related Products	36,000	33,000	+ 9.1	2,256	1,351	67.0
Rubber and Plastic Products	34,000	32,000	+ 6.3	1,633	1,110	47.1
Paper and Allied Products	29,000	31,000	− 6.4	2,209	1,566	41.1
Stone, Clay, and Glass Products	21,000	21,000	0.0	1,771	1,020	73.7
Apparel and Textiles	19,000	25,000	−24.0	887	770	15.2
Furniture and Fixtures	18,000	24,000	−25.0	828	813	1.8
Petroleum and Coal Products	14,000	16,000	−12.5	7,147	4,162	71.7
Lumber and Wood Products	9,000	8,000	+12.5	511	295	73.2
Leather and Leather Products	4,000	7,000	−42.9	182	117	55.6
Miscellaneous Manufacturing	29,000	31,000	− 6.5	1,430	1,120	27.7
TOTAL	952,000	1,011,000	− 5.8%	$88,082	$59,747	47.4%

Source: Chicago Association of Commerce and Industry.

million workers. Of these 919,000 were engaged in manufacturing; 779,000 were in wholesale and retail trade; 677,000 in service; 490,000 in government; 230,000 in finance, insurance, and real estate; 210,000 in transportation and public utilities; 130,000 in construction; and the remainder in a variety of other occupations. Service-producing, white-collar employment has shown the greatest gains in recent years, while employment in manufacturing has declined from over a million (table 6.1). There are, however, decided yearly fluctuations due to changing economic conditions.

During this century, the location, facilities, and products of Chicago's industry have changed greatly. The leading products of the pre-World War I period—meat packing, men's clothing, furniture, agricultural implements, and railway equipment—have declined in relative importance. At the same time, Chicago's industrial base has undergone widespread and healthy diversification until today it includes almost every kind of industry. In addition to industrial diversification, its strong commercial, transportation, service, and government employment components give the area one of the most diversified and best balanced economies in the nation, and usually make it less vulnerable than many other areas to recessions.

Metropolitan Chicago is the nation's leading producer of radios, television sets, telephone equipment, electrical machinery, and household appliances. Such companies as Motorola, Zenith, Sunbeam, Bell and Howell, and McGraw-Edison have their headquarters here. They represent just one facet of the 10 percent of the nation's largest corporations that are headquartered in Chicago and its suburbs.

Table 6.1 shows Chicago's manufacturing ranked on the basis of employment and sales. Chicago is usually the nation's leading producer in many of these fields, including steel, metal wares, confectionery products, surgical appliances, railroad engines and equipment, soap, paint, cosmetics, cans, industrial machinery, commercial printing, and sports goods. To supply these industries, millions of tons of iron ore, coal, chemicals, petroleum, lumber, paper and farm products are brought into the area annually. To meet the increasing energy needs of the area, Commonwealth Edison Company in recent years has greatly expanded its generating capacity, including the addition of three nuclear power plants producing more nuclear power than any other utility in the nation. The plants are at Zion on Lake Michigan, Cordova (Quad Cities plant) on the Mississippi River, and near Morris, Illinois (Dresden plant) on the Illinois River. Over 40 percent of the company's energy generation is now nuclear power. When three other nuclear power plants—at Byron, Seneca, and Braidwood, Illinois—come into operation, the proportion of energy from nuclear power will increase to about 60 percent of the total.

Table 6.2 shows the largest private employers in the Chicago area in 1975—those employing 1,000 or more workers. The list reveals the diversity of Chicago enterprise, for only half of the largest private employers are manufacturers. The list includes fourteen financial and insurance companies, twelve universities and hospitals, ten retailers, nine transportation companies, and six public utilities. Unlike some cities, Chicago's employment is not dominated by one or just a few giant companies. The 119 employers listed in table 6.2 have a total of approximately 650,000 workers, with the top ten employers accounting for only about one-third of the total number of workers.

The average employment in all Metropolitan Chicago business establishments is 233 employees, up from 170 employees in 1962. Since 1962 more than half a million jobs have been added to the Chicago area's private sector employment, and investment in industrial plants and equipment has exceeded that of any

TABLE 6.2
Chicago's Major Private Employers 1975*
(In Order of Chicago Metropolitan Area Employment)

Rank	Company	Chicago Area Employees	Rank	Company	Chicago Area Employees
1.	United States Steel	40,000	15.	Electro-Motive Division, General Motors Corporation	10,000
2.	Illinois Bell Telephone	35,812	16.	FMC Corporation	10,000
3.	Sears Roebuck and Company	30,000	17.	Walgreen Company	9,650
4.	Inland Steel Company	25,900	18.	Illinois Central Industries	8,800
5.	Jewel Companies	21,865	19.	National Tea Company	8,500
6.	International Harvester	19,932	20.	Continental Illinois National Bank and Trust	8,291
7.	Western Electric Company	15,165	21.	Ford Motor Company	8,200
8.	Marcor	15,000	22.	Standard Oil Company (Indiana)	8,100
9.	Commonwealth Edison	14,956	23.	Beatrice Foods	8,000
10.	University of Chicago	14,700	24.	Motorola	7,500
11.	Marshall Field and Company	14,500	25.	Outboard Marine Corporation Central District	7,000
12.	Zenith Radio Corporation	12,200	26.	United States Industries	6,500
13.	United Air Lines	10,500			
14.	General Telephone and Electric Corporation, Automatic Electric	10,020			

Source: *Commerce*, Chicago Association of Commerce and Industry, May 1975, pp. 43-50, 78.

*Some Chicago area employers with 1,000 or more employees are not listed because pertinent information was not available.

TABLE 6.2 (continued)

Rank	Company	Chicago Area Employees	Rank	Company	Chicago Area Employees
27.	CNA Financial	6,000	74.	Danly Machine Corporation	2,090
28.	Carson Pirie Scott and Company	6,000	75.	Wm. Wrigley, Jr. Company	2,064
29.	J. C. Penney Company	6,000	76.	Walter E. Heller, International	2,054
30.	Continental Can Company	6,000	77.	Bunker Ramo Corporation	2,043
31.	First Chicago Corporation	5,868	78.	Sherwin-Williams Company	2,000
32.	Northern Indiana Public Service Corporation	5,628	79.	General American Transporation Corporation	2,000
33.	Hart Schaffner and Marx	5,600	80.	Barber-Greene Company	2,000
34.	Spiegel	5,527	81.	Chicago Rawhide Manufacture Company	1,950
35.	Borg-Warner Corporation	5,500	82.	Central Steel and Wire Company	1,940
36.	Allstate Insurance Companies	5,000	83.	Chicago Milwaukee Corporation	1,840
37.	Interlake	5,000	84.	Chicago Title and Trust Company	1,826
38.	Stewart Warner Corporation	5,000	85.	Mount Sinai Hospital	1,810
39.	W. F. Hall Printing Company	5,000	86.	Illinois Masonic Medical Center	1,800
40.	Bankers Life and Casualty Company	4,700	87.	National Steel Corporation	1,791
41.	Bell and Howell Company	4,700	88.	Nalco Chemical Company	1,700
42.	Peoples Gas Company	4,587	89.	Bell Laboratories	1,670
43.	General Dynamics Corporation Material Service Corporation	4,562	90.	Westinghouse Electric Company	1,600
44.	Michael Reese Hospital	4,300	91.	National Can Corporation	1,600
45.	Allis-Chalmers Corporation	4,200	92.	Saint Francis Hospital	1,600
46.	Illinois Tool Works	4,000	93.	Campbell Soup Company	1,600
47.	Loyola University of Chicago	3,800	94.	American National Bank and Trust Company of Chicago	1,533
48.	YMCA of Metropolitan Chicago	3,800	95.	Oscar Mayer and Company	1,500
49.	Yellow Cab Company	3,500	96.	Washington National Corporation	1,490
50.	Prudential Insurance Company	3,500	97.	Edgewater Hospital	1,450
51.	Elaine Revell	3,500	98.	Alberto Culver Company	1,400
52.	American Airlines	3,400	99.	Schwinn Bicycle Company	1,395
53.	Sargent and Lundy	3,300	100.	Resurrection Hospital	1,361
54.	Northern Trust Company	3,144	101.	DeSoto, Incorporated	1,355
55.	Harris Bankcorp	3,024	102.	Memorial Hospital Du Page	1,350
56.	American Can Company	3 000	103.	Joslyn Manufacturing Company	1,350
57.	A. B. Dick Company	2,986	104.	Saint Joseph Hospital-Joliet	1,325
58.	Illinois Institute of Technology	2,900	105.	Sun Electric Corporation	1,323
59.	Northern Illinois Gas Company	2,862	106.	Wyman-Gordan Company	1,320
60.	Reynolds Metals Company	2,821	107.	Fansteel	1,300
61.	Amsted Industries	2,800	108.	Children's Memorial Hospital	1,300
62.	Universal Oil Products	2,650	109.	Libby, McNeill and Libby	1,300
63.	Victor Graphics Systems	2,580	110.	Central Telephone of Illinois	1,300
64.	Skil Corporation	2,500	111.	Commerce Clearing House	1,211
65.	American Hospital Supply	2,500	112.	Morton-Norwich Products	1,201
66.	Oak Industries	2,300	113.	Hillman's	1,200
67.	Baxter Laboratories	2,264	114.	Whiting Corporation	1,177
68.	Kemper Insurance Companies	2,263	115.	The Quaker Oats Company	1,157
69.	Trans World Airlines	2,200	116.	Playskool	1,050
70.	McGraw-Edison Company	2,200	117.	West Suburban Hospital	1,049
71.	Household Finance Corporation	2,184	118.	Chicago Bridge and Iron	1,000
72.	Sante Fe Industries	2,131	119.	Chemetron Corporation	1,000
73.	Burlington Northern	2,097			

Figure 6.5. Aerial view of Goose Island, about 1925. This 160 acre island was created in the 1850s when the North Branch Canal was dug from Chicago Avenue to North Avenue through low-lying clay pits—thus, creating more waterway frontage and short-circuiting the bend in the North Branch of the Chicago River. Before being taken over almost completely by railroads and factories, including a number of tanneries that followed some early packing plants, the island in the last century contained the cottages and cabbage patches of over 500 immigrant families, mainly Irish. Many of the men of the island served in the police and fire departments, as ward bosses, and one, William E. Dever, became mayor of Chicago. Halsted Street crosses the southeastern tip of the island and Division Street bisects it in an east-west direction. (Photograph courtesy Chicago Historical Society.)

other metropolitan area in the nation. Twenty-three of *Fortune's* 500 largest companies are now headquartered in Chicago and others are in its suburbs.

Traditionally, industrial location in the Chicago area was concentrated along the rivers and railroads, more on the South and West sides than on the North Side which was more residential than the others. In recent years there has been increasing industrial develop-

ment near expressways, near O'Hare International Airport, and in organized industrial districts. A growing proportion of the area's industrial establishments, including numerous concerns once situated in the inner city, is now found outside the city proper. The area between downtown and the suburbs in recent years has lost heavily in factories and jobs—mainly those of blue-collar workers and especially on the West and South sides of the

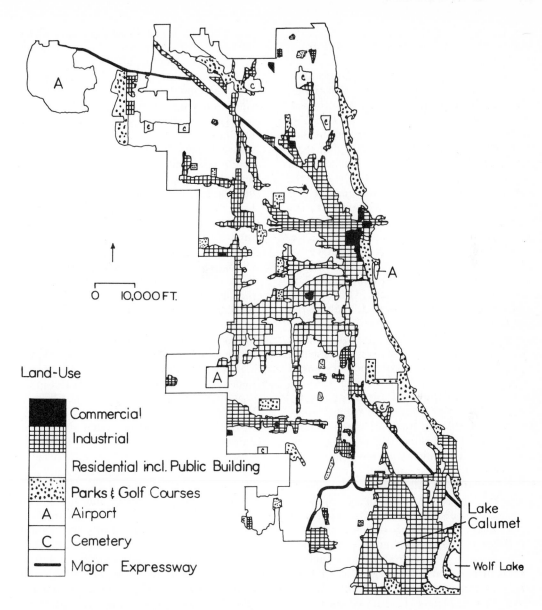

Figure 6.6. Land use in Chicago, 1960. Residential areas also include commercial streets. (From Ying Cheng Kiang, *Chicago,* 1968.)

city. Declining population and jobs led to the loss of 5,000 of Chicago's shops and stores in the 1970s.

More than one-third of the approximately 15,000 manufacturers and over half of the industrial jobs in the metropolitan area are now located outside the city limits of Chicago. Some suburban industries were established well before the turn of the century, but most are of recent origin, especially since World War II. The shift of industry to the suburbs is due to such factors as limited acreage and high land costs in Chicago, as well as to the general problems which plague most large cities today—congestion, plant obsolescence, high tax and insurance rates, inadequate tax base, political uncertainties, insensitive government, crime, poor schools, racial conflict, labor problems, and pollution. Although the suburbs are not free from these difficulties, the problems are usually less severe. Furthermore, many suburban areas can still offer large tracts of vacant land at relatively reasonable cost—land that meets modern industry's need for expansive one-story plants and acres of parking and landscaping. Railroad and water sites, in which Chicago excels, are not as essential to increasingly truck-oriented industry.

Chicago has also lost jobs to small towns and the Sun Belt which often have the advantage of certain living amenities, as well as lower expenses, usually in regard to land, taxes, and wages. Increased foreign competition has cost jobs, as has also the lack of a proportionate share of U.S. defense contracts.

Chicago-area communities employing large numbers of industrial workers include Cicero, Bedford Park, Waukegan, North Chicago, Aurora, Melrose Park, Joliet, Skokie, Elgin, Chicago Heights, and La Grange in Illinois and Gary, Hammond, East Chicago, and Whiting in adjacent northwestern Indiana. In the post-World War II period there was a strong movement of industry to the north, northwest, and west suburban areas based probably on good transportation, desirable environmental factors, and minimal racial problems. More recently, lower-priced and sizable tracts of land and improved transportation in the south and southwest suburbs have made that area more attractive for industrial plants. Increasingly, suburbanites have been able to earn their livelihood in the suburbs, with only about one-third now commuting to Chicago for their work.

The industrial migration out of the city has hurt Chicago's economic base and increased unemployment among the city's poorly educated and unskilled, especially the blacks and Hispanics. These groups find it difficult to take on jobs in the suburban areas far from their residences in the inner city, although reverse commuting from the city to the suburbs is increasing. More jobs are now found in the surrounding metropolitan area than in Chicago itself. In fact, Metropolitan Chicago has more jobs than ever; however, their location has changed significantly. In 1960 over 60 percent of manufacturing employment was in Chicago; in 1980 such employment had dropped to about 40 percent. Some of the suburban industry is new, but much has relocated from Chicago causing a net loss of jobs there. Some 211,000 industrial jobs were lost in Chicago in the 1960s, with the biggest losses on the West Side and Near South Side. In contrast, the suburban area gained 500,000 jobs during that period. During the 1960s also, Chicago lost almost 2,000 manufacturing establishments, while the suburbs gained about that many. In the 1970s Chicago lost another one-fourth of its factories and another one-fifth of its manufacturing jobs. The number of manufacturing jobs in the city has been declining at an average rate of about 20,000 jobs a year. One result of declining manufacturing jobs is that about 20 percent of Chicago's population, mainly concentrated in minority groups, receive some kind of public aid. Twenty years ago only 7 percent of the city's people were on welfare.

Wholesale and Retail Trade

The dollar volume of the Chicago area's wholesale trade equals that of its manufacturing industries. Chicago is a principal market for grain, machine tools, produce, fish, and

Figure 6.7. Randolph Street at Haymarket Square, 1892, looking westward toward Halsted Street. This area still serves as a wholesale and retail produce market. The statue of the policeman in the right foreground commemorates the seven policemen who were killed during the Haymarket Riot of 1886. After two bombings of the statue in recent years, the statue was removed and eventually housed in the police training center. (Photograph courtesy Chicago Historical Society.)

flowers. Its giant Merchandise Mart contains the displays—mainly furniture and home furnishings—of 5,000 manufacturers and designers. Across the street from the Merchandise Mart is the Apparel Center, which opened in 1977. There, more than 4,000 lines of men's, women's, and children's apparel are shown. For the convenience of the buyers, the upper floors of the building contain a Holiday Inn.

The Chicago Board of Trade and the Chicago Mercantile Exchange are among the world's largest commodity markets. They have pioneered many new market concepts. The area's advantages as a distribution center have also helped make it the home headquarters of four of the nation's largest mail order concerns—Sears, Montgomery Ward, Spiegel, and Aldens.

Because of its huge wholesale trade, its accessibility, and its facilities, Chicago has long ranked as the nation's convention capital. About 1,500 conventions and trade shows are held annually, bringing into the city nearly $900 million. To accommodate the annual influx of well over 2 million conventioneers and buyers, Chicago offers 250 hotels and motels, 4,000 restaurants, and numerous exhibition facilities, including the giant McCormick

Figure 6.8. South Water Street, 1905. Located between Lake Street and the main stem of the Chicago River, this was the wholesale produce market of Chicago until it was closed in 1925 to make way for the construction of Wacker Drive. The market was moved about three miles to the southwest around 14th Street and Blue Island Avenue and thus eliminated some downtown traffic. Today the newer facility is also obsolete and hopelessly congested. (Photograph courtesy Chicago Historical Society.)

Place. In recent years many hotels and motels with convention and business meeting facilities have opened in the O'Hare Airport area and in the area just north of the Loop.

Chicago's facilities and location have helped attract the national headquarters of 731 associations with paid staffs totaling 12,000 and an annual budget of about $200,000,000. Among the larger associations headquartered in the city are the American Medical Association, American Dental Association, American Bar Association, American Library Association, National Restaurant Association, American Marketing Association, and the American Public Works Association. Additionally, the headquarters of the three largest service organizations—Lions, Rotary, and Kiwanis—and two of the largest fraternal organizations—the Elks and the Polish National Alliance—are located in the area.

Another important aspect of the economy of Chicago is the retail trade, which generally grosses about half of the dollar volume of the wholesale trade. A hierarchy of retail areas

Figure 6.9. South Water Market looking east on 15th Street from Aberdeen Avenue, 1941. It is the major wholesale fruit and vegetable market in the city with annual sales of about $400,000,000. It opened in 1925 to replace the South Water Street market in downtown Chicago. The market consists essentially of six long buildings containing 166 virtually identical units. The advent of the long trailer truck has severely congested the market streets and brought periodic proposals for the construction of a new market. Both South Water Market and the Randolph Street Market have declined in importance partly due to obsolete facilities and also the advent of chain supermarkets which are usually their own wholesalers. South Water Market now mainly serves restaurants, hotels, hospitals, small retail chains, independent stores, and smaller wholesale markets of the region. (Photograph courtesy Chicago Historical Society.)

has developed in the city headed by downtown. The downtown area is followed by major outlying shopping areas that developed at major transit intersections (such as 63rd and Halsted, and Irving Park, Milwaukee and Cicero). The shopping areas scale downward to the strip developments along some streets, and finally to the little corner grocery stores. Many of these shopping facilities have experienced relative declines as the automobile, changing populations, and modern shopping centers have changed the old shopping patterns.

Organized Industrial Districts and Parks

Chicago has been a leader in a modern industrial trend—the development of the organized industrial district and its more modern version, the *industrial park*. These are planned developments designed to physically accommodate industries in a wholesome and functional relationship to each other and to the community, and to provide industries with such services as transportation, security, utilities, dining facilities, maintenance, financing, and architectural engineering. Industry is provided with a complete location package and usually can either rent or purchase the facility. The accelerating growth of such developments has countered the previous tendency of often locating industry indiscriminately throughout residential areas, a tendency which often resulted in blight.

Chicago's Union Stock Yards and Pullman were pioneering forerunners of organized industrial districts. One of the largest, the Central Manufacturing District, was begun in 1902 to develop a tract of land immediately north of the Union Stock Yards. This industrial development proved so successful that ten others, containing a total of over 300 industrial plants, have been established by the same company in the Chicago Metropolitan Area. The CMD industrial parks now include developments toward the fringe of the metropolitan area in Itasca, St. Charles, and Aurora.

The Clearing Industrial District was established by the railroads in 1909 in Bedford Park, just south of today's Midway Airport. The company operated ten separate industrial tracts containing over 275 plants in the southern and western fringes of the city and in some suburbs before being fragmented by the sale of industrial parks. By 1975 the Chicago area had 354 industrial districts. Table 6.3 shows their distribution.

The biggest growth in recent years of industrial parks has been in northern Cook County, especially in the vicinity of O'Hare Airport and Schaumburg and to a lesser extent in the Oak Brook-Lisle-Naperville area in Du

TABLE 6.3
Chicago Area Industrial Parks 1975*

	Number of Industrial Parks 1975	Total Number of Acres of Land in Parks 1975
City of Chicago	36	3,539
Suburban Cook County, Illinois	156	15,341
North Cook	75	8,523
West Cook	32	1,556
South Cook	49	5,262
Du Page County, Illinois	56	11,269
Kane County, Illinois	34	5,796
Lake County, Illinois	25	2,866
McHenry County, Illinois	2	313
Will County, Illinois	28	8,751
Lake County, Indiana	15	3,063
Porter County, Indiana	2	287
CHICAGO METROPOLITAN AREA	354	51,225

Commerce, Chicago Association of Commerce and Industry, July, 1975, p. 62.

Page County. These areas contain prestigious industrial and office complexes, and are near prime residential areas. Unlike the older railway-oriented organized industrial districts, these parks are mainly expressway-oriented. Lincolnwood, Skokie, Morton Grove, and Niles north of Chicago also contain numerous high status industrial parks. One of the newer parks, Tam-O-Shanter Industrial Fairways in Niles, is built on nine holes of a former championship golf course. Sites in some of the most desirable parks are selling for over $100,000 an acre ($40,500 per ha). Lake and Kane counties in Illinois have also had a rapid recent growth in industrial parks, as have parts of south Cook County where low land costs and an expanded expressway network have been attractions.

The largest industrial park in the Chicago area is Centex Industrial Park, begun in 1956, northwest of O'Hare Airport. Unlike earlier industrial districts, Centex is part of a larger complex, Elk Grove Village, which includes planned residential and commercial areas as well as industrial sections. In the original Centex Industrial Park about 600 plants (plus another 400 in other adjacent industrial parks) conform to the modern trend of well-landscaped one-story buildings with adequate parking facilities for the automobile-oriented workers. As in other developments, the industries are mainly of a light manufacturing or service nature.

In the city of Chicago, industrial parks have recently been proposed or partially developed in such areas as the former Stock Yards, Goose Island, Pullman-Lake Calumet, the former West Side site of International Harvester, and the southwestern part of the Humboldt Park community.

The Calumet Industrial Complex

The heavy industry of the Chicago area is confined largely to the extreme southeastern part of the city and eastward around the southern end of Lake Michigan beyond Gary to the new Burns Harbor development. In Chicago the six miles (9.7 km) along the Calumet River from its mouth to Lake Calumet contains one of the great industrial complexes of the world. The river is lined with a maze of steel plants, grain elevators, shipping facilities, chemical plants, and other enterprises.

Industry began its development on a large scale in the Calumet area about a century ago. Available at low cost were large tracts of vacant, swampy, and sandy land near plenty of fresh water, and strategically located near a great and growing market, but outside the urban areas. The lake, rivers, and railroads offered virtually unexcelled transportation.

A variety of heavy industries developed. Oil refineries concentrated around Whiting, Indiana, making it one of the largest inland refinery areas in the world. Major producers of railway equipment were scattered throughout the area, including plants of Pullman, Union Tank Car, and General American Transportation. Huge soap, paint, chemical, and cement plants were constructed. Some of these plants are related to the Calumet area's main industry—steel. The Calumet Industrial Complex is the nation's leading steel producing area and one of the greatest steel centers in the world. Its production, averaging about 27 million tons annually, is greater than that of Britain, France, or the Ruhr District of Germany and constitutes about 22 percent of United States steel production.

Chicago's steel industry was originally located north of downtown on Goose Island in the Chicago River. Later it moved to South Chicago, where it spread out along both the Lake Michigan shore and the Calumet River. It also expanded into the sand dune and swamp area of adjacent Lake County, Indiana, and in the 1960s, farther eastward along the lake into Porter County, Indiana. The area's accessibility by low-cost water transportation to the Lake Superior iron ore ranges has been a major advantage.

Today there are nine operating steel plants in the area owned by seven different companies. Two of these plants rank among the largest in the nation. They are the Inland Steel plant established in 1901 on the east side of the Indiana Harbor Canal in East Chicago and jutting a mile and a half (2.4 km) out into the lake on artificial landfill, and the Gary Works of U.S. Steel, on miles of former duneland on the southern shore of Lake Michigan. The establishment of the Gary Works led to the founding of the city of Gary in 1906 and the city's subsequent rapid growth. Today it is Indiana's third largest city. In the 1960s Midwest Steel and Bethlehem Steel were established in the dunes east of Gary in the Burns Harbor area. The Bethlehem Steel plant, according to some plans, will eventually become the largest integrated steel plant in the nation.

BIRDSEYE VIEW OF SOUTH CHICAGO---CALUMET HARBOR.

1. South Chicago Hotel.
2. Site Sinclair's Woolen Mills, & Kent, Baldwin & Co.'s Machinery Manufactory.
3. Railroad Station Buildings of Pittsburgh & Fort Wayne and Michigan Sonthern Railroads.
4. Location of Docks, Rolling Mills, Blast Furnaces, Elevators, Saw Mills, Etc.
5. Location of Ship Yard Dock.
6. Location of Cotton Mills.
7. Location of proposed Ship Canal to Lake Calumet.
8. Casgrain House.
9. Office of Calumet and Chicago Canal & Dock Co.
10. South Chicago Planing Mill and Lumber Yard.
11. Lake Calumet---three miles long and navigable for reach.
12. Congregational and Lutheran Church.
13. United States Government Engineer's Office.
14. United States Light House.

Figure 6.10. The Calumet River and Harbor, from an engraving originally published in 1874. (Illustration courtesy Chicago Historical Society.)

Figure 6.11. Aerial view looking northward from about 92nd Street and the Calumet River, 1936. The area shown is mainly the community of South Chicago. Along the lake from the Calumet River to 79th Street is the South Works of the United States Steel Corporation. Northwest of the plant, in the upper left, is the neighboring community of South Shore. (Photograph courtesy Chicago Historical Society.)

Despite the construction of new steel plants, the expansion of most of the older steel mills, and the installation of the newest technology, including continuous casting and the basic oxygen process, the Chicago area often required more steel than it produced. Its steel plants were sometimes unable to meet fully the varied demands of the 15,000 manufacturing plants in the Chicago area and the thousands more in Chicago's hinterland, including nu-merous automobile plants. However, in recent years due to a variety of economic and technological reasons and foreign competition, the steel industry has not been operating near capacity and there have been layoffs and the closing of some marginal facilities.

The steel industry has been a major employer in the Chicago area and its presence has undoubtedly aided the establishment of

Figure 6.12. View of part of Calumet industrial area of northwestern Indiana, looking northward, 1936. In the upper right is the Indiana Harbor area of East Chicago with the Y-shaped Indiana Harbor Canal. To the west of the mouth of the canal is the Youngstown Sheet and Tube Company Plant (now Jones and Laughlin Steel), and on the eastern bank is the western tip of the giant Inland Steel Company plant, which extends almost two miles into the lake on an artificial peninsula. In the center are the oil refineries and storage tanks of East Chicago and Whiting, with the latter being to the north near the lake and containing the huge facilities of the Standard Oil Company (Indiana). On the extreme left is the city of Hammond. (Photograph, Chicago Aerial Survey. Courtesy Chicago Historical Society.)

many other industries. But the older steel mills helped bring appalling air and water pollution; dirt and grime and congestion blighted the surrounding areas. Only in recent years, under public pressure, have strenuous efforts been made that have successfully reversed some of the conditions that had led to numerous air pollution alerts. The noxious air conditions were aggravated not only by the emissions of industrial plants and power generating stations but also by space heating and especially by the millions of motor vehicles in the area.

Figure 6.13. South Works of United States Steel Corporation along the Calumet River looking northeast from the 92nd Street Bridge. The almost 600-acre plant has been in South Chicago for over a century. (Photograph, Ted Farrington. Courtesy Chicago Historical Society.)

The Changing Role of the Central Business District

Downtown Chicago, where the city began, is now the heart of a great metropolitan area, but its structure and functions are changing rapidly. The elevated trains still encircle the Loop on their raised tracks as they have since 1897, but missing are the bustle of hundreds of boats on the river, the clanging of the old red streetcars, much of the manufacturing activity, the South Water Street produce market, and the stately residences of Michigan and Wabash avenues. In their place are the ubiquitous motor vehicle, the roaring subway, and the array of new office and residential high-rises, occasionally relieved by small plazas.

Chicago's downtown until recent years was relatively compact, circumscribed by physical barriers—to the east the lake, to the north and west the river, and to the south a maze of railroad facilities. Enhancing the area's importance was its position as the <u>hub</u> of one of the nation's greatest concentrations

Figure 6.14. Aerial view of Interlake's Riverdale, Illinois steel making facility in the bend of the Little Calumet River. The river separates Riverdale from Chicago. Hot metal is shipped to the Riverdale plant in torpedo cars from another company plant about five miles away in Chicago. (Photograph courtesy Interlake, Inc.)

of rail, waterway, and road transportation. It was also the focal point of the highly developed internal transit system of the city. For about half a century the downtown area even had a network of about sixty miles (96.5 km) of narrow-gauge freight railroad tracks located some forty feet (12.2 m) below the downtown streets. Over these tracks were carried coal, garbage, and mail, as well as a variety of freight between freight terminals and Loop buildings.

Lake Street, just south of the river and its wholesale activity, was the main commercial street of early Chicago, with the major commercial intersection at Lake and Clark streets. State Street—which was later to become "that great street"—was a narrow, muddy, shoddy street until Potter Palmer, one of Chicago's most successful retail, wholesale, and real estate entrepreneurs purchased three-quarters of a mile (1.2 km) of land along State Street. He quickly and dramatically used his

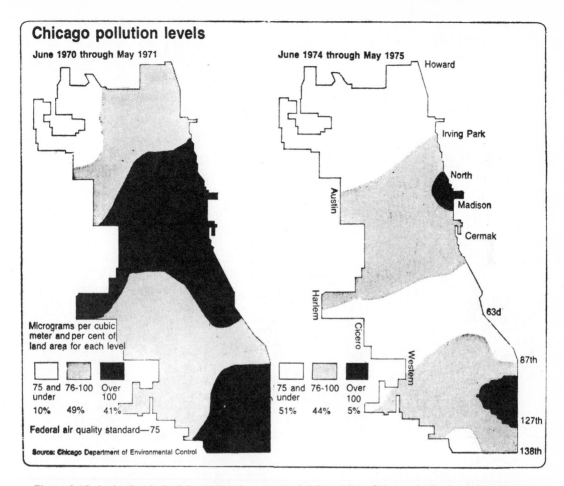

Chicago pollution levels

June 1970 through May 1971

June 1974 through May 1975

Howard

Irving Park

North

Madison

Cermak

Austin

Harlem

Cicero

Western

63d

87th

127th

138th

Micrograms per cubic meter and per cent of land area for each level

75 and under — 10%   76-100 — 49%   Over 100 — 41%

Federal air quality standard—75

75 and under — 51%   76-100 — 44%   Over 100 — 5%

Source: Chicago Department of Environmental Control

Figure 6.15. In the first half of the 1970s the amount of "dirty air" in Chicago declined considerably as shown by the comparative maps. In 1971 only 10 percent of the city's air met federal clean air standards of less than 75 micrograms of dust and soot particles per cubic meter. In 1975, 51 percent of the city met these standards; only 5 percent of the city's air was seriously polluted with dust and soot, mainly around Chicago's downtown area and near the South Side steel mills. Much of the improvement of the quality of the air was due to Chicago's clean air ordinance of 1970 which outlawed the use of dirty sulfur coal for heating purposes, controlled garbage incinerators, and banned open burning and leaf burning. (Courtesy *Chicago Tribune.*)

influence to have the street widened, drainage improved, public transportation instituted, and commercial structures erected, including a hotel bearing his name. He persuaded Field, Leiter and Company (the forerunner of the present Marshall Field & Company) to move from Lake Street to a new luxurious store on State Street. By the time of the Chicago Fire

of 1871, State Street was already Chicago's "main street."

Although State Street was completely gutted by the fire, it was quickly rebuilt on an even grander scale. The post-fire building boom helped to develop the modern skyscraper and the world-famous innovative Chicago School of Architecture which included Louis

Figure 6.16. The Auditorium Building at Michigan Avenue and Congress Parkway in about 1950. The building was designed by Adler and Sullivan and completed in 1889. It is one of Chicago's most famous cultural and architectural landmarks—and one that has been preserved. The building united hotel, offices, and an acoustically superb theater in one structure. After about a half century of full and profitable use the building went bankrupt in 1941. During World War II it was used by the United Service Organization and in 1946 the building became the home of Roosevelt University. With the aid of a public fund raising drive, the theater was restored to operation in 1967. (Photograph, Ralph Line. Courtesy Municipal Reference Library.)

Sullivan, Dankmar Adler, William Le Baron Jenney, John Wellborn Root, Henry Hobson Richardson, and more recently, Frank Lloyd Wright, Ludwig Mies van der Rohe, and Harry Weese. Among the monumental buildings erected in downtown Chicago in the late 1880s were the Auditorium, the Old Chicago Stock Exchange, the Carson Pirie Scott store, the Rookery building, and the Monadnock building. In 1891 Maitland's *Dictionary of* *American Slang* defined the new term *skyscraper* as "a very tall building such as are now being built in Chicago." These were the forerunners of today's high-rise buildings.

The fire also helped indirectly in the development of Chicago's impressive Grant Park (originally called Lake Park). Some of the debris from the fire was dumped into the lake along the original shoreline east of Michigan Avenue. This debris eventually formed the

Figure 6.17. State and Madison streets about 1905. The Louis Sullivan designed Carson Pirie Scott store is on the right, and the Mandel Brothers (Wieboldt's) store is on the opposite side of Madison Street. (Photograph courtesy Chicago Historical Society.)

base of much of the park, which today forms the attractive facade of Chicago's downtown area.

The commercial and manufacturing activities of the downtown area grew with the expansion of the city's population from a half million people in 1880 to well over 3 million a half century later. The growth in the activities of the downtown area was accompanied by a specialization of functions. What was probably the world's most concentrated shopping district, including a half dozen major department stores, stretched for almost a mile along State Street. The wholesale produce area was situated along the main stem of the river; La Salle Street became a major financial center; Market Street was the heart of the garment district; and entertainment facilities were spread along Randolph Street. Small enclaves contained concentrations of millinery, florist, furniture, music, and other specialty establishments. Multistory buildings used for light manufacturing were located to the west and to a lesser extent to the north of the downtown area.

Historically, retail expansion had been slow to develop north of the river, partly due to fear by the merchants south of the river of

Figure 6.18. State Street—"that great street"—looking north from Washington Street with Marshall Field's to the right and Marina City in the background. For about ten blocks from Congress Street to Wacker Drive, State Street, recently transformed into the State Street Mall, is one of the world's most highly concentrated shopping streets. (Photograph courtesy Chicago Convention and Tourism Bureau.)

new competition. (At one time they had even burned a bridge over the river leading to North Side establishments). A major breakout of the concentrated downtown commercial area occurred with the opening of the double-deck Michigan Avenue bridge in 1920. This started the development of the Magnificent Mile of luxury shops, hotels, and office buildings north of the Loop, a development that coincided with a major downtown building boom in the 1920s. However, with the coming of the

depression and then World War II, virtually all major construction was brought to a standstill.

After almost a quarter century of construction stagnation, the completion in 1957 of the 41-story Prudential Building on the air rights over the Illinois Central tracks launched the greatest era of construction that downtown Chicago has yet experienced. The John Hancock Center soars 100 stories tall. The Sears Tower rises to 110 stories, to become the

Figure 6.19. The double-deck Michigan Avenue Bridge over the Chicago River, when opened in 1920, helped spark the development of the fashionable Magnificent Mile along North Michigan Avenue. Viewed in 1972, the buildings from left to right are the Wrigley Building (1921, 1924), Tribune Building (1925), and Equitable Building (1965). Fort Dearborn was located to the west of the bridge along the south bank of the river. (Photograph courtesy Chicago Convention and Tourism Bureau.)

Figure 6.20. Michigan Avenue's "Magnificent Mile" had a long way to go in 1921 when this view was taken looking north from the new Wrigley Building. The opening of the Michigan Avenue Bridge the previous year helped to start the rapid development of the street as the site of luxury retail stores, hotels, and office buildings. The Water Tower and the Drake Hotel, toward the top left center of the photo, are the only structures of prominence still remaining. (Photograph courtesy Chicago Historical Society.)

Figure 6.21. Chicago's changing skyline at the start of the 1970s. The building in the right foreground is the new 60-story First National Bank Building. Behind it is the spire of the First United Methodist-Chicago Temple, the world's tallest church, a contrast to the log cabin in which this church was founded across the river in 1831. When completed in 1923, the Chicago Temple was the tallest building in Chicago. The Brunswick Building is to the right of the spire. Beyond the spire are the Daley Civic Center and, in the distance, the round towers of Marina City. In the far left background is the 100-story John Hancock Center. (Photograph courtesy Chicago Convention and Tourism Bureau.)

Figure 6.22. Examples of Chicago skyscraper architecture, including three of the five tallest buildings in the world. Left to right: Sears Tower, the world's tallest building, rises to a height of 110 stories (1,454 ft; 443 m). Its design consists of nine modular tubes of varying heights. Over 16,000 persons work in the building. The twin towers of the 62-story (588 ft; 179 m) Marina City form a concentrated complex of apartments and commercial and recreational facilities, with the first 18 stories being a continuously rising parking space. The world's fifth tallest building, the 100-story (1,127 ft; 343.5 m) John Hancock Center has its floors divided almost equally between commercial and residential use. The gleaming, white terra-cotta 32-story (398 ft; 121 m) Wrigley Building, built about 60 years ago, is an interesting link to Chicago's earlier office building architecture. The 80-story (1,136 ft; 346 m) Standard Oil Building is the world's fourth tallest and the highest marble-faced building in the world. (Photograph courtesy Chicago Convention and Tourism Bureau.)

world's tallest building. It dwarfs such other Chicago giants as the First National Bank Building (60 stories), Marina City (62 stories), Lake Point Tower (70 stories), Water Tower Place (74 stories), and Standard Oil Building (80 stories). Measured in feet Chicago contains three of the five tallest buildings in the world.

Chicago's downtown business district shows a viability and growth in employment that few downtowns of large cities can match. Downtown employment has moved up to about 500,000 workers, or over 30 percent of the total number of jobs in the city. However, the functions of the downtown area have been changing significantly.

The once very important manufacturing and wholesale activities have declined drastically due to economic and technological changes. The structures, often obsolete, in which these activities were conducted, are being replaced by office buildings and, increasingly, on the fringe of the Loop by tall apartment buildings. Some buildings, such as John Hancock Center and Water Tower Place, combine residential, retail, and office functions. The entertainment function of the downtown area (largely a nighttime activity) has also been declining, spreading into the Old Town and New Town areas to the north, and into the suburbs.

Banking remains strong in the downtown area. In recent years a number of banks have expanded their facilities, over fifty foreign banks have established branches or representative offices in downtown Chicago, and an increasing number of savings and loan associations of the city have opened downtown branches. Each of the two largest banks in the city, Continental Illinois and First National, has assets of over $25 billion.

Banks are the third largest user of downtown office space, trailing insurance companies which rank first and attorneys who rank second. Other large office-space users in downtown Chicago, in descending order, are accountants and engineers, retailing companies, printing and publishing, oil and gas companies, printing and publishing, oil and gas companies, machinery companies, nonprofit groups, communications, and stockbrokers. Downtown pays an estimated 40 percent of the entire city's property tax.

Retail growth in the downtown area has been handicapped by the dispersal of many of the higher income families to the suburbs and the proliferation toward the perimeter of the city and in the suburbs of 150 small and large shopping centers geared to the auto age. Downtown retail business has also been hurt by the concentration of low-income minority groups around the downtown area and by problems of safety, congestion, and parking. In recent years there has been a decline in the number of stores and retail workers in the downtown area. Its proportion of retail sales

of the entire metropolitan area is off significantly from the pre-World War II period.

An increasing percentage of downtown workers and customers are blacks. In the evenings a majority of the people patronizing the Loop movie theaters, restaurants, and many of the other recreational facilities are blacks, reflecting their increasing numbers and affluence, the elimination of racial barriers, good public transportation to the Loop, and the decline of adequate facilities in their own neighborhoods.

Shopping in the old downtown area is being affected by the "new downtown" which is expanding rapidly north of the river in the area of the Magnificent Mile along North Michigan Avenue. In 1980 North Michigan Avenue had sales of $345,000,000. Here high-quality stores, elegant restaurants, and luxury hotels cater to higher income clientele. Climaxing the opening of numerous new fashionable facilities along Michigan Avenue was the opening in 1975 of Water Tower Place, a 74-story, $150 million, multiuse building which contains Marshall Field and Lord & Taylor stores, nearly 100 specialty shops, the 450-room Ritz-Carlton Hotel, and 260 luxury condominiums. The Magnificent Mile now is one of the world's great fashion meccas, with Water Tower Place accounting for about 40 percent of its retail sales. Starting in the 1960s, over $5 billion has been invested in the Magnificent Mile and its Gold Coast neighborhood to the north and northeast and in Streeterville to the east.

Streeterville is named after one of Chicago's more colorful squatters, Captain George Wellington Streeter. In 1886 his steamboat ran aground on a sandbar about 400 yards (365.8 m) east of the beach at approximately Chicago Avenue (800 N). Sand drifted about the boat and he invited building contractors to dump on his newly formed land and expand it. Eventually Captain Streeter claimed about 186 acres (75.3 ha) of filled-in lakefront as his domain. Despite government opposition, he sold lots and built a small shanty town around his tavern. After years of legal wrangling with the city and nearby residents, and following a number of bloody altercations, one of which resulted in the killing of a policeman in 1918, Captain Streeter was finally evicted from his "District of Lake Michigan" and the shanties were burned. Today Streeterville is a prime residential and office building area and the location of a sizable segment of Chicago's communication media industry.

In sharp contrast to North Michigan Avenue is the relatively recent development, just to the northwest, of shopping and entertainment of a more unique, artsy-craftsy, faddish, small shop type—first in Old Town centered along Wells Street (200 W) and, more recently, slightly farther north in New Town. The New Town entertainment and shopping facilities extend along Lincoln Avenue, Clark Street, Halsted Street, and Broadway Avenue. It caters less to tourists than Old Town, and more to the lifestyle of the young adults who live in the area.

Despite its increased competition, commerce in the old downtown area has almost held its own. The area serves some 800,000 people daily and sells almost $1 billion worth of merchandise annually, many times as much as the largest shopping center. Well over half of these sales are on State Street, where shopping and sales have been improved by the development of a nine-block mall—one of the world's largest—and by a refurbishing of some of the street's stores. The mall, dedicated in 1979, has greatly curtailed vehicle traffic on the street and has provided widened sidewalks, kiosks, trees, and pushcart food and flower vendors. After declining for almost two decades, dollar sales volume along State Street has moved upward gradually since the mid-1960s, although part of the sales growth is attributed to inflation.

As the core of an ever larger metropolitan area, the downtown area is by far the front runner in many important categories. It still has the highest concentration of daytime population within the metropolitan area, the highest land values, the greatest building density, and the largest array of services. The downtown area has the best accessibility for shoppers and employees, with commuter railroads and the CTA having been augmented by a series of expressways which focus on downtown Chicago from most parts of the city and suburbs.

Numerous new office, hotel, and residential projects are taking place or being planned for parts of the downtown area, and the wave of redevelopment is pushing outward. Immediately south of the Loop, a 335-acre (135.7 ha) "South Loop New Town" is being planned and developed. It is to be mainly residential, with some industrial, commercial, and public facility space. This has been an area where development was blocked by a maze of railroad and trucking facilities, now largely outmoded. The first major residential development of rentals, townhouses, and condominiums is 51-acre (20.7 ha) Dearborn Park, south of Polk Street (800S). It opened for occupancy in 1979 and when completed will contain 3,000 housing units occupied by about 7,000 people. Dearborn Park is tied to the Loop by what is known as "Printing House Row." It consists of conversions of former printing and other facilities into artist-lofts, condominiums, and rentals. Printing House Row is along Dearborn and adjacent streets from Polk Street north to Congress Parkway. The biggest conversion into rental units is the formerly vacant 22-story Transportation Building at Dearborn and Harrison streets. Just to the north of Congress Parkway on Dearborn Street, the landmark Manhattan, Old Colony, and Fisher buildings are being rehabilitated into residential and office space. About $1 billion in private investment is under way or planned for the South Loop area.

Illinois Center, a major multistructure office, hotel, and residential high-rise complex, is partially completed on an 83-acre (33.6 ha) site bounded approximately by the Chicago River on the north, Michigan Avenue on the west, Randolph Street on the south, and the lake on the east. It is being built over Illinois Central Gulf air rights. This estimated $2 billion project already contains eleven tall buildings, with many more contemplated in a very dense, crammed arrangement of varied architecture. To relieve congestion Illinois Center plans call for a small park and a new multi-level road system. The latter includes the extension of Columbus Drive north across the river, of Wacker Drive eastward, and the re-routing of North Lake Shore Drive closer to the lakefront. The latter project would eliminate the dangerous S-curve where the drive now crosses the river.

Within the Loop itself, numerous high-rises were built in the 1970s and more were being erected in the early 1980s, including the architecturally interesting State of Illinois

Center on the site of the recently demolished Sherman House at Randolph and Clark streets. The largest concentration of new construction was five new buildings near the First National Bank Building and its plaza at Madison and Dearborn streets. Although tall, none of the new downtown buildings approaches the heights of the John Hancock Center, the Standard Oil Building, or Sears Tower—probably a reflection of a changing economy and higher energy costs. A number of the new downtown buildings have plazas, a few containing interesting and unique works of art. In the warmer

Figure 6.23. Art in the Loop by distinguished artists. Top left to right: the Picasso sculpture in the Daley Center Plaza; the "Flamingo," a stabile by Alexander Calder in the Federal Center Plaza; and "Universe," a moving mural by Calder in the lobby of Sears Tower. The lower photo is "The Four Seasons," a mosaic by Marc Chagall located at the First National Bank Plaza. (Photograph courtesy Chicago Convention and Tourism Bureau.)

months, some of the plazas come alive with people and varied activities.

The most controversial of the downtown projects is that of the much-delayed plans for rebuilding the North Loop—a seven block redevelopment project which would probably be the most ambitious renewal of any downtown area in the country. The North Loop site stretches irregularly from approximately State Street to LaSalle Street and from Wacker Drive to Washington Street, an area that contains numerous parking lots and mainly older and often rundown buildings. There are, however, a few landmark office buildings which preservationists would like to save. There are also several theaters which many would like to have retained as the nucleus of a revitalized downtown cultural center. The plan is for the city, using its urban renewal powers, to purchase the land and resell it to developers who would invest well over $1 billion in the development of the area by 1990. In addition to the State of Illinois Center, which is within the North Loop, major features would be a transit center, possibly a

large hotel on Wacker Drive west of State Street, and residential housing along the river. Other sections would contain shopping, office, and parking facilities. In the early 1980s the prolonged, controversial debate on the North Loop plan was still raging.

The building boom has been especially active along Wacker Drive, a wide road that parallels the river, and where in 1981 about ten new high-rises were either under construction or on the planning boards. Building has also been very active to the north of the river, with numerous new office and residential buildings, including some loft conversions. To the west of the river, a few buildings have been built and a large residential complex is contemplated west of the Chicago & North Western railroad station.

Cultural and Recreational Facilities

The numerous cultural and recreational facilities of Chicago are an important facet of the economy of the city. Besides being used by the local people, they are also a major attrac-

Figure 6.24. A favorite view for Chicagoans and tourists of Chicago's skyline, with Grant Park, Chicago's downtown lakefront, and one of the city's eight yacht harbors in the foreground. At the extrme left is the 110-story Sears Tower, and toward the extreme right are the 80-story Standard Oil Building, the 100-story John Hancock Center, and the 74-story Water Tower Place. (Photograph courtesy Chicago Convention and Tourism Bureau.)

Figure 6.25. The Museum of Science and Industry in Jackson Park—the nation's most heavily visited museum. The museum is housed in the restored Fine Arts Building of the World's Columbian Exposition of 1893. It contains some 75 major exhibit areas with 2,000 displays that explain the principles of science and how they are applied in industry and everyday life. (Photograph courtesy Chicago Convention and Tourism Bureau.)

tion for the 6 million people who visit Chicago annually and spend over $600 million. These pleasure visitors and also the more than 2 million persons attending conventions and trade shows support about 150,000 jobs in the area.

Chicago has an extensive system of parks, beaches, zoos, forest preserves, and sports arenas. Chicago also contains numerous museums, including some of international renown. The latter include the Museum of Science and Industry (Chicago's number one tourist attraction), Field Museum of Natural History, Shedd Aquarium, Adler Planetarium, and Oriental Institute. In the arts and music, the Art Institute of Chicago, the Chicago Symphony Orchestra, the Lyric Opera, and the Ravinia Music Festival have been widely acclaimed.

The metropolitan area, with 58 colleges and universities, is also a major center of higher education. Forty-nine Nobel prize win-

Figure 6.26. Popular exhibit of the Field Museum of Natural History. (Photograph courtesy Chicago Convention and Tourism Bureau.)

ners have been associated with the University of Chicago alone, and the university was the site where, on December 2, 1942, Enrico Fermi and his colleagues achieved the world's first controlled nuclear chain reaction.

Chicago is also noted for its medical facilities, many of which are operated by the universities. It has six medical schools and three major medical centers. One of every five physicians in the United States has received all or part of his or her training here.

Chicago has a number of important specialized libraries which attract scholars in many fields of interest. These include the John Crerar Library in science, the Newberry Library in the humanities, and the Library of International Relations.

Through the years distinguished educators, artists, and writers have been associated with the city and felt its influence—some for short periods, others for long periods. William Rainey Harper, John Dewey, and Ella Flagg

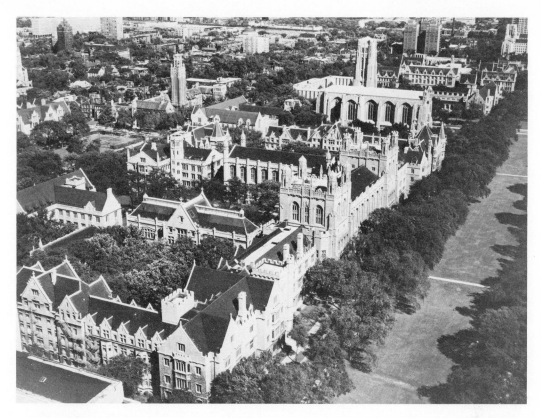

Figure 6.27. Aerial view of part of the University of Chicago looking northeast from 59th Street and Ellis Avenue, 1965. (Photograph courtesy University of Chicago.)

Young were prominent in education; Lorado Taft in sculpture; Ivan Albright in painting; and Louis "Satchmo" Armstrong, Gene Krupa, and Benny Goodman in jazz and swing music.

Among the numerous writers whose work was strongly influenced by their association with Chicago were Eugene Field, Ben Hecht, Sherwood Anderson, Carl Sandburg, Finley Peter Dunne, Edgar Lee Masters, James T. Farrell, Meyer Levin, Richard Wright, Willard Motley, Nelson Algren, Saul Bellow. Gwendolyn Brooks, and Harry Mark Petrakis. Writers whose work was influenced by so-

journs in Chicago included George Ade, Upton Sinclair, Theodore Dreiser, Frank Norris, Edna Ferber, and Ernest Hemingway. A Chicago school of writers left a strong impact on twentieth-century American literature. The current variety of the city's many publications range from the *Encyclopaedia Brittanica* to *Playboy* magazine.

In addition to the distinguished Chicago "schools" of writing and of architecture, other prominent "schools" is the Chicago school of economics which included such scholars as Friedrich von Hayek, Frank H. Knight, and Milton Friedman. The Chicago school of

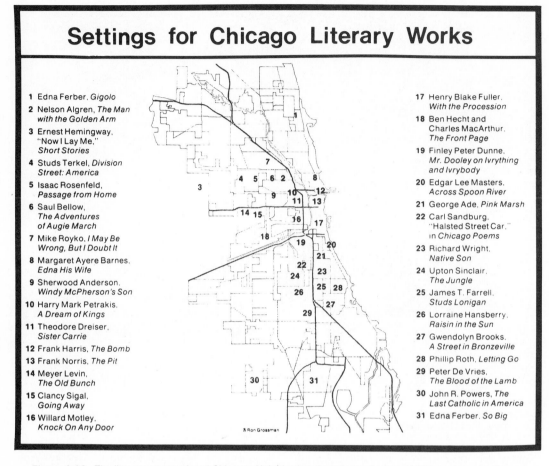

Settings for Chicago Literary Works

1 Edna Ferber, *Gigolo*
2 Nelson Algren, *The Man with the Golden Arm*
3 Ernest Hemingway, "Now I Lay Me," *Short Stories*
4 Studs Terkel, *Division Street: America*
5 Isaac Rosenfeld, *Passage from Home*
6 Saul Bellow, *The Adventures of Augie March*
7 Mike Royko, *I May Be Wrong, But I Doubt It*
8 Margaret Ayere Barnes, *Edna His Wife*
9 Sherwood Anderson, *Windy McPherson's Son*
10 Harry Mark Petrakis, *A Dream of Kings*
11 Theodore Dreiser, *Sister Carrie*
12 Frank Harris, *The Bomb*
13 Frank Norris, *The Pit*
14 Meyer Levin, *The Old Bunch*
15 Clancy Sigal, *Going Away*
16 Willard Motley, *Knock On Any Door*

17 Henry Blake Fuller, *With the Procession*
18 Ben Hecht and Charles MacArthur, *The Front Page*
19 Finley Peter Dunne, *Mr. Dooley on Ivrything and Ivrybody*
20 Edgar Lee Masters, *Across Spoon River*
21 George Ade, *Pink Marsh*
22 Carl Sandburg, "Halsted Street Car," in *Chicago Poems*
23 Richard Wright, *Native Son*
24 Upton Sinclair, *The Jungle*
25 James T. Farrell, *Studs Lonigan*
26 Lorraine Hansberry, *Raisin in the Sun*
27 Gwendolyn Brooks, *A Street in Bronzeville*
28 Phillip Roth, *Letting Go*
29 Peter De Vries, *The Blood of the Lamb*
30 John R. Powers, *The Last Catholic in America*
31 Edna Ferber, *So Big*

Figure 6.28. The literary geography of Chicago. Neighborhood settings of some of Chicago's major literary works. (From the March 1980 *Chicago* magazine. Map copyrighted by Ron Grossman.)

urban sociology, which included Robert E. Park, Ernest W. Burgess, and Louis Wirth, produced a series of classical monographs on cities with special emphasis on Chicago. Other Chicago "schools" are less well-known but are also influential in their fields.

Chicago is viewed in a myriad of ways by its millions of inhabitants and visitors:

To many people Chicago has been more than a hustling midwestern city. To some it has meant the world's largest commercial building (the Merchandise Mart), the world's largest grain market (the Board of Trade) and the world's largest farmers' market (the Chicago Mercantile Exchange). To others it has meant the center of the American transportation system for during the years of extensive train travel no passenger train went through Chicago. A traveler had to change from one train to another or from one station to another. To these travelers Chicago represented an inconvenience to be borne nobly. But they kept coming for passenger trains arrived and departed almost every minute. To others, it still

Figure 6.29. Points of interest and visitors' facilities in the central area of Chicago, 1979. (Courtesy Chicago Association of Commerce and Industry.)

Figure 6.30. Aerial view of Chicago's lakefront and downtown area looking northward from approximately 23rd Street, 1974. In the right foreground is the giant McCormick Place exposition center. At the extreme right is Meigs Field on man-made Northerly Island. Toward the center is the recreational-cultural complex of Soldier's Field, Field Museum of Natural History, Shedd Aquarium, and the Grant Park Music Shell. The tallest buildings in the background from left to right are Sears Tower (110 stories), First National Bank Building (60 stories), Standard Oil (80 stories), and the John Hancock Center (100 stories). (Photograph by Kee T. Chang. Courtesy Chicago Association of Commerce and Industry.)

represents a city of wickedness where vice is rampant, where gangsters rule the municipal government and terrorize the citizens. To some it is the center of the only truly American music, and they come searching for the small bistros which had given rise to jazz in the twenties. To some it is the center of American architecture with the emphasis upon the "Chicago construction," and they come hoping to find the old buildings of Adler and Sullivan, forgetting that Chicago tears down in order to rebuild. To some few it represents a cultural center, and they come to tramp through some of the world's greatest museums and most beautiful parks. Whatever else it might appear to be, it is a city to be seen, and millions of people pour into the city each year with cameras swinging on their shoulders and wonder in their eyes. It makes no difference that many of the old buildings are gone, that many of the gangsters have died, that jazz has since moved to New York, or that the Chicago for which many search is so elusive. Yet visitors and residents alike pursue the legend that is CHICAGO.[2]

Notes

1. James Parton, "Chicago," *Atlantic Monthly*. XIX (March, 1867), pp. 325–45.
2. Kenny J. Williams, *In the City of Men* (Nashville: Townsend Press, 1974), p. 5.

Figure 7.1. View of Chicago River from Rush Street Bridge looking toward Lake Michigan about 1869. In the background to the right are the Sturges and Buckingham grain elevators in the Illinois Central terminal complex. (Photograph courtesy Chicago Historical Society.)

Chapter Seven

TRANSPORTATION—
EXTERNAL AND INTERNAL

From Portage to World Port

At first by water and wagon route, then by railway and finally by motor highway and through the air, the transportation systems of metropolitan Chicago branched out like the arteries of a growing organism, knitting the agricultural settlements and trade centers into an economic unit and joining the Chicago Region with the outside world.[1]

Chicago contains one of the greatest multilayered transportation networks in the world. Its passenger facilities are among the busiest in the nation; its freight facilities are geared to handle the millions of tons of raw materials needed by the nation's largest steel industry as well as the millions of packages shipped annually by its unrivaled complex of mail-order houses. It is a major focal point both for national freight movement and for local traffic interchange. An estimated 86 tons of goods per capita are handled annually by the area's transportation network compared to 54 tons per capita nationally.

Its role as a regional, national, and even international focus for the various forms of transportation has been one of Chicago's greatest assets. Table 7.1 shows the division of freight traffic entering and leaving metropolitan Chicago by different modes of transportation. Since this most recent survey was made, evidence has indicated that the absolute tonnage of all modes has been increasing steadily in recent years. The area has been struggling, however, with mixed results, to keep its ever increasing volume of passenger and freight traffic flowing smoothly and efficiently, both internally and externally. Improvements in the waterways have helped domestic and overseas water linkages, while the spreading expressway network has stimulated new land use and travel patterns; by contrast in recent years mass transit and railroad service generally have continued to have very serious problems. The huge freight operations of the area are handled by a vast complex of facilities, as shown in table 7.2.

The relative importance of the various modes of transportation to Chicago has changed through the years. Water transportation dominated the early era of Chicago; it has been said that Chicago was a port before it was a city.

Chicago was blessed with natural waterways. These waterways were used by the Indians, early explorers, and settlers. But the eventual development of Chicago as an important port depended on a series of manmade improvements, both near and far. These included the opening of the Erie Canal in 1825; the numerous improvements to the Chicago harbors starting with the first federal funds in

TABLE 7.1
Estimated Modal Division of External Freight Traffic in Metropolitan Chicago, 1965

Mode	Percent of Total	Tons
Rail	54.2%	319,000,000
Truck	22.4	132,000,000
Water	12.2	72,000,000
Pipe	11.1	65,000,000
Air	0.1	445,055
	100.0	588,445,055

James R. Blaze, "Estimating Metropolitan Chicago's Freight Traffic," *C.A.T.S. Research News* (September-October, 1968), p. 3.

TABLE 7.2
Freight Facilities of the Chicago Metropolitan Area

Rail
17 line haul railroads
4 belt line railroads
8 industrial switching
   railroads

Truck
1,200 local carriers
   400 intercity carriers

Air
23 scheduled carriers of
   air cargo

Water
14 barge lines
64 commercial waterway
   terminals

Pipe
21 carriers of petroleum
   and petroleum
   products and 6
   refineries
3 carriers of natural
   gas
4 utility companies

Other Services
138 warehouses
56 freight forwarders

Modified from Chicago Area Transportation Study and Lake-Porter County Regional Transportation and Planning Commission, *Regional Transportation Interior Plan and Program* (Chicago, 1971), p. 49.

1833; the Illinois and Michigan Canal in 1848; the Chicago Sanitary and Ship Canal in 1900; the Calumet Sag Channel completed in 1922 with a sixty foot width (18.3 m), since widened to 225 feet (68.6 m); and the opening of the St. Lawrence Seaway in 1959. These improvements allowed Chicago to take advantage of its location at the junction of major water routes by making water connections with the Atlantic Ocean, the Gulf of Mexico, and thereby with the world.

Canal and port traffic reached a peak in the 1880s when the arrivals and clearances of over 26,000 vessels were recorded annually for a number of seasons. The banks of the Chicago River in the downtown area were almost continuously lined with wharves. For the next half century, however, water traffic decreased, chiefly because of competition from the railroads. The once flourishing canal barges and the package freight disappeared, although on the whole the bulk industrial water traffic in iron ore, coal, and limestone for the steel mills continued to increase.

Water traffic began to revive with the completion of the Illinois Waterway in 1933. This made possible barge traffic of a 9-foot (2.7 m) draft all the way from Chicago to the Gulf via the Illinois and Mississippi rivers, as well as into a number of the latter's tributaries. In 1959 Queen Elizabeth II and Prince Philip aboard the royal yacht *Britannia* led a procession of fifty vessels from Montreal into Chicago to inaugurate the long awaited opening of the modern version of the St. Lawrence Seaway—an event that was to make Chicago a major world port. Smaller ships had been operating through the old seaway for many years. As early as 1856 the schooner *Dean Richmond* carried a cargo of grain from Chicago to Liverpool.

Water transportation generally is the cheapest form of transportation, especially for bulk commodities. But it also provides for substantial savings on manufactured goods, especially if transshipments are eliminated. For example, there is usually a saving of between $30 and $40 in shipping costs on the importation of a foreign automobile via the St. Lawrence Seaway as against shipment by water to New York and then by rail to Chicago. An additional benefit for the area is that for every ton of cargo handled by city dockworkers, an estimated $40 is pumped into the local economy through the generation of jobs and business.

Figure 7.2. The Goodrich Line wharf on the south bank of the Chicago River east of the Rush Street Bridge in 1871 after the fire. The landing was used by the steamboat company's vessels from Civil War times until the 1930s, connecting Chicago with ports on both the east and west shores of Lake Michigan. (Photograph courtesy Chicago Historical Society.)

The Modern Port of Chicago

Today the ports of the Chicago area usually handle over 80 million tons of freight annually (50 percent greater than the amount handled by the Panama Canal), making it one of the largest ports in the world in tonnage. About a third of the tonnage consists of barge traffic on the inland waterways. Much of the total tonnage is bulk cargo—iron ore, coal, limestone—destined for the numerous steel mills in the Calumet area; some is coal for utilities, building materials, chemicals, and grain; and only a small amount, averaging less than 3 million tons annually, is in general cargo to and from overseas ports.

Chicago area port facilities now account for almost a third of the value of Great Lakes overseas trade. The port, however, is served by a declining number of ship lines, although they still reach dozens of countries. In past years Chicago normally received between 500 and 800 calls by vessels engaged in overseas trade, but in recent years the number has declined and ranges between about 150 to 400 ships annually. These vessels discharge autos, steel, fish, whiskey, beer, wine, olives, and furniture. They load with scrap metal, machinery, farm equipment, animal and vegetable oils, hides, lumber, and a variety of food products, especially grain to complete the "topping off" of an overseas vessel.

Figure 7.3. Construction of the Chicago Sanitary and Ship Canal, 1895, showing the limestone bedrock underlying the area. The canal, the "eight wonder of the world," was opened in 1900 after a decade of construction which required more earth excavation than the building of the Panama Canal. (Photograph courtesy Chicago Historical Society.)

The Port of Chicago consists of several harbors. The central area one, Chicago Harbor, included Navy Pier and the Chicago River, but since the phasing out of handling general overseas cargo at Navy Pier, Chicago Harbor is limited largely to the main stem of the Chicago River in the downtown area. The latter was once Chicago's major port, but the river is now mainly a handler of newsprint for the newspaper plants along its north bank. The future of this harbor is limited because of neighboring land congestion, high land values, and limited services. The South Branch of the Chicago River has some facilities for handling bulk cargoes and is a link in the Lakes-to-Gulf Waterway. The North Branch has a 21-foot (6.4 m) channel to North Avenue and a 9-foot (2.7 m) channel to the Commonwealth Edison Company plant near Addison Street (3600 N),

but has relatively little water traffic (mainly barge) because it dead ends to the north. The lack of adequate dredging on the North Branch in recent years has also contributed to the reduction of deep-draft vessels.

The main water traffic of the Chicago area long ago shifted south to the Calumet area. The heavily industralized 6-mile (9.7 km) stretch of the Calumet River from Lake Michigan to Lake Calumet handles more tonnage than any other Chicago waterway. This freight consists of great quantities of raw materials for the numerous steel plants along its banks, as well as grain, chemicals, coal, and general cargo.

The most complete array of services and facilities in the Chicago area is to be found in Lake Calumet Harbor (Senator Dan Dougherty Harbor)—the area's major overseas port,

Figure 7.4. Chicago Harbor. In the foreground is the Lake Shore Drive Bridge over the Chicago River. In the background to the right is the lock of the Chicago River Controlling Works and to the left is Navy Pier before the phasing out of overseas shipping. Navy Pier, completed in 1916, has been used for shipping, recreation, exhibits, training navy personnel, and as the site of the Chicago Undergraduate Division of the University of Illinois. In recent years its chief use has been for recreation and exhibits. (Photograph courtesy *Chicago Tribune.)*

located about a dozen miles southeast of downtown. Here the Chicago Regional Port District operates the largest and most comprehensive facility on the Great Lakes for the handling of ocean, lake, and inland-barge shipping. Grain elevators, transit sheds and warehouses, tank farms, scrap facilities, and a variety of transportation facilities enable Lake Calumet Harbor to handle seventeen ocean freighters at one time. In addition this harbor handles barge traffic from the Illinois Waterway and is a most strategic point of interchange with Great Lakes overseas traffic. The major physical handicaps to the harbor—inadequate depth and obstructive bridge approaches along the 6-mile (9.7 km) Calumet River linkage to Lake Michigan—have been partially rectified.

Lake Calumet Harbor has been the core of the Port of Chicago. Annual traffic tonnage,

however, varies widely, depending on such factors as general economic conditions and product costs at home and abroad, international tensions which can lead to such trade deterrents as grain embargoes, and the competition of other ports and modes of transportation. In recent years the number of foreign vessels using the port has declined substantially.

A free trade zone has been established at Lake Calumet Harbor. In a free trade zone, foreign producers can ship raw materials or semifinished goods duty free to have them stored, processed or assembled, and then reexported without being subject to United States tariffs. Goods destined for the United States may be stored in the free trade zone, with taxes being paid only when the goods are shipped out of the zone. Additionally, any materials wasted in the manufacturing process

Figure 7.5. The Chicago Regional Port District terminal at the south end of Lake Calumet, looking northwest. At the upper left are two 6.5 million bushel grain elevators. Just beyond the lower right of the photo, Lake Calumet joins the Calumet River. (Photograph courtesy Chicago Regional Port District.)

in the free trade zone are not taxed because they are not in the final product that enters the country. Such a zone can encourage new industry and trade.

Two canals—the 16-mile (25.7 km) Calumet Sag Channel and the 28-mile (45.1 km) Chicago Sanitary and Ship Canal—are vital links in the Lakes-to-Gulf Waterway. The Calumet Sag Channel links the Calumet area waterways with the Chicago Sanitary and Ship Canal; the Chicago Sanitary and Ship Canal links the South Branch of the Chicago River with the Illinois and Mississippi rivers. The canals handle bulk barge cargoes and provide scattered facilities for oil, building materials, and other products. Both were originally designed primarily to provide sewage-diversion facilities and to reverse the flow of polluted water away from Lake Michigan—Chicago's source of plentiful, low-cost fresh

water. The canals and other facilities of the Metropolitan Sanitary District of Greater Chicago have helped to protect both Chicago's water supply and its lakefront beaches from the type of pollution that has plagued other Great Lakes cities.

To the east of Chicago in Indiana are the ports of Indiana Harbor, Buffington, Gary, and the new Burns Harbor (in the Indiana Dunes area). The tonnage of these ports is almost wholly bulk cargo destined for the steel industry, although they also service chemical and cement plants and oil refineries. Burns Harbor, with its new grain elevator and other new port facilities, has had some effect on the Calumet River-Lake Calumet traffic.

The Port of Chicago has been handicapped by only a nine-month shipping season, labor problems, a shortage of certain facilities (especially those to handle containers), lack of adequate port promotion, limitation on the size of vessels that can traverse the St. Lawrence Seaway, lack of adequate service to key foreign ports, improved rail competition and that of ocean ports, declining use of waterway frontage by industry, and the absence of a unified port authority between Illinois and Indiana, and until recently, within the city of Chicago itself. These handicaps have hurt mainly overseas general cargo traffic, which, after substantial growth in the 1960s, has declined sharply in the last few years. Illinois is the nation's second-largest exporting state; however, only about 3 percent of this export moves through the Port of Chicago.

Although it is difficult at present for the port to compete with coastal ports for the container trade (which usually requires faster movement and turnaround than can be offered via the St. Lawrence Seaway route), the domestic bulk traffic, in which the Chicago area specializes, has generally shown a slow but steady increase. And port officials are hopeful that even the container trade may show some improvement due to the opening in 1980 at the mouth of the Calumet River of the 194 acre (78.6 ha) Iroquois Landing container facility. Its excellent location eliminates for some vessels the slow and costly 6-mile (9.7 km) Calumet River trip to Lake Calumet Harbor. Despite its problems, the Port of Chicago, based largely on its bulk tonnage, continues to be one of the greatest inland ports in the world, although its hope of becoming a great international seaport has not been realized.

The Railroads Spin a Web

The coming of the railroads helped stimulate the rapid growth of Chicago. The first railroad to Chicago was built in 1848—the same year the Illinois and Michigan Canal was completed. At first the railroads were regarded as supplemental to the waterways, and many of Chicago's railroads terminated at or near the waterways of the downtown area. However, the railroads soon surpassed, and even supplanted, waterway traffic.

In 1848, Chicago's first railroad brought a load of wheat into downtown Chicago from its western terminal at the Des Plaines River, only about 10 miles (16.1 km) away. By 1852 Chicago already was connected by rail with the East Coast; in 1869 service was inaugurated to the West Coast. Soon railroads came into Chicago by twenty-seven converging routes—and Chicago had earned the title of "Player with Railroads and the Nation's Freight Handler." Today Chicago is served by railroad companies representing about one-half of the total railroad mileage in the country and is the world's greatest railroad center.

To facilitate distribution and interchange among the numerous industries and radiating railroads, Chicago developed a web of a dozen intersecting belt, switching, and industrial railroads within the 1,754 square mile (4,543 sq km) Chicago Terminal District. Within this area are 7,708 miles (12,402 km) of track, 131 freight terminal and industrial yards with a capacity of 179,000 cars, 32 freight houses, numerous auxiliary facilities, and until recently, 6 active major downtown passenger terminals. On an average day 35,000 freight cars are loaded or unloaded in Chicago, more than the combined total for New York and St. Louis, and some 1,400 trains move through or leave the terminal district daily. About every third railroad carload in the country originates, moves through, or terminates in the Chicago area.

The railroads strongly affected Chicago's growth, its national role, and the local land use and settlement patterns. First they brought great numbers of laborers to build the roads; thereafter, they brought the permanent settlers who opened up the land. The railroads employed thousands directly, while many more worked in the manufacturing of railroad equipment. By making transportation cheaper, more reliable, and more accessible, and by of-

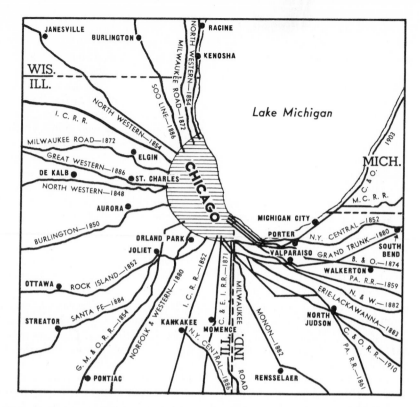

Figure 7.6. Historical map of Chicago's railroad network. Dates mark arrival of railroads to Chicago. (Courtesy *Chicago Tribune*.)

fering service to virtually all parts of the country, the railroads stimulated the growth of agriculture, manufacturing, and commerce in the Chicago area. Many railroads directly fostered industrial development. The railroads also made possible the dispersal of population along the commuter routes into the outlying parts of the city and into the suburbs. They continue to aid the viability of Chicago's downtown area by making it readily accessible to commuters from most parts of the growing metropolitan area.

Although benefiting the city in many ways, the railroads cut it up like a pie. This created neighborhood and traffic barriers and noise and pollution problems. In addition, the facilities of the railroads have blocked the expansion of the downtown area to the south and

preempted long stretches of choice lakefront land.

In recent years rail employment has declined sharply and the once bustling intercity passenger service has virtually disappeared except for the Amtrak service. In 1981, Chicago, as in the past, led the nation in the number of scheduled intercity passenger trains, twenty-six departures daily, but this was drastically off from the many hundreds of such trains that operated daily out of the city a half century ago. Even more passenger trains cuts seem likely. After decades of debate, the coming of Amtrak has finally led to the consolidation of almost all intercity passenger trains into one terminal, Union Station. The elimination of unused terminals and trackage south of the Loop that once served central area pas-

Figure 7.7. The Chicago & North Western Railway Depot at Kinzie and Wells streets about 1885—at the locale occupied today by the Merchandise Mart. The station served from 1881 to 1911 when it was replaced by the terminal at Madison and Canal streets. (Photograph courtesy Chicago & North Western Railway.)

senger stations, manufacturers, and waterway connections has opened sizable and valuable acreage for development, including the new Dearborn Park residential complex. Grand Central, Central (Twelfth Street), and La Salle Street stations have been demolished. The almost century-old Dearborn Street Station is no longer used by the railroads.

Despite increased competition from other modes of transportation, freight volume in the Chicago area continues to hold up well, buoyed by efficient technological changes and the introduction of new methods such as the unit train and piggybacking.

Unit trains carry one commodity, such as coal or grain, and operate intact from origin to destination without stopping at intermedi-

ate classification yards to break up and make up as ordinary trains do. Piggybacking consists of hauling truck trailers on flat cars (TOFC) or containers on flat cars (COFC). The double- and triple-deck auto-rack cars that carry new autos are an adaptation of the piggyback principle. The railroads are carrying an increasing number of truck trailers, containers, and new autos.

One consequence of changing technology and industrial location, along with the merger of railroads, has been the underutilization of some of the maze of railroad facilities which occupy an estimated 52 square miles (134.7 sq km) of rail rights-of-way and yards in the Chicago area. Some of these facilities are outmoded or have been replaced by modern, spa-

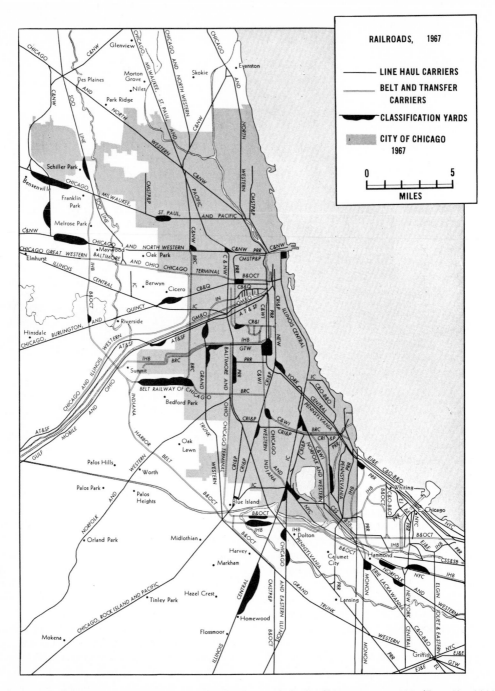

Figure 7.8. Railroad routes and principal classification yards in the Chicago area, 1967. (From Harold M. Mayer and Richard C. Wade, *Chicago: Growth of a Metropolis*, 1969. Reproduced by permission of the University of Chicago Press.)

Figure 7.9. The Milwaukee Road freight yards in Bensenville looking southeastward. This area, just south of O'Hare International Airport and near the Tri-State Tollway, has had substantial industrial growth in recent decades. Chicago's downtown skyscrapers are visible on the horizon. (Photograph courtesy Chicago Association of Commerce and Industry.)

cious, less congested facilities farther out, such as those at Markham, Proviso, Bensenville, and the new yards at Burns Harbor, Indiana. The trend is for the development of huge classification yards even farther beyond the urbanized perimeter. These outlying facilities help alleviate the sometimes long freight car delays often associated with the more complex rail network within the Chicago gateway.

Some facilities have been consolidated as a result of mergers. Some of the older, underused, inner area facilities have been converted into piggyback or new auto-rack yards or into trucking terminals and other uses. But thousands of acres of underutilized railroad land in the metropolitan area are still available for redevelopment.

Road Transportation

About a half century ago, the automobile and motor truck began to challenge the dominance of the railroad. The streets, however, proved to be inadequate for the rapidly increasing number of automobiles. For example, in 1925, with half a million automobile owners

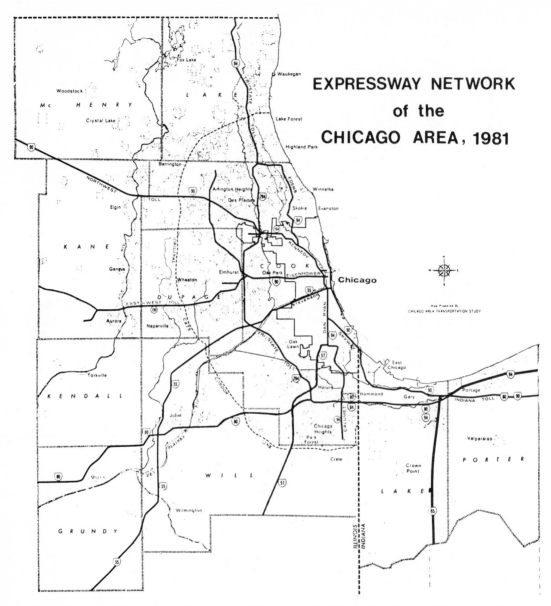

Figure 7.10. The expressway network of the Chicago area in 1981. (Updated from a Chicago Area Transportation Study map.)

Figure 7.11. Lake Shore Drive, one of the earliest prototypes of the expressway, looking south toward downtown from Lincoln Park, 1974. In the foreground is Belmont Harbor; some of Chicago's numerous beaches are visible along the lakeshore. (Photograph courtesy Chicago Association of Commerce and Industry.)

Figure 7.12. The Dan Ryan Expressway from about 47th Street looking northeast, 1969. This stretch of road has been rated the busiest expressway in the nation averaging over 250,000 vehicles per day. In the median strip of the expressway is the rapid transit line of the Chicago Transit Authority and its 47th Street Station. To the east of the expressway are part of the low-income, high-rise Robert R. Taylor homes of the Chicago Housing Authority. In the upper left near the lake are the middle income Lawless Gardens, Lake Meadows, and Prairie Shores high-rise apartment complexes. (Courtesy Wide World Photos.)

in the Chicago region, there were only thirteen paved gateways leading out of the city. There were only 2 miles (3.2 km) of paved roads that could adequately carry four lanes of traffic. Chicago's boulevard system, established in 1869 to connect the city's parks, was one of the few adequate, though limited, road networks.

The next few decades witnessed a massive road building program, designed to provide for the fivefold increase in the number of motor vehicles in the next half century. The road building program called for the widening of many of the major streets, including most of the old diagonal Indian trails, such as Blue Island, Milwaukee, Vincennes, and Archer avenues. The program was climaxed in the 1950s and 1960s by the superimposition on the Chicago area's basic street pattern of a coordinated expressway and tollway system of over 500 miles (804.5 km). Expressways now radiate out from the center of the city in most directions. The proposed very controversial and costly Crosstown Expressway project has recently been eliminated from the contemplated road program. It would have been a circumferential route connecting the major expressways in the city. This would have helped alleviate some of the expressway congestion in the downtown area, but it would have added greatly to the estimated 50,000 Chicagoans already displaced from their homes and businesses by the expressway system.

Of the area's three tollway systems, the Indiana and Illinois tollways have exceeded load expectations and have been successful financially. In contrast, the 7.5 mile (12.1 km) Chicago Skyway, which was hurriedly completed in 1958 to handle the expected dumping of Indiana Toll Road traffic into the already congested southeastern corner of Chicago, has been a financial disaster. The Chicago Skyway traffic projections were grossly overestimated and the Skyway was also hurt by the subsequent construction of alternate freeway routes. Very substantial toll fee increases have also hampered traffic growth.

As in the case of railroading, Chicago has become the nation's largest trucking center, with daily scheduled service to more than 54,000 communities. Trucks now handle about one-fourth of the intercity freight tonnage. Truck freight has grown steadily, and trucking has exhibited a greater locational flexibility than have the other modes of transportation. The truck terminal facilities have been moving generally outward—away from their former close ties with rail and water facilities, and away from congested inner city areas with their small, poorly located facilities. The movement has been especially into the southwestern part of the city and into the southwestern suburbs. Large new terminals have been built, usually in areas that have ready access to expressways and tollways and in proximity to other carriers for convenient interline exchange of goods. To serve some localized traffic, some major companies have established satellite terminals in such cities as Waukegan, Elgin, Aurora, Joliet, and Chicago Heights where building and operating costs are generally lower and there is less congestion than in Chicago.

There are indications that Chicago has lost some interchange business because of high cost, the emergence of bypass routes, and the rash of recent trucking company mergers which created more through routes. Despite the trend toward consolidation of trucking companies, the Chicago area is still served by 1,200 local trucking firms and almost 400 intercity carriers. However, the greater flexibility of the trucking industry does not allow Chicago to attain the degree of dominance it has in railroad transportation.

The automobile and an improved road pattern are playing a major role in the location and dispersal of population and economic activities, especially in suburban areas. Settlement need no longer be aligned along railway routes. The automobile has made huge new areas accessible for residential, commercial, and industrial uses. The expressway system, in particular, has altered area traffic patterns and has lessened the use of other modes of transportation, especially mass transit. However, the recent rapid escalation of fuel and automobile costs, coupled with the high costs of new homes, has somewhat slowed the outward movement of population and renewed interest in the use of mass transit.

Pipelines

Pipelines, with their limited visibility which often masks their crucial importance, are also one of the area's fastest growing freight transport modes, handling in 1975 an estimated one-eighth of the freight tonnage of the area. The subterranean network of pipelines into the area has helped to make Chicago a major inland hub for the petroleum and natural gas industry.

The Chicago area has a total network of twenty-four pipelines that carry petroleum, natural gas, and refined products; seven underground gas storage facilities; and six active oil refineries. Two of the latter, including one of the nation's largest, owned by Standard Oil of Indiana, are located in the Whiting-East Chicago, Indiana, area. The other four are along the inland waterway network south and southwest of the city. The area's facilities were substantially increased by the opening in 1971 of the Union Oil refinery near Lemont and, in 1973, of the Mobil Oil refinery near Joliet. The Chicago area is the nation's largest inland oil refinery center. Most of the area's oil and natural gas supply comes via pipelines from Texas, Oklahoma, Louisiana, Wyoming, Kansas, and Canada. The pipelines range in size from 8 inches (20.3 cm) in diameter to the 26-inch (66 cm) Chicap pipeline which carries oil from Louisiana and the 34-inch (86.4 cm) Lakehead oil pipeline from Canada.

Air Transportation

Transportation did not undergo major changes for thousands of years. Then in relatively quick succession came the steamboat, railroad, motor vehicle, and most recently and dramatically—the airplane. And as it had with other modes of transportation, Chicago soon became a leading air center.

The first government airport opened in 1916 at Ashburn Field at Crawford Avenue (4000 W) and 83rd Street. A decade later Chicago Municipal Airport (now Midway) at 63rd Street and Cicero Avenue (4800 W), on Chicago's Southwest Side, was dedicated. It featured cinder runways, boundary lights, and a revolving beacon for night landings. With many improvements and enlargements this field served as Chicago's main airport for over three decades. For a time it was the busiest airport in the world, handling nearly 10 million passengers a year at its midcontinent location.

Most private planes were handled by the nearly three dozen small scattered airfields that had grown up in the early days of aviation when airfields were primitive and costs low. Many of these small fields disappeared as the sites became much more valuable for real estate developments. For example, Sky Harbor Airport is now an industrial park, York Township Airport is a shopping center, and Hinsdale and Chicagoland airports were sold for commercial development. Many of the approximately 4,000 small, privately owned planes based in the area are experiencing increasing difficulties in securing adequate and convenient airport facilities.

Many private and commuter planes now use Meigs Field, opened in 1948 on Northerly Island in Burnham Park. Its convenient location on the lakefront, just a few minutes from the Loop, has helped to make it one of the busiest single-runway commercial airports in the world. However, due to its location on prime recreational land, ecological and weather problems, and the technical dangers associated with a lakefront location in an area of increasingly taller buildings, some groups have suggested that the facility be phased out.

The rapid growth of commercial jet aviation soon made Midway Airport unable to handle Chicago's commercial aviation. The new large jets needed longer runways than Midway's one square mile (2.59 sq km) of area could provide; furthermore, substantial expansion of the field was not feasible because of the built-up area around the airport. Fortunately the city was able to acquire a huge airfield some 18 miles (29 km) northwest of the Loop that had been developed during the World War II period as a test field in conjunction with the Douglas Aircraft Company plant on the site. Chicago annexed the territory and developed it as O'Hare Field, spending hundreds of millions of dollars on airport terminals, runways, parking facilities, and access roads, with more major improvements contemplated. The field is more than ten times the size of Midway Airport.

Today, O'Hare International Airport is the world's busiest airport, although it is receiving competition for that title from Atlanta's airport. About 30,000 workers are employed at O'Hare. It averages around 1,700 arrivals and departures daily, or better than a plane a minute on a 24-hour basis. It is served by 24 scheduled carriers, including 18 with direct international services. The airport now handles almost 50 million passengers and over 800,000 tons of freight annually and is already overcrowded despite periodic expansion of both passenger and cargo facilities. Approximately 50 percent of the passengers are travelers who land at O'Hare to take a connecting flight.

Efforts to reactivate Midway Airport as a major airport have been only partially successful as yet. Facilities have been renovated,

Figure 7.13. O'Hare International Airport—the world's busiest, 1974. View is northeast from Terminal 2. Behind the terminal is the control tower, the O'Hare Hilton Hotel, and one of the world's largest parking garages, with room for 9,250 vehicles. (Photograph courtesy Chicago Association of Commerce and Industry.)

and, like O'Hare, Midway now has good expressway connections to the downtown area, which is only 10 miles (16 km) away, compared to O'Hare's 18 miles (29 km). Nevertheless, the return of air traffic has been very slow because of service limitations (only smaller jets with a range of about 1,000 miles, 1,609 km, can use the field), the lack of a large number of connecting flights, and the reluctance of airlines to set up costly duplicate service facilities. Beginning in 1979, however, commercial passenger flights using Midway

Airport increased substantially, due mainly to the flights of new Midway Airlines.

The sharp decline in passengers at Midway Airport has had a drastic, deteriorating effect on its once bustling ancillary commercial area of hotels, motels, and restaurants. On the other hand, while increased air traffic at O'Hare has brought problems of high noise levels and of congestion in the air and on roads leading to the airport, O'Hare has also spawned rapid commercial and industrial development in surrounding areas, as well as a very substantial suburban residential growth. Numerous hotels and motels have been built in the area to accommodate air travelers and the growing number of meetings and conventions held in the vicinity of the airport.

To help alleviate a parking problem at O'Hare, the city in 1973 opened one of the world's largest parking structures with room for 9,250 vehicles. Parking problems will be further reduced with the completion to O'Hare Field of the 7.6 mile (12.2 km) extension of the CTA's (Chicago Transit Authority) West-Northwest line, mainly in the median strip of the Kennedy Expressway. Also, badly needed new international facilities are being contemplated to handle more expeditiously the 3 million international passengers who use the airport annually.

There has been some discussion of the eventual need for a third major airport. If the need is ascertained, the main problems will be those of cost and location. Speculation on a site centers on areas southwest or southeast of the city or on an airport in the lake some 8 to 10 miles (13–16 km) east of the city. The land sites would be cheaper but more distant from the heart of the city and would pose a noise problem for the surrounding area. The lake site would be costlier, could have weather problems, and could affect the ecology of the lake, but it would be closer to the heart of the city and to a large work force. However, with the recent slowing in the growth rate of air travel and the increased use of planes with greater passenger capacities, the number of projected plane landings has been decreased and pressure for a third airport has been alleviated, at least temporarily. Serious consideration of a third airport has now essentially subsided, although the possibility is still mentioned occasionally.

The CTA and Its Predecessors

When Chicago was small in area, people lived close to their places of employment and usually could easily walk to work or travel by horse and buggy. In 1850, for example, Chicago was less than 10 square miles (25.9 sq km) in area; most of the industry and population was located in and around what is now the downtown area. As the city expanded rapidly to its present size of 228 square miles (590.9 sq km) and people and industry spread throughout the city and into the suburbs, internal transportation for the metropolitan area became a major problem. Through the years efforts have been made to cope with the problem by developing various modes of transportation.

Chicago's first mass transportation line was established in 1859, when the city's population had passed 100,000. This line consisted of horse drawn street railway cars operating on State Street between Randolph (150 N) and 12th streets. With numerous extensions that helped spread urbanization, the horsecars dominated the city's public transportation until 1882 when they began to be replaced by cable cars which rattled and groaned at a speed of up to fourteen miles (22.5 km) per hour. Cable cars had a brief life, for in 1892 the electric streetcar was introduced into Chicago. Electric streetcars soon operated throughout the city, along nearly all section-line streets, diagonal streets, and even along some half-section streets. A streetcar line was within easy walking distance of nearly everyone in the city. In 1913 the entire fragmented streetcar system was unified under the management of the Chicago Surface Lines, with a resulting track network of about 1,000 miles (1,609 km) and a passenger count which, in 1929, reached nearly 900 million.

In 1892, also, the elevated railroad was introduced into Chicago. Originally it ran from downtown to 39th Street, but by 1893 it had been extended to Jackson Park in time for the World's Columbian Exposition. This "L" line was rapidly followed by lines to various parts of the city, with some eventually reaching into the northern and western suburbs. Until 1897, the "L" trains were pulled by small steam engines.

Figure 7.14. Cable cars in the 3800 block of Cottage Grove Avenue on October 8, 1893, en route to "Chicago Day" at the World's Columbian Exposition. (Photograph courtesy Chicago Historical Society.)

"L" lines converged on the downtown area where they swung around the "Loop," which connected the various independent lines and provided a steel girdle of raised tracks and screeching cars around the major part of the downtown area. In 1913 the various elevated companies were unified into the Rapid Transit Lines creating for the first time a through route connecting the North and South sides.

The streetcars and particularly the fast elevated trains helped to spread population to the far corners of the city and even beyond. High density apartment buildings were built, especially in the vicinity of the elevated lines.

Access to the Loop was particularly good, and by 1910 about 750,000 persons were pouring into the downtown area every day by elevated or, primarily, by streetcar.

While the electric streetcar and the elevated lines were carrying most of Chicago's passengers, a new form of transportation that was to have far reaching effects appeared—the motor vehicle. The use of the automobile and the bus grew very rapidly. In 1917 the Chicago Motor Coach Company began motor bus service using mainly boulevard routes; its route network soon encompassed about 170 miles (273.5 km). Equipment included breezy

Figure 7.15. Cable cars on Cottage Grove Avenue, 1903. This type of car operated on the street from 1882 to 1906 when it was replaced by the electric trolley. The Cottage Grove operation was part of what became the world's largest cable car system. Cable cars were pulled on tracks by gripping a moving cable under the roadway. (Photograph courtesy Chicago Historical Society.)

open-top, double-deck buses that often were also used for pleasure riding, sightseeing, or a romantic interlude under the stars. By the end of the 1920s buses were also being used on some routes of the Chicago Surface Lines; a few years later came the electric trolley bus. By 1958 the two forms of transportation had completely replaced the familiar electric streetcar. In turn, the electric trolley bus was phased out in the early 1970s leaving motor buses on the streets for public mass transportation.

Chicago's mass transit system long was hampered by the absence of subway lines. Chicago lagged decades behind some of the large eastern cities in subway construction. A large part of the problem was physical. In New York the subway was constructed for the most part through solid rock which supported the tubes, but in Chicago the subsoil is soft, watery clay, and requires thick, steel reinforced concrete to support the subway tubes.

Finally, in 1943, Chicago's first subway, less than 5 miles (8 km) in length, was opened beneath State Street; in 1951 the 3.85-mile (6.2 km) Milwaukee-Dearborn Street subway was placed in operation. But while Chicago lagged in subway construction, it was a pioneer in the construction of rapid transit facilities in the median strip of expressways—

Figure 7.16. Electric trolley cars on Madison Street looking westward from Clinton Street, 1906. These streetcars ran on tracks and were powered electrically by current drawn through a trolley pole from a suspended overhead wire. (Photograph courtesy Chicago Historical Society.)

first in the Eisenhower Expressway in 1958, and more recently in the Dan Ryan and Kennedy expressways. The successful 5 mile (8 km), high-speed, nonstop Skokie Swift service along an abandoned interurban rail line was successfully established in 1964 between the Howard Street Rapid Transit Station (7600 N) and Dempster Street in Skokie. A rapid transit extension to O'Hare Field is currently under construction.

Meanwhile, the problem of the lack of unification of the transit facilities was overcome by the creation in 1947 of the Chicago Transit Authority (CTA). This publicly-owned but privately-financed agency took over the operations of the Chicago Surface Lines, the Rapid Transit Lines, and the Chicago

Motor Coach Company. It now provides transit service throughout Chicago and into 36 nearby suburbs.

The creation of the CTA brought about improvements in transfer privileges, efficiency of maintenance, and coordination of schedules. But some of the basic problems which had plagued its predecessors also continued to keep the CTA in deep financial trouble despite repeated increases in fares, which, in turn, have decreased the number of riders by over two-thirds since 1947.

One such problem is that the expensive CTA equipment and facilities are used mainly during the two rush hour periods and remain idle or underused most of the rest of the time. A very major problem of the CTA is related

Figure 7.17. Chicago's traffic problems are not new. View, about 1910, south on Dearborn Street from Randolph Street. (Photograph courtesy Chicago Historical Society.)

to the increasing competition from private automobiles in the metropolitan area. People insist on using their own automobiles to go to work, even though the cost factor usually favors public transportation. This is especially true if one needs to pay for parking downtown which many thousands do. The result has been that about one-sixth of the downtown land area is now devoted to parking. Furthermore, the automobile, for the number of people it carries, is a great fuel consumer. The automobile is also the major source of the city's air pollution—a problem of growing concern in an area which also has substantial heavy industry and in which at times one-third of the natural sunlight is lost due to air pollution. The great number of automobiles clogging the highways slows down public bus transportation, resulting in reduced bus patronage.

Table 7.3 shows that total ridership dropped over 30 percent between 1960 and 1980, although the decline in ridership slowed considerably in the 1970s as the cost of operating private automobiles accelerated rapidly.

Figure 7.18. A double-deck bus of the Chicago Motor Coach Company southbound on Michigan Avenue near Chicago Avenue, 1923. The company operated mainly on boulevard routes. The open-top bus was also used by passengers for pleasure riding and sightseeing. It carried 39 passengers on the open deck and 28 inside. This model was retired from service in 1937. (Photograph Kaufman & Fabray. Courtesy Chicago Historical Society.)

TABLE 7.3
Mass Transportation Ridership: 1960–1980

	Millions of Riders			Percentage of Change	
	1960	1970	1980	1960–1970	1970–1980
CTA Surface System	421.8	296.2	280.1	−29.8%	− 5.4%
CTA Rapid Transit	112.9	105.6	90.6	− 6.5	−14.2
Commuter Railroads	61.1	65.7	80.8	+ 7.5	+23.0
Suburban Bus Systems	51.6	29.4	38.2	−43.0	+30.0
TOTAL	647.4	496.9	489.7	−23.2%	− 1.4%

Based on data from the Governor's Transportation Task Force, Regional Transportation Authority, and Chicago Transportation Authority.

There was actually a slight increase in CTA ridership in the late 1970s; however, substantial fare increases and service cuts in 1981 reversed the trend. In the 1950–1980 period, the number of automobiles registered in the city doubled to almost a million, or from one car for every 6.4 persons to one car for 3.5 persons.

The decline in CTA ridership has been largely in bus passengers. Ridership on the elevated-subway rapid transit system has declined only very slightly due to faster, more reliable service and the opening of four new routes in recent years—the Skokie Swift and the routes in the median strips of three expressways. On a typical day 400,000 passengers originate on the 89 miles (143.2 km) of the eight rapid transit lines, while another 800,000 passengers originate on the 138 bus routes that operate on 2,200 miles (3,539.8 km) of city and suburban streets.

Surveys show that since 1926 the number of people entering the downtown area daily has remained fairly constant at between 800,000 and 1 million persons. However, during this period the number entering by public transit street vehicles has declined about two-thirds, while the number coming by automobile has almost doubled to over 250,000, or about 30 percent of those coming downtown. Only transportation modes having their own right of way, such as the elevated, subway, and suburban rail services, have been generally able to maintain their passenger counts. Today they bring in well over a quarter of a million people daily.

For a while the CTA managed to live out of its fare box revenues by instituting major operating economies, such as complete conversion from the two-man streetcar to the one-man bus, and the installation of automatic door controls on elevated-subway trains, thus permitting operation by a two-man crew. But after these conversions, apparently no other major economies were possible and the CTA has been experiencing deficits since 1964. Declining ridership, due partly to the declining city population, inflation, spiralling labor and fuel costs, new expressway competition, lack of independent taxing authority, deteriorating equipment, and a large bonded indebtedness compelled the CTA to increase fares and then to solicit growing governmental aid to combat its deficits. Although large federal grants have been received for the purchase of new equipment, and funds are also provided by the Regional Transportation Authority, in the early 1980s the CTA experienced one of its worst financial crises which led to some curtailment of service.

The Commuter Railroads

Table 7.3 shows that the commuter railroads are the only mode of mass transportation in the Chicago area that increased in ridership in each of the last two decades. Unlike those in other cities, Chicago's commuter railroads, whose extensive network converges at the downtown area, have managed to keep in operation (with the exception of a few electric interurban lines) and even to grow in ridership. Furthermore, the commuter railroads have improved service by the introduction of double-deck, air-conditioned cars. They now carry about 138,000 passengers daily. But, as with the CTA, a basic problem of the commuter railroads stems from their use mainly to carry workers to and from work. This function is largely concentrated into about two rush hours in the morning and about the same number of hours in the late afternoon, five days a week. The rest of the time the costly equipment remains largely idle. As a result of this pattern, not enough equipment can be economically justified to provide every rush hour rider with a seat. Consequently rush hour riding has been accompanied by overcrowding and straphanging.

Unlike the CTA, the total ridership on the commuter railways has held up well overall in recent years, although results vary among the individual railroads, depending on the quality of their service, the population growth of their service areas, the travel-to-work characteristics of the people served, and competitive rail

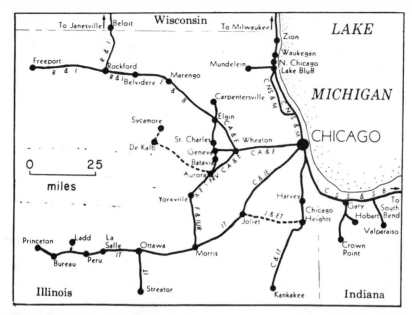

Figure 7.19. The Interurban Electric Railway Network of the Chicago area, 1925, just before the start of their rapid decline. Dashed lines indicate routes abandoned in the early 1920s. The only interurban still operating is the Chicago South Shore and South Bend Railroad. (From Harold M. Mayer and Richard C. Wade, *Chicago: Growth of a Metropolis*, 1969. Reproduced by permission of the University of Chicago Press.)

TABLE 7.4
Annual Passenger Traffic of Major Commuter Railroads

	1961	1971	1979	% Change 1961–1979	% Total 1979
Chicago & North Western	20,107,000	25,000,000	30,279,000	+51%	38%
Illinois Central Gulf	19,675,000	18,000,000	16,554,000	−16	21
Burlington Northern	9,262,000	10,000,000	14,095,000	+52	17
Milwaukee Road	5,037,000	6,000,000	11,191,000	+122	14
Rock Island	6,995,000	5,900,000	6,334,000*	−9	8
South Shore	3,937,000	2,000,000	1,623,000	−59	2

Based on Governor's Transportation Task Force and Regional Transportation Authority data.

*Rock Island inoperative Aug. 28–Oct. 2, 1979 due to strike.

and expressway patterns. Table 7.4 shows that in recent years three of the railroads gained a substantial number of passengers, while three declined. Those which gained serve the fast growing suburbs to the north, northwest, and west.

Like the CTA, and for many of the same reasons, the railroads, with the possible exception of the Chicago & North Western Rail-

way, have consistently lost money on their commuter service. To combat their financial difficulties, the railroads have curtailed service, raised fares repeatedly, cut costs whenever possible and abandoned close-in stations to concentrate on longer hauls. In recent years the commuter railroads have also increasingly depended on government aid to alleviate their financial difficulties. In 1981, due to a sizable

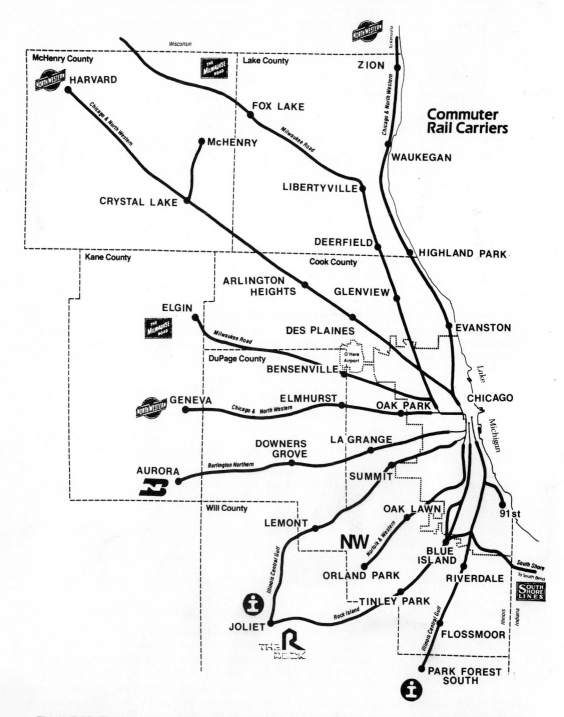

Figure 7.20. The commuter rail carriers of the Chicago area, 1981. Ridership on the commuter railroads increased 23 percent in the decade of the 1970s reaching 80,800,000 riders in 1980. (Map modified from a Regional Transportation Authority map.)

decline in government aid, the commuter railroads increased their fares substantially with a subsequent significant decline in ridership.

Transportation Trends

The area's public transportation system is geared especially to serve the downtown area. Complicating the traffic pattern is the dispersal of industry and population into the outlying areas at densities usually too low to support adequate mass transportation. Unlike jobs in the downtown areas, where transportation routes converge, jobs in the suburbs are difficult to reach by mass transportation methods. The result is a further decentralization of population and the growing phenomenon of reverse commuting by auto from Chicago to suburban jobs. The poor in the city who do not have automobiles find it difficult to commute to suburban jobs, and even more difficult to move near to these jobs.

The 300,000 automobiles that enter the city each morning are now joined by 200,000 cars (double the 1960 number) leaving Chicago daily with workers for jobs in the suburbs. For example, in highly industrialized Elk Grove Village, adjacent to O'Hare Airport, about 75 percent of the 25,000 people employed there reside in Chicago. With increasing frequency, the result is two-way, rush hour traffic jams.

A number of major proposals for improving the area's transportation network have been offered. These include renovation efforts of the "L" system, the construction of a rapid transit line to the Southwest Side, new distributor subways and a riverbank line in the downtown area, southeast and southwest extensions of the Dan Ryan rapid transit, and a lakefront rapid transit line. All of the projects are currently being held in abeyance due to the lack of adequate funding.

Potentially the most important development in recent years in the field of public transportation was the creation in 1974 of the Regional Transportation Authority for the six counties of Northeastern Illinois. This agency

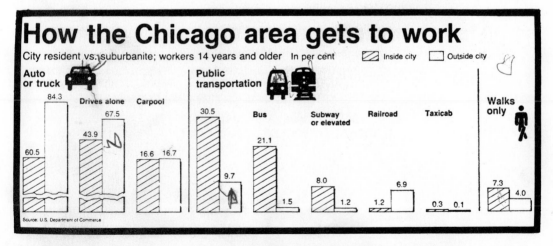

Figure 7.21. Illustration is based on a 1976 survey. Despite the energy crisis, the majority of workers in Chicago and an even higher percentage in the suburbs were still driving their cars to work. Most were driving alone. A much higher percentage of Chicagoans than of suburbanites were using public transportation, which is much more available to city residents than to suburbanites. The average commuting trip of a Chicago area worker is about 10 miles (16.1 km). (*Chicago Tribune* Graphic. Used with permission.)

has the mandate, backed by some taxing powers, to preserve and improve the operations of the ailing CTA, commuter railroads, and suburban bus companies throughout the politically fragmented but economically interwoven metropolitan area.

The RTA has helped maintain, expand, standardize, and coordinate suburban bus and commuter rail service. It has helped provide new equipment and financial aid to these carriers, as well as to the CTA. But like the CTA, it has been plagued by frequent and severe financial crises due chiefly to escalating costs and inadequate funding sources. The RTA has also been handicapped by political wrangling and persistent opposition from some of the suburban areas, especially those more distant from Chicago. It has, however, helped improve service and been instrumental in generally keeping some of the suburban bus lines and commuter railroads from ceasing operations completely. Since the advent of the RTA, suburban bus lines have shown the largest percentage increase, although their passenger load per bus is still small compared to the CTA. To meet its financial requirements, fares throughout the RTA system have been increased, and long-needed attempts have been instituted to make the entire transit system more efficient and economical.

The extensive multimodal mass transit system, consisting of commuter railroads, sub-

Figure 7.22. The Kennedy Expressway during the afternoon rush hour. In the median strip is the CTA Rapid Transit and on the overpass is a Chicago & North Western Railway double-deck commuter train. (Photograph courtesy Chicago & North Western Railway.)

urban bus lines, and the giant Chicago Transit Authority, with its elevated, subway, and bus lines, has long been instrumental in establishing the urban form of the Chicago area and, by its central-area focus, in preserving the viability of the downtown area. In recent decades, the growing use of the automobile, the establishment of an expensive expressway network, the dispersal of the population into areas of lower population density, and rising costs have resulted in rapidly declining ridership and financial difficulties for the mass transit system. However, the energy and pollution crisis, renewed government interest in mass

transportation because of its relative cheapness and efficiency, and the establishment of the Regional Transportation Authority to aid mass transit are all examples of trends which hold some promise of reversing or at least stabilizing the steady decline of mass transportation in the area.

Note

1. Daniel H. Burnham, Jr., and Robert Kingery, *Planning the Region of Chicago* (Chicago: Chicago Regional Planning Association, 1956), p. 81.

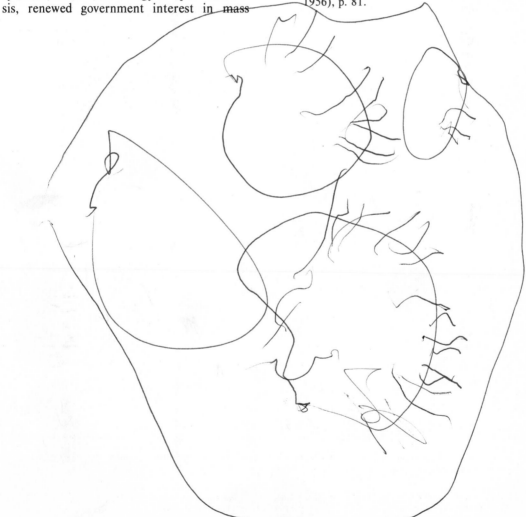

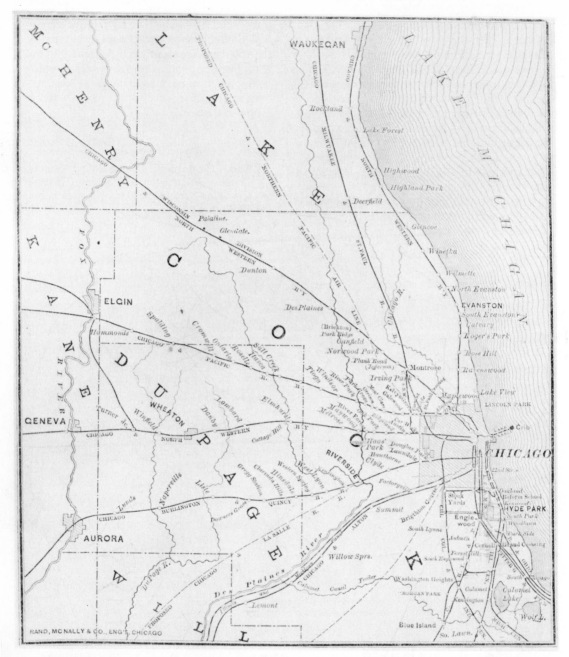

Figure 8.1. Chicago and vicinity, 1873. (From a suburban real estate promotion map. Courtesy Chicago Historical Society.)

Chapter Eight

EXPANSION
OF THE CHICAGO
METROPOLITAN AREA

Suburban Growth

The greater Chicago Metropolitan Area is a mosaic of eight counties and hundreds of variegated, competitive, and fiercely independent communities, stretching approximately from the Wisconsin state line into northwestern Indiana. The area has a total population of almost 8 million, with about 39 percent of the people living in the city of Chicago, down from 80 percent in 1900. And while Chicago continues to lose population, the sprawling suburban "Outer City" now has more people, more jobs, a faster rise in political power, and an immensely greater growth potential than the struggling, but still powerful city of Chicago.

The 1980 census showed that while the city of Chicago had a net loss of about 364,000 persons, or almost 11 percent of its population, between 1970 and 1980, the remainder of the Chicago-Northwestern Indiana Standard Consolidated Area, outside of Chicago, had a net gain of about 495,000 persons, or about 12 percent. (The Illinois portion of the Chicago-Northwestern Indiana Standard Consolidated Area includes Du Page, Kane, Lake, McHenry, and Will counties and Cook County outside of Chicago. In Indiana it includes

Lake and Porter counties. See figure 8.2.) Somewhat similar population trends had been evident between 1960 and 1970, when Chicago experienced a 5 percent decrease in population, whereas the remainder of the area showed an increase of 1,001,000 persons, or about 31 percent. During that decade an estimated one-fifth of Chicago's people, most of them white families with school-age children, had moved to the suburbs, while the movement from the suburbs to the city was comparatively small. The latter consisted mainly of young adults without families and older adults whose children had grown.

Although a few suburbs are almost as old as Chicago, rapid suburban growth around the city of Chicago is largely a phenomenon of the post-World War I period. Chicago itself is, in fact, largely an amalgamation of suburbs that in years past found it advantageous to be annexed to the city which could more readily supply needed services. Suburbs annexed by Chicago make up many of its communities—Lake View, Hyde Park, Jefferson Park, Washington Heights, West Roseland, Rogers Park, West Ridge, Norwood Park, Austin, Edison Park, Morgan Park, Clearing, Mt. Greenwood, etc. In the last half century, however,

CHICAGO-NORTHWESTERN INDIANA STANDARD CONSOLIDATED AREA

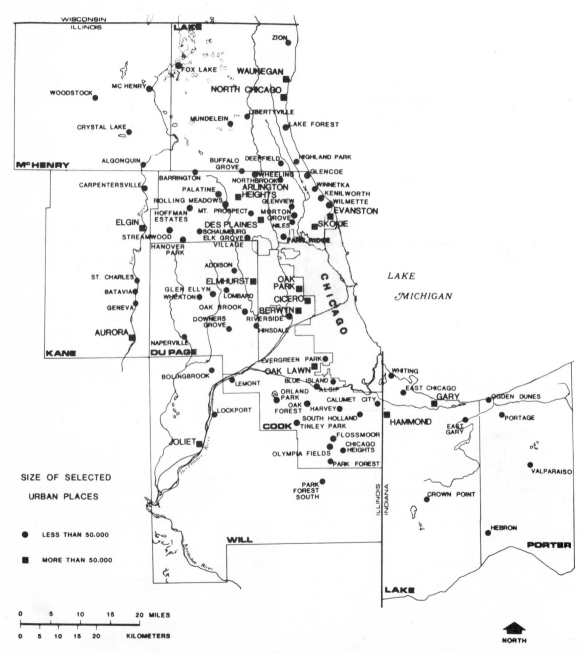

Figure 8.2. Chicago-Northwestern Indiana Standard Consolidated Area. (U.S. Bureau of the Census.)

annexation of suburban areas by Chicago has been minimal, as the remaining suburbs have preferred not to become politically attached to the big city with its multiplicity of problems.

The growth of Chicago's suburbs has been closely related to development of transportation facilities. Some early communities were established along the waterways; later, ribbons of suburbs developed along the railroads; more recently, with the advent of the motor vehicle, suburban settlement has become extremely diffuse.

Before the coming of the railroads there were a few water-oriented communities and a number of small farm-service villages outside Chicago. With the relatively fast transportation of the railroads, however, people for the first time could live some distance from downtown Chicago and still commute there to work. As the railroads radiated out from downtown, stops were located every few miles. Around these stops, homes and often a few shops were built and the nucleus of a suburb developed. More than a century ago, settlements resembling widely-spaced beads on a string had grown up along the main commuter railroads. Along the present Northwest Line of the Chicago & North Western Railway, the communities of Des Plaines, Palatine, and Barrington had already been incorporated; along the North Line of the Chicago & North Western Railway the communities of Evanston, Wilmette, Winnetka, Glencoe, Highland Park, and Lake Forest had been established. The villages were small, usually numbering only a few hundred people, since the inhabitants had to live close to the local railroad station.

The increasing use of the automobile, especially after World War I, resulted in a rapid increase in suburban growth. The growth was substantially slowed during the Great Depression of the 1930s and the World War II period, but thereafter it rose at an unprecedented rate. At first, the automobile chiefly allowed people to reside farther from the commuter railroad stations; later, following improvements in roads, it allowed them to commute to work independent of the railroads. The result was a surge of population outward from the city into the areas between the railroad radials.

There are numerous examples of rapid suburban growth. To the north of Chicago, Skokie was a small village with a population of 783 in 1920. Its truck-farming economy served the Chicago market. The general exodus to the suburbs and improved transportation, especially the opening of Edens Expressway, have resulted in an increase in Skokie's population to 60,000 today. To the south of Chicago, the planned community of Park Forest, which was farmland until the late 1940s, now has a population of 26,000. Similarly, Oak Lawn to the southwest increased from 3,483 in 1940 to over 60,000 today, and Addison to the west increased from 819 in 1940 to over 28,000 today.

In recent years the largest amounts of new housing construction have been recorded in the northwest suburb of Schaumburg and the southwest suburb of Bolingbrook. In Schaumburg the population increased from 18,000 in 1970 to 52,000 in 1980. During the same period, the population of Bolingbrook increased from 7,000 to 37,000. Other leading areas in housing construction and population growth include Hoffman Estates, Wheeling, Elk Grove Village, Vernon Hills, Buffalo Grove, and Hanover Park to the north and northwest; Bloomingdale, Carol Stream, and Glendale Heights to the west; and to the south and southwest, Naperville, Woodridge, Palos Hills, Orland Park, and Tinley Park.

There are many reasons for the decline in the population of Chicago and for the growth in the suburban population (a pattern which is being experienced across the nation). The central city itself is fully occupied and has no space for further growth; indeed, recent expressway construction and slum clearance have decreased the population density of Chicago. In addition, many inhabitants of the central city move to the suburbs to escape its negative aspects—racial conflict, slums, crime, high taxes, high land values, congestion, pollution, poor schools, and other problems.

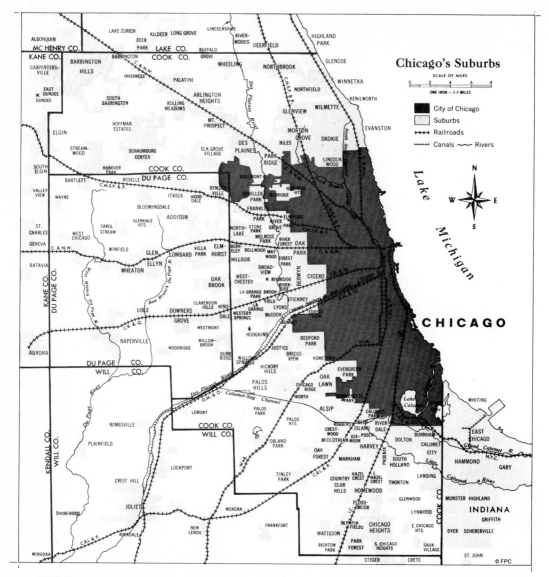

Figure 8.3. Until recent decades Chicago's suburban growth was largely aligned along the railroad routes radiating out of the city. With the advent of the motor vehicle, the land between the railroad routes began to be urbanized also. (Reproduced by permission from M. S. Ratz and C. H. Wilson, *Exploring Chicago,* Follett Publishing Company, 1958.)

REGIONAL GROWTH PATTERNS

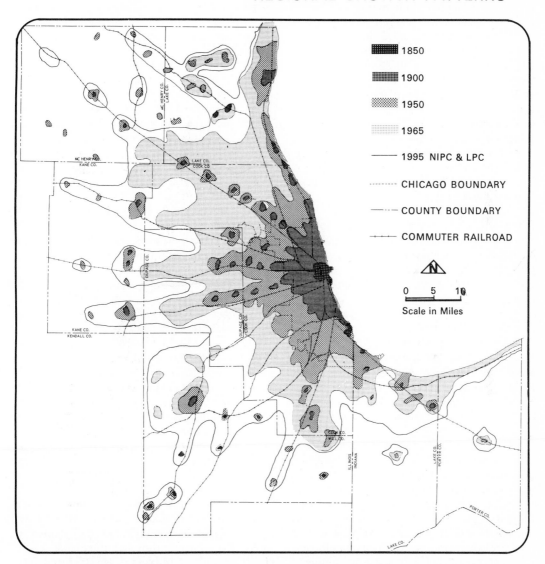

Figure 8.4. Growth of settlement in the Chicago area with projection to 1995, based on data provided by the Northeastern Illinois Planning Commission and the Lake-Porter Regional Transportation and Planning Commission. (Courtesy Regional Transportation Planning Board, 1973.)

The last three decades were, on the whole, periods of prosperity. Automobiles, highways, and homes were built at an unprecedented rate. The "open space, good life" attractions of the suburbs, some real and some imaginary, held strong appeal for young and growing families. Improved transportation, higher standards of living, increased leisure, industrial decentralization, government financial aid, and mass construction of homes all helped accelerate the movement to the suburbs.

In some instances, migration to the suburbs is undoubtedly a response by whites to the approach of blacks; in other cases, it is a flight of the wealthier classes from the poorer classes or of the more "Americanized" from ethnic groups. The smallness of most suburbs makes possible a more homogeneous grouping of people with their own "kind" than is possible in the big city. Even housing may take the form of look-alike structures put up by a single developer in a single effort.

Although the suburban growth rate slowed in the 1970s, largely urbanized stretches now radiate outward from the Loop, especially along the commuter rail lines. In some directions the built-up areas extend about 40 miles (64.4 km) to the vicinity of Waukegan, Barrington, the Fox River Valley cities, Joliet, and to slightly beyond Chicago Heights and Gary. Between the railroad radials, urbanization has been filling in rapidly; there, however, the distance from Chicago of urbanized areas is usually not as great and the movement outward is often discontinuous. Patches of open space occur because of "leap-frogging"—the skipping over some land by developers who decide to get at more distant land because it is more readily available and/or has certain amenity and cost advantages.

Suburban Characteristics

The suburbs of Chicago are far from uniform. They may differ from each other as much as do the individual communities within the city of Chicago. In fact, parts of Chicago are more suburban in character than some suburbs, and some suburbs are more densely populated than the average Chicago community. Chicago's suburbs are rich and poor, new and old, planned and unplanned, white collar and blue collar, industrial and dormitory, close-in and far-out, populated by young and old, succsssful and unsuccessful, with and without previous community tradition, homogeneous and heterogeneous in population—and everything in between. They often differ markedly in race, religion, and ethnic backgrounds, as well as in educational and vocational level. In economic level they range from Kenilworth which had a median family income in 1976 of $42,950 to East Chicago Heights whose median family income was $13,450.

Despite their differences, the suburbs exhibit certain general patterns and trends:

1. Their population density is lower than that of Chicago, as the homes generally occupy larger acreage. Chicago's average population density per square mile is about 13,000 persons (5,019 per sq km), but the city's residential density profile resembles a volcano with a crater of very low density in the central business district, then a sharp rise outward followed by a gradual decline toward the periphery. In the suburbs the density per square mile averages slightly below 5,000 (1930.5 per sq km), although there is a substantial range of variation due to differences in zoning laws and their enforcement. A community's zoning laws control residential density and reflect the attitudes and socioeconomic status of its inhabitants, the transportation facilities, and—an increasingly important consideration—the availability and cost of land.

2. The population density of the suburbs generally decreases as their distance from Chicago increases. Some of the older, larger, close-in suburbs, such as Evanston, Oak Park, and Cicero, built largely in an earlier period and with good rapid transit connections to Chicago, have a relatively

high population density of between 9,000 and 12,000 per square mile (3,475–4,633 per sq km). Some of these mature suburbs are showing signs of deterioration around their commercial cores, just as Chicago is. In a way, such suburbs are simply extensions of the city, with population density decreasing outward from the city.

3. There is an accelerating trend toward building multiple-dwelling units in some suburban areas. In the 1960s, some 150,000 multiple-dwelling units in such forms as apartments, cooperatives, and condominiums, were constructed. Such units help to circumvent high land costs, add to local tax revenue, and often better meet the needs of certain groups, such as singles, young couples, and older people. The rapidly rising cost of single-family homes has priced them out of the range of many families and stimulated the building of smaller homes on smaller parcels of land. In some counties, such as Du Page, the construction of multiple-dwelling units in recent years has exceeded that of new single-family homes.

4. Another trend has been the development of planned, more self-sufficient communities embodying separate compatible locations for residential, commercial, industrial, and recreational functions. Prime examples are Elk Grove Village, near O'Hare Airport, and Park Forest South, 32 miles (51.5 km) south of the Loop. Other suburbs are reserving areas for industrial and commercial use with the aim of broadening their tax base. Some smaller planned developments are being built around recreational facilities, including artificial lakes.

5. A crescent of relatively economically self-sufficient, sizable, industrial satellite cities grew up in an arc about 35 miles (56.3 km) from the Loop, approximately along the route of the Elgin, Joliet, and Eastern Railway (Chicago Outer Belt Line). These cities located at or near the intersection of the belt line and railroads radiating from Chicago, include Waukegan-North Chicago, Elgin, Aurora, Joliet, Chicago Heights, and Gary. Each of these industrial communities was heavily populated by immigrants mainly from Eastern and Southern Europe, and later by a growing black and Hispanic populations.

6. Industry and commerce, as well as population are decentralizing. During the last decade Chicago lost about 2,000 manufacturing establishments, while the suburbs gained about that number. Consequently, increasing numbers of suburbanites are working in the suburbs. In 1980 nearly two-thirds of the suburban work force no longer commuted to Chicago; instead they traveled to other suburbs for their employment. For example, in the 1960s the percentage of the Park Forest labor force working in Chicago declined from 56 percent to 36 percent. In Du Page County, during the decade, the decline of those commuting to Chicago was from 37 to 23 percent, while those working in the county rose from 42 percent in 1960 to 49 percent in 1970.

The percentages vary somewhat with income and occupation. Thus, the suburbs with the highest proportion of rail commuters to Chicago are high income, white collar, residential communities, such as Winnetka, Glencoe, Western Springs, Hinsdale, and Homewood. Conversely, industrial communities, which are large consumers of labor, such as Whiting, Melrose Park, Northlake, Bedford Park and the more distant Aurora, Elgin, Joliet, North Chicago, and Waukegan, supply few commuters. Additionally, in 1970, 18 percent of Chicago's work force was employed in the suburbs, compared to 7 percent in 1960—the big gain being in blue-color jobs which the suburbs often have difficulty filling. But the major increase in suburban workers has been in the white collar category. Suburban commercial office space has increased from 2 percent of the area's total in 1965 to an estimated 30 percent in 1980.

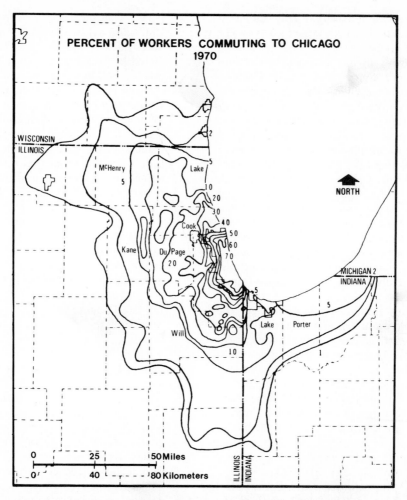

Figure 8.5. Percent of workers from Chicago and the surrounding area working in Chicago, as indicated by the percent numbers on the isolines connecting the points of equal value. Chicago's labor hinterland ranges from 1–2 percent of the workers who live in the southeasternmost counties of Wisconsin to about 70 percent of the workers who reside in Chicago. (Courtesy Brian J. L. Berry, ed., *Chicago: Tranformation of an Urban System,* Ballinger Publishing Co., 1976.)

Table 8.1 shows the change in employment by county from 1959 to 1978 as compiled from U.S. Census data. By percentage the outlying counties have grown much more rapidly in employment than Cook County—led by a spectacular 631.5 increase in Du Page County from 1959 to 1978. Nevertheless, Cook County still accounted for 79.1 percent of the total six-county employment. Cook County's ab-

solute employment increase during this period, mainly in suburban Cook County, was slightly greater than the total absolute increase of the five other counties.

7. Much more than Chicago, the suburban area is strongly oriented toward the automobile. The growing expressway network, in particular, has extended and opened areas for residential, commercial, and industrial development while some-

TABLE 8.1
Trends in Employment Distribution in Northeastern Illinois

	1959		1978		
County	Employment	% of Total Employment	Employment	% of Total Employment	% Changes in Employment 1959–1978
Cook County	1,848,868	90.2%	2,279,902	79.1%	23.3%
Du Page County	33,170	1.6	242,639	8.4	631.5
Kane County	59,027	2.9	107,765	3.7	82.5
Lake County	55,139	2.7	135,747	4.7	146.9
McHenry County	16,096	0.8	40,021	1.4	148.6
Will County	37,992	1.8	76,085	2.7	100.2
TOTAL	2,050,292	100.0%	2,882,159	100.0%	40.5%

Source: Compiled from U.S. Census data.

times reducing commuting time. Residential expansion has been stimulated in the vicinity of almost all of the expressways. Commercial developments, especially in the form of office buildings, have risen near sections of the East-West Tollway and, to the north and northwest, along the corridors of the Tri-State Tollway, the Northwest Tollway, and the Kennedy and Edens expressways.

There is very little effective public transportation for the newer commuting patterns of intersuburban movement and reverse commuting from Chicago to the suburbs—as compared with the old, traditional journey from the suburbs to Chicago's center. The Regional Transportation Authority for the six counties of Northeastern Illinois recently has provided some of the public transportation needed to cope with the new patterns, mainly by establishing numerous new suburban bus routes. In a period of higher fuel and automobile costs, commuters with access to good public transportation are in an advantageous position.

8. In general, the suburbs have a substantially higher median income and higher educational and professional job levels than the city of Chicago. The suburbs have a much smaller foreign-born and black population. Chicago's black population has increased rapidly in recent decades, until it now comprises about 40 percent of the city's population. During the same period, the number of blacks in the suburban area has increased slowly to around 5 percent of the total suburban population. Blacks now live in over half of the approximately 300 communities in the eight-county Chicago Metropolitan Area. However, the majority of blacks are concentrated in fewer than 20 suburbs. In Du Page, McHenry, and Porter counties, blacks still number only about 1 percent or less of the total population. Another developing socioeconomic characteristic is that the newer, more distant suburbs have a younger population than the older, closer suburbs.

9. The growth trends of the past in the suburban areas have varied widely, as is shown by the county data in Table 8.2.

In 1980 the Northeastern Illinois Planning Commission, the official planning body for the six counties of northeastern Illinois, made long-range projections of population growth for the area to the year 2000 showing an increase of 10 percent. The projections were based on such factors as current housing patterns, highway corridors, employment location, local and

Figure 8.6. International Minerals and Chemical Company headquarters along Edens Expressway in Skokie near Old Orchard Shopping Center, 1962. More recently, the building complex has contained the national headquarters of the Brunswick Corporation. Since World War II many companies have located their offices and research facilities in well-landscaped suburban sites, often along expressways which allow for both exposure and accessibility. (Photograph, Robert Foote. Courtesy Chicago Historical Society.)

TABLE 8.2
Population by County, 1950–1980

County	1950	1960	1970	1980	Change 1970–1980	% Change 1970–1980
Cook	4,508,792	5,129,725	5,493,766	5,253,190	−240,576	−4.4%
Du Page	154,599	313,459	490,882	658,177	167,295	34.1
Kane	150,388	208,246	251,005	278,405	27,400	10.9
Lake	179,097	293,656	382,638	440,372	57,734	15.1
McHenry	50,656	84,210	111,555	147,724	36,169	32.4
Will	134,336	191,617	247,825	324,460	76,635	30.9
Lake (Indiana)	368,152	513,269	546,253	522,965	−23,288	−4.3
Porter (Indiana)	40,076	60,279	87,114	119,816	32,702	37.6
Suburban Cook	887,790	1,579,029	2,124,407	2,248,118	123,711	5.8

Source: U.S. Census.

TABLE 8.3
Projected Population Growth of Northeastern Illinois

	1980 (Census)	2000 (Projected)	% Change 1980–2000
Chicago	3,005,072	2,758,800	−8.2%
Suburban Cook County	2,248,118	2,445,000	8.8
Du Page County	658,177	912,000	38.6
Kane County	278,405	394,100	41.6
Lake County	440,372	614,400	39.6
McHenry County	147,724	234,000	58.4
Will County	324,460	455,700	40.4
TOTAL	7,102,328	7,814,000	10.0%

Source: Northeastern Illinois Planning Commission.

county government plans. As shown in Table 8.3, they indicate an uneven growth rate, with Chicago showing a slight decline in population, suburban Cook County a moderate increase, and the five outlying counties showing increases ranging from 38.6 percent to 58.4 percent. McHenry, the most distant county from Chicago and the least populated, shows the greatest projected percentage increase in population.

10. The rapid growth of suburban areas slowed markedly in the 1970s. The suburban population grew 13.5 percent in the decade, with many inner-ring suburbs losing population, middle-ring suburbs tending to post modest gains, and outer-ring suburbs generally growing very rapidly. The shrinking suburb is no longer unique. In the 1960s only 13 suburbs lost population; in the 1970s, 80 in the Chicago Standard Metropolitan Statistical Area showed losses.

The rapid suburban expansion of the 1950–1970 period brought the conversion of an average of 20 square miles (51.8 sq km) of agricultural and vacant land a year into developments. Since 1960 the amount of unincorporated land in Cook County has dropped from 500 of the county's 960 square miles (1,295 of 2,486 sq km) to less than 200 square miles (518 sq km) today. This swift pace of urbanization has recently been curtailed by adverse condi-

tions, including high interest rates, inflation leading to high home costs, the energy crisis, changing family structure, the slowing rate of population increase, and the decline in available land in the areas closer to Chicago. By 1981 the average price of a single-family new home in the Chicago suburbs was over $90,000.

11. While suburban living offers many advantages, it may also have certain drawbacks. These may include poor public transportation, long commuting distances, and inadequate facilities such as for sewage and water, especially if the suburb is new or has grown rapidly. At first there may be a shortage of schools, churches, and shopping facilities. School taxes may be high since the suburbs, particularly the newer ones, usually contain a high proportion of young couples with growing families. In time the children grow up and leave home, marry, and settle in newer communities still farther out from Chicago, where the school-building cycle is repeated. Then the older suburb may decline in population and be saddled with an over-abundance of deteriorating schools and other facilities. At the same time they may lack facilities for the elderly, including low-cost housing.

12. The suburban areas of Chicago can be divided broadly into north, west, and south sectors. These sectors generally differ in rate of growth, economic and social status, and industrial development.

Within each sector, too, there are noticeable, though usually less pronounced, differences.

North Suburban Growth Patterns

The north suburban area includes those suburbs in north Cook County, Lake County, and the adjacent sections of McHenry County. This area ranks higher economically, socially, and educationally than either the western or southern suburbs. Although the northern suburban area contains numerous communities over a century old, it is also the area that has experienced the greatest growth in the post-World War II period.

Population has long been aligned along the three major commuter railroads in the area, with a recent rapid buildup in the sectors between the railroad lines. In addition to well-established transportation facilities, the northern suburbs have certain aesthetic attractions such as (1) the inland lake area with its numerous small lakes and ponds, which developed first as a recreational area and later as the site for permanent homes, (2) rolling topography, such as to the northwest around Barrington, and (3) most important, the Lake Michigan shoreline, which is further enhanced by the picturesque North Shore Ravines from Winnetka to Waukegan. Just south of the Lake County line are the beautiful Botanic Garden of the Chicago Horticultural Society and the Skokie Lagoons. This long-settled lakeshore area, with its attractive physical features, good rail transportation, and freedom from obnoxious industry, contains the greatest number of high income suburbs in the Chicago area.

Figure 5.18 shows that of the twenty-five communities with the highest median incomes in the Chicago area, fifteen are in the north and northwest suburbs (including the top three: Kenilworth, Barrington Hills, and Glencoe). Of these fifteen, seven are aligned along the lake, culminating in Lake Forest, a sylvan community of winding roads and large estates. Unlike communities farther inland, the lake-shore suburbs have now largely achieved maturity, and their prospects for population growth are very limited. Virtually all had small population decreases in the 1970s, caused partially by the declining birthrate. But the suburbs just to the west of the long-established lakeshore suburbs, such as Skokie, Glenview, Northfield, Northbrook, and Deerfield, have grown very rapidly in recent decades because of the availability of land, the opening of the Eden's Expressway with its office building alignments, and their proximity to the prestigious shoreline suburbs. However, even in these suburbs, the growth rate declined in the late 1970s.

Aligned northwest in the corridor of the Chicago & North Western Railway are a group of long-established suburbs—Park Ridge, Des Plaines, Mt. Prospect, Arlington Heights, Palatine, Barrington, and Crystal Lake—populated by families of a generally more modest income than that of the North Shore families. Unlike the North Shore suburbs, these suburbs have experienced rapid growth in recent years. The growth is especially rapid in the communities near O'Hare Airport, such as Schaumburg, Elk Grove Village, Hoffman Estates, Streamwood, and Hanover Park. This area contains many newly-erected prestigious office and hotel complexes, as well as one of the world's largest enclosed shopping centers under one roof—Woodfield Mall in Schaumburg, with annual sales now exceeding $350,000,000. Schaumburg itself increased in population from only 986 in 1960 to 52,000 in 1980. Arlington Heights, the largest community of the area, grew from about 9,000 in 1950 to 66,000 in 1980.

Between 1950 and 1980 the population of this northwest corridor, sometimes referred to as the "golden corridor," more than quadrupled. The growth can be attributed to available land and to a good transportation system, which includes the Chicago & North Western and the Milwaukee Road railroads, plus the Kennedy Expressway-Northwest Tollway, the Tri-State Tollway, and the Lake Street extension of the Eisenhower Expressway. Also, the proximity of O'Hare Airport has attracted a great number of industrial and commercial enterprises.

The areas around O'Hare Airport and Woodfield Mall are the employment nodes of the corridor. The communities around O'Hare Airport employ in excess of 100,000 people in 5,000 industries, with Elk Grove Village alone employing over 40,000 persons. Employment is found not only in industrial concerns but also in a growing number of hotels and office buildings. In 1980 the O'Hare Airport area contained 45 office buildings with 6 million square feet (558,000 sq m) of office space.

In the corridor, about 7 or 8 miles (11.3, 12.9 km) northwest of O'Hare Airport, is the younger, very rapidly growing Woodfield area around Schaumburg, Hoffman Estates, and Rolling Meadows—an area where new office buildings dot the landscape and where there is still plenty of room for growth. The Woodfield area in 1980 contained 63 office buildings with 6.5 million square feet (604,500 sq m) of space. With one exception, all the office buildings have been built since 1965.

The northwest corridor contains facilities of about 300 of *Fortune's* 500 largest corporations, including many familiar names such as Motorola, International Business Machines, Gould, International Telephone and Telegraph, Union Oil, Mobil Oil, Pfizer, United Airlines, International Harvester, Squibb, Quaker Oats, Digital Equipment, and National Can. These are usually located in well-landscaped industrial parks or office complexes. The spectacular growth of the area has brought with it problems, such as growing traffic congestion, noise and pollution from airplanes, and water shortages. The latter may eventually be somewhat alleviated by new water allocations and distribution systems from Lake Michigan. A major problem is a shortage of workers, especially blue-collar workers. They cannot afford to live in the more affluent suburbs of the northwest corridor area and, therefore, must commute longer distances from Chicago. The extension of the CTA rapid

transit line to O'Hare Airport may help alleviate this problem. The extension should also give great impetus to construction of residential, commercial, and industrial facilities along its route.

There are very few lower income suburbs north of Chicago. Among the few examples are North Chicago, Park City, Highwood, Round Lake Park, and Fox Lake. These communities help supply some of the blue-collar workers who are badly needed by industry. The black population is very small and is concentrated in Evanston, Glencoe, Waukegan-North Chicago, and Zion, with the other communities having very few, if any, blacks.

Light industry has expanded rapidly in the northern area, often having moved from Chicago. There is virtually no heavy industry in the northern sector. Much of the light industry is in the growing fields of electronics, chemicals, and pharmaceuticals. Research and office facilities also are increasing rapidly.

The major centers of employment are found in Evanston, North Chicago-Waukegan, Skokie, Niles, Morton Grove, Des Plaines, and Northbrook. The largest city in the northern suburbs is Evanston (1980 population, 73,706), an attractive tree-lined community of homes, apartments, and condominiums, with some industrial areas and a distinguished educational facility, Northwestern University. It is a type of transitional city between Chicago to the south and the lake shore suburbs to the north. Evanston, like most of the lakefront suburbs, lost population in the last decade.

The frontier of urbanization to the north has now pushed deeply, but by no means solidly, into Lake County. Much of the northern third of the county, to the Wisconsin line, is still very largely rural in character, but here and there new developments have been appearing.

Lake County is one of the most heterogeneous of counties, both physically and in population. It is a blend of a variety of urban communities and sizable rural areas. The

Figure 8.7. Fountain Square in downtown Evanston about 1930. City Hall is the towered building on the left, and the Marshall Field store, one of the first suburban branches of a downtown Chicago department store, is in the center background. (Photograph courtesy Chicago Historical Society.)

county is divided by the Des Plaines River as the river flows south from Wisconsin to Cook County. West of the river, the landscape is characterized by rolling topography, farmlands, and numerous small lakes whose shores harbor small moderate-income communities and resort areas. In the northwest corner of the county is the Chain of Lakes State Park, the winding Fox River, and Fox Lake. In the center of the county are the neighboring cities of Mundelein and Libertyville, which have grown rapidly in recent decades. To their south is the small community of Long Grove with its many antique and specialty shops. Just to the south of Long Grove, straddling the Cook County line, is Buffalo Grove, whose

population almost doubled in the 1970s, reaching 22,230 in 1980.

To the east of the Des Plaines River, especially along Lake County's 24 miles (38.6 km) of Lake Michigan shoreline, are some of the wealthiest commuter suburbs in the metropolitan area, including Highland Park, Lake Forest, and Lake Bluff. Also fronting on the lake are two military bases—Fort Sheridan at Highwood and the Great Lakes Naval Training Center at North Chicago. North Chicago and Waukegan are heavily industrialized satellite cities along the lake. To their north, near the Wisconsin border, is Illinois Beach State Park and also the city of Zion. From its founding in 1901 until 1935, Zion was a religious community with a communal society and theocratic government. Today it has a population of about 18,000 and is basically residential with expanding industry, including a nuclear power plant.

The dense population in the eastern part of Lake County helps establish the county as the third most populated in Illinois. Minorities constitute about 11 percent of the county's population, being almost equally divided between blacks and Hispanics. A large blue-collar work force is available in the county for industrial development.

The new population growth in the county has been stimulated by the growth of industry, including huge developments by three medical supply/pharmaceutical companies—Baxter Travenol Laboratories, American Hospital Supply, and Abbott Laboratories; by the opening of two regional shopping centers—Lakehurst at Waukegan and Hawthorne Center (including the adjacent New Century Town community in Vernon Hills); and by the building of the Marriott Great America Theme Recreational Park in Gurnee. The county also contains Ravinia Park, one of the nation's foremost music centers.

The Waukegan-North Chicago-Gurnee complex, aided especially by rapid industrial growth, has had a population increase from 48,671 in 1950 to 113,606 in 1980. Among the larger employers in this area are Outboard Marine, Abbott Laboratories, Johns-Manville, American Hospital Supply, and Fansteel. Growth in the county has been held down somewhat by the lack of adequate water and sewage facilities and by the presence of large estates. Rapid future growth, however, is foreseen for the county. This is partly because land is still available at relatively low cost and in large sections, often from the estates of wealthy Chicagoans who purchased farms years ago and are now willing to sell.

McHenry County to the northwest has the smallest population of any of the metropolitan area counties in Illinois. Its largest city, Crystal Lake, had only 18,590 people in 1980. Agriculture is still a significant industry there, and the county leads the state in milk production. The economic base, however, has gradually shifted to manufacturing, and today the majority of its workers are employed in blue-collar occupations. Because of its geographic remoteness, its immediate growth prospects are relatively limited, although in the 1970s McHenry County led all of the counties in newly incorporated communities with six. The largest of these, McHenry Shores, had a 1980 population of about 1,000.

West Suburban Growth Patterns

The suburbs west of Chicago are more mixed in their characteristics than the suburbs to the north and northwest. Because of Chicago's narrow east-west width, this area includes the suburbs that are closest to the Loop, in some places only about 6 miles (9.7 km) away, such as Cicero, Berwyn, and Oak Park. These are old, sizable, mature suburbs that have had very little room for growth in recent decades. While Berwyn and Oak Park are mainly residential, Cicero is the largest industrial employer of the western area. Oak Park, somewhat like Evanston to the north, is a transitional community that shares characteristics of both the big city and suburbia. It is noted for its beautifully shaded streets and its many homes designed by Frank Lloyd Wright. Like Evanston, it has a large number of apartment and condominium buildings, excellent transportation to Chicago, and an increasing black population.

At the far west, almost 40 miles (64.4 km) from the Loop, are a string of satellite communities aligned along the Fox River in extreme eastern Kane County. The largest of these communities (from north to south) include Carpentersville, Elgin, St. Charles, Geneva, Batavia, and Aurora.

Figure 8.8. View eastward along Lake Street from Harlem Avenue in the central business district of Oak Park, in the late 1920s. Marshall Field store is on the left. (Photograph courtesy Chicago Historical Society.)

All of these communities, with the exception of Carpentersville, had a substantial population increase during the 1970s. These old residential-industrial communities were originally established largely because of their location along the river. The river was also the locale of many summer homes and hotels frequented by Chicagoans. A sizable industrial base, especially in the larger cities such as Elgin (63,798) and Aurora (81,293), combined with their distance from Chicago, has traditionally made for self-sufficiency in employment and, thus, relatively little commuting to Chicago. The Elgin area has facilities of such companies as Simpson Electric, Sherwin-Williams, Stewart-Warner, Elgin Sweeper, Hoffer Plastics, and Illinois Tool Works. The Aurora area contains the facilities of such companies as Caterpillar Tractor, Barber-Greene, Lyon Metal Products, All-Steel, Armour-Dial, and Western Electric.

Only in recent years has the frontier of urban expansion from Chicago reached into the Fox Valley area, leaping over some rural farmland and second-growth prairies. Fox Valley Center, a major regional shopping center, opened in Aurora in 1975. It is part of the new Fox Valley Villages, a planned residential, commercial, and industrial community on the western edge of Du Page County. It is projected to have as many as 50,000 people when completed.

Downtown Aurora is also undergoing improvement with the construction of the Water Street Mall, the restoration of the Paramount Theater, and the start of construction on a new civic center. To the north in Elgin, downtown rehabilitation also is taking place, with a new city hall built as part of a civic center complex. A few miles to the north in West Dundee, the huge Spring Hill Mall shopping center was opened in 1980.

Between the suburbs on the periphery of Chicago and the Fox Valley suburbs is an area that has grown rapidly in the post-World War II period—western Cook County and all of Du Page County. Western Cook County is now almost entirely urbanized. It contains a number of industrial-residential communities with very large industrial employment, such as Melrose Park, La Grange, Bedford Park, Franklin Park, Bellwood, and Maywood. River Forest, Western Springs, and Riverside are attractive, high income suburbs. Riverside was one of the nation's first planned communities, having been laid out in 1868 by the noted landscape architect, Frederick Law Olmsted. It was laid out in parklike fashion, with generous lots and winding roads conforming to the meandering Des Plaines River which it straddles. In western Cook County, only Maywood has a majority of blacks, about 75 percent of its residents. In adjacent Bellwood and Broadview, about one-third of the people are black. Fifteen percent of the population of Melrose Park is Hispanic. In 1980 there were 14,482 Hispanics living in Aurora, about 18 percent of its population, the second-largest Hispanic population in the state.

Du Page County, due west of Chicago, is rapidly urbanizing. In 1950, far more than half the land was still devoted to agriculture, and the entire county population was only 154,599. Since then, the amount of agricultural land has been declining rapidly and the population has climbed to about 658,000. Between 1970 and 1980 the population rose 34.9 percent, the largest percentage of any Illinois county in the Chicago Metropolitan Area. It is the second-most-populated county in Illinois.

Du Page County has the highest median family income in the state, and, in 1970, the fourth highest in the nation. Four of its communities rank among the top twenty-five suburbs of Chicago on the basis of median family income, including Oak Brook in fifth place. The others include Naperville, Hinsdale, and Clarendon Hills. Also the value of homes and the median school years completed are higher in Du Page County than in any other county in the Chicago Metropolitan Area.

Industrial employment is low in Du Page County, and there is no sizable industrial community. However, a number of communities engage in a small amount of manufacturing, with Naperville, West Chicago, and Addison being the largest, although they are relatively small industrial employers. . However, a growing number of nationally known laboratories, research centers, and corporate offices are locating in the county. These facilities are aligned mainly along the East-West Tollway corridor, with major foci in Oak Brook to the east and in the Naperville area toward the west.

Oak Brook, a small village incorporated in 1958, has about 6,700 residents living in spacious homes ranging in price from almost $200,000 to $600,000 and in expensive condominiums. Although it is noted for its polo fields and golf courses, Oak Brook is a major office building and shopping center complex. Twenty thousand workers and 20,000 shoppers come into the village daily, and more than 70 of *Fortune Magazine's* 500 largest companies are headquartered or have office representation in Oak Brook. Companies headquartered there include Ace Hardware, Spiegel, Bliss & Laughlin Industries, Federal Signal, Bunker Ramo, Ceco, Interlake, Nalco Chemical, McDonald's, and Waste Management. Numerous new hotels dot the area, and Oak Brook also contains the second largest regional shopping center in the metropolitan area, Oak Brook Mall. The mall's sales are exceeded only by those of the Woodfield Mall in Schaumburg. A short distance to the north is the Yorktown Shopping Center in Lombard, and farther north is the new Stratford Square shopping center in Bloomingdale. The latter's developers are also planning substantial nearby residential development.

Farther west, for about 5 miles (8 km) in the East-West Tollway corridor, in the general vicinity of Naperville, is an even newer, rapidly growing alignment in a campus-like atmosphere of research centers and office parks—probably one of the fastest-growing private research areas in the country. Among the occupants of this area are Western Electric, Bell Laboratories, Amoco Research Center, Nicor, Nalco Technical Center, Dow Jones, and Fermi National Accelerator Laboratory with the world's largest high-energy particle accelerator. In various stages of planning or construction are facilities for General Motors, Deltak, Burroughs, and Hewlett-Packard corporations. This research and office corridor and Oak Brook have grown rapidly because of available open land and stable residential communities, with growing amenities, such as hotels, shopping centers, and excellent transportation, including easy access to O'Hare Airport or downtown Chicago by automobile. Less than 10 miles (16 km) to the south, in the southern tip of Du Page County, is the 3,700 acre (1,499 ha) Argonne National Laboratory. It is one of the world's leading atomic energy research and development centers.

The residents, although beginning to settle throughout Du Page County, are still predominantly aligned along the two major commuter railroads which serve the county. Along the route of the Chicago & North Western Railway (and also previously served by the now defunct Chicago, Aurora, and Elgin Railroad) are the sizable communities of Elmhurst, Villa Park, Lombard, Glen Ellyn, and Wheaton. The latter community is especially noted for its many religious institutions and Lombard for its annual lilac festival. Larger cities farther south along the Burlington Northern Railroad (which generally parallels the East-West Tollway) include Hinsdale, Downers Grove, and the very rapidly growing, farther out communities of Lisle and Naperville. Naperville, incorporated in 1857, is the oldest community in Du Page

County. In the Lisle area is the Morton Arboretum, a privately endowed, beautiful outdoor nature preserve of thousands of trees and smaller plants. A number of communities not located on the commuter railroads have grown very rapidly and become sizable in the last decade. These include, in particular, Addison, Carol Stream, Bloomingdale, Glendale Heights, and Woodridge.

The high rises that have been built recently in Wheaton, Hinsdale, Oak Brook, and other communities are indicative of the increasingly urbanized nature of the area. The growing population has increased traffic congestion and problems associated with garbage and sewage disposal. Plans are underway to tap Lake Michigan water to supplement the area's well water supply which has been hurt by a falling water table. The county has been the leader in the metropolitan area in the acquisition of new forest preserve land, adding over 10,000 acres (4,050 ha) in the 1968–1977 period and thus increasing its total forest preserve acreage to almost 15,000 acres (6,075 ha).

Minorities in Du Page County constitute just a small fraction of the total population. Blacks comprise only 1 percent of the population and Hispanics 2.6 percent. This may be traceable to early restrictive practices, high home values, and the scarcity of industrial employment opportunities.

Du Page County remains a mosaic of the old and new. Old towns with quiet streets shaded by majestic trees are experiencing renewed growth which sometimes matches that of the new residential municipalities. And scattered around the rapidly disappearing cornfields are sleek new office buildings, busy shopping centers, and vital new industry. In 1950, when Du Page County employed only about 15,000 persons, it was clearly a "bedroom" of Chicago. In 1980, with an employment of over 250,000 persons, a majority of the residents now work within their own county. In the 1970s, Du Page County had by far the greatest percentage increase in jobs of any of the counties of the metropolitan area.

South Suburban Growth Patterns

The southern sector of suburbs forms a large arc stretching from Will County in the southwest, through southern Cook County in the south, into Lake and Porter counties, Indiana, in the southeast. Although the very size of this sector allows for great diversity, in general this area contains the suburbs with the lowest median income, the lowest home value, the lowest levels of schooling, the highest proportion of minorities, and the greatest amount of heavy industry. It also probably has a

greater growth potential than that of the other sectors, although thus far no major new employment complex, such as those at Oak Brook, O'Hare, or Woodfield, have developed.

The area southwest of Chicago's border to Joliet in Will County was at one time one of the slowest-growing suburban segments of the metropolitan area. Will County, for example, was still more than two-thirds farmland in 1970. It was handicapped both by its distance from the Loop and by what was probably the poorest transportation to downtown Chicago of any sector. The recent opening of several expressways plus the existence of one of the few remaining suburban areas with plentiful relatively cheap land has helped it become one of the fastest growing areas

Figure 8.9. Metropolis expanding into the cornfields southwest of Chicago. Development is along the Stevenson Expressway whose opening helped stimulate a building boom in the area. (Reproduced by permission from Rutherford H. Platt, *Open Land in Urban Illinois*, Northern Illinois University Press, 1971.)

around Chicago. Because homes are comparatively moderate in price, many blue-collar workers have moved in, many having left the South Side of Chicago after blacks moved into their neighborhoods. As yet, few blacks live in the southwest suburbs with the exception of Joliet, where blacks in 1980 were 20 percent of the population.

Some of this southwest area is aesthetically attractive, having rolling topography and morainic features, especially in the Mount Forest-Palos area. Due to the proximity of new expressways, such as the Dan Ryan, Stevenson, and Interstate 80, residents now have a greater choice of employment opportunities. In addition, there are industrial centers, such as those located at Bedford Park (the Clearing Industrial District), Alsip, and Joliet. The Joliet region is benefiting from the development of the Chicago-Joliet Livestock Marketing Center, the Louis Joliet Mall, and from a growing petrochemical complex nearby along the Illinois Waterway. Joliet, with a population of 78,000, has a strong industrial base that includes facilities of such companies as Caterpillar Tractor, Olin Chemical, Economics Laboratory, and Uniroyal. Its location along the Chicago Sanitary and Ship Canal also benefits the area.

Among the faster growing communities to the southwest are Alsip, Justice, Tinley Park, Orland Park, Oak Forest, Hickory Hills, Romeoville, Bolingbrook, and Oak Lawn. For example, the population of Oak Lawn more an doubled in the last two decades to 60,590 in 1980; it now ranks second only to Joliet among the cities of the area. From 1970 to 1980, Bolingbrook, along Interstate 55, increased its population fivefold to 37,261 persons. Romeoville, formerly noted mainly for its limestone quarries, grew from 3,574 people in 1960 to 15,519 in 1980.

Due south of Chicago in south Cook County, spilling over into Will County, in an area served by the Illinois Central Gulf and Rock Island railroads, are a large number of small and medium-sized communities. Most

are older, mature suburbs, but a number developed after World War II. A few communities, such as Blue Island, Riverdale, and especially Harvey and Chicago Heights, are highly industrialized.

Among the larger industrial employers in Harvey are Allied Tube & Conduit, Allis-Chalmers, Atlantic Richfield, Whiting, and Wyman-Gordon. In Chicago Heights the larger employers include Stauffer Chemical, Ford, Thrall Car Manufacturing, Owens-Illinois, Hobart, and Calumet Steel. Many communities are a combination of industrial and residential development, containing a population with a low to moderate income range and educational level. The suburbs of East Chicago Heights, Robbins, Phoenix, Chicago Heights, Harvey, and Dixmoor, for example, rank among the poorest in the Chicago area. However, there are a few notable exceptions, especially the residential suburbs of Flossmoor and Olympia Fields. In income, these two commuter communities along the Illinois Central Gulf Railroad rank among the top ten suburbs in the Chicago area.

An interesting moderate income suburb is Park Forest, started in 1947 as one of the first large carefully planned communities in the country. It was developed essentially by a single corporation. It consists of a series of neighborhood units tied together by common community and service facilities, including a major shopping center. Park Forest offers abundant open spaces, curved streets, and a mixture of townhouse apartments, cooperatives, and single family homes. Adjoining it is an even newer planned community partially completed—Park Forest South in Will County.

After a long period of slow growth, this due-south area also is now developing more rapidly. This is the result partly of new expressways into the area, the availability of cheap land, and the mitigation of some drainage problems in the eastern section. In recent years many of the long-established Dutch and German farmers of the area have sold their

Figure 8.10. A section of the post-World War II planned community of Park Forest, 1952, showing some of the curvilinear street patterns. It is located about 30 miles (48 km) south of the Loop. (Photograph, Owen Kent. Courtesy Chicago Historical Society.)

land, although a few of the onion set farmers of Dutch ancestry still remain.

Some of the growth has been due to an influx of blacks into the area, continuing the southward movement of blacks from the heart of Chicago. Many have been attracted to the area by jobs in heavy industry, especially in the numerous steel plants nearby. Despite the fact that the south suburban area contains the largest percentage of blacks of any suburban sector around Chicago, most of the communities have few, if any, blacks. On the other hand, a few communities contain large percentages of black residents. These include Dixmoor, Harvey, Park Forest South, Markham,

Chicago Heights, East Chicago Heights, Phoenix, and Robbins. The population of the latter three communities is almost all black.

Across the state line in adjacent Lake County, Indiana, the area exhibits characteristics quite different from those in other sectors around Chicago. This is an area of very heavy industry, steel in particular, and oil refining and chemicals to a lesser extent. This narrow industrial corridor fronts on Lake Michigan and part of the Indiana Dunes. Surface drainage is poor and severe pollution problems have been precipitated by the heavy industry of the area. Northern Lake County contains the good-sized industrial cities of Hammond,

Figure 8.11. Broadway, main north-south artery of Gary, 1908. The tracks are those of an electric trolley line. The community had been incorporated in 1906 on U.S. Steel land in conjunction with the building of the company's huge new steel plant in the dunes area along the Lake Michigan shoreline. The community was named for the chairman of the board of the corporation, Elbert H. Gary. (Photograph courtesy Chicago Historical Society.)

Whiting, East Chicago, and Gary—some large enough to be considered metropolitan areas. Gary, with a 1980 population of 151,953, and Hammond, with a population of 93,714, are the second- and third-largest cities in the eight-county metropolitan area. Unlike more rural southern Lake County, this is an area of stagnant residential growth and, in some instances, of declining population brought on at least partially by the conditions created by industry and its expansion. All four of the cities lost population in the 1970–1980 decade.

As a whole, the area ranks low in median income, home values, and educational levels. There are very sizable black communities in Gary and East Chicago; in Gary 71 percent and in East Chicago 30 percent of the population is now black. A substantial Hispanic population also lives in northern Lake County, especially in East Chicago, where 42 percent of the 1980 population was Hispanic. East Chicago, population 39,786 in 1980, is actually physically divided into two parts by railroads and the Indiana Harbor Ship Canal. The "Twin Cities" include the eastern part, Indiana Harbor, where the blacks and Hispanics live and have their own business area, and the western part, usually identified as East Chicago, which is largely white and has its own business district.

Less than 10 miles (16 km) south of Gary, along Interstate 65, is the community of Merrillville, Indiana, established in the 1960s. Its population almost doubled in the last decade to 27,677 persons in 1980. Many of the residents are white steel workers who moved out of Gary and were followed by many of their doctors, lawyers, churches, clubs, stores, and restaurants. Merrillville is also the site of a large shopping csnter.

Farther east, Porter County, Indiana, is still the least populated of the eight counties— 120,000 persons in 1980 compared with Lake County's 523,000. However, its population increased 37.5 percent in the 1970s. The cities of Porter County are all small. Its growth, however, has been accelerating largely as a result of the construction within the last decade of two huge steel mills. These flank the new deep-water Port of Indiana at Burns Harbor on the lakeshore east of Gary. One of the largest cities, Valparaiso, with 22,247 people in 1980, is perched on the Valparaiso Moraine and is a manufacturing and university center and the county seat. Somewhat larger, with a population of 27,409, is the relatively new community of Portage, incorporated in 1959. It spans three miles (4.8 km) of Lake Michigan shoreline and includes the new port and much of the two new steel mills. The importance of the steel industry to both Lake and Porter counties is evident by the fact that about two-thirds of all employed residents of each county have occupations associated with the primary metals industry.

Indiana Dunes National Lakeshore

Porter County contains Indiana Dunes State Park and Indiana Dunes National Lakeshore. The latter has been described as "America's first urban park." It took years of bitter conflict before federal legislation established it in 1972. Conservationists, who wished to preserve more of the scenic dunes for the benefit of the burgeoning population of the area, were opposed by commercial and industrial interests desirous of stimulating economic growth by taking advantage of the area's excellent location for industry. After recent land acquisitions, the National Lakeshore occupies 12,535 acres (5,077 ha), including 10 miles (16 km) of Lake Michigan shoreline—about a fourth of Indiana's entire lakefront. In addition to long beaches, the park includes high dunes, wooded ravines, tree graveyards, interdunal lagoons and swamps, arctic bogs, tropical orchids, desert cactus, and interesting wildlife.

Almost 70 years ago, Professor Eliot R. Downing described the wildlife of the dunes in its natural setting:

> . . . it is an extensive stretch of wild country with plenty of cover in which small animals find shelter; it is consequently also the haunt of some of the larger predaceous animals now nearly extinct elsewhere hereabouts. In the last five years I have found the gray timber wolf there once, foxes several times, raccoons, porcupines, rattlesnakes, and nearly every year the bald eagle has been nesting somewhere in the region. . . . Just as the flora of the dunes is a curious mixture of southern and northern species, like the cactus and arbutus, that grow side by side, so there are found animals there as neighbors that represent the desert conditions of the Southwest and the pine barrens of the North. Such representatives of usually widely separate faunas are the six lined lizard that runs to cover with such celerity and the ruffed grouse that as a rule only nests in the pine forest several hundred miles farther north. Yet both these animals are quite common in

Figure 8.12. First large citizen's gathering to preserve the Indiana dunes. The meeting was held in 1917 on the site of the present Indiana Dunes State Park and was sponsored by the Prairie Club of Chicago. (Photograph courtesy Chicago Historical Society.)

the dunes. . . . You also find a group of animals naturally foreign to this latitude but brought here by plants they inhabit. The varying hare, porcupine, and chipmunk are here; such birds as the wood peewee and red eyed vireo nest in the mixed evergreen and birch thickets; the Pickering tree frog peeps his love song; and numerous woodboring beetles and bark tunnelers that infest only the conifers are found abundantly. . . . Because of the congenial cover afforded by the evergreen thickets and the abundant food, many birds are found

during the spring and fall migrations, staying days and weeks in the dunes, that would not loiter at all in the Chicago region were it not for the attractions of this particular section. Such are the raven, cross-bills, kinglets, black-throated green and pine warblers. So too the many lakes and swamps of the region, lying in the depressions between the sand ridges, are ideal shelters for the waterfowl on their way to or from the extensive marshes that lie near to the south. Wild geese, ducks of all sorts, loons, coots, gallinules, rails and a variety of

Figure 8.13. Aerial view of part of Bethlehem Steel Corporation's new Burns Habor, Indiana plant located along the lakeshore in the Indiana dunes area, 1971. The plant, when fully completed, will be one of the largest steel plants in the world. (Photograph courtesy Bethlehem Steel Corporation.)

snipes are all annual visitors and some of them regular residents.[1]

Some of the wildlife have vanished due to encroachment by man, but there are still an estimated 40 different mammals left, including the raccoon, opossum, weasel, muskrat, skunk, and white-tail deer, as well as between 250 and 300 species of birds.

The National Lakeshore park in the Chicago area urban complex is also unique in a number of other respects:

The Indiana Dunes National Lakeshore is America's first urban park. It is within easy driving distance of millions of Americans. . . . [It] is a mosaic park where great industrial complexes, residential conmunities and a web of railroad tracks and highways are interspersed with areas of great physical beauty which remain substantially untouched by man. Though the Lakeshore's land holdings are not contiguous, they include the recreational, aesthetic, and historical elements which typify all of our country's great parks.[2]

Regional Shopping Centers

The retail heart of many Chicago suburban areas is the automobile-oriented regional shopping center. These huge modern shopping complexes usually contain from two to four major department stores, and from 50 to 200 specialty stores (the majority are stores of regional or national chains). Chicago's department store giants have over 50 stores in these suburban centers. The centers are surrounded by acres of parking space, with some being able to accommodate as many as 10,000 cars. Few have adequate public transportation.

TABLE 8.4
Major Chicago Area Regional Shopping Centers

Name of Center	Municipality	Land Area (Acres)[a]	Building Area (Sq. Ft.)[b]	Parking Spaces	Number of Stores	Year Opened	Approximate 1979 Sales
1. Park Forest Plaza	Park Forest	53	900,000	4,600	65	1949	N.A.[c]
2. Evergreen Plaza	Evergreen Park	38	1,250,000	5,000	125*	1952	$145,000,000
3. Hillside	Hillside	53	471,000	4,000	67*	1956	N.A.
4. Old Orchard	Skokie	98	1,245,000	6,200	60	1956	169,000,000
5. Golf Mill	Niles	88	900,000	6,500	78	1960	110,000,000
6. Oak Brook	Oak Brook	125	1,250,000	6,900	70	1962	242,000,000
7. Randhurst	Mt. Prospect	100	1,200,000	7,000	86*	1962	125,000,000
8. Ford City	Chicago	100	1,300,000	7,000	153*	1965	190,000,000
9. River Oaks	Calumet City	100	1,250,000	6,000	53	1966	182,000,000
10. Yorktown	Lombard	133	1,500,000	10,000	130*	1968	180,000,000
11. Deerbrook Mall	Deerfield	48	500,000	3,298	65*	1969	N.A.
12. Lakehurst	Waukegan	98	1,272,696	6,500	129*	1971	125,000,000
13. Woodfield	Schaumburg	169	2,267,000	10,800	235*	1971	348,000,000
14. Lincoln Mall	Matteson	110	1,216,158	5,650	132*	1973	100,000,000
15. Hawthorne Center	Vernon Hills	113	1,400,000	6,800	140*	1973	130,000,000
16. Jefferson Square	Joliet	56	543,736	3,700	67*	1974	N.A.
17. Southlake Mall	Merrillville, Ind.	94	1,368,667	5,800	135*	1974	N.A.
18. Fox Valley Center	Aurora	120	1,497,656	8,135	190*	1975	148,000,000
19. North Riverside Park	North Riverside	64	1,115,000	4,827	120*	1976	135,000,000
20. Orland Square	Orland Park	100	1,240,000	8,085	150*	1976	149,000,000
21. Northbrook Court	Northbrook	140	1,200,000	4,863	136*	1976	108,000,000
22. Water Tower Place	Chicago	3	750,000	660	123*	1976	125,000,000
23. Brickyard	Chicago	50	1,000,000	3,800	130*	1977	N.A.
24. Louis Joliet Mall	Joliet	63	1,000,000	5,200	107*	1978	N.A.
25. Spring Hill Mall	West Dundee	120	1,200,000	8,137	100*	1980	N.A.
26. Stratford Square	Bloomingdale	100	1,400,000	7,000	180*	1981	N.A.
27. Chicago Ridge Mall	Chicago Ridge	74	572,000	4,183	108*	1981	N.A.

Source: Compiled largely from *Directory of Shopping Centers in the United States and Canada.* 21st ed. Burlington, Iowa: The National Research Bureau, Inc., 1980; and data of the Chicago Tribune Research Services Division.

*Enclosed Mall

[a]To convert acres to hectares multiply by 0.405.

[b]To convert square feet to square meters multiply by 0.093.

[c]N.A.—Not Available

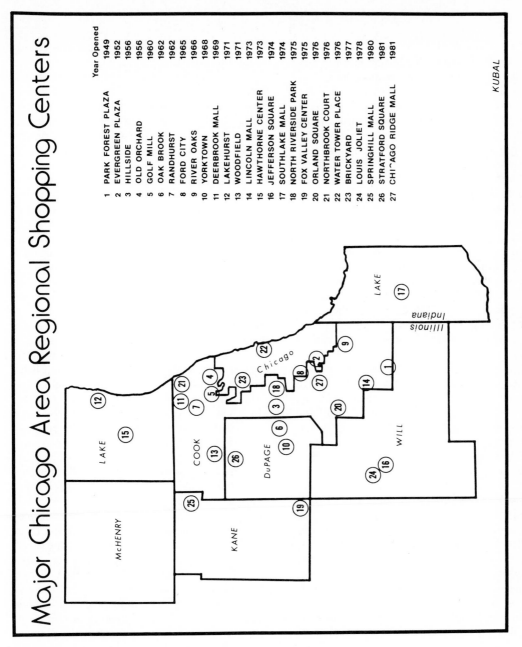

Figure 8.14. Major Chicago area regional shopping centers. (Compiled from *Directory of Shopping Centers in the United States and Canada.* 21st ed. The National Research Bureau Inc., Burlington, Iowa, 1980.)

The centers are in some respects the downtowns of suburbia and the pattern of retailing has oriented itself to these new retail nodes. In addition to retail activities, there are usually numerous professional services, recreational facilities, and often cultural events. They are often the gathering places for various age groups. Design and landscaping are usually attractive, with the newer centers having enclosed malls for more convenient and pleasurable shopping.

The Chicago area now contains 27 regional shopping centers and over 100 smaller plaza-type centers. The first regional shopping centers in the area were opened about a quarter century ago, but until 1960 there were only 4 in the area. These were well spaced, at least 15 miles (24 km) from each other and more than a dozen (19 km) from the Loop. Since 1960, 23 additional major regional shopping centers have opened. (See table 8.4 and figure 8.14).

Many of the centers now are closely spaced, with overlapping hinterlands. In the western suburbs, Hillside (opened in 1956), Oak Brook (1962), Yorktown (1968), and North Riverside Mall (1976) are just a few minutes drive from one another. To the north of Chicago, aligned in the vicinity of Golf Road in a stretch of only about 17 miles (27.4 km), are four major regional shopping centers—Old Orchard (1956), Golf Mill (1960), Randhurst (1962), and Woodfield (1971). The pattern of the opening of the new centers, as illustrated by these cases, has generally been an ever-outward movement toward the periphery of the metropolitan area. Some of the newer centers, in areas where large tracts of land are available, are the hubs of a complementary residential development, such as the planned New Century Town adjacent to Hawthorne Center, or the Fox Valley Villages development—which includes Fox Valley Center. The shopping center often is a catalyst for important residential and commercial growth, such as is occurring around the Woodfield and Oak Brook shopping centers. Some centers have been established prematurely for their areas and are counting on rapid population growth to increase the market potential. Additional major new shopping centers under various stages of planning or construction are contemplated for Lansing, Orland Park, and Rosemont.

The community containing the regional shopping center usually finds that its roads have become more congested and that it has to provide additional police and fire protection; however, this is usually more than compensated for by greatly increased real estate and sales tax revenue as well as improved shopping and employment opportunities for its residents. Adjacent communities often feel the adverse effect of the shopping center, for not only do their streets usually bear some of the increased traffic, but their shopping facilities suffer from the competition of the new modern center. As a consequence there has often been strong opposition by neighboring communities to the development of large shopping centers. In a few rare cases, adjoining suburbs have agreed to share in some fashion the revenue generated by a new shopping center.

A new major shopping center can have an adverse effect on an old, established suburban downtown area, as has happened in such communities as Chicago Heights, Aurora, Oak Park, Waukegan, and Evanston. For example, Evanston, although larger in population than adjacent Skokie, has only about half the retail sales of Skokie which contains the very busy Old Orchard Shopping Center; Park Ridge has only about half the retail sales of the adjacent and smaller community of Niles which contains the Golf Mill Shopping Center; Oak Brook, with less than one-eighth the population of Oak Park, has substantially greater retail sales due to the presence in Oak Brook of the huge Oak Brook Shopping Center. Some major suburban shopping centers not

Figure 8.15. The Oak Brook Shopping Center is located in Oak Brook, Illinois near the intersection of the East-West and Tri-State tollways. It ranks second in sales among the area's 27 regional shopping centers. Its opening in 1962 stimulated rapid growth in the area of office buildings, industry, hotels, and residential development. (Photograph by Hedrich-Blessing. Courtesy Draper and Kramer, Inc.)

only compete with long-established suburban downtown stores, but also attract customers from the city of Chicago.

The Rural-Urban Fringe

The farm acreage around Chicago continues to decline as urbanization expands outward from the central city. The once-productive truck and dairy farms of Cook County have largely disappeared. The same process is accelerating in the adjoining counties, although all but Du Page County (21 percent) and Lake County, Indiana (44 percent) still have 60 percent or more of their land in farms. In 1978 the percentage of land devoted to farming in Metropolitan Chicago ranged from 8 percent in Cook County to 75 percent in Kane County.

The change of an area from rural to urban generally follows a pattern with accompanying problems. First, there is an influx of nonfarm rural residents.

They come to the countryside for cheaper land and lower taxes, sunshine and open spaces, room to relax and enjoy outdoor living, a safe and healthy environment in which to raise their children, a place to grow a garden and perhaps a few chickens, refuge during misfortune, and a home in their declining years.

The change in the rural scene often begins when a farmer sells off a front lot or two or perhaps a front tract or an acre or so. The price the farmer received was high compared with the value per acre of his farm as a whole. Because of this, other farmers are induced to sell off their frontages. More houses follow. Later, entire farms are broken up into tracts and subdivided. The change continues and as the years go by, country roads begin to look like residential streets. As the nonfarm population grows land is bought for gas stations and roadside stores and shops, then for other business and industrial uses.[3]

If the area is unincorporated and without adequate government regulations, new construction may be substandard, a honky-tonk atmosphere may be created, and the natural environment may be defaced. This intrusion of nonfarm rural residents often creates problems that virtually force farmers to sell out. Whereas an 80-acre (32 ha) farm may contain one family, an 80-acre subdivision may hold 120 families. Without adequate advance planning and zoning, the farmers may find their schools suddenly crowded; new problems of water, sewage disposal, and drainage; increased traffic; and higher taxes. Often there is a time lag before the subdivision assumes its full tax load, and the farmer may be assessed at land values similar to those of subdivisions. Highway relocations may divide farms. There may be zoning disputes. Also, the lack of large, undivided, or expandable farms makes it difficult for farmers to take full advantage of large, cost-reducing farm machinery or other improvements. Thus, some of the urban-area farmers are producing vegetables because these typically are more profitable on small parcels of land than is the production of grain. However, the bulk of the farmland in the area is still devoted to growing corn, soybeans, oats, winter wheat, hay, and alfalfa.

The aggressive farmer may feel himself hemmed in as far as expansion is concerned. He may even have to put up fencing against trespassers. He may have to use his land more intensively in order to pay the higher taxes. Necessary farm services are often curtailed as an area becomes more urbanized, and a farmer so isolated may encounter difficulty, for example, in arranging for a truck to collect his milk. The result of these problems, plus the

attraction of high land prices, is that the farmer sells his land.[4]

Actually very few farmers are deeply disappointed when urban interests buy them out for a thousand dollars per acre or more. For agricultural purposes the soil itself is generally worth no more than a fraction of the selling price. The sale of the land may mean giving up a favorite spot, but even the old homestead loses its appeal when all the farms around it go into industry, residential developments, and shopping centers. The capital gain that comes when a farmer surrenders to the city is a handsome reward. He naturally feels much better about the deal than the suburbanite who follows him with a split-level on an 80 foot lot and a thirty-year mortgage. The "poor farmer" can grieve at his leisure on Miami Beach while the "rich city slicker" works the rest of his able lifetime to pay for taking his land.[5]

In time this distant "exurbia" becomes suburbia and another tier of suburbs develops around Chicago. Since 1960, the farmland acreage in the six county Chicago metropolitan statistical area has declined an estimated 15 percent to about a million acres (405,000 ha) in the early 1980s. The average annual loss of farmland has been about 17,000 acres (6,885 ha)—predominantly in the smaller farms close to Chicago. The number of farms in the six county area has declined by an estimated 3,000, or over 45 percent, since 1960, a small number through farm mergers, but the vast majority because of the spread of urbanization.

The 1978 Census of Agriculture listed 454 farms still remaining in Cook County, down 59 from the 1974 census. The average size of these farms was 127 acres (51 ha). Soybeans occupied the most acreage of any crop in the county, followed in order by corn, hay, and vegetables. In 1981, one farm of 64 acres (25.9 ha), originally started by two Dutch immigrants in 1863, still existed in the city of Chicago at 111th Street and Pulaski Road (4000

W)—in an area which at one time was mainly farm land.

Midwest Megalopolis

By early in the twenty-first century, it is likely that the suburbs of Chicago will have virtually merged with the suburbs of Milwaukee and the other large communities to form a giant mainly urbanized area whose basic framework is clearly evident. Chicago is now the nucleus of this large developing urbanized sprawl—a Midwest Megalopolis—that stretches almost 300 miles (482.7 km) between approximately Elkhart, Indiana, and Green Bay, Wisconsin. This urbanizing area, encompassing about six thousand square miles (15,540 sq km), is roughly L-shaped, around the southern and western shores of Lake Michigan through such cities as South Bend, Gary, East Chicago, Hammond, Chicago and its suburbs, and northward through Waukegan, Kenosha, and Racine, to Milwaukee and beyond. This area of developing urban coalescence already contains a population of over 10 million people. The dominance of the Chicago area is seen in the fact that the city of Chicago now contains about one-third of this population and that its surrounding metropolitan area contains slightly more than another third of the total population of the megalopolis.

The orderly, harmonious, and efficient development of the emerging megalopolis, with its changing scope and nature of urban settlement, is one of the problems confronting the Chicago area.

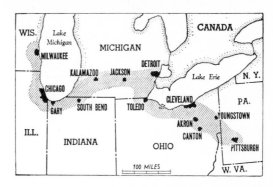

Figure 8.16. Shaded area represents a future "megalopolis" predicted by some planners for the next century. The "midwest megalopolis" forms the western part. (Map courtesy *Chicago Tribune*.)

Notes

1. S. T. Mather, *Report on the Proposed Sand Dunes National Park, Indiana* (Washington, D.C.: Dept. of the Interior, National Park Service, 1917), pp. 93–94.
2. Jean Komaiko and Norma Schaeffer, *Doing the Dunes* (Beverly Shores, Ind.: Dunes Enterprises, 1973), p. 5.
3. U.S. Department of Agriculture, *The Why and How of Rural Zoning.* Agriculture Information Bulletin no. 196 (Washington: Government Printing Office, 1958), p. 1.
4. Irving Cutler, *The Chicago-Milwaukee Corridor: A Geographic Study of Intermetropolitan Coalescence.* Northwestern University Studies in Geography no. 9 (Evanston: Northwestern University, 1965), pp. 126–27.
5. Jean Gottman, *Megalopolis* (New York: Twentieth Century Fund, 1961), pp. 131, 333.

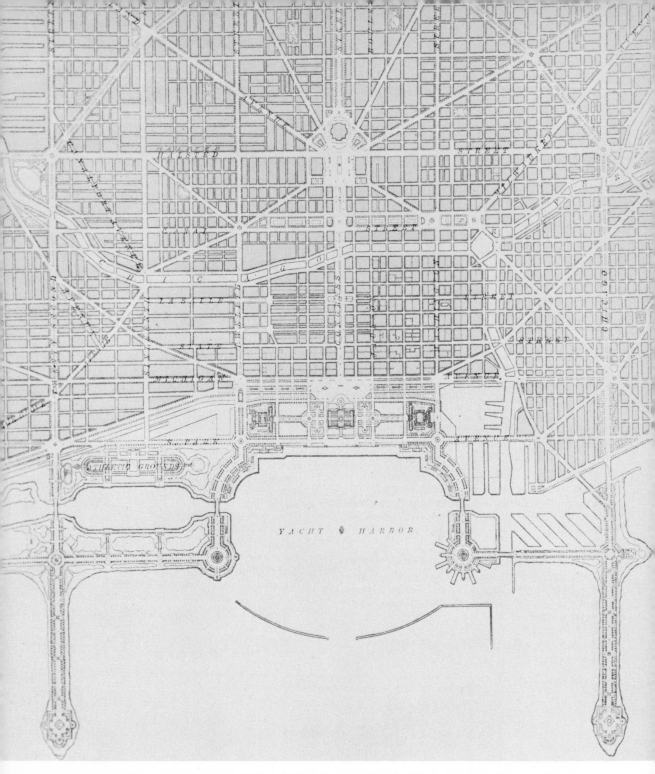

Figure 9.1. A portion of Burnham's Plan of Chicago, 1909. Some important proposals shown on the map that have been implemented, generally in accordance with the plan, are Northerly Island, Grant Park, and Navy Pier (from left to right in the foreground), the straightening of the South Branch of the Chicago River, the widening of major streets and the construction of the Eisenhower Expressway. The campus of the University of Illinois at Chicago Circle is now located in the area of Burnham's proposed monumental civic center plaza around Halsted and Congress streets. (From *Plan of Chicago,* 1909. Courtesy Chicago Historical Society.)

Chapter Nine

PLANNING FOR THE FUTURE

Problems and Principles

Chicago is plagued by the problems that confront most large cities today—housing, pollution, traffic, racial strife, employment, welfare, crime, schools, land use, and recreation. Chicago has made extensive efforts in some of these fields, but they are still not adequate. For example, billions of dollars have been spent for new expressways and rapid transit service, yet acute traffic problems still remain. There have been extensive public and private slum clearance projects, yet there are still slums. Chicago has developed a fine recreational system of parks, beaches, and some of the best museums in the country, yet there are not enough readily accessible recreational facilities. Because of high costs and uncertain tax sources, financing improvements is becoming increasingly difficult. The same problems, on a smaller scale, are now also affecting many other parts of the metropolitan area whose destinies are inextricably interwoven with the central city.

Part of the problem is due to the rapid growth of the area, changing lifestyles and technology, governmental shortcomings, the inadequate tax base, and most important, the lack of foresight and planning, all of which have resulted in haphazard growth. In the beginning there was no plan for Chicago; once a city is developed and populated it is most difficult to change. Unraveling the chaos and making the area a good place to live will take the highest level of planning, dedication, and financial contributions.

A plan to support the optimum development of the area should be based on certain principles and objectives: (1) the community should decide "where it wants to go;" that is, what kind of community is desired, based on the citizens' views of what constitutes a better community and better living; (2) the plan should be a blueprint to guide future development as well as correcting the mistakes of the past; (3) it must try to anticipate future population trends and technological innovations; (4) it should be flexible, comprehensive, and practical as to financing and implementation; and (5) the plan should encompass human aspects as well as physical conditions—for the city is really its people.

The Burnham Plan

Fortunately, Chicago has been a pioneer in city planning and some of its finest features are the result of such planning. In 1869 Frederick Law Olmsted laid out the basic park and connecting boulevard system which has served Chicago so well for a century. A semi-circular basic park pattern was developed in which Jackson and Washington parks on the South

Side and Lincoln Park on the North Side were linked by a belt of boulevards with Humboldt, Garfield, and Douglas parks on the West Side.

In 1893 the World's Columbian Exposition gave Chicago a glimpse of the advantages of urban design that incorporated an orderly arrangement of structure and space. And in 1909 the renowned architect Daniel H. Burnham, who had presided over the construction of the World's Columbian Exposition, proposed a monumental long-range *Plan of Chicago* which introduced comprehensive city planning to Chicago and the nation.

The Burnham Plan was encouraged and backed financially by the Commercial Club, whose members included many of Chicago's foremost business and civic leaders. Although Burnham did not adequately foresee such problems as housing, neighborhood redevelopment, and the enormous effects of the automobile, his plan was bold in imagination, metropolitan in scope, and comprehensive in its incorporation of the advanced concepts of the time. It saw Chicago primarily as a dynamic industrial and commercial city. It was designed to free industry and commerce from congestion and to make the city an agreeable place to work and live—a city that would be aesthetically pleasing as well as convenient and practical. It stressed the "city beautiful" trend with wide, tree-lined boulevards, parks, vistas, and civic centers. It became the official plan of Chicago and guided public improvements for many years. Although not all of Burnham's specific suggestions have been implemented, some outstanding features of present-day Chicago were either proposed or advanced by the plan, and more than half-a-billion dollars has been expended in its implementation. Much of its success can be credited to the promotional and educational work on its behalf carried out by such men as Charles H. Wacker and Walter D. Moody to win public support and carry necessary bond issues. *The Wacker Manual,* a noteworthy civics textbook, explained the plan to two generations of local schoolchildren.

Major recommendations and achievements of the Burnham Plan include:

1. The creation of a regional highway system extending up to 60 miles (96.5 km) outside the city—a metropolitan approach which has been at least partially implemented by the expressway system.
2. The widening of major thoroughfares including the section-line streets. Michigan Avenue was bridged and partially double-decked, Canal Street widened, Ogden Avenue extended, and the mile-long Roosevelt Road viaduct and the double-deck Wacker Drive were built.
3. The consolidation of railway terminals, still not fully achieved but anticipated to be further implemented in the near future. The Union Station was built as the plan suggested.
4. The construction of new docks and navigation facilities. Navy Pier was built, Lake Calumet developed, the South Branch of the Chicago River straightened, and a number of new bridges constructed.
5. The development of a continuous lakefront park has been largely achieved, with 25 miles (40.2 km) of the city's 29 miles (46.7 km) of lakeshore devoted to recreational and cultural facilities, including numerous beaches and yacht basins. Only one (Northerly Island) of the string of contemplated offshore islands has been completed.
6. The substantial extension of the outlying forest preserves, especially along the river floodplains.

An incidental but far reaching result of the Burnham Plan was the organizing of planning on a permanent basis. The plan stimulated the development of two organizations, one for the city's planning, the other for planning on a more regional basis. From these earlier agencies have evolved the city's present policy-making Chicago Plan Commission and its administrative arm, the Department of

Figure 9.2. Looking northeast toward Lake Michigan, with Sears Tower, the world's tallest building (1,454 ft; 443 m) dominating the skyline, 1977. In the center foreground is the world's largest post office, with the Eisenhower Expressway going through it. Although the building preceded the expressway by almost three decades, it was constructed to allow for the passage of the future expressway in accordance with the Burnham Plan of 1909. (Photograph courtesy Chicago Convention and Tourism Bureau.)

Planning. Serving six counties of the northeastern part of the state is the Northeastern Illinois Planning Commission.

Recent Chicago Planning

Through the years other measures were taken to ensure the orderly development of Chicago, but none of these has as yet matched the overall impact of the Burnham Plan. In 1923, Chicago's first zoning ordinance was passed. Two decades later a complete land use survey of Chicago was finished. The documents based on this survey provided significant data information for planners; the

information has been updated periodically. Special agencies have been created to deal with specific problems, such as the Medical Center Commission to redevelop the area surrounding Cook County Hospital; the Urban Renewal Agency to undertake slum clearance, redevelopment, and aid in the conservation and rehabilitation of rundown areas; the Chicago Area Transportation Study to develop a comprehensive transportation plan; and the city's Environmental Division of the Department of Consumer Services.

In 1946, the Chicago Plan Commission published a map to show the Preliminary Comprehensive City Plan of Chicago. The plan recommended patterns of residential, commercial, industrial, recreational, and transportation development. Included were designated boundaries for 514 self-contained neighborhoods, each centered around an elementary school, and 59 larger community units, each centered around a high school. The document has served as a general guide for subsequent activities in urban renewal, zoning, and public works.

In 1966, after prolonged study and discussion, the city proposed the Comprehensive Plan of Chicago. This plan was designed to guide the growth of Chicago into the 1980s and to alleviate some of the city's most pressing problems. More than any of the previous efforts, this plan concentrated on the human and economic element. It stated some rather obvious basic aims, such as to improve the quality of family life and the environment, expand opportunities for the disadvantaged, create job opportunities through economic development, provide for efficient movement of people and goods, and plan for proper land use. The plan, however, did not deal with the serious problem of segregation or the continued flight of whites to the suburbs.

To supplement the basic plan, the Department of Planning published a lavishly illustrated, detailed plan for each of sixteen geographic areas of Chicago. Each plan made specific recommendations, complete with colorful detailed maps, for improving the various facets of the area, such as housing, shopping, schools, recreation, transportation, industry, public safety, and health. After discussion with members of each community and if the plan received official city approval, appropriate improvements were to be made part of the capital improvements program of Chicago.

A decade and a half after being issued, the proposed Comprehensive Plan still has not received official city approval, and extensive major implementation seems doubtful. It is now outmoded and disregarded, due largely to political, community, and racial bickering, and a new Comprehensive Plan consisting of

goals and policies for the city is being prepared. Certain of the proposals, however, are being put into effect independently. As one critic of this laissez faire approach to planning in Chicago cynically observed: "Bend the zoning a little. Give the big money boys a tax break. Bring on the skyscrapers. Build more expressways. Let the cement mixers roll."

Recent planning recommends high-density communities along the lakefront, in the downtown area, and along mass transportation routes; low density housing in the outlying parts of the city; and medium-density development in between. In some areas there will be a "mix" of housing.

Major development projects for the central area of Chicago include the Illinois Center project east of Michigan Avenue and north of Randolph Street, which is already partially completed; additional construction in the area east of North Michigan Avenue and north of the Chicago River; the seven-block North Loop redevelopment plan; and the "South Loop New Town" on the largely unused railroad land just beyond the southern edge of the Loop. These developments are all part of the all-encompassing Chicago 21 Plan which deals with the future of the central area communities. This plan includes downtown Chicago and the adjacent lands to the north, west, and south which are bounded by the lake on the east, Ashland Avenue (1600 W) on the west, North Avenue (800N) on the north, and the Stevenson Expressway on the south.

The Chicago 21 Plan, proposed in 1973, is sponsored by a nonprofit organization composed mainly of business and real estate people. The plan, if substantially implemented by various private and public sources, will provide innovative guidance and coordination into the twenty-first century. It proposes to stabilize and improve the central area and includes plans for substantial new residential development. A major aim is to have more people— including many members of non-minority groups—live, shop, work, and be entertained in the central area. In addition to substantial

Figure 9.3. Aerial view of the Chicago River and its many bridges looking eastward toward Lake Michigan in the late 1960s. The tall buildings toward the foreground are Marina City (left) and the United of American Building (right). The bridge in the center of the picture, toward the end of the curve in the river, is the double-deck Michigan Avenue Bridge. In the background from left to right are the Central District Filtration Plant, Lake Point Tower, Navy Pier, and the lock of the Chicago River Controlling Works. Since the late 1960s substantial progress has been made toward implementing some of the plans for the underutilized south bank area of the river near its mouth (right background). A number of high-rise office and residential buildings and a major hotel have been built on the Illinois Central Gulf land and Wacker Drive has been extended to join Lake Shore Drive. (Photograph courtesy Chicago Association of Commerce and Industry.)

housing and commercial development in or near the Loop, the plan proposes a variety of public transportation improvements; more open space, especially along the lakefront; and preservation of certain landmarks.

Since the plan was presented in 1973, its proposals have met with some notable successes, although some of its lofty goals have not yet been achieved. Several thousand new residential units have been opened on the perimeter of the Loop, including the Dearborn Park development in the "South Loop New Town," the adjoining "Printing House Row" development, and a few scattered high-rise residential buildings. Many more thousands of new residential units are under construction or planned for the area around the Loop.

An impressive number of new commercial buildings—about 40—have been completed or announced since 1973, accounting for most of the nearly 80,000 new jobs that have been created. The State Street Mall has been completed, and the new Loop College building is scheduled to be completed in 1982. Such landmark structures as the Marquette, Monadnock, and Fine Arts buildings have been renovated. Navy Pier has been improved and the Prairie Avenue Historic Area established. And the extension of Columbus and Wacker drives has progressed.

Little or no progress, however, has been made on proposals of the Chicago 21 Plan for new downtown subways, removal of the Loop elevated tracks, conversion of Meigs Airport into a public recreational area, erection of a giant sports arena, development of "River City" along the South Branch of the Chicago River, or for significant rehabilitation of some of the outlying areas. In fact, some of these proposals have met with decided opposition. Many of the plans for the rehabilitation and improvement of Chicago, as for the operation of some of the city's programs, have depended on federal and state aid—which may not be as readily available in the future.

Two elaborate waterfront development plans have been proposed by the city itself. In 1973 the city published the Lakefront Plan of Chicago, designed to complete, extend, and improve Chicago's lakefront park system, make the lakefront facilities more accessible, increase recreational opportunities, and improve the ecological aspects of the lake and lakeshore. The following year the Riveredge Plan of Chicago proposed the improvement of the 1½ mile (2.4 km) main branch of the Chicago River from Lake Michigan to Wolf Point at the junction of the North and South branches of the river.

The Riveredge Plan proposes the development of recreational and open spaces along both sides of the river. It includes a type of grand pedestrian promenade along part of its north bank, a new landfill park near the river mouth, and significant artwork and other cultural and historical attractions. Appropriate public and private riveredge development, including residential buildings will be encouraged. Efforts will be made to improve the water quality of the river and its use for recreational as well as commercial purposes. No significant financial arrangements have been made to carry out either of these elaborate plans for the waterfront, and little has been done, as yet, to implement either proposal.

Chicago's planning, development, and investment in recent decades have been heavily concentrated in the central area, often to the neglect of many of the poorer parts of the city. The city has been renewing itself from the core outward. The vitality of the downtown area, however, has helped in the renovation of some of the choice nearby areas, especially to the north, such as the Near North, Lincoln Park, and Lake View communities. These areas are increasingly inhabited by white middle- and upper-income persons, mainly professionals— young couples, singles, and "empty nesters," some of the latter returning from the suburbs. Often poor minority groups are replaced in the process, and they crowd into poorer, neglected areas where they aggravate already crowded conditions.

Around the city center and the fashionable Near North area is a huge crescent of mainly black and Hispanic residents, many having arrived in the city at the time manufacturing jobs were moving out from the city. This largely economically depressed section of the city, between the central area and the remaining old ethnic communities to the southwest and northwest, is the part that is especially in need of sound planning which will lead to improvement in residential, educational, shopping, and employment facilities of the area.

Planning for the Metropolitan Area

In the metropolitan area there are both localized and widespread planning problems; often the two are interwoven. A planner of a new suburban development would have to give serious consideration to a number of important questions:

As the planner gazes out over the rural-urban fringe he must face such questions as: Where should schools be located? How much land should be set aside for each school? Where should major thoroughfares be located? How should interstitial areas between thoroughfares be laid out—with winding street patterns, or grids, or some other design? What areas should be zoned for apartments, for large-lot single-family dwellings, for small-lot single-family structures? Should land be set aside for shopping centers? If so, how much and where should it be located? Will there be a need for land for industrial uses? (If so, it should be demarcated in large parcels—at least a few hundred acres—zoned to keep other users out and situated near railways, main highways, and on land which is not too valuable.) The general thinking by planners now is that at least five percent of a city's land should be set aside for recreational purposes. Hence, the need for deciding what parts of the farm land to be annexed should be devoted to parks, golf courses, wildlife refuges, or other types of recreational uses. Additional questions deal with matters like positioning storm sewers in such a manner that heavy rains and melting snow can run off with no flooding. Rural land adjoining a city usually is not faced with a serious problem at this point (unless it

is in a valley bottom) since most of the earth's surface is covered with soil into which much of the water seeps. Water which isn't absorbed by the soil often is retarded in its run off by pasture grasses or other ground cover. But when such land is transformed into city, it is almost entirely resurfaced—and water proofed. Roofs, streets, driveways, and sidewalks absorb no water—neither do they impede its run off. Heavy rains and melting snow produce volumes of water which must be quickly conducted away to prevent flooding.[1]

Many of the problems of the Chicago metropolitan area defy purely local solutions. Rainwater falling in one community may create flood problems for other communities; traffic problems in the heart of the central city may cause expressway backups all the way out into the suburbs; disease, pollution, and crime do not stop at political boundaries. The major obstacle to solving these problems is that although the area has a certain economic unity, it is a fragmented, overlapping, disorganized, political checkerboard—often offering inadequate, conflicting, and uncoordinated solutions at the local level. The "real Chicago" encompasses more than 1,500 governmental units, ranging from counties to mosquito abatement districts, and it even crosses state lines. This multiplicity of government has led to an absence of coordination and efficiency in road construction, the use of open space, water control, mass transit development, air pollution control, and refuse disposal. It has also resulted in increased costs because each community, regardless of size, must usually provide its own police, fire, garbage disposal, schools, and other services. Attempts to consolidate some local governmental units and to eliminate duplicate layers of government in order to provide a more efficient structure are usually met with strong opposition. This opposition is based on a variety of reasons, including fierce local independence, distrust of larger governmental units, apprehension about Chicago's domination, racial antipathy, and fear of the loss of jobs, patronage, and political power.

Probably the most disruptive political boundary is that between Chicago and its surrounding suburbs, despite the fact that both have problems that neither can solve alone. Chicago provides employment and a variety of services for suburban commuters, who do not share proportionately in the cost. The suburbs, on their part, generally refuse to become enmeshed in the many problems and burdens of the central city. Political party rivalry has often widened the gap between Chicago and surrounding areas—in recent decades Chicago has consistently voted Democratic, while the suburbs generally have tended to vote Republican. Racial, religious, and economic differences between Chicago and the suburbs have also been devisive.

Fortunately, there is a growing trend toward cooperation among the numerous governmental units. Chicago supplies water to some 74 other communities, and the Metropolitan Sanitary District of Greater Chicago, a pioneer in certain aspects of regional planning for the area, handles the sewage of 110 cities and villages. Groups of suburbs have concluded cooperative pacts dealing with such services as police, fire, and health protection; library cooperation; joint purchasing; transit improvement; refuse disposal; water supply; and street construction and maintenance. Some suburbs have even considered the possibility of merging in order to pool tax dollars, provide better services, and exercise uniform control over development. The Comprehensive Plan of Chicago has been developed in a metropolitan context and recommends principles of development for the metropolitan area.

The agency officially designated by the state of Illinois to guide the development of the six counties in the Chicago area is the Northeastern Illinois Planning Commission, created in 1957. Shortly thereafter, the private non-profit Chicago Regional Planning Association, which had been established in 1925 to plan for the greater Chicago area, was merged into the new commission. The commission is becoming increasingly important in the general planning of the six counties in the area. It is largely an advisory agency, funded by voluntary contributions from state, county, municipal, and private sources. It also receives occasional federal grants for specific projects. However, the lack of financial independence and the dependence on uncertain sources for its funding has handicapped the agency since its inception.

The commission consists of twenty-five members. Five are appointed by the governor, five by the mayor of Chicago, three by the president of the Cook County Board, and one by each of the other five counties. In addition, the Chicago Transit Authority and the Metropolitan Sanitary District of Greater Chicago each appoints a member, and the mayors and village presidents of all municipalities outside Chicago elect five members to represent the suburbs. The commission conducts research into problems such as flooding, water supply, open space, industrial development, housing, land use, population growth, and refuse disposal, and then makes reports and recommendations. It assists local governments with their problems and planning and tries to coordinate efforts. It reviews and makes recommendations on all requests for federal funds, with the requests in some years exceeding $2 billion. And it has prepared a comprehensive regional plan for the area.

To guide future development of the suburban area the commission drafted the so-called "finger plan." This Comprehensive General Plan, adopted in 1968, was selected from eleven alternative plans originally considered after extensive study and consultation with community groups.

The finger plan called for the orderly development of the suburban area along the major transportation routes, or "fingers," radiating out of Chicago. Communities would concentrate most of their industrial, commercial, educational, medical, and other service facilities, as well as high density residential areas, including skyscraper complexes, along the corridors of the main transportation routes. Residential areas of deceasing density would be placed farther out, although close enough to transportation facilities. In the wedges between the corridors would be open

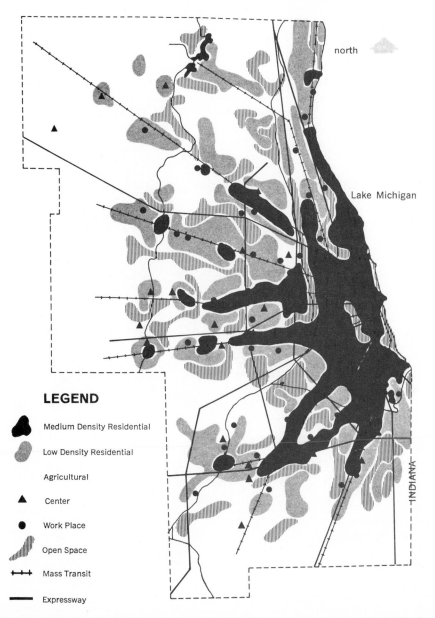

Figure 9.4. The "finger plan" for the future development of the Chicago area as proposed by the Northeastern Illinois Planning Commission in the late 1960s. (Map courtesy Northeastern Illinois Planning Commission.)

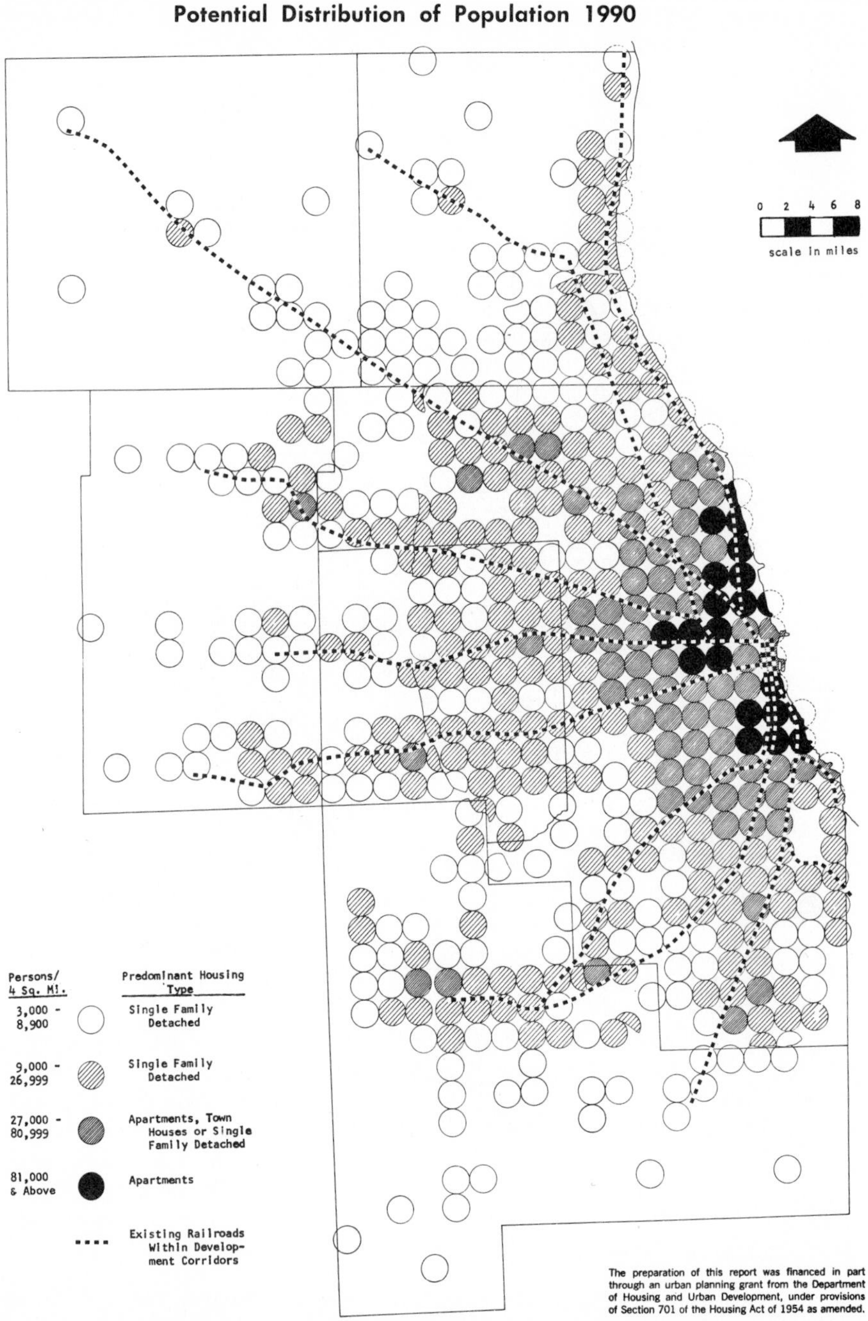

Potential Distribution of Population 1990

Figure 9.5. Potential distribution of population and housing types, 1990. (From the *Comprehensive General Plan for the Development of the Northeastern Illinois Counties Area,* Northeastern Illinois Planning Commission, 1968.)

space and recreational facilities which would also serve to absorb pollution. The plan was designed as a framework to maximize the use of land and transportation facilities, and to prevent the entire area from being covered by unplanned, congested, and polluted urbanization. It would enhance accessibility by centralizing transportation facilities in the corridor. Due, however, to various conflicting economic and political pressures, and the lack of adequate enforcement powers, the plan was not implemented and the encroachment on the open space area continued.

In 1976 the Northeastern Illinois Planning Commission updated its Comprehensive General Plan of 1968 to reflect important and rapid changes that had taken place in the intervening years. These changes included chronic high inflation, energy shortages, tight government budgets, escalating suburban land costs, widespread environmental concerns, and housing abandonment in older neighborhoods. The updated plan envisioned better synchronization of land use, transportation, and utility services in order to minimize further environmental incursions and large capital expenditures.

In lieu of further urban encroachment into even more distant farm areas, with heavy expenditures for new roads, utilities, and schools, the 1976 updated plan recommends improvement, redevelopment, and maintaining or increasing population in existing cities. These include satellite cities and suburbs, as well as Chicago whose established public facilities and services are underutilized and whose population has declined. Urban investments were to be concentrated in municipal areas, not in unincorporated areas, and the trend of not investing in certain built-up municipalities was to be discouraged and reversed. This policy should, if implemented, conserve open space, revitalize existing urban areas, guide new growth into compact, economical forms, while countering some of the problems of high energy and building costs.

Thus, Chicago in recent years has had many elaborate official plans—the Comprehensive Plan of 1966, the "finger plan" and its later update, the Lakefront Plan, the Riveredge Plan—all presented with much fanfare and colorful illustrative material. While some of these plans are too new to have generated any results as yet, most plans of recent years have become bogged down and stymied by the realities of political dealings and expediency, racial conflict, self-interest, and financial difficulties.

The Challenge

In just a century and a half the Chicago area has been transformed from a virtual wilderness into the nucleus of a burgeoning megalopolis. The crude cabins have been replaced by soaring skyscrapers, the muddy trails by multi-lane expressways, the canoes by the ocean freighters of the world, and the handful of settlers by almost 8 million people of every race, religion, and nationality.

Step by step, millions of people fired by ideals, ambitions, and an "I Will" spirit built the city. They utilized its important locational assets and surmounted its natural deficiencies. They drained the marshes, built canals, and reversed the rivers. Despite the devastation of a catastrophic fire, periods of crime and corruption, and economic downturns, they developed major industrial, commercial, and transportation facilities and created outstanding universities, medical centers, and cultural institutions. Internationally known leaders in the scientific, literary, educational, and social fields flourished in the Chicago area.

Though the area's accomplishments have been great, much remains to be done. Unfortunately, bigger did not always lead to better. Rapid, largely uncontrolled urban sprawl, coupled with changing socioeconomic conditions and inflation, often exacerbated old problems and created new ones, such as Chicago's loss of people and jobs, and an inadequate tax

Figure 9.6. Aerial view of downtown Chicago and the surrounding area looking northeast from approximately Racine Avenue, 1975. In the foreground are the Eisenhower Expressway and the campus of the University of Illinois at Chicago Circle. To the left, on the perimeter of downtown are numerous multistory factory buildings, many old and obsolete. The tall buildings in the background from left to right are John Hancock Center (100 stories), Water Tower Place (74 stories), Lake Point Tower (70 stories), Standard Oil Building (80 stories), First National Bank Building (60 stories), and Sears Tower (110 stories). (Photograph by Airpix.)

base. Some of the problems are indigenous to Chicago; many are common to most metropolises, although on the whole Chicago's progress compares favorably with that of most other large American cities.

In the future the Chicago area will continue to need the dynamism and innovativeness that have characterized its past. It is clear that as the metropolitan area and its problems grow, bold, imaginative, large-scale plans are needed along with the commitment and ability to carry them out. In an age when man can split the atom and reach the moon, he should also be able to resolve some of his major urban

problems. In such areas as housing, transportation, employment, ecology, education, government, public safety, and racial relations, the technology and concepts needed to provide for wholesome growth and development in a pleasant environment either exist or can be created. As one of Chicago's greatest dreamers and planners, Daniel H. Burnham, counseled more than 70 years ago:

Make no little plans; they have no magic to stir men's blood and probably will not be realized. Make big plans, aim high in hope and worth, remembering that a noble, logical diagram once recorded will never die, but long after we are gone will be a living thing, asserting itself with ever-growing insistency. Remember that our sons and grandsons are going to do things that would stagger us.

Note

1. John W. Alexander. *Economic Geography* (Englewood Cliffs, N.J.: Prentice-Hall, 1963), pp. 639–40.

Appendix A

SELECTED INFORMATION ABOUT CHICAGO

Facts about Chicago

Location

Latitude, 41°50′N. Longitude, 87°37′W.

On the waterway connecting the Great Lakes-St. Lawrence Seaway and the Mississippi Waterway.

Airline distance from Chicago to New York City is 714 miles (1,149 km); to Washington, D.C., 596 miles (959 km); to San Francisco, 1,859 miles (2991 km).

About 275 miles (442 km) northeast of the center of population of the United States.

About 150 miles (241 km) north of the center of the greatest industrial region on earth.

Near the heart of the largest food producing region on earth.

Population and Area

	Area of Chicago Square Miles	Square Km	Population Chicago	Population Metropolitan Chicago (SMSA)
1830	0.4	1.0	est. 50	
1840	10.2	26.4	4,470	35,616
1850	9.3	24.1	29,963	115,285
1860	17.5	45.3	112,172	259,384
1870	35.2	91.2	298,977	493,531
1880	35.2	91.2	503,185	771,250
1890	178.1	461.3	1,099,850	1,391,890
1900	189.6	490.8	1,698,575	2,084,750
1910	190.2	492.6	2,185,283	2,702,465
1920	198.2	513.3	2,701,705	3,394,996
1930	207.2	536.6	3,376,438	4,449,646
1940	212.9	551.4	3,396,808	4,569,643
1950	212.9	551.4	3,620,962	5,177,868
1960	212.9	551.4	3,550,404	6,220,913
1970	227.3	588.7	3,369,357	6,981,347
1980	228.1	590.8	3,005,072	7,102,328

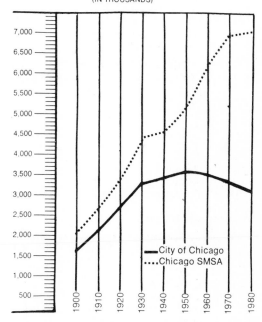

POPULATION CHANGE 1900-1980 (IN THOUSANDS)

— City of Chicago
····· Chicago SMSA

According to the 1980 U.S. Census, of the 3,005,072 persons in the city of Chicago, 49.6% classified themselves as white; 39.8%, black; 14.0%, Spanish origin (who often classified themselves also as black or white); 2.3%, Asian/Pacific Islanders; 0.2%, American Indian; 8.1%, Other.

The Chicago Standard Metropolitan Statistical Area (SMSA) consists of McHenry, Lake, Cook, DuPage, Kane, and Will counties in Illinois. Its area is 4,653 square miles (12,051 sq km).

Of the 7,102,328 persons in the Chicago SMSA in 1980, 73.3% were white. For the United States, 83.2% of the population was white.

There were 13,173 persons per square mile (2.59 sq km) in Chicago in 1980, down from peak of 17,011 in 1950. There were 1,526 persons per square mile in 1980 in Metropolitan Chicago (SMSA). For the United States, the figure in 1980 was 62.6 persons per square mile.

The following are comparisons of the populations of Chicago, Metropolitan Chicago (Chicago SMSA), and the Chicago-Northwestern Indiana Standard Consolidated Area (CNISCA=Chicago SMSA + Gary-Hammond-East Chicago, Indiana, SMSA).

	Chicago	Chicago SMSA	CNISCA
1900	1,699,000	2,085,000	2,142,000
1970	3,369,000	6,981,000	7,614,000
1980	3,005,000	7,102,000	7,745,000

Weather and Climate

	Average Temperature °F	Average Precipitation Rainfall Inches	Snowfall
January	24.3	1.85	9.7
February	27.4	1.59	8.1
March	36.8	2.73	8.0
April	49.9	3.75	1.2
May	60.0	3.41	Trace
June	70.5	3.95	0.0
July	74.7	4.09	0.0
August	73.7	3.14	0.0
September	65.9	3.00	0.0
October	55.4	2.62	0.4
November	40.4	2.20	2.6
December	28.5	2.11	9.7

	°C	Centimeters	
January	−4.3	4.70	24.6
February	−2.6	4.04	20.6
March	2.7	6.93	20.3
April	9.9	9.53	3.0
May	15.6	8.66	Trace
June	21.4	10.03	0.0
July	23.7	10.39	0.0
August	23.2	7.98	0.0
September	18.8	7.62	0.0
October	13.0	6.65	1.0
November	4.7	5.59	6.6
December	−1.9	5.36	24.6

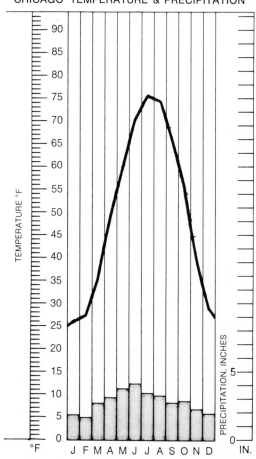

CHICAGO TEMPERATURE & PRECIPITATION

Average annual temperature, 50.8°F (10.4°C). This is about 6°F (2.85°C) colder than the world mean.

Highest recorded temperature, 105°F (40.6°C) in 1934.

Lowest recorded temperature, −27°F (−32.8°C) in 1985.

Average annual precipitation, 34.44 inches (87.48 cm). This is about 6 inches (15.24 cm) less than the world mean.

Number of days per year with precipitation of 0.01 inches (0.025 cm) or more, 122 days.

Average annual snowfall, 39.7 inches (100.8 cm). Greatest seasonal snowfall, 89.7 inches (227.8 cm), 1978–1979.

Average annual relative humidity; 7 A.M., 75%; 1 P.M., 58%.

Average annual percent of possible sunshine, 57%; summer, 68%; winter, 44%.

Average annual wind speed, 10.4 miles (16.7 km) per hour.

The wind blows from the southwest more than from any other direction.

General Facts

The name Chicago is seemingly derived from "Che-ca-gou," the name applied by the Indians to the strong-smelling wild onions of the mud flats.

Chicago's altitude is 578.5 feet (176.3 m) above sea level. The highest point is at 92nd Street and Western Avenue—672.4 feet (204.9 m).

The center of the city is approximately 3700 South Honore (1832 W).

Chicago has 3,679 miles (5,920 km) of streets. There are 53.7 miles (86.4 km) of expressways.

Chicago has 29 miles (46.7 km) of shoreline.

Over half the nations of the world have fewer people than Metropolitan Chicago.

Metropolitan Chicago has 3.1% of the United States population but accounts for 4.4% of the nation's gross national product.

Only eleven foreign nations have a gross national product higher than that of Metropolitan Chicago.

About 70 million people live within a 500-mile (805 km) radius of Chicago. Within this area, 40% of the nation's manufacturing and one-third of its wholesale and retail sales are found.

In 1980 Metropolitan Chicago had retail sales of $34 billion and the value of manufactured goods amounted to over $90 billion.

The median family income in Chicago in 1978 was $19,468.

Chicago has about 1,175,000 housing units of all kinds, with over one-third being owner occupied and almost three-quarters being over 40 years old. About 24% of all Chicago families live in single-family houses; 35% live in buildings with two, three, or four apartments; and the remainder live in large apartment or condominium buildings.

The daily per capita consumption of water is 255 gallons. The daily average pumpage is 977 million gallons. There are 65 miles (104.6 km) of water supply tunnels under the lake and the land. There are 4,184 miles (6,732 km) of water mains in Chicago. The Chicago water system also supplies 74 suburbs.

Chicago has 4,300 miles (6,919 km) of sewer facilities.

Chicago has 6,756 acres (2,736 ha) used for park purposes. There are 574 parks, 31 beaches, and 8 yacht harbors.

Chicago has approximately 924,000 passenger motor vehicles and 70,000 trucks.

There are 52 movable and 36 fixed bridges in Chicago.

Chicago has 1,777 grocery stores, 1,724 beauty shops, 1,029 barber shops, 844 pharmacies, and 339 hardware stores.

Chicago has 20 major museums and more than 30 art galleries.

Chicago has 850 Protestant churches, 263 Roman Catholic churches, and 65 synagogues.

Chicago has 480 public elementary schools and 56 public high schools; 228 Catholic elementary schools and 42 Catholic high schools; 31 Lutheran elementary schools and 2 Lutheran high schools; 5 Jewish elementary schools and 2 Jewish high schools.

Chicago has 58 colleges and universities, including 6 medical schools, 3 dental colleges, a pharmacy college, and a college of osteopathy. One of every 5 doctors in the United States has received all or part of his/her training in Chicago.

In Metropolitan Chicago about 54% of the adults over 25 years of age have completed at least one year of college.

The median age of people living in the Chicago area is about 29 years.

The average life expectancy in Chicago is 68.8 years. For the United States it is 73.8 years.

Chicago has 62 hospitals containing 20,324 beds.

There are 233 physicians per 100,000 population in Metropolitan Chicago. The figure for the United States is 155.

Chicago has 100 cemeteries. Oakwood on the South Side is the oldest. Rosehill on the North Side is the largest.

In 1980 the crime rate per 100,000 in Chicago was 6,640. The figure for Cook County was 6,037.

Chicago has a Mayor-Council form of government with 50 aldermen in the City Council.

Cook County, in which Chicago is located, has more political administrative units than any other county in the United States— 592.

The Chicago Flag

The Chicago flag is white with two blue stripes and four red stars.

The white, a composite of all colors, represents the composite of nationalities living in peace. The top white represents the North Side, the middle white the West Side, and the bottom white the South Side.

The two blue stripes represent the magnificent waterways—Lake Michigan, the Chicago River, and the great canal.

The four stars represent:
Fort Dearborn—1803
Chicago Fire—1871
World's Columbian Exposition—1893
A Century of Progress—1933

Chicago's Firsts

Manufacturing

Metropolitan Chicago is number one in steel production. It accounts for almost one-fourth of the nations' output. There are 9 major operating steel plants in this area.

Chicago is first in commercial printing. There are 1,100 printing firms in Chicago and 2,200 in the suburbs. They print three-fourths of the United States paperbacks, and phone directories for some 9,000 cities. They produce everything from gum wrappers to encyclopedias.

Chicago is the appliance manufacturing center of our nation. Admiral, Hotpoint, and Sunbeam are well-known names.

More candy is produced in Chicago than in any other city in the United States. Leading candy producers include Mars, Tootsie Roll, Reed, Peter Paul Cadbury, Brach, and Curtis.

Chicago is number one in telephone equipment manufacturing. Both the Bell System and the General Telephone System get much of their supplies here.

Metropolitan Chicago is the industrial machinery capital of our country. The products range from conveyor systems to giant stamping machines.

Chicago is number one in metal products manufacturing. The products range from pots and pans to water towers.

About 25% of all musical instruments manufactured in our country come from Metropolitan Chicago. They range from drums to electric organs. Chicago ranks first in this field.

Metropolitan Chicago is first in the manufacture of diesel engines, railroad equipment, metal furniture, cosmetics, plastic products, radios, TV sets, snuff, boxes, metal cans, surgical appliances, mortician supplies, mattresses, petroleum and coal byproducts, office machines, business forms, lampshades, saws, sporting goods, screws and bolts, soaps, paints, cut stone products, paving and roofing materials, cookies, sausages, and canned and frozen foods.

Transportation

Chicago has the world's busiest airport—O'Hare International Airport. A plane lands or leaves every 46 seconds. Almost 50 million people annually pass through Chicago's three principal airports—O'Hare, Meigs, and Midway.

Chicago is the world's greatest ground transportation center. Seventeen trunk line railroads, representing half of the nation's railway mileage, come into Chicago. Over 35,000 freight cars are handled each day. About 1,200 buses and 12,000 trucks converge on Chicago every 24 hours. On an average day railroads bring 138,000 persons (mainly commuters) to Chicago; buses bring 35,000.

Chicago is the only connecting link between the Great Lakes-St. Lawrence Seaway and the Lakes to Gulf Waterway. It is a regular port of call for most of the ships involved in Great Lakes-overseas trade.

Trade

Chicago sells more goods to foreign countries than any other city in the United States. It exports well over $1 billion worth of manufactured goods annually. This is over 3% of the national total.

Chicago leads in the mail order business. Four of the largest mail order concerns in the nation—Sears, Montgomery Ward, Spiegel, and Aldens—are headquartered in the area.

Conventions and Tourists

Chicago ranks first in the convention business. It hosts almost 1,500 conventions and trade shows annually, attracting over 2 million people. Conventions and trade shows bring nearly $900 million to Chicago each year. The convention or trade show visitor stops for an average of 3.1 days and spends over $400 while in Chicago. McCormick Place is the world's largest exposition center.

Almost 6 million pleasure tourists visit Chicago each year, staying for an average of 2.5 days and spending about $110 during their stay. About 850,000 of the visitors are from points outside the United States.

Historical Firsts

Chicago produced the first steel frame skyscraper, stainless steel building, electric iron, electric cooking range, Pullman car, refrigerator car, grain reaper, reactor to produce electricity from atomic energy, cafeteria, zipper fastener, elevated railway, window envelope, two-pants suit of clothes.

Atomic fission was first brought under control at the University of Chicago. The world's most powerful particle accelerator is located 30 miles (48.3 km) west of Chicago's Loop at Weston.

The Biggest and Busiest

Chicago has the:

Tallest building in the world—Sears Tower. (110 stories; 1,454 feet or 443.2 m)

Tallest bank building—First National. (60 stories; 852 feet or 259.7 m)

Tallest apartment-office building—John Hancock Center. (100 stories; 1,105 feet or 336.8 m)

Tallest apartment building—Lake Point Tower. (70 stories; 640 feet or 195 m)

Tallest reinforced concrete building—Water Tower Place. (74 stories; 871 feet or 265.5 m)

Largest post office.

Largest water filtration plant.

Largest sewage disposal plant.

Leading futures trading market—Chicago Board of Trade.

Leading commodity exchange—Chicago Mercantile Exchange.

Largest newspaper plant—*Chicago Tribune.*

Busiest street corner—State and Madison.

Longest continuous street within a city limit—Western Avenue. (24.5 miles or 39.4 km)

Significant Dates

ca 11,500 B.C.—Last glacier receded from area.

ca 10,000 B.C.—Glacial Lake Chicago broke through its confining moraines to drain southwest into the Illinois and Mississippi rivers.

1673—Marquette and Jolliet explored the region.

1696—Father Pierre Pinet established the shortlived Mission of the Guardian Angels.

1779—First home and fur-trading station built by Jean Baptiste Point du Sable.

1803—Fort Dearborn erected.

1812—Fort Dearborn Massacre.

1816—Fort Dearborn rebuilt.

1831—Cook County organized with Chicago as county seat.

1833—Chicago, with 350 inhabitants, incorporated as a town.

1837—Chicago, with a population of about 4,000, incorporated as a city; William B. Ogden, first mayor.

1845—First permanent school building erected.

1847—McCormick, inventor of the reaper, started making farm implements.

1848—Chicago Board of Trade founded.
 —Illinois-Michigan Canal opened.
 —Chicago and Galena Union Railroad built.

1854—Cholera claimed 1,424 victims.

1855—City began raising level of streets up to 12 feet (3.7 m).
 —"Beer riots" after enforced closing of saloons on Sunday.

1856—Chicago Historical Society founded.

1859—First horse drawn railway line went into operation.

1860—Abraham Lincoln was made a presidential candidate in the "Wigwam."

1865—Union Stock Yards established south of city boundary.

1867—A sanitary water system installed.

1871—Great Chicago Fire of October 8–10.

1872—Ordinance outlawing wooden buildings in downtown area.

1879—Art Institute of Chicago incorporated.

1880—George Pullman built his car shop and the town of Pullman.

1885—Home Insurance Building, major progenitor of the true skyscraper, erected.

1886—Haymarket riot.

1889—Hull House founded by Jane Addams.
 —Annexations increased area of city from 36 to 168 square miles (93–435 sq hm).
 —Chicago Sanitary District established.

1891—Chicago Symphony Orchestra formed.

1892—University of Chicago opened.

1893—Carter H. Harrison elected mayor for a fifth term. Assassinated by disgruntled office seeker.
 —World's Columbian Exposition.
 —Museum of Natural History founded.

1894—Pullman car plant strike led to a railroad strike.

1897—Chicago Loop encircled by new "L" lines.

1900—Chicago Sanitary and Ship Canal opened; flow of Chicago River reversed.

1903—Iroquois Theater fire killed 602 people.

1909—The Chicago Plan was originated by Daniel Burnham.

1911—Present-day City Hall and County Building completed.
—Carter H. Harrison, Jr., elected mayor for a fifth term.

1915—Excursion steamer *Eastland* overturned in the Chicago River, killing 812 people.

1916—Municipal Pier (later called Navy Pier) completed.

1918—Influenza epidemic killed thousands.

1919—A bloody race riot left 15 whites and 23 blacks dead.

1920—New Michigan Avenue Bridge completed.

1924—Despite prohibition, there were 15 breweries and 20,000 retail alcoholic beverage outlets operating illegally in Chicago.

1925—Relocated South Water Street produce market opened.

1927—Chicago's first municipal airport (later called Midway Airport) opened.

1930—Adler Planetarium and Shedd Acquarium dedicated.

1933—Museum of Science and Industry officially opened.

1933–1934—Century of Progress Exposition ran successfully for two years.

1934—Gulf to Lakes Inland Waterway opened with Chicago as northern terminus.

1937—Eleven killed in labor dispute at Republic Steel.

1942—World's first atomic reaction achieved at the University of Chicago.

1943—Chicago's first passenger subway opened beneath State Street.

1947—Chicago Transit Authority created.

1953—Chicago became world's steel capital.

1955—O'Hare Airport opened.

1959—St. Lawrence Seaway opened.

1960—McCormick Place opened.

1965—University of Illinois at Chicago Circle opened.

1967—Record 23 inch (58.4 cm) snowfall of January 26–27 paralyzed city.

1968—Riots and fires occurred in parts of Chicago's West Side following assassination of Dr. Martin Luther King, Jr.
—Disorders erupted during the Democratic National Convention.

1971—Stockyards closed.
—McCormick Place reopened after original building was damaged by fire in 1967.

1974—World's tallest building, Sears Tower, opened.
—Regional Transportation Authority established.

1975—Mayor Richard J. Daley died while serving a record 6th term.

1979—Record total winter snowfall of 89.7 inches (227.8 cm) crippled city.
—Jane M. Byrne elected Chicago's first woman mayor.

1983—Harold Washington elected Chicago's first black mayor.

Historic Sites

This list of Chicago's more important historic sites is slightly modified and enlarged from one prepared by the Municipal Reference Library of the City of Chicago. Wherever it is known that suitable memorial plaques and historical markers have been erected, that fact is shown. The list is in approximate chronological order.

Chicago Portage—Near this site began the portage used by Marquette and Jolliet in 1673 between the Des Plaines River and the South Branch of the Chicago River about six miles to the northeast. (Harlem Avenue and 49th Street.)

Marquette Cabin—Near this spot stood the cabin to which came Jacques Marquette, Priest of the Society of Jesus, on December 14, 1674. He spent the ensuing winter there. In September 1673, Louis Jolliet and Father Marquette first passed this spot. (At north end of Damen Avenue bridge and 26th Street. Wooden cross marker.)

Guardian Angel Mission—Near this site from 1696 to 1699 stood Father Pinet's Mission of the Guardian Angel from which he conducted his evangelical labors among the Miami Indians. (On the North Branch at Foster Avenue.)

Fort Dearborn—One of the military posts established by Thomas Jefferson to protect the new frontier. Built by Captain John Whistler in 1803 near the mouth of the Chicago River. Destroyed by Indians, August 16, 1812—the day after the Fort Dearborn Massacre. A second Fort Dearborn was built in 1816 and stood until 1856. (Southwest corner of Michigan Avenue and Wacker Drive. Landmark plaque.)

Du Sable Cabin—Near this site stood the Du Sable cabin, later remodeled into the Kinzie Mansion, 1784–1832, home of Point du Sable, Le Mai, and John Kinzie. Here was born the city's first white child, Ellen Marion Kinzie, in 1805. (Northeast corner of Michigan Avenue and the Chicago River.)

Old Vincennes Road—This historic trail into Chicago from the south, now Vincennes Avenue, was originally used by the Indians to unite all villages of the Potawatomi nation. It later became the thoroughfare from Ohio and Wabash River settlements.

Little Fort Road—Here began the Little Fort Road, now Lincoln Avenue, an Indian trail which became the main road to Little Fort or Waukegan, the first important settlement north of Chicago. (Head of Wells Street and Lincoln Avenue.)

Fort Dearborn Massacre—The garrison at Fort Dearborn, under command of Captain Nathan Heald, evacuated the fort and marched southward along the lake to a point now marked by a tablet at 18th Street and Prairie Avenue, where it was attacked by Indians and 53 killed, including several women and children, on August 15, 1812.

Antoine Ouilmette—Near this site stood the home of the French interpreter Antoine Ouilmette, after whom the suburb Wilmette was named. Following the Fort Dearborn Massacre (1812) Ouilmette was Chicago's only white inhabitant. (West of Michigan Avenue on the north bank of the Chicago River.)

Indian Boundary Line—In 1816 the Indians ceded land from Lake Calumet on the south to Rogers Avenue on the north. Rogers Avenue from Sheridan Road to Ridge Avenue was part of the Indian Boundary Road.

Jean Baptiste Beaubien—On this site, then the lakeshore, Jean Baptiste Beaubien, an early settler, in 1817 built a "mansion" to which he brought his bride, Josette La Framboise. It remained their home until 1845. (Southwest corner of Randolph Street and Michigan Avenue.)

Sauganash Hotel—A popular hotel built in 1827 by Mark Beaubien. In 1833 a meeting to incorporate Chicago was held there. Destroyed by fire in 1851. (Southeast corner of Lake Street and Wacker Drive.)

Wolf Point—In early days this elbow of land, formed by junction of the North Branch of the Chicago River with the main river, was the site of Chicago's first tavern, Wolf Tavern, built in 1828 by James Kinzie.

Billy Caldwell's House—Here stood the home of Billy Caldwell, half-breed Potawatomi Indian known as "Sauganash" (The Englishman). It was built in 1828 by U.S. Department of Indian Affairs in recognition of his friendly efforts to preserve peace. (State Street and Chicago Avenue.)

"Cobweb Castle"—Near this site on Wolcott (now State) Street stood Agency House, known as 'Cobweb Castle." It was the home of Dr. Alexander Wolcott, Government Indian Agent at Chicago (1819–

1830). (North side of river near foot of State Street.)

City's First Church and First Methodist Church—On June 14, 1831, the Rev. Jesse Walker founded this church. The 10 members held their first services in a log cabin at Wolf Point on the North Branch of the Chicago River. (Today it is the Chicago Temple-First United Methodist Church at Washington and Clark streets.)

Green Bay Road—From this point Green Bay Road ran northwesterly to Clark Street and North Avenue, and followed Clark Street's present route to the vicinity of Peterson Avenue. This road connected Fort Dearborn with Fort Howard, Green Bay, Wisconsin. (North end of Michigan Avenue Bridge.)

City's First Baptist Church—Near this site in the "Temple Building," Chicago's first Baptist church held services. The congregation was organized October 19, 1833, by Rev. Allen B. Freeman. (Southwest corner of South Water and Franklin streets.)

City's First Catholic Church—On this site, old St. Mary's, Chicago's first Catholic church, was erected in 1833 and dedicated in October of that year. Father John Mary Iranaeus St. Cyr was the first pastor. (Southwest corner of State and Lake streets.)

City's First Presbyterian Church—Near this spot was erected in 1833 Chicago's first Presbyterian church, organized June 26, 1833, by Rev. Jeremiah Porter. The building was dedicated January 4, 1834. (Near southwest corner of Lake and Clark streets.)

First Post Office—Near this site in 1833, the log store of John S. C. Hogan was this section's only post office, serving settlers from miles around. Eastern mail was delivered once a week from Niles, Michigan. (Near the corner of Lake Street and Wacker Drive. Memorial plaque.)

Green Tree Tavern—Built near this site in 1833 and opened by David Clock. Re-named Stage House in 1835, Chicago Hotel a few years later, and afterward Lake Street House. (Northeast corner of Milwaukee Avenue, Lake and Canal streets.)

Old Treaty Elm—The tree which stood here until 1933 marked the northern boundary of the Fort Dearborn Reservation, the trail to Lake Geneva, the center of Billy Caldwell's (Chief Sauganash) reservation, and the site of the Indian Treaty of 1833. (Intersection of Rogers, Kilbourn, and Caldwell avenues.)

South Water Street—This was Chicago's main business street in 1834, connecting the village with Fort Dearborn. Years before this also was the site of a trading post with the Indians. (Now Wacker Drive between State and Clark streets.)

Dearborn Street Drawbridge—First drawbridge over Chicago River was constructed at Dearborn Street in 1834 by Nelson R. Norton. A primitive wooden affair, 300 feet (91 m) long with a 60-foot (18 m) opening, the council removed it in 1839. (Dearborn Street at river.)

"Hubbard's Folly"—On this site, about 1834, Gurdon S. Hubbard built Chicago's first warehouse, for storing pork and other pioneer produce. Because of its size and substantial construction, early skeptics called the building "Hubbard's Folly." (Corner of La Salle and South Water streets, now Wacker Drive. Memorial plaque.)

First U.S. Land Office—Near this site the first United States Land Office was erected in 1835. (On the south side of Lake Street between Clark and Dearborn streets.)

First City Cemeteries—This was the site of one of Chicago's first two cemeteries and comprised sixteen acres (6.5 ha). It was laid out in August 1835 and enclosed in September, after which burials elsewhere on the South Side were forbidden. (Near the lake and 23rd Street.)

Chicago's Oldest House—This home, said to be Chicago's oldest house, was built by Henry B. Clarke in 1836 at Michigan

Avenue and 16th Street. John Chrimes bought it in 1871 and moved it to 4526 Wabash Avenue from where it was recently moved to 1855 S. Indiana Avenue in the vicinity of its original site. It is now in the Prairie Avenue Historic District. (Landmark plaque.)

"Saloon Building"—So called because of the upper floor salon where entertainments were held. The Common Council having leased one of the rooms, the building was the City Hall from 1837 to 1842. (Southeast corner of Lake and Clark streets.)

First Mayor's House—In the center of this block, Chicago's first mayor, William B. Ogden, built a home in 1837. It was the city's first house designed by an architect. (Block bounded by Erie, Rush, Ontario and Cass [now Wabash Avenue].)

Toll Bridge—This bridge, in use from 1839 to 1843, was built of planking and timbers upon the barge principle of construction. Gideon M. Jackson was the first toll man. (At 92nd Street and Calumet River.)

First Wheat Cargo—Near this site stood Newberry and Dole's warehouse. On the brig *Osceola,* in 1839 they shipped the first cargo of wheat from the port of Chicago. (North bank of river near Rush Street.)

Stagecoach Office—On this site Frink and Walker, successors to Dr. John Temple, pioneer stagecoach operator, built their terminal and office about 1840. Dr. Temple began his line in 1834. (Southwest corner of Dearborn and Lake streets.)

Washington Square—This area was deeded to Chicago in 1842, upon condition that it be enclosed with "a handsome post, board, or picket fence within five years and kept enclosed forever as a public square." (Dearborn Street, Delaware Place, Clark Street, and Walton Place.)

First City Hospital—Near this site stood Chicago's first city hospital, built in 1843 and originally used as a rest house for smallpox patients, on ground purchased for a cemetery. Burned in 1845, it was rebuilt the same year. (Just north of North Avenue on Clark Street.)

First City-owned School—On this site was erected in 1844 a two-story frame building, Chicago's first city-owned school. Known as "Old District School," and sometimes called the Rumsey School. (Southeast corner of Madison and Dearborn streets. Memorial plaque.)

Historic Cow Path—This areaway, 10 × 117 × 18 feet (3 × 36 × 6 m), is reserved forever as a cow path, by terms of the deed of Willard Jones in 1844, when he sold portions of the surrounding property. (Under 100 West Monroe Street.)

St. Paul's Church—On this site, 1846–48, stood the first St. Paul's Evangelical Lutheran Church and Chicago's first Lutheran parochial school. Pastor Selle preached the first Lutheran sermon here, Easter Sunday, April 12, 1846. (Southwest corner of Ohio and La Salle streets.)

McCormick Reaper Works—On this site in 1847 Cyrus Hall McCormick began his reaper factory. International Harvester is the industrial giant that grew from this first factory and its home office today is in the Equitable Building on the site of the original factory. (Along the north bank of the Chicago River just east of Michigan Avenue.)

First Permanent Theater—Near this site, John B. Rice, in 1847, built Chicago's first permanent theater a frame building 40 × 80 feet (12 × 24 m) on plan of old coliseum. He paid $25 monthly license for operating it. (South side of Randolph Street, a little east of Dearborn Street.)

First Board of Trade—Near this spot in 1848 was held the first session of the Board of Trade of the City of Chicago now the world's largest grain exchange. (Clark and Wacker. Memorial plaque.)

First Cattle Market—From "Bull's Head Stockyards," established near this site in 1848, began Chicago's advance to become world's greatest livestock and packing center. (Corner of Madison Street and Ogden Avenue.)

First Railway Depot—Here stood Chicago's first railway depot, a wooden structure built in 1848 by the Galena and Chicago Union Railroad. From its cupola the president and dispatchers watched trains advance across the prairie. (Southwest corner of Canal and Kinzie streets. Memorial plaque.)

First Plank Road—Southwestern road was constructed in 1848 from Chicago to Doty's Tavern, Riverside, a distance of ten miles (16 km). It generally parallels what is now Ogden Avenue. By 1852, it was extended to Naperville, connecting with a network of southwestern improved roads.

Chicago's First Synagogue—On this site stood Chicago's first synagogue which was dedicated in 1851 with Rabbi Ignatz Kunreuther in charge of the congregation. (Clark Street between Quincy and Adams streets. Plaque on Kluczynski Federal Building.)

Kennison, David—A granite boulder marks the grave of David Kennison—the last survivor of the Boston Tea Party. He died in 1852 at the age of 115. (Boulder in Lincoln Park near the intersection of Wisconsin and Clark streets.)

Junction Grove—Around this intersection of the Michigan Southern Railroad with the Rock Island Railroad in 1852 started the settlement called Junction Grove, later Chicago Junction, and finally Englewood. (63rd and La Salle streets.)

St. Patrick's Church—Constructed during the period 1852 to 1856, it is the oldest church building in Chicago and one of the few buildings to escape the Great Fire of 1871. (Northwest corner of Adams and Desplaines. Landmark plaque.)

First Black Church—Here stood Quinn Chapel, African Methodist Episcopal Church, named in honor of Bishop William P. Quinn. The building, dedicated November 20, 1853, was Chicago's first black house of worship and also a civic and social center. (Jackson Boulevard and Federal Street.)

Blue Island Plank Road—Built in 1854, it ran north on the line of Western Avenue to Blue Island Avenue, thence into the heart of the city. Thirteen miles (20.9 km) long, it was a direct route for heavy southern transportation.

Lakeview House—On this site stood the first lakeside hotel. Built by James H. Reese and Elisha E. Hundley, and opened July 4, 1854, it became the center of a fine residential section. (Northwest corner of Grace Street and Sheridan Road.)

Grand Crossing—A collision here of two trains in 1854 caused a railroad controversy, which resulted in legislation requiring all trains to stop at this intersection, and the consequent development of a village nearby. (75th Street and Woodlawn Avenue.)

Chicago's First High School—This site contained Chicago's first high school, completed in 1856 in accordance with Common Council ordinance of 1855. (748 W. Monroe Street.)

Andersonville School—On this site stood the Andersonville School, in the northeastern corner of the subdivision called Andersonville. Here in 1857, arrangements were made for Lake View Township's first election. (Southwest corner of Foster Avenue and Clark Street.)

The Wigwam—Temporary wooden building erected in 1860, for the Republican National Convention. Here Abraham Lincoln was nominated for the first time for the presidency. (Southeast corner Lake Street and Wacker Drive. Plaque on building.)

Camp Douglas—Camp Douglas built in 1861 during the Civil War; was a training camp for Union soldiers and later a Confederate prison. It covered 60 (24.3 ha) acres along Cottage Grove Avenue, 31st and 33rd streets, and Giles Avenue.

Douglas, Stephen A.—Democratic leader and United States Senator, died June 3, 1861. In 1868 a monument was erected to his memory and his body placed in the crypt at its base. In smallest state park, which is on land that was once part of his 53-acre (21.5 ha) estate. (East end of 35th Street.)

Refuge for Slaves—South of what was then Chicago, in the midst of the prairie, stood the Gardner Home and Tavern. Built in 1836, it was bought by William Wilcox in 1844 and became a refuge for slaves during the Civil War. (At 9955 Beverly Avenue.)

Lind Block—This building, one of Chicago's first "skyscrapers," built in the 1860s, 90 feet (27 m) high, with seven stories, is celebrated for its escape from the Chicago Fire. (Northwest corner of Randolph Street and Wacker Drive.)

Camp Fry—On this site, formerly known as Wright's Grove, stood Camp Fry, assembly and mustering point for Civil War troops. The 132nd and 134th Illinois Infantry Regiments were organized here in 1864. (Corner Clark Street and Diversey Parkway.)

Mrs. Lincoln's Home—On this site stood the home Mrs. Lincoln bought in 1866 and occupied for about a year with her son "Tad." (1238 West Washington Street.)

Old Water Tower—This water tower, completed in 1869, marks the establishment of Chicago's second water works and stands as a memorial of the Chicago Fire of 1871. (Chicago and Michigan avenues. Landmark plaque.)

Mrs. O'Leary's Home—On this site stood the home and barn of Mrs. O'Leary where the Chicago Fire of 1871 started. Although there are many versions of the story of its origin, the real cause of the fire has never been determined. The Chicago Fire Academy now occupies the site, which also includes a sculpture, "Pillars of Fire" by Egon Weiner. (558 De Koven Street. Landmark plaque.)

Chicago Fire's Limits—The northern limits of the Fire of 1871 extended along the line of Fullerton Avenue from Lincoln Park on the east to the Chicago River on the west. The last building burned was the frame house of Dr. John Foster, near the northeast corner of Belden Avenue, Sedgwick and Clark streets.

Ogden Home—The home of Mahlon D. Ogden was the only house in the path of the Chicago Fire which was not burned. It is now the site of the Newberry Library. (60 West Walton Place. Plaque in building.)

Lake View Town Hall—On this site stood the Town Hall of the Township of Lake View, a two-story building erected in 1872. When this section was a separate municipality, the Town Hall was its "City Hall." (Northwest corner Halsted and Addison streets.)

Calaboose—On this site stood the Calaboose of the original town of Lake View. It was a predecessor of the Little Jail at the old Town Hall. (At approximately the corner of Byron and Clark streets.)

Union Stock Yard Gate—The gate, erected in 1875, is one of the few visual reminders of Chicago's past supremacy in the livestock and meat packing industries. (Exchange Avenue at Peoria Street. Landmark plaque.)

Pullman—The first completely planned company town in the United States; erected by George M. Pullman in the early 1880s. (Approximately from 103rd Street to 115th Street and from Cottage Grove Avenue eastward to the Lake Calumet area. Landmark plaque.)

Prairie Avenue—This street, from about 1800 South for a few blocks, around the turn of the century contained the mansions of many of Chicago's elite including Marshall Field, George Pullman, Philip Armour, William Kimball, and John Glessner. The Glessner House, 1800 S. Prairie Avenue, designed by H. H. Richardson in 1886, contains a landmark plaque. Main street now of Prairie Avenue Historic District.

Haymarket Square—Here on May 4, 1886, a bomb was thrown into a group of policemen who had come to disperse a labor protest meeting. Many died, including seven policemen. The bomb thrower was never positively identified. Eight anarchist leaders were convicted, and four were later hanged. Only the pedestal stands of a historic landmark monument that formerly contained a memorial statue of a policeman. (Randolph Street between Halsted and Des Plaines streets.)

Hull House—One of the most important and influential social settlement complexes in America, established by Jane Addams in 1889. (800 S. Halsted Street, now part of the University of Illinois at Chicago Circle campus. Landmark plaque.)

Eugene Field Home—In 1895 Eugene Field bought a home on this site in Buena Park, then a suburb of Chicago. After enlarging and remodeling the building, Field called his place "The Sabine Farm." (4242 Clarendon Avenue.)

Michigan Avenue Bridge—Opened in 1920; near this site were located Fort Dearborn, the Du Sable cabin, the start of the Green Bay Trail, and the McCormick Reaper Works. (Michigan Avenue and Wacker Drive. Numerous memorial plaques and stoneworks.)

First Nuclear Reaction—On this site on December 2, 1942, man established the first self-sustaining controlled nuclear reaction under the grandstands of Stagg Field Stadium. Contains twelve foot (3.7 m) bronze sculpture by Henry Moore entitled "Nuclear Energy." (South Ellis Avenue between 56th and 57th streets. Landmark plaque.)

Appendix B

Statistical Data for Incorporated Communities of Chicago Area

| | Population | | | | Median Family Income 1979 | Distance from Loop | |
Place	1980 Census	1970 Census	1960 Census	1970-1980 % Change		Miles	Km
Cook County							
Alsip	17,134	11,608	3,770	47.6%	$25,731	19	31
Arlington Heights	66,116	65,058	27,878	1.6	33,323	27	43
Barrington	9,029	8,581	5,434	5.2	36,805	37	60
Barrington Hills	3,631	2,805	1,726	29.4	52,874	38	61
Bedford Park	988	583	737	69.5	N.A.*	15	24
Bellwood	19,811	22,096	20,729	−10.3	24,959	13	21
Berkeley	5,467	6,152	5,792	−11.1	28,779	15	24
Berwyn	46,849	52,502	54,224	−10.8	23,178	10	16
Blue Island	21,855	22,629	19,618	− 3.4	20,772	18	29
Bridgeview	14,155	12,506	7,334	13.2	24,764	15	24
Broadview	8,618	9,623	8,588	−10.4	25,373	13	21
Brookfield	19,395	20,284	20,429	− 4.4	25,679	13	21
Buffalo Grove	22,230	12,333	1,492	80.2	32,338	29	47
Burbank (South Stickney)	28,461	29,900	—	− 4.8	26,367	13	21
Burnham	4,030	3,634	2,478	10.9	26,019	21	34
Calumet City	39,673	33,107	25,000	19.8	25,628	23	37
Calumet Park	8,788	10,069	8,448	−12.7	23,793	16	26
Chicago	3,005,072	3,369,357	3,550,440	−10.8	18,776	—	—
Chicago Heights	37,026	40,900	34,331	− 9.5	21,206	28	45
Chicago Ridge	13,473	9,187	5,748	46.7	22,392	17	27
Cicero	61,232	67,058	69,130	− 8.7	20,804	8	13
Country Club Hills	14,676	6,920	3,421	112.1	27,794	29	47
Countryside	6,538	2,864	—	128.3	25,543	15	24
Crestwood	10,712	5,770	1,213	85.6	24,604	19	31

*N.A. Not available

Statistical Data for
Incorporated Communities
of Chicago Area (continued)

Population

Place	1980 Census	1970 Census	1960 Census	1970–1980 % Change	Median Family Income 1979	Distance from Loop Miles	Km
Cook County, cont.							
Des Plaines	53,568	57,239	34,886	− 6.4%	$28,807	21	34
Dixmoor	4,175	4,735	3,076	−11.8	20,236	20	32
Dolton	24,766	25,990	18,746	− 4.7	27,747	20	32
East Chicago Heights	5,347	5,000	3,270	6.9	11,240	30	48
East Hazel Crest	1,362	1,885	1,457	−27.7	N.A.*	22	35
Elk Grove Village	28,907	20,346	6,608	42.1	30,578	22	35
Elmwood Park	24,016	26,160	23,866	− 8.2	25,851	11	18
Evanston	73,706	80,113	79,283	− 8.0	28,264	12	19
Evergreen Park	22,260	25,921	24,178	−14.1	26,376	14	23
Flossmoor	8,423	7,846	4,624	7.4	46,495	26	42
Forest Park	15,177	15,472	14,452	− 1.9	23,040	10	16
Forest View	764	927	1,042	−17.6	N.A.*	11	18
Franklin Park	17,507	20,348	18,322	−14.0	26,151	15	24
Glencoe	9,200	10,542	10,472	−12.7	56,136	21	34
Glenview	30,842	24,880	18,132	24.0	36,344	20	32
Glenwood	10,538	7,416	882	42.1	30,649	24	39
Hanover Park	28,850	11,735	451	145.8	27,036	30	48
Harvey	35,810	34,636	29,071	3.4	20,441	20	32
Harwood Heights	8,228	9,060	5,688	− 9.2	24,806	15	24
Hazel Crest	13,973	10,329	6,205	35.3	28,057	23	37
Hickory Hills	13,778	13,176	2,707	4.6	27,363	19	31
Hillside	8,279	8,888	7,794	− 6.9	28,877	14	23
Hodgkins	2,005	2,270	1,126	−11.7	N.A.*	18	29
Hoffman Estates	38,258	22,238	8,296	72.0	29,865	29	47
Hometown	5,324	6,729	7,479	−20.9	21,728	14	23
Homewood	19,724	18,871	13,371	4.5	31,247	24	39
Inverness	4,046	1,674	—	141.7	54,434	33	53
Justice	10,552	9,473	2,803	11.4	22,118	18	29
Kenilworth	2,708	2,980	2,959	− 9.1	66,950	16	26
La Grange	15,681	17,814	15,285	−12.0	31,915	14	23
La Grange Park	13,359	15,459	13,793	−13.6	30,100	15	24
Lansing	29,039	25,805	18,098	12.5	26,707	26	42
Lemont	5,640	5,080	3,397	11.0	24,478	29	47
Lincolnwood	11,921	12,929	11,744	− 7.8	38,453	11	18
Lynwood	4,195	1,042	255	302.6	26,323	29	47
Lyons	9,925	11,124	9,936	−10.8	23,820	12	19
Markham	15,172	15,987	11,704	− 5.1	24,714	24	39
Matteson	10,223	4,741	3,225	115.6	29,168	30	48
Maywood	27,998	29,019	27,330	− 3.5	21,668	11	18
Melrose Park	20,735	22,716	22,291	− 8.7	22,503	12	19
Merrionette Park	2,054	2,303	2,354	−10.8	N.A.*	17	27
Midlothian	14,274	14,422	6,605	− 1.0	24,481	22	35
Morton Grove	23,747	26,369	20,533	− 9.9	31,898	16	26

**Statistical Data for
Incorporated Communities
of Chicago Area (continued)**

Population

Place	1980 Census	1970 Census	1960 Census	1970–1980 % Change	Median Family Income 1979	Distance from Loop Miles	Km
Cook County, cont.							
Mount Prospect	52,634	34,995	18,906	50.4%	$30,617	24	39
Niles	30,363	31,432	20,393	− 3.4	28,447	16	26
Norridge	16,483	17,113	14,087	− 3.7	27,665	15	24
Northbrook	30,735	25,422	11,635	20.9	42,297	24	39
Northfield	5,807	5,010	4,005	15.9	37,515	19	31
Northlake	12,166	14,191	12,318	−14.3	25,657	16	26
North Riverside	6,764	8,097	7,989	−16.5	23,452	11	18
Oak Forest	26,096	19,271	3,724	35.4	28,027	25	40
Oak Lawn	60,590	60,305	27,741	0.5	27,8,13	15	24
Oak Park	54,887	62,511	61,093	−12.2	27,413	9	14
Olympia Fields	4,146	3,478	1,503	19.2	52,422	26	42
Orland Park	23,045	6,391	2,592	260.6	31,229	26	42
Palatine	32,166	26,050	11,504	23.5	33,443	31	50
Palos Heights	11,096	8,544	3,775	29.9	36,126	22	35
Palos Hills	16,654	6,629	3,766	151.2	28,939	18	29
Palos Park	3,150	3,297	2,169	− 4.5	35,705	21	34
Park Forest	26,222	30,638	29,993	−14.4	25,156	30	48
Park Ridge	38,704	42,614	32,659	− 9.2	34,131	18	29
Phoenix	2,850	3,596	4,203	−20.7	15,363	20	32
Posen	4,642	5,498	4,517	−15.6	24,503	20	32
Prospect Heights	11,808	13,333	—	−11.4	28,750	25	40
Richton Park	9,403	2,558	933	267.6	25,951	30	48
Riverdale	13,233	15,806	12,008	−16.3	24,047	19	31
River Forest	12,392	13,402	12,695	− 7.5	36,312	10	16
River Grove	10,368	11,465	8,464	− 9.6	23,278	12	19
Riverside	9,236	10,357	9,750	−10.8	32,326	11	18
Robbins	8,119	9,641	7,511	−15.8	16,287	20	32
Rolling Meadows	20,167	19,178	10,879	5.2	27,144	27	43
Rosemont	4,137	4,825	978	−14.3	23,835	20	32
Sauk Village	10,906	7,479	4,687	45.8	25,046	31	50
Schaumburg	52,319	18,531	986	182.3	29,257	30	48
Schiller Park	11,458	12,712	5,687	− 9.9	25,457	15	24
Skokie	60,278	68,322	59,364	−11.8	30,858	13	21
South Chicago Heights	3,932	4,923	4,043	−20.1	20,988	29	47
South Holland	24,977	23,931	10,412	4.4	30,706	23	37
South Stickney, now Burbank							
Stickney	5,893	6,601	6,239	−10.7	24,648	10	16
Stone Park	4,273	4,429	3,038	− 3.5	22,807		23
Streamwood	23,456	18,176	4,821	29.0	26,947	33	53
Summit	10,110	11,569	10,374	−12.6	21,584	13	21
Thornton	3,022	3,714	2,895	−18.6	28,263	26	42
Tinley Park	26,171	12,572	6,392	108.2	26,901	29	47
Westchester	17,730	20,033	18,092	−11.5	30,309	14	23

**Statistical Data for
Incorporated Communities
of Chicago Area (continued)**

Population

Place	1980 Census	1970 Census	1960 Census	1970–1980 % Change	Median Family Income 1979	Distance from Loop	
						Miles	Km
Cook County, cont.							
Western Springs	12,876	13,029	10,838	− 1.2%	$36,210	16	26
Wheeling	23,266	13,243	7,169	75.7	26,301	27	43
Willow Springs	4,147	3,318	2,348	25.0	28,658	19	31
Wilmette	28,229	32,134	28,268	−12.2	41,304	15	24
Winnetka	12,772	14,131	13,368	− 9.6	54,900	18	29
Worth	11,592	11,999	8,196	− 3.4	24,918	19	31
Du Page County							
Addison	28,836	24,482	6,741	17.8	27,413	20	32
Bartlett	13,254	3,501	1,540	278.6	28,360	32	51
Bensenville	16,124	12,956	9,141	24.5	26,008	20	32
Bloomingdale	12,659	2,974	1,262	325.7	30,943	25	40
Burr Ridge	3,833	1,637	299	134.1	39,726	19	31
Carol Stream	15,472	4,434	836	248.9	23,892	27	43
Clarendon Hills	6,857	6,750	5,885	1.6	33,615	20	32
Darien	14,968	7,789	—	92.2	33,428	21	34
Downers Grove	39,274	32,544	21,154	20.7	31,478	22	35
Elmhurst	44,251	46,392	36,991	− 4.6	30,578	17	27
Glendale Heights	23,163	11,406	173	103.1	27,496	23	37
Glen Ellyn	23,649	21,909	15,972	7.9	33,506	23	37
Hinsdale	16,726	15,918	12,859	5.1	39,104	18	29
Itasca	7,948	4,638	3,564	71.4	29,796	24	39
Lisle	13,625	5,329	4,219	155.7	30,141	26	42
Lombard	37,295	34,043	22,561	9.6	28,404	21	34
Naperville	42,330	22,794	12,933	85.7	36,685	30	48
Oak Brook	6,641	4,164	324	59.5	59,067	19	31
Oak Brook Terrace	2,285	1,126	1,121	102.9	N.A.*	18	29
Roselle	16,948	6,207	3,581	173.0	30,368	28	45
Villa Park	23,185	25,891	20,391	−10.5	27,251	19	31
Warrenville	7,519	3,281	3,134	129.2	27,983	30	48
West Chicago	12,550	9,988	6,854	25.7	22,823	32	51
Westmont	16,718	8,832	5,997	89.3	25,438	21	34
Wheaton	43,043	31,138	24,312	38.2	31,185	26	42
Willowbrook	4,953	1,457	157	239.9	35,777	19	31
Winfield	4,422	4,285	1,575	3.2	35,409	28	45
Wood Dale	11,251	8,831	3,071	27.4	29,113	22	35
Woodridge	22,322	11,028	542	102.4	29,582	25	40
Kane County							
Aurora	81,293	74,389	63,715	9.3	23,035	39	63
Batavia	12,574	9,060	7,496	38.8	26,072	37	60
Carpentersville	23,272	24,059	17,424	− 3.3	24,224	42	68

Statistical Data for
Incorporated Communities
of Chicago Area (continued)

Population

Place	1980 Census	1970 Census	1960 Census	1970-1980 % Change	Median Family Income 1979	Distance from Loop Miles	Km
Kane County, cont.							
East Dundee	2,618	2,920	2,221	−10.3%	$26,295	41	66
Elburn	1,224	1,122	960	9.1	N.A.*	45	72
Elgin	63,798	55,691	49,447	14.6	23,193	38	61
Geneva	9,881	9,049	7,646	9.2	30,846	37	60
Hampshire	1,735	1,611	1,309	7.7	N.A.*	53	85
Montgomery	3,363	3,278	2,122	2.6	24,509	41	66
North Aurora	5,205	4,833	2,088	7.7	26,406	39	63
St. Charles	17,492	12,945	9,269	35.1	27,379	37	60
Sleepy Hollow	2,000	1,729	311	15.7	N.A.*	44	71
South Elgin	6,218	4,289	2,624	45.0	23,706	37	60
Sugar Grove	1,366	1,230	326	11.1	N.A.*	46	74
Valley View	2,112	1,723	1,741	22.6	N.A.*	40	64
West Dundee	3,502	3,295	2,530	6.3	22,896	42	68
Lake County							
Antioch	4,419	3,189	2,268	38.6	23,241	53	85
Bannockburn	1,316	1,359	466	− 3.2	N.A.*	30	48
Deerfield	17,430	18,876	11,786	− 7.7	41,383	27	43
Deer Park	1,368	726	476	88.4	N.A.*	34	55
Fox Lake	6,831	4,511	3,700	51.4	19,630	53	85
Grayslake	5,260	4,907	3,762	7.2	25,545	44	71
Gurnee	7,179	2,738	1,831	162.2	30,189	39	63
Hawthorn Woods	1,658	939	239	76.6	N.A.*	36	58
Highland Park	30,611	32,263	25,532	− 5.1	42,903	26	42
Highwood	5,452	4,973	4,499	9.6	20,797	27	43
Island Lake	2,293	1,973	1,639	16.2	N.A.*	44	71
Lake Bluff	4,434	5,008	3,494	−11.5	41,440	33	53
Lake Forest	15,245	15,642	10,687	− 2.5	52,691	31	50
Lake Villa	1,462	1,090	903	34.1	N.A.*	49	79
Lake Zurich	8,225	4,082	3,458	101.5	30,277	37	60
Libertyville	16,520	11,684	8,560	41.4	34,953	37	60
Lincolnshire	4,151	2,531	555	64.0	54,897	31	50
Lindenhurst	6,220	3,141	1,259	98.0	29,368	47	76
Long Grove	2,013	1,196	640	68.3	N.A.*	32	51
Mundelein	17,053	16,128	10,562	5.7	27,394	38	61
North Barrington	1,475	1,411	282	4.5	N.A.*	39	63
North Chicago	38,774	47,275	22,938	−18.0	16,850	38	61
Park City	3,673	2,906	1,408	26.4	20,833	38	61
Riverwoods	2,804	1,571	96	78.5	50,828	29	47
Round Lake	2,644	1,531	997	72.7	20,838	47	76
Round Lake Beach	12,921	5,717	5,011	126.0	23,849	46	74
Round Lake Heights	1,192	1,144	—	4.2	N.A.*	47	76

Statistical Data for
Incorporated Communities
of Chicago Area (continued)

Population

Place	1980 Census	1970 Census	1960 Census	1970-1980 % Change	Median Family Income 1979	Distance from Loop	
						Miles	Km
Lake County, cont.							
Round Lake Park	4,032	3,148	2,565	28.1%	$21,524	45	72
Vernon Hills	9,827	1,056	123	830.6	29,060	31	50
Wadsworth	1,104	756	—	46.0	N.A.*	44	71
Wauconda	5,688	5,460	3,227	4.2	24,052	42	68
Waukegan	67,653	65,134	55,719	3.9	22,692	39	63
Winthrop Harbor	5,438	4,794	3,848	13.4	26,615	47	76
Zion	17,861	17,268	11,941	3.4	22,212	46	74
McHenry County							
Algonquin	5,834	3,515	2,014	66.0	29,209	44	71
Cary	6,640	4,358	2,530	52.4	28,202	43	69
Crystal Lake	18,590	14,541	8,314	27.8	28,142	49	79
Fox River Grove	2,515	2,245	1,866	12.0	25,000	41	66
Harvard	5,126	5,177	4,248	− 1.0	20,495	70	113
Hebron	786	781	701	0.6	N.A.*	66	106
Huntley	1,646	1,432	1,143	14.9	N.A.*	51	82
Lake in the Hills	5,651	3,240	2,046	74.4	26,201	46	74
Marengo	4,361	4,235	3,568	3.0	22,538	56	90
McCullom Lake	947	873	759	8.5	N.A.*	54	87
McHenry	10,908	6,772	3,336	61.1	23,814	53	85
Richmond	1,068	1,153	855	− 7.4	N.A.*	61	98
Woodstock	11,725	10,226	8,897	14.7	22,671	57	92
Will County							
Beecher	2,024	1,770	1,367	14.4	N.A.*	37	60
Bolingbrook	37,261	7,651	—	387.0	27,679	28	45
Braidwood	3,429	2,323	1,944	47.6	24,779	60	97
Channahon	3,734	1,505	—	148.1	27,776	48	77
Crest Hill	9,252	7,460	5,887	24.0	22,256	37	60
Crete	5,417	4,656	3,463	16.3	29,792	32	51
Frankfort	4,357	2,325	1,135	87.4	30,815	32	51
Joliet	77,956	78,827	66,780	− 1.1	22,694	39	63
Lockport	9,017	9,861	7,560	− 8.6	25,623	36	58
Manhattan	1,944	1,530	1,117	27.1	N.A.*	43	69
Mokena	4,578	1,643	1,332	178.6	24,318	32	51
Monee	993	940	646	5.6	N.A.*	36	58
New Lenox	5,792	2,855	1,750	102.9	27,653	36	58
Park Forest South	6,245	1,748	—	257.3	24,366	34	55
Peotone	2,832	2,345	1,788	20.8	22,761	42	68
Plainfield	4,485	2,928	2,183	53.2	26,849	37	60
Rockdale	1,913	2,015	1,272	− 5.1	N.A.*	41	66
Romeoville	15,519	12,888	3,574	20.4	25,453	32	51
Shorewood	4,714	1,749	499	169.5	31,235	44	71
Steger	9,269	8,104	6,432	14.4	20,582	30	48
Wilmington	4,424	4,335	4,210	2.1	23,873	54	87

**Statistical Data for
Incorporated Communities
of Chicago Area (continued)**

Population

Place	1980 Census	1970 Census	1960 Census	1970-1980 % Change	Median Family Income 1979	Distance from Loop	
						Miles	Km
Lake County, Indiana							
Cedar Lake	8,754	7,589	5,766	15.4%	$22,190	43	69
Crown Point	16,455	10,931	8,443	50.5	27,365	44	71
Dyer	9,555	4,906	3,993	94.8	27,761	31	50
East Chicago	39,786	46,982	57,669	−15.3	20,945	22	35
Gary	151,953	175,415	178,320	−13.4	19,477	30	48
Griffith	17,026	18,168	9,483	− 6.3	26,660	32	51
Hammond	93,714	107,983	111,698	−13.2	22,978	22	35
Highland	25,935	24,947	16,284	4.0	29,039	28	45
Hobart	22,987	21,485	18,680	7.0	25,586	38	61
Lake Station	14,294	9,858	9,309	44.9	22,049	35	56
Lowell	5,827	3,839	—	51.8	24,367	50	81
Merrillville	27,677	15,918	—	73.9	27,653	38	61
Munster	20,671	16,514	10,313	25.2	33,259	26	42
New Chicago	3,284	2,231	—	47.2	23,204	33	53
St. John	3,974	1,757	—	126.2	31,501	35	56
Schererville	13,209	3,663	2,875	260.6	27,568	33	53
Whiting	5,630	7,054	8,137	−20.2	23,991	18	29
Porter County, Indiana							
Burns Harbor	920	1,284	—	−28.3	N.A.*	41	66
Chesterton	8,531	6,177	4,335	38.1	25,467	47	76
Hebron	2,696	1,624	—	66.0	25,652	55	88
Ogden Dunes	1,489	1,361	—	9.4	N.A.*	39	63
Portage	27,409	19,127	11,822	43.3	26,225	39	63
Porter	2,988	3,058	—	− 2.3	25,254	45	72
Valparaiso	22,247	20,020	15,227	11.1	25,619	53	85

Appendix C

SELECTED BIBLIOGRAPHY BY CHAPTERS

Chapter 1. Introduction—References and General Readings

Andreas, Alfred T. *History of Chicago.* 3 vols. Chicago: A. T. Andreas, 1884–86.

Bach, Ira J., ed. *Chicago's Famous Buildings.* 3rd ed. Chicago: University of Chicago Press, 1980.

Bach, Ira J. *Chicago on Foot: Walking Tours of Chicago's Architecture.* 3rd ed. Chicago: Rand McNally & Co., 1977.

Bailey, Janet. *Chicago Houses.* New York: St. Martin's Press, 1981.

Berry, Brian J. L., et al. *Chicago Transformations of an Urban System.* Cambridge, Mass.: Ballinger Publishing Co., 1976.

Bishop, Glenn A., and Gilbert, Paul T. *Chicago's Accomplishments and Leaders.* Chicago: Bishop Publishing Co., 1932.

Bonner, Thomas N. *Medicine in Chicago, 1850–1950.* New York: American Book-Stratford Press, 1957.

Bross, William. *History of Chicago.* Chicago: Jansen, McClurg & Co., 1876.

Campbell, Edna Fay; Smith, Fanny R.; and Jones, Clarence F. *Our City—Chicago.* New York: Charles Scribner's Sons, 1930.

Chicago Department of Development and Planning. *Historic City: The Settlement of Chicago.* Chicago, 1976.

———. *The People of Chicago: Who We Are and Who We Have Been.* Chicago, 1976.

Chicago Department of Public Works, Bureau of Maps and Places. *Atlas of City of Chicago.* Chicago, 1977–78.

Commission on Chicago Historical and Architectural Landmarks. *Chicago Landmarks, 1980.*

———. *Landmark Neighborhoods of Chicago, 1981.*

Condit, Carl W. *The Chicago School of Architecture: A History of Commercial and Public Building in the Chicago Area, 1875–1925.* Chicago: University of Chicago Press, 1964.

———. *Chicago 1910–29: Building, Planning, and Urban Technology.* Chicago: University of Chicago Press, 1973.

———. *Chicago 1930–70: Building, Planning, and Urban Technology.* Chicago: University of Chicago Press, 1974.

Currey, Josiah Seymour. *Chicago: Its History and Its Builders: A Century of Marvelous Growth.* 5 vols. Chicago: S. J. Clark Publishing Co., 1912.

Cutler, Irving, ed. *The Chicago Metropolitan Area: Selected Geographic Readings.* New York: Simon & Schuster, 1970.

Dedmon, Emmett. *Fabulous Chicago.* 2nd ed. New York: Atheneum, 1981.

Drury, John. *Old Chicago Houses.* Chicago: University of Chicago Press, 1941.

Farr, Finis. *Chicago: A Personal History of America's Most American City.* New Rochelle, N.Y.: Arlington House, 1973.

Federal Writers Project. *Illinois, A Descriptive and Historical Guide.* 2nd ed. Chicago: A. A. McClurg & Co., 1947.

Fiedler, D. E., ed. *The Chicagoland Atlas.* Arlington Heights, Ill.: Creative Sales Corp., 1980.

Furer, Howard B. *Chicago: A Chronological and Documentary History, 1784–1970.* Dobbs Ferry, N.Y.: Oceana Publications, 1974.

Gilbert, Paul, and Bryson, Charles Lee. *Chicago and Its Makers.* Chicago: Felix Mendelsohn, 1929.

Goode, J. Paul. *The Geographic Background of Chicago.* Chicago: University of Chicago Press, 1926.

Graham, Jory. *Chicago—An Extraordinary Guide.* Chicago: Rand McNally & Co., 1968.

———. *Instant Chicago. How to Cope.* Chicago: Rand McNally & Co., 1973.

Grossman, Ron. *Guide to Chicago Neighborhoods.* Piscataway, N.J.: New Century Publishers, 1981.

Halper, Albert, ed. *The Chicago Crime Book.* Cleveland: World Publishing Co., 1967.

———, ed. *This Is Chicago: An Anthology.* New York: Henry Holt & Co., 1952.

Hansen, Harry, ed. *Illinois: A Descriptive and Historical Guide.* New York: Hastings House, Publisher, 1974.

Havighurst, Robert J. *The Public Schools of Chicago: A Survey for the Board of Education of the City of Chicago.* Chicago: Chicago Board of Education, 1964.

Heise, Kenan. *Is There Only One Chicago?* Richmond, Va.: Westover Publishing Co., 1973.

Herrick, Mary J. *The Chicago Schools: A Social and Political History.* Beverly Hills: Sage Publications, 1971.

A History of Chicago: Its Men and Institutions. Chicago: Inter Ocean, 1900.

Horowitz, Helen Lefkowitz. *Culture & the City: Cultural Philanthropy in Chicago from the 1800s to 1917.* Lexington: University Press of Kentucky, 1976.

Jensen, George Peter. *Historic Chicago Sites.* Chicago: Creative Enterprises, 1953.

Karlen, Harvey. *The Governments of Chicago.* Chicago: Courier Publishing Co., 1958.

Kiang, Ying Cheng. *Chicago.* Chicago: Adams Press, 1968.

Kirkland, Joseph. *The Story of Chicago.* 3 vols. Chicago: Dibble Publishing Co., 1892–1894.

Kitagawa, Evelyn M., and Taeuber, Karl E., eds. *Local Community Fact Book: Chicago Metropolitan Area, 1960.* Chicago: Chicago Community Inventory, University of Chicago, 1963.

Krantz, Leslie J. *Chicago Art Review.* 2nd ed. Chicago: Chicago Review Press, 1980.

Lewis, Lloyd, and Smith, Henry Justin. *Chicago, the History of Its Reputation.* New York: Harcourt, Brace & Co., 1929.

Longstreet, Stephen. *Chicago, 1860–1919.* New York: David McKay Co., 1973.

Lowe, David. *Chicago Interiors.* Chicago: Contemporary Books, 1979.

McManis, John T. *Ella Flagg Young and a Half-Century of the Chicago Public Schools.* Chicago: A. C. McClurg & Co., 1916.

McPhaul, John J. *Deadlines and Monkeyshines: The Fabled World of Chicago Journalism.* Englewood Cliffs, N.J.: Prentice Hall, 1962.

Mark, Norman. *Chicago: Walking, Bicycling, and Driving Tours of the City.* Chicago: Chicago Review Press, 1977.

Masters, Edgar Lee. *The Tale of Chicago.* New York: G. P. Putnam's Sons, 1933.

Mayer, Harold M. *Chicago: City of Decisions.* Papers on Chicago, No. 1. Chicago: Geographic Society of Chicago, 1955.

Mayer, Harold M., and Wade, Richard C. *Chicago: Growth of a Metropolis.* Chicago: University of Chicago Press, 1969.

Nash, Jay Robert. *People to See: An Anecdotal History of Chicago's Makers and Breakers.* Piscataway, N.J.: New Century Publishers, 1981.

Northeastern Illinois Planning Commission. *A Social Geography of Metropolitan Chicago.* Chicago, 1960.

———. *Suburban Fact Book.* Chicago, 1973.

Olcott's Land Values Blue Book of Chicago & Suburbs. Chicago: George C. Olcott & Co., 1980.

Pierce, Bessie Louise. *A History of Chicago.* 3 vols. New York: Alfred A. Knopf, 1937–57.

———. *As Others See Chicago—Impressions of Visitors. 1673–1933.* Chicago: University of Chicago Press, 1933.

Poole, Ernest. *Giants Gone—Men Who Made Chicago.* New York: McGraw Hill Book Co., 1943.

Rex, Frederick. *Mayors of the City of Chicago from March 4, 1837 to April 13, 1933.* Chicago: Municipal Reference Library, 1947.

Riedy, James L. *Chicago Sculpture.* Urbana: University of Illinois Press, 1981.

Schackleton, Robert. *The Book of Chicago.* Philadelphia: Penn Publishing Co., 1920.

Smith, Henry Justin. *Chicago, A Portrait.* New York: D. Appleton-Century Co., 1931.

Tallmadge, Thomas Eddy. *Architecture in Old Chicago.* Chicago: University of Chicago Press, 1941.

Wagenknecht, Edward. *Chicago.* Norman: University of Oklahoma Press, 1964.

Williams, Kenny J. *Prairie Voices: A Literary History of Chicago from the Frontier to 1893.* Nashville, Tenn.: Townsend Press, 1980.

Winslow, Charles S. *Historical Events of Chicago.* Chicago: Soderlund Printing Service, 1937.

Chapter 2. The Physical Setting

Atwood, Wallace W., and Goldthwait, James. *Physical Geography of the Evanston-Waukegan Region.* Bulletin No. 7. Urbana: Illinois State Geological Survey, 1908.

Benton, Chris. *Chicagoland Nature Trails.* Chicago: Contemporary Books, 1978.

Bretz, J. Harlan. *Geology of the Chicago Region.* Part 1, *Geology of the Chicago Region,* 1939; Part 2, *The Pleistocene,* 1955. Bulletin No. 65. Urbana: Illinois State Geological Survey.

Cain, Louis P. *Sanitation Strategy for a Lakefront Metropolis.* De Kalb: Northern Illinois University Press, 1978.

Cowles, Henry C. *The Plant Societies of Chicago and Vicinity.* Bulletin No. 2. Chicago: Geographic Society of Chicago, 1901.

Cox, Henry J., and Armington, John H. *The Weather and Climate of Chicago.* Bulletin No. 4. Chicago: Geographic Society of Chicago, 1914.

Cressey, George B. *The Indiana Sand Dunes and Shore Lines of the Lake Michigan Basin.* Bulletin No. 8. Chicago: Geographic Society of Chicago, 1928.

Duddy, Edward A. *Agriculture in the Chicago Region.* Chicago: University of Chicago Press, 1929.

Fryxell, F. M. *The Physiography of the Region of Chicago.* Chicago: University of Chicago Press, 1927.

Knight, Robert, and Zeuch, Lucius H. *The Location of the Chicago Portage of the Seventeenth Century.* Chicago: University of Chicago Press, 1920.

Salisbury, Rollin D., and Alden, William C. *The Geography of Chicago and Its Environs.* Bulletin No. 1. Chicago: Geographic Society of Chicago, 1899.

Schmid, James A. *Urban Vegetation.* Research Paper No. 161. Chicago: University of Chicago, Department of Geography, 1975.

Shelford, Victor E. *Animal Communities in Temperate America, As Illustrated in the Chicago Region: A Study in Animal Ecology.* Bulletin No. 5. Chicago: Geographic Society of Chicago, 1913.

Wilman, H. B. *Summary of the Geology of the Chicago Area.* Circular 460. Urbana: Illinois State Geological Survey, 1971.

Chapter 3. The Evolution of Chicago

Andrews, Wayne. *Battle for Chicago.* New York: Harcourt, Brace & Co., 1946.

Angle, Paul M. *The Great Chicago Fire, October 8–10, 1871, Described by Eight Men and Women Who Experienced Its Horrors and Testified to the Courage of Its Inhabitants.* Chicago: Chicago Historical Society, 1971.

Asbury, Herbert. *Gem of the Prairie: An Informal History of the Chicago Underworld.* Garden City, N.Y.: Garden City Publishing Co., 1942.

Badger, R. Reid. *The Great American Fair: The World's Columbian Exposition and American Culture.* Chicago: Nelson-Hall, 1979.

Bancroft, Hubert Howe. *The Book of the Fair: An Historical and Descriptive Presentation Viewed through the Columbian Exposition at Chicago in 1893.* 2 vols. Chicago: Bancroft Co., 1895.

Burg, David F. *Chicago's White City of 1893.* Lexington: University Press of Kentucky, 1976.

Chicago, Department of Public Works. *Chicago Public Works: A History.* Chicago: Rand McNally & Co., 1973.

Chicago Plan Commission. *Housing in Chicago Communities.* 75 vols. Chicago, 1940.

Colbert, Elias, and Chamberlain, Everett. *Chicago & the Great Conflagration.* Chicago: J. S. Goodman & Co., 1871.

Cromie, Robert, and Lieberman, Archie. *Chicago.* Chicago: Rand McNally & Co., 1980.

David, Henry. *History of the Haymarket Affair.* New York: Farrar & Rinehart, 1936.

Demaris, Ovid. *Captive City.* New York: Lyle Stuart, 1969.

Duis, Perry. *Chicago: Creating New Traditions.* Chicago: Chicago Historical Society, 1976.

Fanning, Charles. *Finley Peter Dunne and Mr. Dooley. The Chicago Years.* Lexington: University Press of Kentucky, 1978.

Fehrenbacher, Don E. *Chicago Giant: A Biography of "Long John" Wentworth.* Madison, Wis.: American History Research Center, 1957.

Ginger, Ray. *Altgeld's America: The Ideal Versus Changing Realities.* New York: Funk & Wagnall Co., 1958.

Harrison, Carter H. *Stormy Years.* Indianapolis: Bobbs-Merrill Co., 1935.

Illinois Archaeological Survey. *Chicago Area Archaeology.* Bulletin No. 3. Urbana: University of Illinois, 1961.

Kennedy, Eugene. *Himself! The Life and Times of Mayor Richard J. Daley.* New York: Viking Press, 1978.

Kinzie, Juliette A. *Wau-Bun.* Chicago: Rand McNally & Co., 1901.

Knudtson, Thomas. *Chicago, The Rising City.* Chicago: Chicago Publishing Co., 1975.

Kobler, John. *Capone: The Life and World of Al Capone.* New York: G. P. Putnam's Sons, 1971.

Kogan, Herman, and Cromie, Robert. *The Great Fire: Chicago 1871.* New York: G. P. Putnam's Sons, 1971.

Kogan, Herman, and Kogan, Rick. *Yesterday's Chicago.* Miami, Fla.: E. A. Seemann Publishing Co., 1976.

Kogan, Herman, and Wendt, Lloyd. *Chicago: A Pictorial History.* New York: Bonanza Books, 1958.

Lohr, Lenox Riley. *Fair Management, the Story of A Century of Progress Exposition: A Guide for Future Fairs.* Chicago: Cuneo Press, 1952.

Lowe, David. *Lost Chicago.* Boston: Houghton Mifflin Co., 1975.

———. *The Great Chicago Fire.* New York: Dover Publications, 1979.

Mark, Norman. *Mayors, Madams, & Madmen.* Chicago: Chicago Review Press, 1979.

Merriam, Charles Edward. *Chicago: A More Intimate View of Urban Politics.* New York: Macmillan Co., 1929.

O'Conner, Len. *Clout: Mayor Daley and His City.* Chicago: Henry Regnery Co., 1975.

Quaife, Milo M. *Checagou: From Indian Wigwam to Modern City, 1673–1835.* Chicago: University of Chicago Press, 1933.

———. *Chicago and the Old Northwest, 1673–1835.* Chicago: University of Chicago Press, 1913.

Quimby, George Irving. *Indian Life in the Upper Great Lakes, 11,000 B.C. to A.D. 1800.* Chicago: University of Chicago Press, 1960.

Rakove, Milton. *Don't Make No Waves— Don't Back No Losers.* Bloomington: Indiana University Press, 1975.

Reckless, Walter C. *Vice in Chicago.* Chicago: University of Chicago Press, 1933.

Royko, Mike. *Boss: Richard J. Daley of Chicago.* New York: E. P. Dutton, 1971.

Schaaf, Barbara C. *Mr. Dooley's Chicago.* Garden City, N.Y.: Anchor Press/Doubleday, 1977.

Smith, Henry Justin. *Chicago's Great Century, 1833–1933.* Chicago: Consolidated Publishers, 1933.

Stead, William F. *If Christ Came to Chicago.* Laird & Lee Publishers, 1894.

Wendt, Lloyd, and Kogan, Herman. *Big Bill of Chicago.* Indianapolis: Bobbs-Merrill Co., 1953.

———. *Lords of the Levee.* Indianapolis: Bobbs-Merrill Co., 1943.

Chapters 4 & 5. People and Settlement Patterns

Abbott, Edith. *The Tenements of Chicago, 1908–1935.* Chicago: University of Chicago Press, 1936.

Abrahamson, Julia. *A Neighborhood Finds Itself.* New York: Harper & Brothers, 1959.

Addams, Jane. *Twenty Years at Hull House.* New York: Macmillan, 1910.

Adelman, William J. *Pilsen and the West Side.* Chicago: Illinois Labor History Society, 1977.

Allswang, John M. *A House for All Peoples: Ethnic Politics in Chicago, 1890–1936.* Lexington: University Press of Kentucky, 1971.

Beijbom, Ulf. *Swedes in Chicago: A Demographic and Social Study of the 1846–1880 Immigration.* Sweden: Historiska Institutionen at University of Uppsala/Chicago Historical Society, 1971.

Berkow, Ira. *Maxwell Street.* Garden City, N.Y.: Doubleday & Co., 1977.

Block, Jean F. *Hyde Park Houses.* Chicago: University of Chicago Press, 1978.

Bowly, Devereux, Jr. *The Poorhouse: Subsidized Housing in Chicago, 1895–1976.* Cardondale: Southern Illinois University Press, 1978.

Chicago Department of Development and Planning. *Chicago's Black Population: Selected Statistics.* Chicago, 1975.

———. *Chicago's German Population: Selected Statistics.* Chicago, 1976.

———. *Chicago's Irish Population: Selected Statistics.* Chicago, 1976.

———. *Chicago's Italian Population: Selected Statistics.* Chicago, 1976.

———. *Chicago's Polish Population: Selected Statistics.* Chicago, 1976.

———. *Chicago's Spanish-Speaking Population: Selected Statistics.* Chicago, 1973.

Czechoslovak National Council of America. *Panorama: An Historical Review of Czechs and Slovaks in the United States of America.* Cicero, Ill., 1970.

De Vise, Pierre. *Chicago's Widening Color Gap.* Chicago: Interuniversity Social Research Committee, 1967.

Drake, St. Clair, and Cayton, Horace R. *Black Metropolis: A Study of Negro Life in a Northern City.* 2 vols. New York: Harcourt, Brace & World, 1970.

Duncan, Otis Dudley, and Duncan, Beverly. *The Negro Population of Chicago: A Study of Residential Succession.* Chicago: University of Chicago Press, 1957.

Fainhauz, David. *Lithuanians in Multi-Ethnic Chicago until World War II.* Chicago: Lithuanian Library Press and Loyola University Press, 1977.

Frazier, Franklin E. *The Negro Family in Chicago.* Chicago: University of Chicago Press, 1932.

Greeley, Andrew M. *Neighborhood.* New York: The Seabury Press, 1977.

Grossman, Ronald P. *The Italians in America.* Minneapolis: Lerner Publications Co., 1966.

Gutstein, Morris A. *A Priceless Heritage.* New York: Bloch Publishing Co., 1953.

Heimovics, Rachel Baron. *The Chicago Jewish Source Book.* Piscataway, N.J.: New Century Publishers, 1981.

Hofmeister, Rudolph A. *The Germans of Chicago.* Champaign, Ill.: Stipes Publishing Co., 1976.

Holli, Melvin G., and Jones, Peter d'A. *The Ethnic Frontier.* Grand Rapids, Mich.: Wm. B. Eerdmann Publishing Co., 1977.
————. *Ethnic Chicago.* Grand Rapids, Mich.: Wm B. Eerdmann Publishing Co., 1981.

Holt, Glen E., and Pacyga, Dominic A. *Chicago: A Historical Guide to the Neighborhoods, the Loop and South Side.* Chicago: Chicago Historical Society, 1979.

Jones, Jayne Clark. *The Greeks in America.* Minneapolis: Lerner Publications Co., 1969.

Kantowicz, Edward R. *Polish-American Politics in Chicago, 1888–1940.* Chicago: University of Chicago Press, 1975.

Koenig, Harry C., ed. *A History of the Parishes of the Archdiocese of Chicago.* vols. 1 & 2. Chicago: The Archdiocese of Chicago, 1980.

Kopan, Andrew T. "Education and Greek Immigrants in Chicago, 1892–1973: A Study in Ethnic Survival." Ph.D. Dissertation, University of Chicago, 1974.

Kourvetaris, George A. *First and Second Generation Greeks in Chicago.* Athens, Greece: National Center of Social Research, 1971.

Lane, George A. *Chicago Churches and Synagogues: An Architectural Pilgrimage.* Chicago: Loyola University Press, 1981.

Linn, James Weber. *Jane Addams.* New York: D. Appleton-Century Co., 1935.

McCaffery, Lawrence J. *The Irish Diaspora in America.* Bloomington: Indiana University Press, 1976.

Meites, Hyman L., ed. *History of the Jews of Chicago.* Chicago: Jewish Historical Society of Illinois, 1924.

Nelli, Humbert S. *The Italians in Chicago 1880–1930. A Study in Ethnic Mobility.* New York: Oxford University Press, 1970.

Olson, Ernst W. *History of the Swedes of Illinois.* 2 vols. Chicago: Engberg-Holmberg Publishing Co., 1908.

Philpott, Thomas Lee. *The Slum and the Ghetto: Neighborhood Deterioration and Middle Class Reform, Chicago 1880–1930.* New York: Oxford University Press, 1978.

Poles of Chicago, 1837–1937. Chicago: Polish Pageant, 1937.

Pomrenze, Seymour Jacob. "Aspects of Chicago Russian-Jewish Life, 1893–1925." In *The Chicago Pinkus,* edited by Simon Rawidowicz. Chicago: College of Jewish Studies, 1952.

Residents of Hull-House. *Hull-House Maps and Papers.* New York: Thomas Y. Crowell & Co., 1895.

Ropka, Gerald William. "The Evolving Residential Pattern of the Mexican, Puerto Rican, and Cuban Population in the City of Chicago." Ph.D Dissertation, Michigan State University, 1973.

Saloutos, Theodore. *The Greeks in the United States.* Cambridge, Mass.: Harvard University Press, 1964.

Schiavo, Giovanni. *The Italians in Chicago: A Study in Americanization.* Chicago: Italian American Publishing Co., 1928.

The Sentinel's History of Chicago Jewry, 1911–1961. Chicago: Sentinel Publishing Co., 1961.

Short, James F., Jr. *The Social Fabric of the Metropolis: Contributions of the "Chicago School of Urban Sociology."* Chicago: University of Chicago Press, 1971.

Spear, Allan H. *Black Chicago: The Making of a Negro Ghetto, 1980–1920.* Chicago: University of Chicago Press, 1967.

Strand, A. E. *A History of the Norwegians of Illinois.* Chicago: John Anderson Publishing Co., 1905.

Thrasher, Frederic M. *The Gang.* Chicago: University of Chicago Press, 1927.

Townsend, Andrew Jacke. "The Germans of Chicago," *Deutch-Amerikanische Geschichtblatter* 32 (1932). Reprinted from Ph.D. dissertation, University of Chicago, 1927.

Travis, Dempsey J., *An Autobiography of Black Chicago.* Chicago: Urban Research Institute, 1981.

Tuttle, Wm. M., Jr. *Race Riot: Chicago in the Red Summer of 1919.* New York: Atheneum, 1970.

Vandenbosch, Amry. *The Dutch Communities of Chicago.* Chicago: Knickerbocker Society of Chicago, 1927.

Vecoli, Rudolph. "Chicago's Italians Prior to World War I: A Study of Their Social and Economic Adjustment." Ph.D. dissertation, University of Wisconsin, 1962.

Wirth, Louis. *The Ghetto.* Chicago: University of Chicago Press, 1928.

Zorbaugh, Harvey W. *The Gold Coast and the Slum.* Chicago: University of Chicago Press, 1929.

Chapter 6. The Economy of Chicago

Adelman, William J. *Touring Pullman.* Chicago: Illinois Labor History Society, 1972.

Appleton, John B. *The Iron and Steel Industry of the Calumet District.* University of Illinois Studies in the Social Sciences, vol. 13, no. 2. Urbana: University of Illinois, 1925.

Berry, Brian J. L. *Commercial Structure and Commercial Blight.* Research Paper No. 85. Chicago: University of Chicago, Department of Geography, 1963.

Bird's-Eye Views and Guide to Chicago. Chicago: Rand McNally & Co., 1898.

Breese, Gerald W. *The Daytime Population of the Central Business District of Chicago.* Chicago: University of Chicago Press, 1949.

Buder, Stanley. *Pullman: An Experiment in Industrial Order and Community Planning 1880–1930.* New York: Oxford University Press, 1967.

Carter, Peter. *Mies van der Rohe at Work.* New York: Praeger Publishers, 1974.

Casson, Herbert N. *Cyrus Hall McCormick.* Chicago: McClurg & Co., 1909.

Corplan Associates, IIT Research Institute. *Technological Change: Its Impact on Industry in Metropolitan Chicago.* 8 vols. Chicago: IIT Research Institute, 1964.

De Meirleir, Marcel J. *Manufactural Occupance in the West Central Area of Chicago.* Research Paper No. 11. Chicago: University of Chicago, Department of Geography, 1950.

Hines, Thomas S. *Burnham of Chicago: Architect and Planner.* Chicago: University of Chicago Press, 1974.

Hoyt, Homer. *One Hundred Years of Land Values in Chicago 1830–1933.* Chicago: University of Chicago Press, 1933.

Industrial Chicago. 6 vols. Chicago: Goodspeed Publishing Co., 1891–1896.

Kornblum, William. *Blue Collar Community.* Chicago: University of Chicago Press, 1974.

Leech, Harper, and Carroll, John. *Armour and His Times.* New York: D. Appleton-Century Co., 1938.

Lindsay, Almont. *The Pullman Strike.* Chicago: University of Chicago Press, 1942.

Morrison, Hugh. *Louis Sullivan: Prophet of Modern Architecture.* New York: W. W. Norton & Co., 1935.

Randall, Frank A. *History of the Development of Building Construction in Chicago.* Urbana: University of Illinois Press, 1949.

Solomon, Ezra, and Bilbija, Zarko G. *Metropolitan Chicago: An Economic Analysis.* Glencoe, Ill.: The Free Press, 1959.

Solzman, David M. *Waterway Industrial Sites, A Chicago Case Study.* Research

Paper No. 107. Chicago: University of Chicago, Department of Geography, 1966.

Twombly, Robert C. *Frank Lloyd Wright: An Interpretive Biography*. New York: Harper & Row, 1973.

University of Chicago Center for Urban Studies. *Mid-Chicago Economic Development Study*. 3 vols. Chicago: Mayor's Committee for Economic and Cultural Development, 1966.

Wendt, Lloyd. *Chicago Tribune: The Rise of a Great American Newspaper*. Chicago: Rand McNally & Co., 1979.

Wendt, Lloyd, and Kogan, Herman. *Give the Lady What She Wants!* Chicago: Rand McNally & Co., 1952.

Werner, Morris R. *Julius Rosenwald*. New York: Harper & Brothers, 1939.

Chapter 7. Transportation—External and Internal

Chicago Area Transportation Study. *Final Report*. 3 vols. Chicago, 1959, 1960, 1962.

The Chicago Freight Tunnels. Chicago: Chicago Tunnel Terminal Corp., 1928.

Davis, James L. *The Elevated System and the Growth of Northern Chicago*. Studies in Geography No. 10. Evanston, Ill.: Northwestern University, Department of Geography, 1965.

Draine, Edwin H. *Import Traffic of Chicago and Its Hinterland*. Research Paper No. 81. Chicago: University of Chicago, Department of Geography, 1963.

Fellman, Jerome D. *Truck Transportation Patterns of Chicago*. Research Paper No. 12. Chicago: University of Chicago, Department of Geography, 1950.

Hansen, Harry. *The Chicago*. Rivers of America Series. New York: Farrar & Rinehart, 1942.

Helvig, Magne. *Chicago's External Truck Movements*. Research Paper No. 90. Chicago: University of Chicago, Department of Geography, 1964.

Hilton, George W., and Due, John F. *The Electric Interurban Railways in America*. Stanford, Calif.: Stanford University Press, 1960.

Lind, Alan R. *Chicago Surface Lines: An Illustrated History*. Park Forest, Ill.: Transport History Press, 1974.

Mayer, Harold M. *The Port of Chicago and the St. Lawrence Seaway*. Research Paper No. 49. Chicago: University of Chicago, Department of Geography, 1957.

————. *The Railway Pattern of Metropolitan Chicago*. Chicago: University of Chicago, Department of Geography, 1943.

Middleton, William D. *North Shore: America's Fastest Interurban*. San Marino, Calif.: Golden West Books, 1968.

————. *South Shore: The Last Interurban*. San Marino, Calif.: Golden West Books, 1970.

————. *The Interurban Era*. Milwaukee: Kalmbach Publishing Co., 1961.

Public Transportation in Northeastern Illinois. Report by the Governor's Transportation Task Force, January, 1973.

Putnam, James Williams. *The Illinois and Michigan Canal: A Study in Economic History*. Chicago: University of Chicago Press, 1918.

Quaife, Milo M. *Chicago's Highways Old and New: From Indian Trails to Motor Road*. Chicago: D. F. Keller & Co., 1923.

Taaffe, Edward J. *The Air Passenger Hinterland of Chicago*. Research Paper No. 24. Chicago: University of Chicago, Department of Geography, 1952.

Chapter 8. Expansion of the Chicago Metropolitan Area

Ahmed, G. Munir. *Manufacturing Structure and Patterns of Waukegan-North Chicago*. Research Paper No. 46. Chicago: University of Chicago, Department of Geography, 1957.

Andreas, Alfred T. *History of Cook County, Illinois: From the Earliest Period to the*

Present Time. Chicago: A. T. Andreas, 1884.

Bach, Ira J. *A Guide to Chicago's Historic Suburbs, on Wheels and on Foot.* Chicago: Swallow Press/Athens, Ohio: Ohio University Press, 1981.

Canine, Gerald C., ed. *Chicagoland's Community Guide, 17th Annual Edition.* Chicago Law Bulletin Publishing Co., 1981.

Chamberlain, Everett. *Chicago and Its Suburbs.* Chicago: T. A. Hungerford & Co., 1874.

Cramer, Robert E. *Manufacturing Structure of the Cicero District, Metropolitan Chicago.* Research Paper No. 27. Chicago: University of Chicago, Department of Geography, 1952.

Cutler, Irving. *The Chicago-Milwaukee Corridor: A Geographic Study of Intermetropolitan Coalescence.* Studies in Geography No. 9. Evanston, Ill.: Northwestern University, Department of Geography, 1965.

Federal Writers Project. *The Calumet Region Historical Guide.* Gary, Ind.: Garman Printing Co., 1939.

Harper, Robert A. *Recreational Occupance of the Moraine Lake Region of Northeastern Illinois and Southeastern Wisconsin.* Research Paper No. 14. Chicago: University of Chicago, Department of Geography, 1950.

Johnson, Charles B. *Growth of Cook County: A History of the Large Lake-Shore County That Includes Chicago.* Chicago: Board of Commissioners of Cook County, 1960.

Kenyon, James B. *The Industrialization of the Skokie Area.* Research Paper No. 33. Chicago: University of Chicago, Department of Geography, 1954.

Klove, Robert C. *The Park Ridge-Barrington Area: A Study of Residential Land Patterns and Problems in Suburban Chicago.* Chicago: University of Chicago, Department of Geography, 1942.

Komaiko, Jean, and Schaeffer, Norma. *Doing the Dunes.* Beverly Shores, Ind.: Dunes Enterprises, 1973.

Lane, James B. *"City of the Century": A History of Gary, Indiana.* Bloomington: Indiana University Press, 1978.

League of Women Voters of Chicago. *The Key to Our Local Government: Chicago, Cook County Metropolitan Area.* 4th ed. Chicago: Citizens Information Service of Illinois, 1978.

Miller, John J. *Open Land in Metropolitan Chicago.* Chicago: Midwest Open Land Association, 1962.

Moore, Powell A. *The Calumet Region. Indiana's Last Frontier.* Indianapolis: Indiana Historical Bureau, 1959.

Northeastern Illinois Planning Commission. *Open Space in Northeastern Illinois.* Technical Report No. 2. Chicago, 1962.

Platt, Rutherford H. *Open Land in Urban Illinois.* De Kalb: Northern Illinois University Press, 1971.

Stetzer, Donald Foster. *Special Districts in Cook County: Toward a Geography of Local Government.* Chicago: University of Chicago, Department of Geography, 1975.

Chapter 9. Planning for the Future

Burnham, Daniel H., and Bennett, Edward H. *Plan of Chicago.* Chicago: Commercial Club, 1909.

Burnham, Daniel H., Jr., and Kingery, Robert. *Planning the Region of Chicago.* Chicago: Chicago Regional Planning Association, 1956.

Chicago Department of Development and Planning. *Chicago 21: A Plan for the Central Area Communities.* Chicago, 1973.

———. *The Comprehensive Plan of Chicago.* Chicago, 1966.

———. *The Lakefront Plan of Chicago.* Chicago, 1972.

———. *The Riveredge Plan of Chicago.* Chicago, 1974.

Chicago Land Use Survey. vol. 1: *Residential Chicago.* vol. 2: *Land Use in Chicago.* Chicago: Chicago Plan Commission, 1942, 1943.

Chicago Plan Commission. *Forty-Four Cities in the City of Chicago.* Chicago, 1942.

————. *Master Plan of Residential Land Use of Chicago.* Chicago, 1943.

Hillman, Arthur, and Casey, Robert J. *Tomorrow's Chicago.* Chicago: University of Chicago Press, 1953.

Meyerson, Martin, and Banfield, Edward C. *Politics, Planning, and the Public Interest.* Glencoe, Ill.: The Free Press, 1955.

Midwest Open Land Association. *Preservation of Open Space Areas.* Chicago, 1966.

Moody, Walter D. *Wacker's Manual of the Plan of Chicago.* Chicago: H. C. Sherman & Co., 1911.

Moore, Charles. *Daniel Burnham: Architect, Planner of Cities.* 2 vols. New York: Houghton Mifflin Co., 1921.

Northeastern Illinois Metropolitan Area Local Governmental Services Commission. *Governmental Problems in the Chicago Metropolitan Area.* Edited by Leverett S. Lyon. Chicago: University of Chicago Press, 1957.

Northeastern Illinois Planning Commission. *The Comprehensive Plan for the Development of the Northeastern Illinois Counties Area.* Chicago, 1968.

Ranney, Victoria Post. *Olmsted in Chicago.* Chicago: Open Lands Project, 1972.

Rossi, Peter H., and Dentler, Robert A. *The Politics of Urban Renewal: The Chicago Findings.* New York: Free Press of Glencoe, 1961.

Simpson, Dick, ed. *Chicago's Future: An Agenda for Change.* Champaign, Ill.: Stipes Publishing Co., 1976.

Willie, Lois. *Forever Open, Clear and Free: The Historic Struggle for Chicago's Lakefront.* Chicago: Henry Regnery Co., 1972.

Fiction, Poetry, Reflections

Ade, George. *Chicago Stories.* Chicago: Henry Regnery Co., 1963.

Algren, Nelson. *Chicago: City on the Make.* Garden City, N.Y.: Doubleday, 1951.

————. *Man with the Golden Arm.* Garden City, N.Y.: Doubleday, 1949.

Anderson, Sherwood. *Windy McPherson's Son.* New York, Cape, 1916.

Bellow, Saul. *Adventures of Augie March.* New York: Viking Press, 1953.

Brashler, William. *City Dogs.* New York: Harper & Row, 1976.

Brooks, Gwendolyn. *Maud Martha.* New York: AMS Press, 1953.

Casey, Robert J. *Chicago Medium Rare.* Indianapolis: Bobbs Merrill Co., 1952.

Cleaver, Charles. *Early Chicago Reminiscences.* Fergus Historical Series No. 19. Chicago: Fergus Printing Co., 1882.

Cook, Frederick F. *Bygone Days in Chicago.* Chicago: A. C. McClurg & Co., 1910.

Dreiser, Theodore. *Sister Carrie.* New York: Doubleday, Page & Co., 1900.

————. *The Financier.* New York: Harper & Brothers, 1912.

Dubkin, Leonard. *My Secret Places: One Man's Love Affair with Nature in the City.* New York: McKay, 1972.

Farrell, James T. *Studs Lonigan: A Trilogy.* New York: Vanguard Press, 1935.

Ferber, Edna. *So Big.* Garden City, N.Y.: Doubleday, Page & Co., 1924.

Field, Eugene. *Sharps and Flats.* New York: C. Scribner's Sons, 1900.

Fuller, Helen Blake. *The Cliff Dwellers.* New York: Harper & Brothers, 1893.

Gale, Edwin O. *Reminiscences of Early Chicago.* Chicago: F. H. Revell Co., 1902.

Halper, Albert. *On the Shore: Young Writer Remembering Chicago.* New York: Viking Press, 1934.

Hansberry, Lorraine. *Raisin in the Sun.* New York: Random House, 1959.

Harris, Frank. *Bomb.* Chicago: University of Chicago Press, 1963.

Hecht, Ben. *Gaily, Gaily.* Garden City, N.Y.: Doubleday, 1963.

Hecht, Ben, and MacArthur, Charles. *The Front Page.* New York: Covici-Friede, 1928.

Herrick, Robert. *The Web of Life.* New York: Irvington Publishers, 1900.

Kupcinet, Irv. *Kup's Chicago.* Cleveland: World Publishing Co., 1962.

Levin, Meyer. *The Old Bunch*. New York: Viking Press, 1937.

———. *Compulsion*. New York: Simon & Schuster, 1956.

Liebling, Abbott J. *Chicago: The Second City*. New York: Alfred A. Knopf, 1952.

Meeker, Arthur. *Chicago with Love*. New York: Alfred A. Knopf, 1955.

———. *Prairie Avenue*. New York: Alfred A. Knopf, 1949.

Morley, Christopher D. *Old Loopy: A Love Letter for Chicago*. Chicago: Argus Book Shop, 1937.

Motley, Willard. *Knock on Any Door*. New York: D. Appleton-Century Co., 1947.

Norris, Frank. *The Pit*. New York: Doubleday, Page & Co., 1903.

Petrakis, Harry Mark. *A Dream of Kings*. New York: D. McKay & Co., 1966.

———. *Pericles on 31st Street*. Chicago: Quadrangle Books, 1965.

Port Chicago Poets. Chicago: Chicago International Manuscripts, 1966.

Powers, John R. *The Last Catholic in America*. New York: Saturday Review Press, 1973.

Sandburg, Carl. *Chicago Poems*. New York: H. Holt & Co., 1916.

Sinclair, Upton. *The Jungle*. New York: Doubleday, Page & Co., 1906.

Smith, Alston J. *Chicago's Left Bank*. Chicago: Henry Regnery Co., 1953.

Smith, Mark. *The Death of the Detective*. New York: Avon, 1977.

Terkel, Louis (Studs). *Division Street: America*. New York: Pantheon Books, 1967.

Williams, Kenny J. *In the City of Men*. Nashville: Townsend Press, 1974.

Wright, Richard. *Native Son*. New York: Harper & Brothers, 1940.

Index

*Chicago's neighborhood communities

*Chicago's neighborhood communities

*Chicago's neighborhood communities

*Chicago's neighborhood communities

*Chicago's neighborhood communities

*Chicago's neighborhood communities

The Chicago area as taken from the Skylab manned orbital laboratory on September 19, 1973. (Courtesy National Aeronautics and Space Administration.)